D1356920

Native American Bibliography Series

Advisory Board

A Biobibliography of Native American Writers 1772-1924: A Supplement

Native American Bibliography Series, No. 5

by
Daniel F. Littlefield, Jr.
and
James W. Parins

The Scarecrow Press, Inc.
Metuchen, N.J., & London 1985

320592

Library of Congress Cataloging in Publication Data

Littlefield, Daniel F.
  A biobibliography of native American writers,
1772-1924. Supplement.

  (Native American bibliography series ; no. 5)
  Includes indexes.
  1. Indians of North America--Biography. 2. American
literature--Indian authors--Bibliography. 3. United
States--Imprints. I. Parins, James W. II. Title.
III. Series.
Z1209.2.U5L57 Suppl. [E77] 016.973'0497   85-2045
ISBN 0-8108-1802-7

CONTENTS

EDITOR'S FOREWORD

In compiling this supplement to the original 1981 <u>A Biobibliography</u> <u>of Native American Writers, 1772-1924</u>, Daniel F. Littlefield and James W. Parins have located additional Native American writers so that over 1,200 writers are included within the two volumes. The compilers cross-reference from this supplement to the previous volume to inform users of the supplemental volume that additional materials by writers can be found in the earlier publication. Together these two volumes contain the names and writings of more Native American writers than any other bibliographical work.

Among the very large number of American Indian persons writing in English from Colonial times until 1924, some were known by only one writing, or a few more. But there were also many notable writers during these times, including Gertrude Bonnin, Ella Deloria, Charles A. Eastman, John N. B. Hewitt, William Jones, Francis La Flesche, Charles Montezuma, John B. Oskison, Arthur C. Parker, Alexander L. Posey, Will Rogers, and Muriel H. Wright.

The compilers have improved this work by adding annotations while continuing the practice of including only Native Americans who composed their own writings in English, and by giving biographical sketches. These two volumes, the Supplement and the 1981 edition, will be valuable and essential research tools for those studying the writings of Native Americans for the 150 years preceding 1924.

Jack W. Marken

PREFACE

This volume adds to the information provided by A Biobibliography of Native American Writers, 1772-1924, published in 1981, on works written in English by American Indians and Alaska Natives from Colonial times to 1924. The scope of this second volume remains the same as the first, including not only literary works of fiction, drama, and poetry, but also political essays and addresses, published letters, dialect pieces, historical works, myths and legends, and other genres. We stayed close to the original plan for the 1981 volume, too, in the matter of identifying writers included in the main bibliography. In this volume as well as in the first, writers' personal claims of American Indian or Alaska Native citizenship were corroborated before their works were included. Some examples of corroboration are inclusion on tribal rolls, attendance at government schools that were limited to Native Americans, and various kinds of published data. In this volume as in the last, we have included a bibliography of writers known only by pen names. These writers were included primarily on the basis of self-identification as Indians.

In identifying members of larger tribal groups, we have tried to indicate an individual's reservation or band as well as the tribal designation where that information was available. We have attempted, too, to use the accepted current nomenclature and spelling of these designations.

Some added features appear in the second volume. Most bibliographic entries--excluding those with obviously descriptive titles-- have been annotated. We hope these brief remarks are useful to the scholars who use this volume. In addition, we have provided some citations for sources on the biographical entries. We do not mean to suggest that the ones listed are the only sources available, but offer these as aids to scholars wishing to make further inquiry concerning individual writers. When biographical information has been derived from the work cited in the bibliography, we have not included a citation after the biography. Another feature is information on the periodical publications which were searched for the works of American Indians and Alaska Natives included in this volume.

This supplement contains the works of some 1192 writers. Works of 250 of these were included in the first biobibliography: 942 new writers were represented here.

v

The information contained in this volume significantly expands the body of known writings by American Indians and Alaska Natives during the period 1772 to 1924. We hope that this information aids the work of scholars in Native American studies.

Daniel F. Littlefield, Jr.
James W. Parins

USER'S NOTE

Users of this bibliographic guide will discover some bibliographic nightmares: weeklies that occasionally or for several months running issued a monthly in the place of a weekly issue; volume numbers out of order; the same volume sequences of the same title, published at different times by the same organization, but without a series designation; and several periodicals with the same title, but published by different organizations. We have retreated to common sense in dealing with those matters.

We have taken certain steps to assist the user. First, we have arranged the entries for each writer in chronological order. We assumed that the user will not be familiar with most of the work included and that a chronological arrangement would reflect a writer's range and development much better than would an alphabetical listing of his his work.

Second, the writers are listed in alphabetical order, and after each name is a tribal designation. For those users who are interested in tribal groups or tribal literatures, the first Index is a list of writers according to their tribal affiliation. In listing their affiliation, we have used the designations that the writers or their publishers used in identifying them. If the information was available, we have further identified the band, tribal division, or reservation of members of large or scattered groups such as the Sioux and Chippewas. Further information on the writers and their backgrounds appears in the biographical notes in Part III. However, the reader should realize that these are simply notes and are not offered as complete biographical statements.

Third, each entry in the bibliography is preceded by a number, after which appears a letter that designates the general genre category into which the work fits. Following is a key to the genre designations:

A = Address   M = Myth or legend
C = Collection or compilation   N = Nonfiction prose
D = Drama   P = Poetry
E = Edition   S = Sermon
F = Fiction   T = Translation into English
L = Letter

Last, for those users who are interested in themes, ideas, or subjects, the Subject Index is a general guide to the bibliographic entries.

PART I

A BIBLIOGRAPHY OF NATIVE AMERICAN WRITERS

ADAIR, BRICE MARTIN (Cherokee)
  1L "From the Cherokee Nation," Arkansian, November 18, 1859. Concerns Cherokee affairs.

ADAIR, WALTER SCOTT (Cherokee)
  2L Letter, Cherokee Advocate, March 12, 1849. Concerns Indian schools.
  3L Letter, Cherokee Advocate, October 29, 1850. Concerns an affray at Evansville, Arkansas.

ADAIR, WILLIAM PENN (Cherokee)
  4A "Address of Hon. W. P. Adair, before the Indian International Agricultural Fair, at Muskogee, Oct. 3, 1878," Council Fire, 1 (October, 1878), 156-157. Concerns "civilization" of the Indians and their condition.
See also 1981 Biobibliography, 58-82.

ADAMS, JOHN F. (Siletz)
  5A "That the Negro Is Superior to the Indian," Red Man, 12 (January-February, 1894), 4. Argues the negative side.

ADAMS, JOSEPH E. (Sioux)
  6L Letter, Ogalalla Light, 1 (June 1, 1900), 4. Concerns the benefits of the Oglala Boarding School.

ADAMS, SUSIE (Sioux)
  7L Letter, Ogalalla Light, 1 (May 1, 1900), 4. Urges others to attend the Oglala Boarding School.

AITSAN, LUCIAN BEN (Kiowa)
  8L "An Indian's Appeal," Indian's Friend, 12 (March, 1900), 10-11. Appeals for supression of the whiskey trade.
See also 1981 Biobliography, 98.

ALFORD, PIERREPONT (Absentee Shawnee)
  9F "The First Easter," Talks and Thoughts, 15 (July, 1901), 4. Fantasy.
  10N "The Shawnees of the Past," Talks and Thoughts 17 (July, 1903), 3-4. Concerns Shawnee history.

1

11N   "Catching Runaways," Talks and Thoughts, 19 (December, 1905), 4.

ALFORD, REESE (Absentee Shawnee)
12N   "School Days," Talks and Thoughts, 17 (December, 1903), 4. Concerns his school experiences.

ALFORD, THOMAS WILDCAT (Absentee Shawnee)
13L   Letter, Council Fire, 3 (March, 1880), 39. Concerns his experiences at Hampton Institute.
14L   Letter. In Ten Years' Work for Indians at Hampton Institute. Hampton, VA: Hampton Institute, 1888, pp. 47-51. Concerns Hampton's Indian education program.
15L   Letter, Talks and Thoughts, 3 (February, 1889), 1. Concerns Christmas in an Indian Territory school.
See also 1981 Biobibliography, 107-117.

ALFORD, WEBSTER (Absentee Shawnee)
16N   "Painting--Stains," Indian Leader, June 23, 1911. Describes characteristics and methods of applying.

ALLEN, DOROTHEA (Klamath)
17N   "Capitola Meditations," Sherman Bulletin, April 20, 1910.
18P   "Sherman the Beautiful," Sherman Bulletin, December 21, 1910.

ALLMAN, PANSY (Sioux)
19N   "Items from Classrooms," Oglala Light, 20 (January 15, 1920), 3. Reports classroom activities at the Oglala Boarding School.
20N   "Items from the Class Rooms," Oglala Light, 20 (February 15, 1920), 3. Reports classroom activities at the Oglala Boarding School.
21N   "Items from the Class Rooms," Oglala Light, 20 (March 1, 1920), 3. Reports classroom activities at the Oglala Boarding School.

AMAGO, SORTERO (Mission)
22N   "An Indian Paper," Indian's Friend, 13 (August, 1901), 8. Discusses the conditions of the La Jolla Indians.

ANAKARTUK, JOHN (Eskimo)
23N   Article on Herding, Eskimo, 1 (January, 1917), 3. Concerns reindeer herding.

ANDERSON, PHENIA (Konkow)
24F   "The Bears' Christmas," Carlisle Arrow, January 8, 1909. Story about toys.
25M   "Why the Ground Mole Is Blind--An Indian Legend," Carlisle Arrow, February 19, 1909.
See also 1981 Biobibliography, 151.

ANNEBUCK
    See BUCK, ANNE

ANOWOLUKWUK, ANDREW G. (Eskimo)
    26L   Letter, Eskimo, 1 (June, 1917), 6. Concerns reindeer herd-
            ing.

ANTONIO, CALLISTRO (Mission)
    27L   "Very Clever: Will Answer in Next Issue," Mission Indian,
            1 (November, 1895), 5. Concerns snow on the mountain-
            tops.

APES, WILLIAM (Pequot)
    28N   "The Indians--the Ten Lost Tribes," Monthly Repository and
            Library of Entertaining Knowledge, 1 (August, 1830), 63-
            65, and 1 (September, 1830), 115-116. Discusses the pop-
            ular theory on the origin of Indians.
    29P   "Indian Hymn," Word Carrier, 18 (April-May, 1889), 1. In
            dialect, about Christianity. Attributed to Apes.
    30P   "Indian Hymn," Word Carrier of Santee Normal Training
            School, 39 (January-February, 1910), 6. In dialect, about
            Christianity. Attributed to Apes. Reprinted from Orange
            Scott, ed., New and Improved Camp Meeting Hymn Book.
            Boston, 1836.
    See also 1981 Biobibliography, 160-165.

APPLE, JENNIE (Sioux)
    31L   Letter, Ogalalla Light, 1 (May 1, 1900), 4. Praises the
            Oglala Boarding School.

ARCASA, ALEXANDER (Colville)
    32N   "Practical Training in Agriculture," Carlisle Arrow, April
            8, 1910. Describes his work as a student in the outing
            system.
    See also 1981 Biobibliography, 166.

ARCHER, ADA (Cherokee)
    33N   "The Indian Territory," Wowapi, November 7, 1883, 9-12.
            Describes political situation in Indian Territory, including
            allotment schemes.

ARKEKETAH, MARY (Oto)
    34N   "Our Duty to Our People," Indian Leader, April 20, 1906.
            Argues the need for education of Indians.

ARMELL, JOSEPHINE (Winnebago)
    35N   "Twenty-Ninth Anniversary of Hampton Institute," Talks and
            Thoughts, 13 (June, 1897), 1-2. Describes events at the
            anniversary celebration.

ARMELL, LOUIS H. (Winnebago)
    36A "Citizens for God and Country," Talks and Thoughts 12
        (March, 1897), 6. Concerns education and the Indians.

ARPAN, AMELIA (Cheyenne River Sioux)
    37L Letter, Word Carrier of Santee Normal Training School, 36
        (January-February, 1907), 4. Autobiographical statement.

ARTESHAW, MARIE (Bad River Chippewa)
    38N "Conditions at Bad River," Arrow, December 20, 1907. De-
        scribes changes in dress, housing, and occupations.
    39N "Crawling Stone Lake," Carlisle Arrow, June 3, 1910. Dis-
        cusses legends about the lake in northern Wisconsin.
    See also 1981 Biobibliography, 171.

ATKINS, LOU (Creek)
    40N "Sleep," Creek Boys' and Girls' Monthly, December, 1870.
        Argues the importance of adequate sleep.

ATKINS, MARY (Creek)
    41N "Religious Life Among Our People," Word Carrier of Santee
        Normal Training School, 42 (November-December, 1913),
        42. Discusses religious life among the Creeks.

ATKINS, MINNIE (Creek)
    42N "A Creek Girl Writes of Our Trip to Philadelphia," School
        News, 3 (November, 1882), 1, 4. Describes student ex-
        cursion to Philadelphia.

AZULE, ESTHER (Pima)
    43N "Class History," Purple and Gold. Riverside, CA: Sher-
        man Institute, 1923, pp. 6, 11. Concerns graduating
        students at Sherman Institute.

BAGNELL, AMY T. (Rogue River, i.e., Shasta)
    44N "The Oregon Country," Indian Leader, June 3, 1903. De-
        scriptive historical sketch of Oregon.
    See also 1981 Biobibliography, 179-181.

BAHR, SUSAN WAMBDISUS (Santee Sioux)
    45N "A Santee Graduate's Description of Her Home Life," Word
        Carrier of Santee Normal Training School, 33 (March-April,
        1904), 8. Reprinted from Talks and Thoughts.
    46L Letter, Word Carrier of Santee Normal Training School, 34
        (March-April, 1905), 6. Concerns her life on the farm
        and her Christian endeavors.

BAIRD, ELIZABETH J. (Oneida)
    47A "Bandaging," Arrow, April 3, 1908. Describes the process.

BALDWIN, MARIE L. BOTTINEAU (Chippewa)
48L   Letter, Chemawa American, 17 (October, 1914), 1-2. Concerns Indian exhibitions at fairs.
See also 1981 Biobibliography, 183-184.

BALENTI, MICHAEL R. (Southern Cheyenne)
49N   "My Northfield Trip," Arrow, July 20, 1906. Concerns a
YMCA excursion.
50N   "King Philip," Arrow, May 1, 1908. Anecdote about, and
biographical sketch of, King Philip.
51N   "Pontiac," Arrow, June 19, 1908. Biographical sketch of
Pontiac.
52N   "Indian History--The Comanches," Carlisle Arrow, September 25, 1908. Historical sketch of the Comanches.
53N   "Kiowa Indians," Carlisle Arrow, October 23, 1908. Historical sketch of the Kiowas.
54N   "Basketry and Pottery," Carlisle Arrow, December 4, 1908.
Describes the crafts in many tribes.
55A   "Seven Lamps of Architecture," Carlisle Arrow, February
12, 1909. Concerns man's soul in relation to God.
56M   "Origin of the Iroquois," Carlisle Arrow, March 12, 1909.
Relates the Hiawatha legend.
57N   "Julius Caesar," Carlisle Arrow, April 9, 1909. Historical
sketch of Caesar.
See also 1981 Biobibliography, 185-188.

BALL, JOSEPH (Klamath)
58N   "The Sign of Equality," Red Man and Helper, June 19, 1903.
Argues for equal education for Indians and whites. Reprinted from Native American.
See also 1981 Biobibliography, 190.

BALMER, JAMES (Chippewa)
59N   "The Advantages of Skilled Labor," Indian Leader, July 1,
1899.

BALMER, WILLIAM (Chippewa)
60N   "What Is Your Aim?" Indian Leader, June 22, 1900. Concerns student career goals.

BANKS, JESSIE (Crow Creek Sioux)
61L   "Vacation in Westfield," Talks and Thoughts, 5 (November,
1890), 4. Describes the author's vacation.

BANKS, MARY (Mission)
62L   "Well Done, Mary," Mission Indian, 1 (December 15, 1895),
5. Concerns women's roles.

BANKS, SARAH (Mission)
63L   "Very Good for First Attempt," Mission Indian, 1 (December
15, 1895), 5. Concerns boarding school life.

BARADA, LOTTIE (Omaha)
64N "An Indian Christmas Story," Indian Leader, December 23, 1910. Concerns dances.

BARBY, GRACE (Sioux)
65L Letter, Sina Sapa Wocekiye Taeyanpaha, April, 1894. Urges others to attend school.

BARKER, ALFRED H. (Santee Sioux)
66L "World's Fair Correspondence," Talks and Thoughts, 8 (July-August, 1893), 1-2. Describes a trip to the fair.

BARNABY, JOSEPHINE E. (Omaha)
67L Letter, Talks and Thoughts, 1 (August, 1886), 3. Describes a trip to Lyrington, Massachusetts.
See also 1981 Biobibliography, 195-198.

BARRETT, EMMA (Yankton Sioux)
68N "The Furnishings of a Bedroom," Indian Leader, June 28, 1907.

BARTLETT, EDITH (Bannock)
69N "What I Am Going to Do When I Leave School," Red Man and Helper, June 7, 1901. Discusses her ambition to be a teacher.

BARTON, INEZ M. (Navajo)
70N "Industrial Activities," Purple and Gold. Riverside, CA: Sherman Institute, 1923, pp. 17-20. Concerns the Industrial Department at Sherman Institute.

BASKIN, EUNICE KITTO (Santee Sioux)
71N "Mrs. Ellen Kitto, 1838-1918," Word Carrier of Santee Normal Training School, 48 (January-February, 1919), 3. Biographical sketch.
72N "Boys' Cottage, Santee Normal Training School," Word Carrier of Santee Normal Training School, 48 (November-December, 1919), 21. Describes school routine. Reprinted from Work at Home.

BASKIN, SAMUEL (Santee Sioux)
73N "King Birds," Talks and Thoughts, 7 (January, 1893), 3.
74N "Father Marquette and Fernando de Soto," Talks and Thoughts, 9 (December, 1894), 7. Historical sketch of Father Marquette and de Soto.
75T "Ite Waste, or Fair Face: An Indian Story," Talks and Thoughts, 11 (September, 1895), 1.
76A "What the White Man Has Gained from the Indian," Talks and Thoughts, 11 (May, 1896), 3. Concerns the Indian's contribution to American society.

77A   "What the White Man Has Gained from the Indian," Indian's
       Friend, 10 (October, 1897), 10. Concerns the Indian's
       contribution to American society.
See also 1981 Biobibliography, 200.

BASTIAN, JOHN (Puyallup)
  78N   "My Summer Vacation," Carlisle Arrow, October 29, 1909.
       Describes his outing in New Jersey.
  79F   "The Story of the Bluejay," Carlisle Arrow, June 17, 1910.
       Tale about how the jay got his characteristics.
  80M   "Stick-Injun," Carlisle Arrow, December 30, 1910. Legend
       about a mysterious person who lives in the Washington
       mountains.
See also 1981 Biobibliography, 201-202.

BATTICE, C. WALTER (Sac and Fox)
  81N   "Education War-path Meetings," Talks and Thoughts, 1
       (May, 1886), 2-3. Describes the effects of education on
       the Indian.
  82F   "A Dream," Talks and Thoughts, 1 (July, 1886), 3. Fan-
       tasy on "What the man in the moon told me."
  83N   "Olden Time," Talks and Thoughts, 1 (August, 1886), 2.
       Concerns his experiences at Hampton Institute.
  84N   "Our Trip," Talks and Thoughts, 2 (July, 1887), 2-3. De-
       scribes a trip to Hampton Roads.
  85L   Letter, Talks and Thoughts, 2 (February, 1888), 1-2. Con-
       cerns the religious traditions of the Sac and Fox.
  86N   "Good Words from Walter Battice," Talks and Thoughts, 4
       (September, 1889), 1, 4. Argues for education of the
       Indian.
See also 1981 Biobibliography, 204-207.

BAYHYLLE, LOUIS (Skeedee Band Pawnee)
  87L   Letter, Red Man and Helper, December 5, 1902. Concerns
       Pawnee students formerly at Carlisle.

BEAR, JOSEPH L. (Sioux)
  88M   "Legend of Elkhorn Butte," Carlisle Arrow, February 11,
       1910. Concerns rattlesnakes.
See also 1981 Biobibliography, 212.

BEAR, SAMSON (Santee Sioux)
  89N   "The Santee Indians," Word Carrier of Santee Normal Train-
       ing School, 33 (March-April, 1904), 6-7. Describes con-
       ditions among the Santees.

BEAR, STELLA VANESSA (Arickara)
  90F   "An Indian Story," Talks and Thoughts, 16 (April, 1903),
       4. Concerns hunting.
  91M   "How People First Came to the World," Talks and Thoughts,
       16 (May, 1903), 4. Arickara creation legend.

92F   "An Enemy's Revenge," Talks and Thoughts, 18 (February, 1905), 1. A story.

93N   "Laundry Work," Arrow, October 5, 1906. Describes work in the laundry room at Carlisle.

94N   "Chief Black Hawk," Arrow, December 13, 1907. Biographical sketch.

95F   "How the Woodpecker Got Its Red Top Knot," Arrow, December 20, 1907. A tale.

96N   "Some Peculiarities of My People," Carlisle Arrow, February 25, 1910. Concerns Arickara story telling, burial, kinship, and other customs.

97M   "Ghost Bride Pawnee Legend," Carlisle Arrow, March 4, 1910.

98N   "The Chestnut Tree," Carlisle Arrow, March 25, 1910. Describes uses of the tree.

99M   "An Arickaree Legend," Talks and Thoughts, 16 (March, 1910), 4.

100M   "Indian Legend--Creation of the World," Carlisle Arrow, April 1, 1910. Arickara legend.

101M   "Indian Legend--How the World Was Peopled," Indian Orphan, 7 (January, 1911), 3. Arickara legend.

See also 1981 Biobibliography, 213-215.

BEARSKIN, GLADYS (Wyandot)

102N   "Demonstration," Sherman Bulletin, June 2, 1915. Concerns how to develop a household budget.

BEAUDOIN, WILLIAM (Chippewa)

103N   "The Calumet and Hecla," Carlisle Arrow, January 1, 1909. Discusses copper mines in Michigan.

BEAULIEU, C. H. (White Earth Chippewa)

104L   Letter, Council Fire, 1 (November, 1878), 167. Argues against moving Indian Bureau to the War Department.

See also 1981 Biobibliography, 218-229.

BEAULIEU, GUSTAVE H. (White Earth Chippewa)

105N   "Why He Objects to the Treaty," Progress, December 3, 1887.

See also 1981 Biobibliography, 231-232.

BEAULIEU, PAUL H. (White Earth Chippewa)

106A   "Civilization--'On the Wrong End,'" Progress, December 17, 1887. Delivered to the U.S. Senate.

BEAULIEU, T. B. H. (Leech Lake Chippewa)

107L   "Pillager School," Council Fire, 2 (November, 1879), 175. Concerns education and conditions among the Chippewas.

108N   "Leech Lake Agency," Council Fire, 3 (March, 1880), 46-47. Describes church, Christmas activities, New Year's Day, and old people.

109L   "A Bundle of Fagots," Council Fire, 4 (June, 1881), 86.
Concerns the boarding and industrial school at Leech
Lake.

110N   "Friend of the Indian Cause," Southern Workman, 10 (October, 1881), 93.

BEAULIEU, THEODORE H. (White Earth Chippewa)

111N   "Pioneer Personal--the Early Fur Trade in the Northwest--
Reminiscences of Traders, Trappers, and Couriers Du
Bois," Progress, March 16, 1889.

112N   "Early Days" Reminiscence of the Fur Trade Half a Century Ago Related by Old Traders, Trappers, Voyageurs,"
Progress, May 26, 1888.

133N   "Grand Medicine: Origin of Sacred Rite Among the Chippewa Indians," Chippeway Herald, 1 (January, 1902), 3,
5-6. Reprinted from Salt Lake Tribune.

114N   "Gee-sah-ke-we-ni-ne or Jugglers," Chippeway Herald, 1
(February, 1902), 1. Ojibwa lore concerning jugglers.

115M   "The Indian of Yesterday," Chippeway Herald, 1 (March,
1902), 1. Origin myth and legend of the robin, concerning initiation into manhood.

116M   "Legend of the Robin," Indian Leader, April 4, 1902.
Concerns initiation into manhood. Reprinted from Chippeway Herald.

117M   "Legend of the Robin," Red Man and Helper, April 25,
1902. Concerns initiation into manhood. Reprinted from
Chippeway Herald.

118N   "A Moose Adventure," Chippeway Herald, 1 (September,
1902), 5. Narrative about catching a moose alive. Reprinted from Western Field and Stream.

119M   "Wain-nah-Boo-zho: First Birch Bark Canoe; How the Ojibwa
Vulcan Stole Fire from the Sun God," Chippeway Herald,
1 (November, 1902), 1, 8.

120N   "Killing Deer with Stone; Strange Adventures of a Hunter
on the White Earth Reservation," Chippeway Herald, 2
(February, 1903), 6.

121N   "Two Noted Red Men," Chippeway Herald, 3 (February,
1904), 1, 2. Biographical sketches of Wah-we-yah-cum-
ig (Round Earth) and Gay-gway-ge-way-bin-ung (He who
tries to throw). Reprinted from Minneapolis Journal.

122N   "White Cloud--Wah-Bon-Ah-Quod," Chippeway Herald, 3
(March, 1904), 1. Biographical sketch.

123N   "May-zhuck-ke-ge-shig--Lowering Day," Chippeway Herald,
3 (April, 1904), 1, 2. Biographical sketch.

124N   "Many Moons Ago," Chippeway Herald, 3 (May, 1904), 1.
Describes old Ojibwa customs.

See also 1981 Biobibliography, 236-239.

BEBEAU, GENEVIEVE (Chippewa)

125M   "The Origin of Thunder," Carlisle Arrow, February 24, 1911.

A Chippewa legend.
See also 1981 Biobibliography, 242-243.

BEBEAU, MATILDA (Sioux)
126N   "Opportunities," Peace Pipe, 5 (June, 1916), 8-9. Concerning opportunities through education.

BECK, SAVANNAH (Cherokee)
127N   "The Indian Canoe," Arrow, June 5, 1908. Discusses kinds and uses.

BECK, STACY (Eastern Band Cherokee)
128M   "Legend of the Quail and Turtle," Arrow, December 20, 1907.
129M   "Robert E. Lee," Arrow, May 1, 1908. Biographical sketch.
130N   "The Custom of Scalping," Arrow, May 22, 1908.
131M   "Thunder Tradition," Carlisle Arrow, December 17, 1909. Ojibwa legend concerning "the young thunder."
132M   "Thunder Tradition," Indian's Friend, 25 (July, 1913), 5. Ojibwa legend concerning "the young thunder."
See also 1981 Biobibliography, 265-266.

BELLANGER, CLEMENT (Leech Lake Chippewa)
133N   "Home Building," Indian News, 15 (May, 1913), 3-4.

BEMO, DOUGLAS (Creek)
134N   "Do Right," Creek Boys' and Girls' Monthly, December, 1870. Concerns proper behavior.
135N   "School," Creek Boys' and Girls' Monthly, December, 1870. Concerns the importance of studying.

BEMO, ONIE (Creek)
136N   "Time," Creek Boys' and Girls' Monthly, December, 1870. Concerns the penalties for procrastination.

BEMO, SONIA (Creek)
137N   "Bells," Creek Boys' and Girls' Monthly, December 1870. Concerns their pleasant sound.

BENCHLER, SARAH (Paiute)
138N   "The Sewing Industry at the Carlisle School," Carlisle Arrow, January 8, 1909. Describes what went on there.

BENDER, ANNA (White Earth Chippewa)
139F   "Quital's First Hunt," Talks and Thoughts, 17 (January, 1904), 4. Story told by John Clifford and set in a Sioux camp.
140F   "A Crow Story," Talks and Thoughts, 17 (February, 1904), 1.
141M   "The First Squirrel," Talks and Thoughts, 17 (April, 1904), 1, 4. Legend told by Bertha Mountain Sheep.

142M   "The First Squirrel," Indian Leader, May 6, 1904. Legend
        told by Bertha Mountain Sheep. Reprinted Talks and
        Thoughts.

143N   "A Glimpse of the Old Indian Religion," Talks and Thoughts,
        17 (May, 1904), 4.

144N   "A Glimpse of the Old Indian Religion," Indian Leader,
        September 9, 1904. Reprinted from Talks and Thoughts.

145M   "The Big Dipper," Talks and Thoughts, 18 (November,
        1904), 1, 4. Told by Bertha Mountain Sheep.

146N   "An Indian Girl in Boston," Talks and Thoughts, 18 (De-
        cember, 1904), 4. Describes her experiences in Boston.

BENDER, ELIZABETH (Bad River Chippewa)
  147N   "The Grainfields of North Dakota," Talks and Thoughts,
        20 (December, 1906), 4.

  148N   "The Land of Hiawatha," Talks and Thoughts, 21 (June,
        1907), 1. Describes the Chippewa country.

See also 1981 Biobibliography, 577.

BENDER, TIFFANY (Washo)
  149N   "Tiffany Bender Visits Washington," Red Man and Helper,
        April 15, 1904. Describes a visit to the public buildings
        in Washington, D.C.

BENGE, SAMUEL HOUSTON (Cherokee)
  150A   "An Indian Speech," Indian Missionary, 2 (May, 1886), 3.
        Concerns conditions among the Cherokees.

See also 1981 Biobibliography, 278.

BENOIST, ELSIE (Cheyenne River Sioux)
  151A   "The Art of Study," Indian News, 15 (May, 1913), 1-2.

BENOIST, LAURA L. (Sioux)
  152P   "Class Poem," Indian News, 13 (May-June, 1911), 1-2.

BENSON, DANIEL (Alaska Native)
  153N   "The Coming of the Russians," North Star, 5 (June, 1892),
        1. Concerns Russian occupation of Alaska.

  154N. "Witch-Craft," North Star, 5 (June, 1892), 3. Concerns
        Tlingits and Haidas.

BENT, JULIA (Cheyenne)
  155L   "I Will Talk About in the Chapel," School News, 2 (Octo-
        ber, 1881), 1. Autobiographical statement.

BIG HORSE, LOUIS (Osage)
  156L   "Home Letter," School News, 3 (February, 1883), 1, 4.
        Urges self-help among the Osages.

  157N   "Pittsburg," School News, 3 (March, 1883), 3. Describes
        a trip to Pittsburgh, Pennsylvania.

BIG JIM DRIVER, GOLIATH (Eastern Band Cherokee)
    158N "A Trip to Cherokee," Arrow, August 30, 1907. Describes
        a trip to Cherokee, North Carolina.

BIGWALKER, LELIA (Sac and Fox)
    159N "From a Grain of Wheat," Indian Leader, July 13, 1906.
        Concerns gluten.

BILLY, LUCINDA (Choctaw)
    160N "The Choctaws: Long Ago and Now," Indian School Jour-
        nal, 19 (June, 1919), 35-36. Concerns Choctaw customs.

BIRD, ETTA R. CRAWFORD (Sisseton Sioux)
    161N "Former Santee Pupils Work for Their School," Word Car-
        rier of Santee Normal Training School, 46 (January-
        February, 1918), 1. Reports on work of alumni asso-
        ciation.

BIRD, LULU (Maricopa)
    162M "A Maricopa Legend," Indian's Friend, 25 (October, 1912),
        11. Concerns a fox and quails.

BIRDNECKLACE, ANNIE (Sioux)
    163L Letter, Word Carrier of Santee Normal Training School, 36
        (January-February, 1907), 4. Autobiographical state-
        ment about her days at Oahe School, South Dakota.

BISHOP, LUCIUS (Seneca)
    164N "Our New York Land," Talks and Thoughts, 12 (May,
        1897), 1-2. Concerns allotment.

BISHOP, THOMAS G. (Chimakum, i.e., Skokomish)
    165N "The Court of Indian Offenses," Indian, Unnumbered (Jan-
        uary, 1922), 5. Criticizes the court.

BISHOP, WILLIAM C. (Cayuga)
    166M "The Old Man in the Sky--An Indian Legend," Carlisle Ar-
        row, October 9, 1908. Concerns how the constellation
        came to be.
    167M "The Seven Stars of Pleiades--An Indian Legend," Carlisle
        Arrow, October 23, 1908. Legend of seven Iroquois
        boys.
    168N "Self-Education," Carlisle Arrow, May 14, 1909. Argues
        that work is a requirement for education.
    169M "The Origin of the Turtle Clan," Carlisle Arrow, March 15,
        1912. Concerns the Turtle Clan of the Cayugas.
    170N "The Reward of Persistence," Carlisle Arrow, April 19,
        1912. Concerns success.
    171P "Senior Class Song," Carlisle Arrow, April 19, 1912.

BISSIONETTE, LEONARD (Sioux)
172N "Items from Classrooms," Oglala Light, 20 (January 15, 1920), 3. Reports classroom activities at the Oglala Boarding School.
173N "Items from the Class Rooms," Oglala Light, 20 (February 15, 1920), 3. Reports classroom activities at the Oglala Boarding School.
174N "Items from the Class Rooms," Oglala Light, 20 (March 1, 1920), 3. Reports classroom activities at the Oglala Boarding School.

BISSIONETTE, RICHARD (Sioux)
175N "Items from Classrooms," Oglala Light, 20 (December 1, 1919), 3. Reports classroom activities at the Oglala Boarding School.
176N "Items from Classrooms," Oglala Light, 20 (December 15, 1919), 3. Reports classroom activities at the Oglala Boarding School.
177N "Items from Classrooms," Oglala Light, 20 (January 1, 1920), 3. Reports classroom activities at the Oglala Boarding School.
178N "Items from Classrooms," Oglala Light, 20 (January 15, 1920), 3. Reports classroom activities at the Oglala Boarding School.
179N "Items from the Class Rooms," Oglala Light, 20 (March 1, 1920), 3. Reports classroom activities at the Oglala Boarding School.
180N "Items from the Class Rooms," Oglala Light, 20 (March 15, 1920), 3. Reports on classroom activities at the Oglala Boarding School.
181N "Items from the Class Rooms," Oglala Light, 20 (April 15, 1920), 3. Reports classroom activities at the Oglala Boarding School.

BLACK, THOMPSON (Quileute)
182N "Indians Progressing," Quileute Chieftain, January 26, 1910. Concerns giving up old ways.

BLACK BEAR, THOMAS (Pine Ridge Sioux)
183L "Correspondence," Arrow, March 29, 1907. Reports events at Porcupine, South Dakota.
See also 1981 Biobibliography, 285.

BLACK HAWK, MINNIE (Sioux)
184N "Care of Poultry," Carlisle Arrow, October 9, 1908.
185M "A Sioux Legend--Moon Boy," Carlisle Arrow, November 20, 1908.
186M "The Moon Boy--A Sioux Legend," Native American, December 19, 1908.

BLACK HORSE, WILLIAM (Sioux)
187L   Letter, Ogalalla Light, 1 (May 1, 1900), 4. Urges others
         to attend Oglala Boarding School.

BLACKHAWK, JOSEPH (Winnebago)
188N   "An Indian Method of Preparing Corn for Winter Use,"
         Talks and Thoughts, 17 (November, 1903), 4.
189N   "The Old Roving Live," Talks and Thoughts, 17 (December,
         1903), 1.
190F   "The Old Man or the Stag," Talks and Thoughts, 17 (March,
         1904), 1. Told by Theodore Owl, concerns an old man
         who turns himself into a stag.
191N   "The Making of a Buckskin Suit," Talks and Thoughts, 18
         (June, 1904), 1, 4.
192N   "The Old Pipe-Stone Pipe," Talks and Thoughts, 19 (June,
         1905), 1, 4.
193F   "The Story Teller," Talks and Thoughts, 19 (June, 1905),
         4; (July-August, 1905), 1, 4. A story.
194N   "The Coming of Spring," Talks and Thoughts, 19 (May,
         1906), 1. Concerns how beautiful Hampton Institute is
         in spring.

BLACKHOOP, BENEDICT (Standing Rock Sioux)
195N   "An Indian's Philosophy," Word Carrier of Santee Normal
         Training School, 36 (May-June, 1907), 9. Espouses
         Christianity.
196N   "How the People Are to Live," Word Carrier of Santee Nor-
         mal Training School, 37 (March-April, 1908), 8. Argues
         that Indians must adjust, giving up dancing and liquor.
197N   "An Indian's View of How His People Are to Live," Word
         Carrier of Santee Normal Training School, 37 (May-June,
         1908), 11. Opposes liquor and dancing.

BLACKHOOP, FRANK (Standing Rock Sioux)
198F   "Indian Stories," Word Carrier of Santee Normal Training
         School, 43 (May-June, 1914), 12. Tales of a bear and
         a rabbit.
199L   "A Santee School Letter," Word Carrier of Santee Normal
         School, 43 (July-August, 1914), 16. Concerns school
         work at Santee Normal Training School.

BLACKWATER, EMMA (Pima)
200N   "Christmas on the Pima Reservation," Sherman Bulletin,
         December 24, 1913.

BLACKWATER, JOSEPH (Pima)
201N   "Points on Presswork," Sherman Bulletin, May 27, 1914.
         Concerns printing at Sherman Institute.
202F   "The Story of My Life," Sherman Bulletin, November 25,
         1914. Thanksgiving fantasy.

BLACKWOOD, MARGARET O. (Chippewa)
203F   "A Story of Two Indian Boys, Manteo and Manchese, Chapter IV," Carlisle Arrow, October 15, 1909. Story of a lost colony.
204N   "Klamath-Modoc," Carlisle Arrow, November 5, 1909. Historical sketch of the tribes.
205N   "The Naming of a Town," Carlisle Arrow, March 25, 1910. Concerns how Ontonagon was named.
206M   "Beliefs of the Chippewas," Carlisle Arrow, May 20, 1910. Concerns "Bear Walks," a transformation legend.
207N   "The Indians' Treasure," Carlisle Arrow, September 16, 1910. Concerns copper on Lake Superior.
208N   "How Christmas Is Celebrated at My Home," Carlisle Arrow, December 23, 1910.
See also 1981 Biobibliography, 290-292.

BLAINE, JOHN C. (Sioux)
209M   "Legend of Standing Rock," Red Man, 15 (February, 1900), 6.

BLANDIN, LENORA (Potawatomi)
210N   "Ceremony of Adoption," Indian Leader, September 25, 1908.

BLUEEYES, DORA (Cheyenne River Sioux)
211L   Letter, Word Carrier of Santee Normal Training School, 36 (January-February, 1907), 4. Concerns her life and Oahe School, South Dakota.

BOHANAN, SILAS D. (Choctaw)
212M   "Why the Boy Was a Swift Runner," Indian Leader, 19 (October, 1915), 9. A legend.

BOND, GEORGE M. (Choctaw)
213L   Letter, Indian Citizen, October 4, 1890. Concerns Choctaw education.

BOND, THOMAS J. (Choctaw)
214L   "Editor Oklahoma Star," Oklahoma Star, July 30, 1875. Argues the need for education for the Choctaws.
See also 1981 Biobibliography, 295-302.

BONGA, CECELIA (White Earth Chippewa)
215N   "Success," Peace Pipe, 5 (June, 1916), 12. Concerns success through education.

BONGA, JULIA (Chippewa)
216N   "Indian Customs," Indian Leader, October 15, 1909. Concerns burial customs.

BONNIN, EDNA (Sioux)
   217N   "An Indian Thanksgiving," Indian Leader, November 26,
         1909.

BONNIN, GERTRUDE SIMMONS (Yankton Sioux)
   218N   "A Plea for the Indian Dance," Word Carrier of Santee Nor-
         mal Training School, 31 (January-February, 1902), 2.
         Reprinted from Boston Transcript.
   219F   "Shooting of the Red Eagle," Indian Leader, August 12,
         1904. A story.
   220N   "California Indian Trails and Prayer Trees, Chapter I,"
         California Indian Herald, 1 (January, 1923), 6. Relates
         lore of the Redwoods to illustrate the present plight of
         the Indians. Reprinted from San Francisco Bulletin.
   221N   "Lost Treaties of the California Indians," California Indian
         Herald, 1 (April, 1923), 7.
   222N   "The California Indians of Today," California Indian Herald,
         1 (July, 1923), 10. Discusses the condition of the Cali-
         fornia Indians.
   223N   "Heart to Heart Talk," California Indian Herald, 2 (May,
         1924), 2-3. Offers encouragement to California Indians.
  See also 1981 Biobibliography, 303-331.

BONSER, CLARA (Sioux)
   224N   "Christmas in a Sioux Home," Carlisle Arrow, January 28,
         1910.

BOSIN, JOHN (Kiowa)
   225M   "Indian and White Man," Indian Leader, 17 (October, 1913),
         18. Legend of Sane-day.

BOSWELL, CHRISTINE (Alaska Native)
   226A   "Some Other Girls," Chemawa American, 16 (May, 1914),
         22-24. Concerns economics, life-style, canning season,
         and Christianity in Alaska.

BOUDINOT, ELIAS (Cherokee)
   227F   "Poor Sarah," Religious Intelligencer, January 1 and 8,
         1820. A religious tale, allegedly true, attributed to
         Boudinot. Reported to have been reprinted in Boston
         Recorder, March 11, 1820.
   228F   "Religion Exemplified in the Life of Poor Sarah," Connecti-
         cut Mirror, March 6 and 13, 1820. A religious tale, al-
         legedly true, attributed to Boudinot. Reprinted from
         Religious Intelligencer.
   229F   The History of an Indian Woman. Boston: Crocker &
         Brewster for Samuel T. Armstrong, 1820. A religious
         tale, allegedly true, attributed to Boudinot.
   230F   The Pious Indian: or Religion Exemplified in the Life of
         Poor Sarah. Newburyport, MA: W. & J. Gilman, 1820.
         A religious tale, allegedly true, attributed to Boudinot.

231F The Pious Indian: or Religion Exemplified in the Life of
      Poor Sarah. Newburyport, MA: W. & J. Gilman, for
      Charles Whipple, 1820. A religious tale, allegedly true,
      attributed to Boudinot.

232F Poor Sarah; or Religion Exemplified in the Life and Death
      of a Pious Indian Woman. Philadelphia: Religious Tract
      Society of Philadelphia, 1820. A religious tale, allegedly
      true, attributed to Boudinot.

233L Letter, Missionary Herald, 17 (August, 1821), 257. Thanks
      Baron de Campagne for support of the Cornwall School.

234F Poor Sarah; or Religion Exemplified in the Life and Death
      of a Pious Indian Woman. New York: J. Seymour, for
      the New York Tract Society, 1821. A religious tale, al-
      legedly true, attributed to Boudinot.

235F Poor Sarah; or Religion Exemplified in the Life and Death of
      a Pious Indian Woman. Wilmington, DE: H. Porter, 1821.
      A religious tale, allegedly true, attributed to Boudinot.

236F Poor Sarah, an Indian Woman. Andover, MA: Flagg &
      Gould, Printers, 1822. A religious tale, allegedly true,
      attributed to Boudinot.

237L "Inventing a New Alphabet," Cherokee Advocate, October
      26, 1844. Concerns Sequoyah. Reprinted from Annals
      of Education for 1832.

See also 1981 Biobibliography, 333-354.

BOUDINOT, ELIAS CORNELIUS (Cherokee)

238L Letter, Oklahoma Star, September 17, 1875. Relates to the
      Grand Council's rejection of Caddo Resolutions.

239L "Tom Scott's Projected Railroad," Western Independent,
      September 29, 1875. Signed "Sebastian," complains that
      Scott's proposal ignores the Thirty-fifth Parallel.

240N "Prospectus of the Indian Progress," Oklahoma Star Octo-
      ber 1, 1875. Proposes the establishment of a newspaper
      by that name.

241L "Letter from Boudinot," Oklahoma Star, November 23, 1875.
      Discusses Judge Isaac Parker's decision on Indian citizen-
      ship.

242L "Special Correspondence of the Star," Oklahoma Star, Jan-
      uary 4, 1876. Concerns Indian policy and the upcoming
      Congress.

243L "Special Correspondence of the Star," Oklahoma Star, Jan-
      uary 11, 1876. Relates Washington news about Indian
      affairs and discusses Caddo Resolutions.

244L Letter, Oklahoma Star, February 8, 1876. Attacks W. P.
      Ross and defends the Oklahoma bill.

245L Letter, Oklahoma Star, February 22, 1876. Concerns Wash-
      ington affairs and attacks W. P. Ross.

246L Letter, Oklahoma Star, February 29, 1876. Defends pro-
      posed transfer of Indian Bureau to the War Department.

247L "Day Breaking," Oklahoma Star, April 4, 1876. Defends
      territorial bill for the Indian Territory.

248L   "The Indian Territory," Oklahoma Star, April 18, 1876. To the Baltimore Gazette, arguing for a territorial government.

249L   "Babcock-Kilbourne and the Transfer Bill," Oklahoma Star, April 25, 1876. Concerns proposed transfer of Indian affairs to the War Department.

250L   "Washington," Oklahoma Star, May 16, 1876. Concerns the Oklahoma bill, U.S. centennial, and a bill to transfer Indian affairs.

251L   "Letter from Col. Boudinot," Oklahoma Star, June 6, 1876. Speculation concerning the presidency and the Oklahoma bill.

252L   Letter, Oklahoma Star, June 29, 1876. Concerns James G. Blaine and the transfer of Indian affairs to the War Department.

253L   "Editorial Correspondence," Oklahoma Star, July 20, 1876. Concerns Congress, legislation concerning Indians, and statistics on Indian Territory.

254L   "From Washington," Oklahoma Star, August 3, 1876. Attacks W. P. Ross, charges fraud in Cherokee financial affairs.

255L   Letter, Oklahoma Star, September 28, 1876. Favors opening Indian Territory and defends treaties. Reprinted from Kansas City Times.

256L   "Correspondence," Oklahoma Star, November 16, 1876. Attacks W. P. Ross and discusses Cherokee bounty fraud.

257L   "Washington," Oklahoma Star, January 6, 1877. Supports allotment of land in severalty.

See also 1981 Biobibliography, 355-402.

BOUDINOT, FRANKLIN JOSIAH (Cherokee)

258N   "The Foundation of Earth," Indian Missionary, 1 (February, 1885), 3. Explores possible explanations for earth's existence but settles on God.

259A   "Our Time," Indian Missionary, 2 (February, 1886), 3. Presents Christian testimony.

260A   "The Plan of Salvation," Indian Missionary, 2 (May, 1886), 1. Presents Christian testimony.

See also 1981 Biobibliography, 404-407.

BOUDINOT, WILLIAM PENN (Cherokee)

261P   "There Is a Spectre Ever Haunting," Cherokee Advocate, March 25, 1851. Signed "Cherokee."

262L   Letter, Cherokee Advocate, November 4, 1851. Explains his part in an affray.

263L   "To the Readers of the Cherokee Advocate," Cherokee Advocate, November 17, 1852. Explains the duties of the editor and the role of the paper.

264P   "The Spectre," Indian Missionary, 5 (April, 1889), 1. Allegedly an old poem translated into English by Boudinot.

See also 1981 Biobibliography, 408-425.

BOURASSA, PETER B. (Potawatomi)
265N "An Appeal to My People," Word Carrier of Santee Normal
Training School, 45 (March-April, 1916), 5. Asks them
to stamp out demon whiskey. Reprinted from Indian
Scout.

BOURASSA, SHERMAN (Prairie Band Potawatomi)
266M "The Ground Animals' Creator," Indian Leader, February
15, 1907. A Pueblo legend.
267M "How the Sun and Moon Were Made--An Apache Legend,"
Indian Leader, March 1, 1907.

BOYD, OSCAR (Blackfeet)
268M "The Story of the Sun Dance," Carlisle Arrow, May 28,
1909. Concerns the dance's origin.

BRAVE, BENJAMIN (Lower Brule Sioux)
269L "The Brotherhood of Christian Unity," Talks and Thoughts,
2 (July, 1887), 1. Discusses founding of the Brotherhood.
270L "From an Old Hampton Student," Talks and Thoughts, 5
(December, 1890), 1. Relates activities at Lower Brule.
271A "The Speech," Red Man, 13 (June, 1895), 7-8. Autobiographical statement.
272A "Ben. Brave's Farewell," Talks and Thoughts, 12 (April,
1897), 6. Concerns Hampton Institute and its importance.
See also 1981 Biobibliography, 436-438.

BREAST, SILAS (Sioux)
273L Letter, Ogalalla Light, 1 (May 1, 1900), 4. Urges others
to attend the Oglala Boarding School.

BREUNINGER, AUGUST A. (Menominee)
See UN-A-QUA

BREWER, ELLA L. (Puyallup)
274L "To Our Y.W.C.A.," Chemawa American, 15 (April, 1913),
4. Reminisces about Chemawa and Y.W.C.A. activities.
See also 1981 Biobibliography, 443.

BREWER, OLIVER P. (Cherokee)
275L "From Senator O. P. Brewer," Sallisaw Star, March 13,
1903. Concerns so-called Freedman "fraud."

BRINGSTHEARROW, JULIA (Sioux)
276L Letter, Word Carrier of Santee Normal Training School,
36 (January-February, 1907), 4. Autobiographical statement.

BROKER, CLAUDIA (Chippewa)
277N "Indian Women in the War," Red Lake News, June 1, 1918.

278N "Indian Women in the War," Peace Pipe, 7 (May-June, 1918), 11.

BROKER, JOSEPH HENRY (Chippewa)
279N "Why the Indian Should Celebrate," Carlisle Arrow, July 4, 1912. Concerns the Fourth of July.
See also 1981 Biobibliography, 445.

BROOKS, CHARLES LONEDOG (Sioux)
280L "Santee Graduates' Letters," Word Carrier of Santee Normal Training School, 39 (July-August, 1910), 16. Autobiographical statement.

BROOKS, EMILY (Seneca)
281N "A View on Our Grounds," Talks and Thoughts, 11 (November, 1895), 1.

BROWN, CATHARINE (Cherokee)
282L Letter, Missionary Herald, 17 (August, 1821), 258-259. Presents Christian testimonial. Reprinted from New Haven Religious Intelligencer.

BROWN, DAVID (Cherokee)
283L Letter, Missionary Herald, 17 (August, 1821), 257-258.

BROWN, FANNIE (Little Lakes, i.e., Pomo)
284M "Indian Legends," Indian Leader, April 2, 1909. Concerns the Little Lakes.

BROWN, INEZ (Sioux)
285N "A Vacation at Carlisle," Carlisle Arrow, October 1, 1909. Describes work at Carlisle.
286F "A Story of Two Indian Boys, Manteo and Manchese, Chapter II," Carlisle Arrow, October 1, 1909. Concerns a lost colony.
287N "The Influence of Kind Words," Carlisle Arrow, April 8, 1910.

BROWN, IRENE M. (Sioux)
288N "The Earth Lodge," Carlisle Arrow, November 27, 1908. Describes the lodge.
289N "Mercy Is Sometimes Better Than Justice," Carlisle Arrow, April 9, 1909.
290N "Lincoln's Legacy of Inspiration to Americans," Carlisle Arrow, April 9, 1909.

BROWN, THOMAS (Yankton Sioux)
291N "Onward and Upward," Peace Pipe, 5 (June, 1916), 8. Encourages students to strive.

BRUCE, HAROLD E. (Winnebago)
292N "Educating Sioux Indians at Rosebud, So. Dak.," Word Car-
          rier of Santee Normal Training School, 53 (November-
          December, 1924), 24. Reviews schools and argues that
          Indians must in time assume responsibility for them. Re-
          printed from Sioux Falls Argus-Leader.

BRUNETTE, CECELIA (Menominee)
293N "Religious Conditions Among the Indian People," Word Car-
          rier of Santee Normal Training School, 43 (January-
          February, 1914), 4. Concerns the Menominees.
See also 1981 Biobibliography, 457-458.

BRUNETTE, FRANCES (White Earth Chippewa)
294N "Class History," Peace Pipe, 5 (June, 1916), 5. Concerns
          Pipestone Indian School

BRUNETTE, JOSEPH M. (Menominee)
295N "The Appeal of the Young Indian," Indian Leader, 17 (No-
          vember, 1913), 6-7. Advocates education and "progress"
          for the Indian.

BRUSHELL, SAMUEL J. (Stockbridge)
296N "Trip Across the Mountains," Red Man and Helper, April
          12, 1901. Describes a trip with the Carlisle band.

BRUYIER, JOHN (Crow Creek Sioux)
297N "Our Young Men's Christian Association," Talks and
          Thoughts, 4 (November, 1889), 4. Concerns activities
          at Hampton Institute.
298N "What Next for an Indian Graduate," Talks and Thoughts,
          4 (June, 1890), 3-4. Argues that Indians must continue
          their education.

BRYANT, MICHAEL (Yuma)
299N "With the Band," Sherman Bulletin, May 28, 1913. De-
          scribes activities of the Sherman Institute band.

BUCK, ANNE (Eskimo)
300L "From Far-Off Alaska," Arrow, October 12, 1906. De-
          scribes her trip home from Carlisle.
301L "Letter from Annie Buck," Arrow, July 5, 1907. Describes
          her return to Alaska.

BUFFINGTON, THOMAS MITCHELL (Cherokee)
302A "Pleads for Unity," Fort Smith Elevator, November 14,
          1902. Concerns Cherokee political affairs.
See also 1981 Biobibliography, 465-476.

BULL BEAR, JOCK (Northern Arapaho)
303L "One Indian Boy Helps Another in the Right Way," School

News, 3 (June, 1882), 4. Thanks a friend for introduc-
ing him to Christianity.

BULLEATER, ALBERT (Rosebud Sioux)
304N   "Useful Lives," Word Carrier of Santee Normal Training
School, 37 (March-April, 1908), 8. Urges readers to
give up old ways.

BULLIS, LON S. (San Carlos Apache)
305N   "The Serpent and the Savior," Apache Scout, 2 (June,
1924), 7-8. Concerns the history of the Hebrew Church.
306N   "Good Talk," Apache Scout, 2 (August, 1924), 3-4. Presents Christian testimonial.

BURNEY, BENJAMIN CROOKS (Chickasaw)
307A   "Valedictory," Indian Journal, September 16, 1880. Surveys
Chickasaw affairs as he leaves office.

BURNS, MICHAEL (San Carlos Apache)
308N   "What Michael Burns, an Apache Boy, Thinks on the Indian
Question," School News, 1 (April, 1881), 1. Argues
that "civilization" and education are good for the Indians.
309N   "An Apache Boy Tells What He Thinks About Work," School
News, 2 (August, 1881), 1, 4. Espouses the Protestant
work ethic.
310L   "Communicated," School News, 2 (May, 1882), 1. Urges
students to learn English.

BURSON, RACHAEL (Ute)
311N   "A Ute Christmas," Indian Leader, December 20, 1907.
Describes activities.

BUSCH, ELMER (Pomo)
312N   "Acorn Bread," Indian's Friend, 25 (November, 1912), 8.
Describes how to make it. Reprinted from Red Man.
See also 1981 Biobibliography, 481.

BUSHOTTER, GEORGE (Yankton Sioux)
313A   "Speech of George Bushotter," Council Fire and Arbitrator,
7 (January, 1884), 10. Presents old ways versus the new.
See also 1981 Biobibliography, 482-484.

BUSHYHEAD, DENNIS WOLFE (Cherokee)
314A   "Chief Bushyhead's Speech at Indian University," Indian
Missionary, 1 (June, 1885), 2. Calls for "civilization"
of the Indian.
See also 1981 Biobibliography, 485-514.

BUTLER, BESSIE (Stockbridge)
315N   "The Sewing Department," Indian Leader, May 10, 1901.
Describes type and amount of work at Haskell.

BUTLER, CHARLES W. (Cattaraugus Seneca)
    316N "A Trip to Puerto Rico," Indian Leader, July 24, 1903.
        Describes trip and gives autobiographical statement.

BYANUABA, ELENA (Pueblo)
    317N "An Autobiography," Indian Leader, January 31, 1902.

CABRILLAS, MARIANA (Mission)
    318L "Your Penmanship Is Good," Mission Indian, 1 (December
        15, 1895), 5. Autobiographical statement.

CAJUNE, FRANK (White Earth Chippewa)
    319A Address, Red Man, 14 (January, 1897), 6. Argues that
        the reservation system makes independent citizens of the
        Indians.
See also 1981 Biobibliography, 523.

CALAC, JOSEPH (Mission)
    320N "Our Industrial Work," Sherman Bulletin, May 27, 1914.
        Describes the work at Sherman Institute.

CALLSEN, MINNIE J. (Alaska Native)
    321N "Description of My Home," Red Man and Helper, March 29,
        1901. Describes life at Sitka, Alaska.

CAMPBELL, IRENE (Santee Sioux)
    322N "Leadership," Indian Leader, June 22, 1900. Urges Indians
        to take leadership.
See also 1981 Biobibliography, 233-235.

CAMPBELL, JAMES (Sioux)
    323M "Hiawatha Land," Carlisle Arrow, January 15, 1909. Re-
        tells the Hiawatha story.

CANUP, WILLIAM T. (Eastern Band Cherokee)
    324N "Hostile Comanches. One of Their Many Exploits as Told
        by Old Tom Starr," Cherokee Telephone, September 17,
        1891. Describes a raid near San Antonio, Texas.
    325F "Alluwee Brown and the Tragic End of Unlearned 'Jim,'"
        Cherokee Telephone, November 5, 1891. Short story set
        at Fort Gibson, Cherokee Nation. Reprinted from Cap-
        ital City Daily News.

CARDIN, FRED WILLIAM (Quapaw)
    326N "My Outing," Carlisle Arrow, January 19, 1912. Describes
        his work in the outing system.

CARLOW, ANNA (Sioux)
    327F "An Indian Story," Indian Leader, April 10, 1908. Story
        of a stolen child.

CARPENTER, LINDA L. (Chippewa)
 328N "Salutatory," Peace Pipe, June 20, 1913. Encourages students to strive.

CARR, VIOLA (Navajo)
 329N "How I Made a Little Boy's Waist," Sherman Bulletin, May 29, 1919.

CARTER, BENJAMIN WINSOR (Cherokee)
 330A "An Address Delivered by B. W. Carter at the Female Seminary on the 7th of May," Sequoyah Memorial, July 31, 1856. Concerns Cherokee "progress" and the need to work hard.

CARTER, CALEB W. (Nez Percé)
 331N "Christmas Among the Nez Percés," Carlisle Arrow, January 13, 1911. Describes dances and celebrations.
 332N "How the Nez Percés Trained for Long Distance Running," Carlisle Arrow, April 7, 1911.
 333P "Class Poem," Carlisle Arrow, April 19, 1912. Encourages students to strive.
 334N "Gardening," Carlisle Arrow, May 17, 1912. Stresses the value of gardening.
 See also 1981 Biobibliography, 531-537.

CARY, NELLIE (Apache)
 335L Letter, School News, 1 (March, 1881), 4. Encourages others to attend school.

CASH, A. WARREN (Sioux)
 336N "The Indian of To-day," American Indian Advocate, 3 (Grass Moon, 1922), 5-6. Argues that the Indian is not vanishing but making economic and civic gains.
 See also 1981 Biobibliography, 541.

CASTRO, FELICITA (Mission)
 337L "Father Ubach Plays," Mission Indian, 1 (January 15, 1895), 4. Concerns a missionary at St. Anthony's Industrial School.

CASTRO, MARIE AGNES (Klamath)
 338N "Care of Milk," Sherman Bulletin, March 15, 1911.

CASWELL, BENJAMIN (Chippewa)
 339N "The General Outlook," Red Man, 13 (May-June, 1896), 2-3. Argues for assimilation and citizenship.
 340N "Leech Lake Institute," Chippeway Herald, 3 (January, 1904), 3.
 See also 1981 Biobibliography, 542-543.

CAYOU, FRANK (Omaha)
341A   "Past, Present and Future of the Carlisle Indian School
        Team," Red Man, 14 (January, 1898), 5. Concerns foot-
        ball.

CEDARTREE, CLARA (Southern Arapaho)
342N   "An Old-Time Sun Dance," Indian Leader, June 20, 1902.
        Describes the dance.

CEERLEY, ELIZABETH (Navajo)
343N   "Elizabeth," Word Carrier of Santee Normal Training School,
        46 (January-February, 1917), 4. Relates her conversion
        to Christianity.

CENTER, NANCY (Sioux)
344N   "Items from the Class Rooms," Oglala Light, 20 (April 1,
        1920), 3. Reports classroom activities at the Oglala
        Boarding School.

CETAN SAPA (Sioux)
345N   "The Yankton Sioux," Indian Leader, September 19, 1902.
        Concerns past and present of the Yanktons. Reprinted
        from Twin Territories.
See also 1981 Biobibliography, 544.

CHAPMAN, ARTHUR (White Earth Chippewa)
346P   "Indians in Khaki," Southern Workman, 49 (November,
        1919), 607. Poem concerning World War I. Reprinted
        from American Indian Magazine.
See also 1981 Biobibliography, 545-546.

CHARGING EAGLE, AGNES (Standing Rock Sioux)
347L   Letter, Sina Sapa Wocekiye Taeyanpaha, August, 1892.
        Urges others to attend school.

CHARGING WOLF, LIZZIE (Pine Ridge Sioux)
348N   "Ration Day Out West," Talks and Thoughts, 16 (July,
        1902), 1.
349N   "An Indian Feast," Talks and Thoughts, 16 (March, 1903),
        1. Describes an event of 1896.

CHARLES, JOSEPHINE S. (Oneida)
350N   "Experiences," Arrow, March 27, 1908. Autobiographical
        statement lauding housekeeping.

CHARLES, REUBEN (Tonawanda Seneca)
351N   "Christmas," Arrow, January 3, 1908. Describes activities
        at his home.
352M   "Indian Legend," Carlisle Arrow, September 18, 1908. Iro-
        quois story of O-yo-ga-weh.

353N   "Christmas on the Tonawanda Reservation," Carlisle Arrow,
       January 7, 1910.

CHARLEY, BESSIE M.   (Peoria)
354M   "How the Bear Lost His Tail," Arrow, December 27, 1907.
       A legend.
355N   "Kit Carson," Arrow, May 29, 1908.   Biographical sketch.

CHARLEY, FANNIE   (Peoria)
356L   "Interesting Description of the Bermuda Islands," Carlisle
       Arrow, March 10, 1911.   Describes islands and her trip
       there.

CHECOTE, SAMUEL   (Creek)
357L   Letter, Council Fire, 1 (April, 1878), 61.   Relates news of
       the Creek Nation.
See also 1981 Biobibliography, 552-555.

CHICO, ANTONIO   (Papago)
358F   "The Adventures of a Turkey," Sherman Bulletin, Novem-
       ber 25, 1914.   Fantasy on a Thanksgiving theme.

CHIEF, ANNIE   (Sioux)
359L   Letter, Ogalalla Light, 1 (May 1, 1900), 4.   Concerns
       Hiawatha legend.

CHIEF EAGLE, ALBERT   (Pine Ridge Sioux)
360N   "Describing the German Attack in Champagne," Indian News,
       20 (January, 1919), 3-4.

CHILDERS, CLARENCE   (Creek)
361N   "Valedictory--'Over the Top,'" Indian School Journal, 18
       (June, 1918), 43-45.   Offers encouragement to students
       to strive.

CHILDS, CHRISTINE   (Crow)
362N   "Corn Culture," Red Man and Helper, November 7, 1903.
363N   "Housekeeping," Arrow, March 30, 1906.   Argues the need
       to learn housekeeping.

CHILSON, DANIEL O.   (Citizens' Band Potawatomi)
364L   Letter, Talks and Thoughts, 2 (May, 1887), 4.   Describes
       his home in Shawneetown, Indian Territory.
365L   "To the 'Talks and Thoughts,'" Talks and Thoughts, 6
       (January, 1892), 3.   Relates events at Shawneetown,
       Indian Territory.

CHIMAL, ETTA   (Mescalero Apache)
366N   "Some Customs at Mescalero," Talks and Thoughts, 17 (July,
       1903), 3-4.

CHINGWA, LOUIS F. (Chippewa)
367N "The Carlisle Indian Band," Arrow, March 27, 1908. Relates history and activities of the band.

CHOOROMI, JOHN (Hopi)
368N "Life Among the Hopis," Talks and Thoughts, 16 (April,
1903), 1, 3-4.
369F "A Pretty Girl Who Married a Poor Boy," Talks and
Thoughts, 17 (August-September, 1903), 3.
370F "The Deer and the Coyote," Talks and Thoughts, 17
(August-September, 1903), 6. A tale.
See also 1981 Biobibliography, 566.

CLAIRMONT, PHILIP (Sioux)
371N "The Harness Shop," Carlisle Arrow, December 4, 1908.
Discusses the tools used in the shop.

CLANCY, ALLAN (Sioux)
372N "How We May Be Respected," Word Carrier of Santee Normal Training School, 37 (March-April, 1908), 8. Urges
readers to give up old ways.

CLARK, HOMER (Crow Creek Sioux)
373A "Our Hampton Mother," Talks and Thoughts, 5 (August,
1890), 1. Discusses what Hampton Institute gives the
Indians.

CLARKE, MALCOLM W. (Piegan)
374A "That the Negro Is Superior to the Indian," Red Man, 12
(January-February, 1894), 7. Argues the negative side.
See also 1981 Biobibliography, 571.

CLEMENTE, JOHN C. (Mission)
375L "Will Be Glad to Hear from You Again," Mission Indian,
1 (December 15, 1895), 5. Concerns boarding school
life.

CLEVELAND, MARCHELL (Mission)
376N "A Visit to My Home After Fifteen Years," Indian, Unnumbered (April, 1922), 1. Describes a meeting of Indians
at Somerton, California.

CLIFFORD, JOHN (Pine Ridge Sioux)
377N "Then and Now," Talks and Thoughts, 17 (August-
September, 1903), 5, 6. Discusses how the Sioux have
changed.
378N "Leaders," Talks and Thoughts, 18 (August, 1904), 4.

CLIFFORD, MARY (Sioux)
379L "A Dakota Endeavor," Word Carrier of Santee Normal Training

School, 36 (November-December, 1907), 21. Concerns
her efforts to establish a Christian Endeavor Society.

CLOUD, BENEDICT D. (Sioux)
380N "How the Great Spirit Taught the Dakotas to Pray," Carlisle Arrow, December 1, 1911. Concerns the Ghost
Dance.
See also 1981 Biobibliography, 575-576.

CLOUD, ELIZABETH (Bad River Chippewa)
See BENDER, ELIZABETH

CLOUD, HENRY C. ROE (Winnebago)
381N "Growth of Church Architecture in Europe," Word Carrier,
30 (April, 1901), 12. Concerns cathedrals.
382L "Henry Cloud and Tennent Church," Word Carrier of Santee Normal Training School, 34 (May-June, 1905), 9.
Concerns David Brainerd and Tennent Church.
383L "A Santee Pupil at Yale!" Word Carrier of Santee Normal
Training School, 35 (November-December, 1906), 22.
Reminisces about Santee Normal School and describes his
experiences in the East.
384N "Missionary Work Among the Oklahoma Indians," Word Carrier of Santee Normal Training School, 36 (September-
October, 1907), 18. Describes W. C. Roe's work among
the Comanches and Apaches.
385N "The Winnebago Situation," Word Carrier of Santee Normal
Training School, 38 (July-August, 1909), 13. Concerns
his summer experiences during mission work among the
Winnebago.
386N "A Brave Indian Superintendent," Weekly Chemawa American,
December 16, 1910. Concerns Albert H. Kneale of Winnebago, Nebraska. Reprinted from Southern Workman.
387A "An Appeal to the Christian People of America," Word Carrier of Santee Normal Training School, 39 (November-
December, 1910), 21. Argues that Christian education
is improving the Indian. Reprinted from Indian's Friend.
388N "Education of the American Indian," Weekly Review, January 30, 1915. Reprinted from Southern Workman.
389A "Problems of the American Indian," Indian News, 17 (March,
1915), 2-3.
390N "Alfred Longley Riggs," Word Carrier of Santee Normal
Training School, 45 (July-August, 1916), 14. Offers a
tribute to Riggs at his death. Reprinted from Southern
Workman.
See also 1981 Biobibliography, 578-595.

COACHMAN, WARD (Creek)
391A "The Chief's Message," Council Fire, 1 (October, 1878),
154. Concerns the threat to Indian rights.
See also 1981 Biobibliography, 596.

COLBERT, GEORGE (Chickasaw)
    392L   Letter, Indian Missionary, 1 (May, 1885), 1. Concerns
            Baptists in the Chickasaw Nation.

COLBERT, HUMPHREY (Chickasaw)
    393L   Letter, Indian Missionary, 6 (January, 1890), 1-2. Relates
            religious activities in his community.
    See also 1981 Biobibliography, 602.

COLE, COLEMAN (Choctaw)
    394N   "Unwritten Choctaw Traditions," Council Fire, 2 (September,
            1879), 133-134. Describes old Choctaw life-style and habits.
    395N   "Indian Traditions," Council Fire, 2 (December, 1879), 181.
            Discusses Choctaw clans and funeral practices and white
            influence upon them.
    396N   "Indian Traditions--No. 3," Council Fire, 3 (January,
            1880), 14. Describes the effects of white contact.
    397N   "Indian Traditions Number Five," Council Fire, 3 (March,
            1880), 39. Concerns the United States and its treaty
            obligations.
    See also 1981 Biobibliography, 603-618.

COLEMAN, FRANCIS E. (Chippewa)
    398N   "Ice Harvesting," Carlisle Arrow, April 29, 1910. Concerns
            gathering ice for ice houses.
    399N   "Choosing a Career," Carlisle Arrow, September 29, 1911.
            Encourages hard work and practicality.

COLHOFF, LIZZIE (Sioux)
    400L   Letter, Sina Sapa Wocekiye Taeyanpaha, April, 1894. Urges
            others to attend school.

COLONAHASKI, ABRAHAM C. (Eastern Band Cherokee)
    401L   "What the Indian Should Be Taught," Arrow, December 21,
            1906. Urges self-support for citizenship.

COLVARD, MYRTLE (Cherokee)
    402N   "Chilocco Students in the Great War," Indian School Jour-
            nal, 19 (June, 1919), 18, 21.

COMMAND, JOSEPH (Leech Lake Chippewa)
    403N   "Salutatory," Peace Pipe, 5 (June, 1916), 5. Encourages
            students to achieve.

CONEPACHO, BILLY (Florida Seminole)
    404L   "Letter from a Seminole Boy," School News, 3 (November,
            1882), 4. Urges others to attend school.

CONGER, ALICE CORA (Santee Sioux)
    405F   "Healing of Jarius' Daughter," Word Carrier, 1 (June, 1884),
            24. Retells the story.

406N   "Autobiographies of Pupils," Word Carrier, 20 (June, 1891), 24.

407N   "Early Recollections of Santee," Word Carrier of Santee Normal Training School, 32 (November-December, 1903), 22. Describes her early experiences. Reprinted from Work at Home.

408L   Letter, Word Carrier of Santee Normal Training School, 34 (March-April, 1905), 6. Relates her experiences as a cook at a school in Greenwood, South Dakota.

CONGER, JENNIE IONE (Sioux)

409N   "Growth of Church Architecture in Europe," Word Carrier, 30 (April 1901), 12. Concerns styles of architecture.

410L   "Former Pupils' Letters, I," Word Carrier, 32 (January-February, 1903), 2. Describes what she has done since she left school.

CONGER, LUCILLE I. (Santee Sioux)

411N   "Christmas Holidays," Talks and Thoughts, 11 (January, 1896), 1-2. Concerns Christmas on campus.

412N   "The Many in One," Talks and Thoughts, 13 (July, 1897), 3-4; (August-September, 1897), 6. Concerns the Sioux and their bands.

413N   "The Hemenway Farm," Talks and Thoughts, 16 (January, 1903), 1.

414N   "Indian Childhood," Talks and Thoughts, 17 (July, 1903), 1, 4.

415N   "Anniversary Week," Talks and Thoughts, 17 (July, 1903), 1, 3-4. Describes events at Hampton Institute.

416N   "Indian Customs," Indian Leader, August 14, 1903. Concerns hospitality. Reprinted from Talks and Thoughts.

See also 1981 Biobibliography, 624.

CONGER, MERCY I. (Santee Sioux)

417N   "What the Moon Said," Talks and Thoughts, 1 (November, 1886), 1. Concerns improvement of the educated Indian.

CONGER, SYBIL (Sioux)

418F   "The Medicine Man (a True Story)," Talks and Thoughts, 16 (August-September, 1902), 7.

CONGWHIO, LOMO (Hopi)

419N   "How the Hopi Indians Live," Indian Leader, April 11, 1902. Describes life-style and dances.

COODALOOK, ANNIE (Eskimo)

420L   "From Far-Off Alaska," Arrow, July 26, 1907. Concerns her trip from Carlisle to Nome.

421L   "From Far-Off Alaska," Carlisle Arrow, September 25, 1908. Describes her life at Barrow.

COODEY, DANIEL ROSS (Cherokee)
    422L   Letter, Cherokee Advocate, December 26, 1844. Concerns
           the Starrs.

COOK, CHARLES SMITH (Pine Ridge Sioux)
    423L   "A Native Missionary at Pine Ridge Agency," Morning Star,
           7 (July, 1887), 2. Concerns Carlisle students who have
           returned to Pine Ridge.
    424N   "Indian Names for Indians," Word Carrier, 19 (July-August,
           1890), 22. Opposes giving Indians European names.
See also 1981 Biobibliography, 631-632.

COOK, PHILLIP (Southern Cheyenne)
    425L   "An Indian Letter," Baptist Home Mission Monthly, 22 (Jan-
           uary, 1900), 19. Concerns native practices among the
           Cheyenne.

COOKE, MARY (Mohawk)
    426N   "Physiology," Chippeway Herald, October 29, 1909. Con-
           cerns sprains.

COOKE, MAUDE (Mohawk)
    427P   With Agnes Hatch. "Our Cottage," Carlisle 1917. Carlisle,
           PA: U.S. Indian School, 1917, p. 40. Concerns Model
           Home, a cottage at Carlisle.

COOLIDGE, SHERMAN S. (Northern Arapaho)
    428A   Address, Red Man, 14 (March, 1898), 1. Autobiographical
           statement.
    429N   "The Indian Speaking for Himself," Word Carrier of Santee
           Normal Training School, 41 (September-October, 1912),
           18. Concerns formation of the Society of American In-
           dians. Reprinted from Week.
See also 1981 Biobibliography, 642-650.

COONS, ARTHUR (Pawnee)
    430N   "Weeds," Carlisle Arrow, October 23, 1908. Discusses types
           and the need to control them.
    431N   "Carpentry at Carlisle," Carlisle Arrow, June 4, 1909.

COOPER, MEDORA (Potawatomi)
    432N   "What Domestic Art Means to Us," Indian School Journal,
           18 (June, 1918), 39-40. Argues that it gives independ-
           ence and pride.

COPWAY, GEORGE (Ojibwa)
    433A   "An Eloquent Indian," Mistletoe, 1 (February, 1849), 42.
           Urges temperance.
    434L   "New Indian Republic," Indian Advocate, 5 (September,
           1850), 4. Relates his plan for an Indian territory west
           of the Missouri River.

435N   "Indian Pastime," Indian Advocate, 6 (December, 1851), 1.
Describes Ojibwa ball games.
See also 1981 Biobibliography, 653-714.

CORNELIUS, BRIGMAN (Oneida)
436A   Address, Red Man, 14 (January, 1897), 7. Argues that
the reservation system makes independent citizens.
See also 1981 Biobibliography, 715-716.

CORNELIUS, ISABELLA C. (Oneida)
437L   Letter, Red Man, 14 (May-June, 1897), 3. Urges Indians
to go East to school.

CORNELIUS, LAURA MINNIE (Oneida)
438N   "Building the Indian Home," Indian's Friend, 13 (May, 1901),
2, 11-12. Argues education and self-sufficiency for the
Indians.
See also 1981 Biobibliography, 1882-1884.

CORNELIUS, LAVINIA (Oneida)
439L   "Vacation in Block Island," Talks and Thoughts, 5 (November, 1890), 4.

CORNELIUS, LEILA (Oneida)
440A   "The President's Address," Red Man, 13 (January, 1896),
4. Opens a meeting of the Longstreth Society at Carlisle.

CORNELIUS, LILIAN (Oneida)
441N   "An Indian Estimate," Indian's Friend, 13 (April, 1901),
7. Urges education and the overcoming of stereotypes.

CORNELIUS, REBECCA (Oneida)
442N   "Christmas at Oneida," Talks and Thoughts, 16 (December,
1900), 4. Describes activities.
443N   "Christmas in Oklahoma," Talks and Thoughts, 16 (December, 1900), 1, 4. Describes events there.

CORNELIUS, ROSE (Oneida)
444N   "How I Should Like to Spend the Christmas Holidays," Indian Leader, December 29, 1905. Describes Christmas
activities at her home.

CORNTASSEL, BERTHA (Cherokee)
445N   "Turpentine and Rosen," Interpreter, 2 (November 1, 1917),
11.

COSAR, GALVOS (Creek)
446M   "An Indian Legend," Indian Progress, 1 (March, 1923), 2.
Story of deer and rabbit exchanging feet.
See also 1981 Biobibliography, 726-728.

COUNTING, DORA (Sioux)
> 447L   Letter, <u>Word Carrier of Santee Normal Training School</u>, 36 (January-February, 1907), 4. Concerns school life at Oahe School, South Dakota.

CRANE, JAMES (Umatilla)
> 448N   "Our Visit to the Tailor Shop," <u>Carlisle Arrow</u>, October 2, 1908. Describes what goes on there.

CRAZY GHOST, JULIA (Sioux)
> 449N   "Items from the Class Rooms," <u>Oglala Light</u>, 20 (March 1, 1920), 3. Reports classroom activites at the Oglala Boarding School.

CROOKS, OLIVE (Crow)
> 450F   "The Story of a Worm," <u>Word Carrier</u>, 28 (January, 1899), 4. Fantasy, telling the life cycle of a worm.

CROTZER, ETHEL (Wyandot)
> 451N   "Cooking Meats," <u>Indian Leader</u>, June 24, 1904.

CROTZER, MARTHA BAIN (Sisseton Sioux)
> 452L   Letter, <u>Word Carrier of Santee Normal Training School</u>, 34 (March-April, 1905), 6. Relates her life at Darlington, Oklahoma as a seamstress in an Indian school.

CROWE, NONA (Cherokee)
> 453N   "My Vacation," <u>Carlisle Arrow</u>, September 18, 1908. Describes her summer in Medford, New Jersey.

CROWE, WESLEY (Cherokee)
> 454N   "My People, the Cherokees," <u>Talks and Thoughts</u>, 9 (March, 1895), 6. Describes their life-style.

CROW-EAGLE, THOMAS (Sioux)
> 455L   Letter, <u>Sina Sapa Wocekiye Taeyanpaha</u>, April, 1894. Urges others to attend school.

CROWSGHOST, MORGAN (Gros Ventre)
> 456N   "Christmas at Fort Berthold," <u>Carlisle Arrow</u>, December 31, 1909. Describes church services.

CULBERTSON, MOSES (Sioux)
> 457N   "My Summer Home," <u>Talks and Thoughts</u>, 4 (October, 1889), 1. Describes his experiences at Lexington, Massachusetts.

DAJIDA (San Carlos Apache)
See BULLIS, LON S.

DALE, WILLIAM (Caddo)
    458M "A Legend of the Sun," Carlisle Arrow, March 26, 1909.
          Legend of the fox and the sun.
    See also 1981 Biobibliography, 760-761.

DAUGHERTY, MATHEW (Cherokee)
    459P "To Eliza," Muskogee Morning Times, February 12, 1897.

DAVIS, RICHARD (Southern Cheyenne)
    460N "Courage," Red Man, 8 (December, 1887), 5. Defines
          courage.
    See also 1981 Biobibliography, 766-767.

DAVIS, SAMUEL G. (Haida)
    461N "Klinquan's Progress," Home Mission Monthly, 18 (August,
          1904), 246. Reports on mission efforts.
    462N "The Alaskan Totem," Home Mission Monthly, 19 (June,
          1905), 178-179. Concerns Haidas.
    463N "The Totem and the Potlatch," Indian News, 14 (November,
          1911), 10-11. Reprinted from Home Mission Monthly.
    464N "The Totem and the Potlach," Indian Leader, December 29,
          1911. Reprinted from Home Mission Monthly.
    465N "The Potlach," Word Carrier of Santee Normal Training
          School, 41 (January-February, 1912), 1. Describes the
          old custom and ways it survives.
    466L "Letter from Kasaan," Alaskan Fisherman, 1 (June, 1924),
          10. Concerns citizenship.
    See also 1981 Biobibliography, 768.

DAWSON, ANNA R. (Arickara)
    467L Letter, Ten Years' Work for Indians at Hampton Institute.
          Hampton, VA: Hampton Institute, 1888, pp. 57-58. Con-
          cerns Indian education and returned students.
    468N "Three Little Sun Worshippers," Talks and Thoughts, 5
          (July, 1890), 1. Concerns religion in her early days
          on the Missouri River.
    469N "How Mission Work Has Helped the Indian Woman," Word
          Carrier, 20 (September, 1891), 31.
    See also 1981 Biobibliography, 769-770.

DAY, EUGENE (Paiute)
    470A "Salutatory," Sherman Bulletin, May 24, 1916. Encourages
          students.

DAY, MARTHA (Pueblo)
    471N "Frances E. Willard," Carlisle Arrow, December 25, 1908.
          Biographical sketch.

DAY-DODGE (White Earth Chippewa)
    472N "The Ojibwas: Their Customs and Traditions," Progress,

December 17, 1887. Concerns the origin of the Indian,
naming children, and initiation into maidenhood and manhood.

473N   "The Ojibwas: Their Customs and Traditions," Progress,
December 24, 1887. Concerns courtship and marriage.

474N   "The Ojibwas: Their Customs and Traditions," Progress,
January 21, 1888. Concerns Gee-sah-ke-we-nine or the
Jugglers and faiths and beliefs.

475N   "The Ojibwas: Their Customs and Traditions," Progress,
January 28, 1888. Concerns Ojibwa faiths and beliefs.

476M   "The Ojibwas: Their Customs and Traditions," Progress,
February 4, 1888. Legends of the first birchbark canoe,
Sun's Island, and first fire.

477N   "The Ojibwas: Their Customs and Beliefs," Progress,
February 14, 1888. Concerns the Grand Medicine.

478N   "The Ojibwas: Their Customs and Beliefs," Progress,
February 25, 1888. Describes the Grand Medicine and
initiation.

479M   "The Ojibwas: Their Customs and Traditions," Progress,
April 21, 1888. Legend of Wainahboozho.

480M   "The Ojibwas: Their Customs and Traditions," Progress,
May 12, 1888. Legend of Wainahboozho.

DE CORA, ANGEL (Winnebago)

481N   "The Division of Land in Severalty Among the Indians and
Its Expected Effects Upon Tribal Organization," Talks
and Thoughts, 6 (October, 1891), 1, 4.

482N   "Native Indian Art," Arrow, August 23, 1907. Argues the
need to retain Indian art and opposes assimilationist education.

483N   "Native Indian Art," Chippeway Herald, 7 (September,
1907), 1-2. Argues the need to retain Indian art and
opposes assimilationist education.

See also 1981 Biobibliography, 771-778.

DE CORA, JULIA (Winnebago)

484N   "Napoleon," Talks and Thoughts, 11 (December, 1895),
2-3; (January, 1896), 1-3.

485N   "Indian Superstitions," Talks and Thoughts, 14 (July, 1898),
4. Concerns the Winnebago.

DE COTEAU, LIEN (Sisseton Sioux)

486N   "A Summer's Work," Word Carrier of Santee Normal Training School, 43, (May-June, 1914), 12. Concerns farm
work on the Sisseton Reservation.

DE COTEAU, LOUIS (Sioux)

487N   "Santee Pupils' Association," Word Carrier of Santee Normal
Training School, 36 (July-August, 1907), 16. Reports
on meeting and election of officers.

DEER, JAMES H. (Caddo)
488L   Letter, Indian Missionary, 2 (June, 1886), 1. Describes
      conditions among the Kiowas, Comanches, and Wichitas
      and argues the need to Christianize.

DE FOND, SAMUEL C. (Yankton Sioux)
489L   "What Will Our Education Amount To?" Talks and Thoughts,
      1 (September, 1886), 1.
490N   "Old Indian Ways," Talks and Thoughts, 1 (October, 1886),
      1. Concerns Indian life-style before the whites came.
491N   "My Early School Days," Talks and Thoughts, 1 (Decem-
      ber, 1886), 2-3. Describes his early experiences in pub-
      lic school.
492N   "Teaching," Talks and Thoughts, 2 (December, 1887), 2-3.
      Describes his experiences.
See also 1981 Biobibliography, 780-782.

DEGAN, LILLIAN (Chippewa)
493N   "What We Ought to Do After We Graduate," Peace Pipe,
      February 27, 1914. Argues for higher education.
494N   "Education," Peace Pipe, November 27, 1914.

DEGAN, LOUISE (Chippewa)
495N   "Salutatory," Peace Pipe, June 19, 1914. Encourages stu-
      dents.

DE GRASSE, ALFRED (Mashpee)
496M   "About Poison Ivy," Carlisle Arrow, April 23, 1909.
497M   "The Legend of the Red Eagle," Carlisle Arrow, February
      10, 1911. Story of the eagle killed by a magic arrow.
498N   "My Outing," Carlisle Arrow, May 12, 1911. Describes
      his work at Bethlehem Steel.
See also 1981 Biobibliography, 783-785.

DE LODGE, VICTORIA (Ponca)
499N   "Christmas Customs Among the Ponca Indians," Indian
      Leader, December 20, 1907.

DE LONEY, ELLA (Chippewa)
500F   "My Trip Across the Atlantic and Pacific Oceans," Carlisle
      Arrow, November 20, 1908. Fantasy.
501N   "My Christmas," Carlisle Arrow, January 1, 1909. De-
      scribes activities at her home in Minnesota.
502N   "The Needle," Carlisle Arrow, May 7, 1909. Describes how
      it is made.

DELORIA, ELLA CARA (Yankton Sioux)
503N   "Health Education of Indian Girls," Word Carrier of Santee
      Normal Training School, 53 (March-April, 1924), 6. Urges

such education in government schools. Reprinted from
Southern Workman.
See also 1981 Biobibliography, 787.

DE LORIMIERE, MARGARET I. (Mohawk)
504N "Christmas the Greatest Day," Carlisle Arrow, January 7,
1910. Describes activities at Hogansburg, New York,
her home.

DEMARRIAS, MATT (Sioux)
505L "A Letter from the Indian Who Is Missionary to His Own
People," Word Carrier of Santee Normal Training School,
42 (March-April, 1913), 7. Describes his experiences as
a missionary at Lodge Pole, Montana.

DENNY, JOSEPH H. (Oneida)
506N "School Improvements," Carlisle Arrow, September 18, 1908.
Describes improvements at Carlisle.
507N "Tailoring," Carlisle Arrow, April 2, 1909. Describes activities in the tailor shop at Carlisle.

DENNY, WALLACE (Oneida)
508N "Farming," Arrow, March 30, 1906. Discusses the Indian
as a farmer.

DENOMIE, ALICE H. (Chippewa)
509N "The Soil and the Plant," Arrow, November 9, 1906. Describes food cycle in plants.

DE PELTQUESTANGUE, ESTAIENE M. (Chippewa)
510N "Indian Nurses and Nursing Indians," Sherman Bulletin,
October 20, 1915.
See also 1981 Biobibliography, 795, where she is incorrectly identified as Kickapoo.

DE POE, ROBERT R. (Siletz)
511A Address, Red Man, 14 (January, 1897), 6. Attacks the
reservation system.

DESGEORGES, PATRICK (Pueblo)
512N "Christmas Story," Indian Leader, December 24, 1902. Describes Pueblo celebration of Christmas.
513F "The Iron for the Haskell Wagons," Indian Leader, January
20, 1905. Fantasy, pretending he is iron being proc-
essed.

DOCTOR, MILO (Seneca)
514L Letter, Arrow, October 13, 1905. Concerns his trip to
the Philippines.

515L "Letter from the Philippines," Arrow, January 11, 1907.
Describes events in the Philippines.

DOCTOR, NANCY (Sioux)
516N "About the Puppy and the Hen," Iapi Oaye, 1 (May, 1884),
2.
517N "The Santee Mission," Southern Workman and Hampton
School Record, 15 (May, 1886), 56.

DODSON, JOHN (Shoshoni)
518N "Progress of the Indians," Talks and Thoughts, 18 (March,
1905), 3, 4.
See also 1981 Biobibliography, 803.

DOLPHUS, AMY E. (Sioux)
519M "The Bone Ghost--An Indian Myth," Red Man and Helper,
April 5, 1901.

DOOR, FRANK C. (Cheyenne River Sioux)
520L Letter, Talks and Thoughts, 2 (March, 1887), 1. Advocates "civilization" of the Indians.

DORIAN, ELWOOD (Iowa)
521L Letter, School News, 1 (March, 1881), 4. Urges others
to attend school.

DORMAN, EBEN (Ukie, i.e., Yuki)
522N "The Indian Farmer," Sherman Bulletin, May 12, 1909.

DORMAN, ELLEN (Ukie, i.e., Yuki)
523P "1910 Class Poem," Sherman Bulletin, May 25, 1910, Supplement. Concerns Sherman Institute students.

DOW, LEE (Hupa)
524N "Industrial Education of the Indian," Sherman Bulletin,
June 10, 1908.

DOWNIE, FORDIE (Clallam)
525N "The Hermitage," Chemawa American, 17 (April, 1915), 26-
27. Describes the Hermitage.

DOWNIE, REGINALD (Clallam)
526N "Printcraft," Chemawa American, 16 (June, 1914), 1-3.
Gives a brief history of printing.
527N "Our Dairy Department," Chemawa American, 17 (March,
1915), 28-29. Describes the Dairy Department at Chemawa.

DOWNING, LOUIS (Cherokee)
528N "The Outlook for the Indians of Oklahoma," Indian School

Journal, 18 (June, 1918), 20-21. Argues good effects of white influence.

529N "Senior Class," Indian School Journal, 18 (June, 1918), 59. Concerns students at Chilocco.

DOWNING, LOUISE (Cherokee)

530P "Class Song," Indian School Journal, 18 (June, 1918), 60. Encourages students to strive.

531A "Salutatory--Attention," Indian School Journal, 18 (June, 1918), 19-20. Encourages students.

DOXON, CHARLES (Onondaga)

532A "Our Needs," Talks and Thoughts, 1 (May, 1886), 3-4. Urges "civilization" of the Indians.

533N "The Life in the Wigwam," Talks and Thoughts, 1 (November, 1886), 3-4. Describes campus life at Hampton Institute.

534A "Speech of Charles Doxon," Talks and Thoughts, 2 (August, 1887), 3. Concerning the Fourth of July and its meaning.

535F "A Story from a Tree," Talks and Thoughts, 2 (May, 1888), 3. Fantasy, presenting the history of the Butler School site as told by a tree.

536N "Witnessing the Whole Proceedings of Harrison's Inauguration," Talks and Thoughts, 3 (March, 1889), 1.

537N "An Indian as a Mechanic," Chippeway Herald, 4 (October, 1905), 3. Autobiographical statement.

538P "Hampton," Talks and Thoughts, 19 (February, 1906), 1.

539A "Industrial Education for the Indian," Arrow, February 15, 1907.

See also 1981 Biobibliography, 816-824.

DOXTATER, EDNA (Seneca)

540N "A Syrian," Carlisle Arrow, December 18, 1908. Concerns a Syrian woman who spoke at Carlisle.

DOXTATER, FRED (Oneida)

541N "How to Grow Corn," Arrow, June 29, 1906.

DU BRAY, JOSEPH (Yankton Sioux)

542N "Indians' Accustoms," Talks and Thoughts, 5 (June, 1891), 1, 4. Describes interesting customs.

543N "How to Walk Straight," Talks and Thoughts, 6 (April, 1892), 4. Draws analogies between Indians and crabs.

544F "Moon Nibblers: A Fable," Talks and Thoughts, 8 (August, 1892), 3. Concerns mice.

545F "A Fox and a Wolf," Talks and Thoughts, 8 (September, 1892), 1. A fable.

546M "A Queen, a Half-Wit, and a Prince: An Old Indian Legend," Talks and Thoughts, 7 (January, 1893), 2-3.

547N   "The Sun Dance," Talks and Thoughts, 8 (November, 1893),
        1. Describes dance.

548N   "My Visit to Richmond," Talks and Thoughts, 8 (January,
        1894), 6. Describes his trip.

549N   "The War Bonnet," Talks and Thoughts, 9 (December, 1894),
        1-2. Describes it and its use.

See also 1981 Biobibliography, 829.

DUEL, D. W. (Cherokee)

550L   Letter, Indian Missionary, 4 (April, 1888), 2. Advocates
        Christian teaching in schools.

DUNBAR, JOSEPH (Snohomish)

551N   "Farming," Chemawa American, 15 (June, 1913), 15-16.
        Describes his plans for his farm on the Tulalip Reserva-
        tion.

DUNCAN, DE WITT CLINTON (Cherokee)

552L   "An Indian's Warning," Council Fire, 1 (December, 1878),
        189. Opposes territorial status for Indian Territory.
        Reprinted from Cherokee Advocate.

553F   "A Cherokee Fable," Iapi Oaye, 10 (July, 1881), 56. Anec-
        dote illustrating the white man's broken promises to In-
        dians. Reprinted from Cherokee Advocate.

554F   "A Cherokee Fable," Council Fire, 4 (August, 1881), 125.
        Anecdote illustrating the white man's broken promises to
        Indians. Reprinted from Cherokee Advocate.

555N   "The Indian Problem," Iapi Oaye, 12 (April, 1883), 3.
        Concerns Indian-white relations.

556N   "Carlisle Indian School," Cherokee Telephone, August 27,
        1891. Describes his visit to Carlisle.

557L   "Coercive Throughout," Daily Chieftain, October 3, 1898.
        Concerns the Curtis Act.

558N   "No Remedy Probable," Daily Chieftain, October 7, 1898.
        Concerns the Curtis Act.

559L   "From Vinita," Western Christian Advocate, January 19,
        1905. Reports on Methodism in Vinita, Cherokee Nation.

560N   "The Cherokees in Georgia," Tahlequah Arrow, September
        15, 1906. Concerns how the Republicans have mistreated
        the Cherokees. Reprinted from Vinita Leader.

See also 1981 Biobibliography, 832-997.

DUNCAN, JAMES W. (Cherokee)

561N   "R. L. Owne's Plan Endorsed," Cherokee Telephone, Octo-
        ber 22, 1891. Concerns the Cherokee Strip sale.

See also 1981 Biobibliography, 1000-1005.

DUNCAN, MYRTLE E. (Ukie, i.e., Yuki)

562F   "How the Bear Lost His Tail," Sherman Bulletin, April 6,
        1910.

563N   "Cotton," Sherman Bulletin, March 17, 1909.

564F   "How the Blue Bird Became Beautiful and the Fox Became
Ugly," Sherman Bulletin, April 22, 1914. A tale.

565A   "Salutatory," Sherman Bulletin, May 27, 1914. Encourages
students to strive.

DUNCAN, WALTER ADAIR (Cherokee)

566L   Letter, Cherokee Advocate, December 18, 1848. Concerns
Cherokee affairs.

567L   "To the People of the Nation," Cherokee Advocate, July
30, 1850. Concerns Miss Ellen Stetson, Dwight Mission.

568L   "To the People of the Nation," Choctaw Intelligencer, August 21, 1850. Concerns Miss Ellen Stetson, Dwight
Mission.

569L   "Temperance," Cherokee Advocate, July 15, 1851.

570L   "For the Cherokee Advocate," Cherokee Advocate, May 25,
1853. Attacks Mormonism.

571N   "Hadley's Method with the Cherokee," Cherokee Advocate,
September 21, 1879. Discusses Cherokee linguistics.

572L   "From Delegate Duncan," Afton News, December 28, 1894.
Concerns U.S. citizenship for Indians.

573A   Speech before Committee on the Judiciary, Telephone,
January 25, 1895. Concerns affairs in the Indian Territory.

574N   "Impedigo Contagiosum," Tahlequah Arrow, January 5,
1901. Concerns a disease of the skin.

575N   "Allotment Filings Discussed," Tahlequah Arrow, January
31, 1903.

See also 1981 Biobibliography, 1007-1110.

DUNDAS, ARCHIE (Tsimshian)

576N   "Carpentry," Arrow, March 30, 1906. Describes the carpentry program at Carlisle.

DUNLAP, SADIE (Caddo)

577N   "Caddo," Arrow, December 20, 1907. Discusses Caddo
dress, housing, and allotments.

DU PUIS, LOUIS (Iowa)

578M   "The Creation of Man," Carlisle Arrow, April 28, 1911.
Legend of the good and bad spirit.

579N   "The Making of Butter," Carlisle Arrow, December 30, 1910.

DURAN, JACOB (Pueblo)

580N   "Mining at Home," Indian Leader, April 12, 1901. Concerns
mining in the Santa Fe region.

581N   "Building an Adobe House," Word Carrier, 31 (January-
February, 1902), 4. Reprinted from Indian Leader.

DWIGHT, JONATHAN EDWARDS (Choctaw)

582N   "To the Patrons of the Intelligencer," Choctaw Intelligencer,

January 15, 1851. Presents the aims of the newspaper.

EADES, BESSIE (Nisenan)
583F   "Class Prophecy," Sherman Bulletin, May 22, 1912. Fantasy concerning Sherman Institute students.

EAGLE, DANIEL D. (Sioux)
584N   "Daniel Eagle of the Band Describes the Philadelphia Mint," Red Man and Helper, May 15, 1903.
585A   "Great Indians in History," Red Man and Helper, April 15, 1904. Concerns Osceola, Tecumseh, and Sitting Bull.

EAGLE, SIMON F. (Pawnee)
586N   "Wagon Making," Carlisle Arrow, February 5, 1909. Describes the tools and process.
587N   "Abraham Lincoln," Carlisle Arrow, March 12, 1909. Biographical sketch.

EAGLEBEAR, EDWARD (Sioux)
588N   "Stock Raising," Carlisle Arrow, February 19, 1909. Concerns the Rosebud and Pine Ridge Reservations.

EAGLEMAN, THOMAS ASHLEY (Crow Creek Sioux)
589A   "Developing My Allotment," Arrow, April 3, 1908. Describes plans for his land at Crow Creek.

EASTMAN, CHARLES ALEXANDER (Santee Sioux)
590N   "Asleep Through a Massacre," Indian's Friend, 6 (June, 1894), 8-9. Anecdote about Daniel Hemans, a Santee Sioux.
591N   "The Indian in Literature," Oglala Light, 4 (May, 1903), 1-4. Concerns portrayal of the Indian in literature and history.
592N   "Indian Children at Play, Albuquerque Indian, 1 (February, 1906), 12. Reprinted from St. Nicholas.
593F   "The Gray Chieftain." In William Dean Howells and Henry Mills Alden, eds., Under the Sunset. New York: Harper & Brothers, 1906, pp. 173-187.
594N   "An Indian's First Day at School," Word Carrier of Santee Normal Training School, 36 (July-August, 1907), 15.
595N   "The North American Indian." In Papers on Inter-Racial Problems, Communicated to the First Universal Races Congress, Held at the University of London, July 26-29, 1911. London: P.S. King & Son, 1911, pp. 367-376.
596N   "Song of the Birch Canoe," Craftsman, 23 (October, 1912), 3-11.
597N   "Too Much Expected of the Indian," Indian Leader, March 28, 1913. Concerns Indian education. Reprinted from New York Times.

598N   "Life and Handicrafts of the Northern Ojibways," Oglala
       Light, 16 (March, 1915), 11-15.

599N   "Camping with Indians," Teepee Book, 1 (September, 1915),
       5-12.

600N   "'My People': The Indians' Contribution to the Art of
       America," Weekly Review, January 23, 1915.

601N   "American Eagle an American Symbol: The Real Meaning
       of Indian Head-Dress," American Indian Advocate, 3
       (Grass Moon, 1922), 12-13.

See also 1981 Biobibliography, 1118-1182.

EASTMAN, FRANCIS R. (Sioux)

602A   "The Price of Success," Carlisle Arrow, November 8, 1912.
       Advocates hard work.

EASTMAN, GRACE OLIVE (Sioux)

603N   With Jessie Frazier. "Our Last Year's Class," Word Carrier
       of Santee Normal Training School, 34 (September-October,
       1905), 17. Reports on their experiences at Oxford,
       Ohio.

604N   "A Dakota Teaching the Creeks," Word Carrier of Santee
       Normal Training School, 36 (November-December, 1907),
       21. Concerns her experiences as music teacher at Nuyaka
       Mission, Oklahoma.

605L   "A Letter from the Indian Field," Word Carrier of Santee
       Normal Training School, 39 (March-April, 1910), 7. Con-
       cerns her experiences as teacher of the Cherokees at
       Dwight Mission.

EASTMAN, JOHN (Sisseton Sioux)

606A   "Address by Rev. John Eastman," Word Carrier of Santee
       Normal Training School, 45 (May-June, 1916), 10. Fun-
       eral oration concerning the work of A. L. Riggs.

ECHO HAWK, ELMER (Pawnee)

607M   "The Horse and the Buffalo," Arrow, February 14, 1908.
       Pawnee legend about the Milky Way.

EDDLEMAN, ORA V. (Cherokee)

608F   "An Unwelcome Visitor," Twin Territories, 3 (February,
       1901), 27-28. A short story.

EDDLEMAN, S. GEORGE (Cherokee)

609N   "A Soldier's Life in the Philippines," Twin Territories, 3
       (January, 1901), 14; (February, 1901), 34; (March,
       1901), 56-57.

EDENSHAW, RUFUS (Haida)

610F   "An Indian Story," Weekly Chemawa American, December,
       16, 1910. An Indian doctor tale set in Northern Alaska.

EDER, CHARLES JAMES (Sioux)
   611A "Valedictory--A Link in Life," Chemawa American, 16 (June,
         1914), 13-14. Advocates hard work.

EDGE, MARY (Caddo)
   612N "Sacajawea, a Wonderful Woman," Indian School Journal,
         19 (June, 1919), 16-17.

EDICK, CHARLES (Chippewa)
   613N "What I Intend to Do after Leaving Haskell," Indian Leader,
         May 3, 1901.

EDWARDS, JAMES (Choctaw)
   614L "From Bro. James Edwards," Indian Missionary, 3 (May,
         1887), 6. Concerns his mission efforts at the Wichita
         Agency.

ELGIN, STANFORD (Chippewa)
   615N "How the Apple Tells Us When It Is Ripe," Carlisle Arrow,
         October 2, 1908.

ELK, HENRY (Cayuse)
   616N "Be Kind to Dumb Animals," Chemawa American, 16 (No-
         vember, 1913), 22. Opposes the Pendleton Roundup.

ELLIOTT, HAZEL (Pomo)
   617N "Meat," Sherman Bulletin, March 29, 1911.

ELM, ANDREW N. (Oneida)
   618A "From Fighting to Farming," Talks and Thoughts, 12
         (March, 1897), 3. Concerns "progress" of the Indians.
   619N "Primeval Government," Talks and Thoughts, 14 (April,
         1899), 3. Describes the old government of the Oneidas.
   620N "Military Drill at Hampton," Talks and Thoughts, 14 (May,
         1899), 1, 3.

ELM, IDA (Oneida)
   621F "The Story of a Witch," Talks and Thoughts, 18 (May,
         1905), 4.

ENMEGAHBOWH (Ottawa)
   622N "The Death of Chief I. H. Tuttle." The Church and the
         Indians. New York: Protestant Church, 1874, pp. 1-7.
   See also 1981 Biobibliography, 1195-1196, where he was incorrectly
         identified as Chippewa.

ENOS, JOHNSON (Pima)
   623N "Christmas in Pima Land," Carlisle Arrow, December 31,
         1909. Describes activities among the Pimas and Papagos.
   624M "An Indian Legend," Carlisle Arrow, March 18, 1910. Ari-
         zona Indian legend of the deluge.

625N   With William Nelson. "School Athletics, 1910," Carlisle Ar-
        row, April 8, 1910. Presents the merits of athletics.
See also 1981 Biobibliography, 1197-1199.

ENOUF, JAMES   (Citizens' Band Potawatomi)
626N   "Pony Smoke Dance," Talks and Thoughts, 4 (March, 1890),
        1. Describes the dance.
627N   "The Story of a Bean," Talks and Thoughts, 4 (May, 1890),
        3-4. Describes an experiment in agriculture.

ESTES, ALEXANDER H.   (Yankton Sioux)
628N   "My Early School-Life," Talks and Thoughts, 1 (May, 1886),
        1. Autobiographical statement.
629N   "How Is It?" Talks and Thoughts, 1 (June, 1886), 4.
        Concerns Hampton Institute.
630T   "My People," Talks and Thoughts, 1 (July, 1886), 1. Art-
        icle by Daniel Firecloud, concerns "progress" of the
        Sioux.
631L   "My First Experience in Teaching," Talks and Thoughts, 1
        (September, 1886), 3.
632N   "A Trip to Norfolk and Portsmouth," Talks and Thoughts,
        1 (September, 1886), 2-3. Describes his travels.

ESTES, GRACE   (Lower Brule Sioux)
633N   "Religious Conditions Among the Indian People," Word Car-
        rier of Santee Normal Training School, 43 (January-
        February, 1914), 4. Concerns the Lower Brule Reserva-
        tion.

ETTAWAGESHIK, J. WILLIAM   (Ottawa)
634N   "My Home Locality," Carlisle Arrow, May 7, 1909. De-
        scribes the Harbor Springs, Michigan, area.
635F   "Maple Sugar Sand," Carlisle Arrow, December 30, 1910.
        Tale about a captive.
636P   "The Glow-worm," Carlisle Arrow, January 27, 1911. Pre-
        sents an inspirational theme.
See also 1981 Biobibliography, 1202-1206.

EUBANKS, R. ROGER   (Cherokee)
637F   "Nights with Uncle Ti-ault-ly: How the Terrapin Beat the
        Rabbit," Osage Magazine, 1 (May, 1910), 72-74. Tale
        told in dialect.
638F   "Nights with Uncle Ti-ault-ly: The Ball Game of the Birds
        and Animals," Osage Magazine, 2 (September, 1910),
        45-47. Tale told in dialect.

EXENDINE, ALBERT ANDREW   (Delaware)
639N   "Blacksmithing," Arrow, March 30, 1906. Describes the
        program at Carlisle.

FAIRBANKS, WILLIAM (Chippewa)
>   640N   "Resolved: That Bad Companions Do More Harm Than Bad
>   Books," Peace Pipe, December 19, 1913. Argues the af-
>   firmative side.
>   641N   "Duty," Peace Pipe, February 27, 1914.

FARR, JOHN B. (Chippewa)
>   642A   "Carpentry," Arrow, April 3, 1908. Describes the kinds
>   of work done.

FAST HORSE, WILLIAM (Sioux)
>   643N   "Items from Classrooms," Oglala Light, 20 (December 1,
>   1919), 3. Reports on classroom activities at the Oglala
>   Boarding School.
>   644N   "Items from Classrooms," Oglala Light, 20 (December 15,
>   1919), 3. Reports on classroom activities at the Oglala
>   Boarding School.
>   645N   "Items from Classrooms," Oglala Light, 20 (January 1,
>   1920), 3. Reports on classroom activities at the Oglala
>   Boarding School.
>   646N   "Items from Classrooms," Oglala Light, 20 (January 15,
>   1920), 3. Reports on classroom activities at the Oglala
>   Boarding School.
>   647N   "Items from Class Rooms," Oglala Light, 20 February 15,
>   1920), 3. Reports on classroom activities at the Oglala
>   Boarding School.
>   648N   "Items from the Class Rooms," Oglala Light, 20 (March 15,
>   1920), 3. Reports on classroom activities at the Oglala
>   Boarding School.
>   649N   "Items from the Class Rooms," Oglala Light, 20 (April 1,
>   1920), 3. Reports on classroom activities at the Oglala
>   Boarding School.
>   650N   "Items from the Class Rooms," Oglala Light, 20 (April 15,
>   1920), 3. Reports on Classroom activities at the Oglala
>   Boarding School.

FAULKNER, CLARENCE L. (Shoshoni)
>   651N   "Thoughts from Miss Collins' Talk," Arrow, March 9, 1906.
>   Advocates assimilationist education.

FEATHER, JOHN (Menominee)
>   652N   "My Vacation at Chautauqua," Arrow, August 30, 1907.
>   Describes Lake Chautauqua, New York.

FIELDER, HENRY W. (Cheyenne River Sioux)
>   653N   "The Indian 'Turkish Bath,'" Talks and Thoughts, 8 (May,
>   1894), 1. Describes the sweatbath.
>   654N   "An Account of the Indians at Cheyenne Agency, S. D.,"
>   Talks and Thoughts, 9 (November, 1894), 1. Describes
>   their condition.

655N   "The Ghost Tipi," Talks and Thoughts, 10 (May, 1895),
      3-4.

656N   "Roy Dorsey Stabler," Talks and Thoughts, 12 (November,
      1896), 1, 4. Biographical sketch.

657N   "A Visit to Lincoln Institute," Talks and Thoughts, 12
      (November, 1896), 3. Describes his travels.

658N   "Capt. R. R. Moton," Talks and Thoughts, 12 (January,
      1897), 1. Biographical sketch.

659N   "New Ways," Talks and Thoughts, 12 (February, 1897), 7.
      Concerns the difficulty for the Indian to learn white ways.

660N   "Miss Howard's Mission," Talks and Thoughts, 12 (May,
      1897), 7.

661L   "Correspondence," Talks and Thoughts, 15 (March, 1902),
      3. Reports religious change at Rosebud.

FIELDS, DELILAH (Cherokee)
662L   Letter, Mission Herald, 17 (August, 1821), 259. Argues
      the need for Christianity.

FIELDS, RICHARD F. (Cherokee)
663N   "Help These Women," Cherokee Telephone, July 7, 1892.
664N   "Mexican Society," Indian Sentinel, December 22, 1898.

FIGHT, FRANK (Pine Ridge Sioux)
665N   "An Indian Parable," Word Carrier of Santee Normal Train-
      ing School, 37 (July-August, 1908), 13. Describes Pres-
      byterian mission work at Pine Ridge Reservation.

FIRE THUNDER, ANGELIQUE (Pine Ridge Sioux)
666F   "Brown Eyes," Talks and Thoughts, 18 (December, 1904),
      1, 4. Story of a girl who marries the son of a chief of
      a warring tribe.

FIRE THUNDER, ELLA (Lower Brule Sioux)
667N   "An Indian Childhood," Talks and Thoughts, 18 (October,
      1904), 1, 4. Autobiographical statement.
See also 1981 Biobibliography, 1247-1248.

FIRECLOUD, DANIEL (Sioux)
668N   "Old Indian Ways," Talks and Thoughts, 1 (July, 1886), 2.

FIRECLOUD, GEORGE T. (Fort Totten Sioux)
669N   "What Indian Students Ought to Do," Word Carrier of San-
      tee Normal Training School, 32 (November-December,
      1903), 22. Advocates Christian education.

670N   "The Devil's Lake Indians," Word Carrier of Santee Normal
      Training School, 33 (March-April, 1904), 6. Describes
      their condition.

671N   "The Assinaboine Indians," Word Carrier of the Santee
      Normal Training School, 38 (March-April, 1909), 5.

Describes their condition and his experiences as a preacher among them.

FIRETHUNDER, LYDIA (Sioux)
    672N "Essay on Tuberculosis," Indian Leader, May 10, 1912.
        Describes its treatment.

FIRETHUNDER, WILLIAM (Sioux)
    673M "An Indian Legend," Indian Leader, January 31, 1913. A
        Sioux legend.

FISH, CHARLES L. (Lower Brule Sioux)
    674M "The Arrow Heads," Carlisle Arrow, November 11, 1910.
        Legend concerning how arrowheads became widely dis-
        tributed.
    See also 1981 Biobibliography, 1249.

FISH, FRANK (Peoria)
    675P "Haskell Song," Indian Leader, December 8, 1905.
    676N "Bread and How It Is Made," Indian Leader, February 16,
        1906.

FISHER, JOSIAH (Creek)
    677N "The Bell," Creek Boys' and Girls' Monthly, December,
        1870.

FITE, NANCY DANIEL (Cherokee)
    678N "Historical Statement," Cherokee National Female Seminary.
        Chilocco, OK: Chilocco Indian Agricultural School, 1906.
        Historical sketch of the Cherokee Female Seminary.

FLOOD, THOMAS J. (Pine Ridge Sioux)
    679N "The Indian in Business," Indian Leader, July 10, 1908.

FLORES, VIRGINIA (Mission)
    680L "Good St. Anthony," Mission Indian, 1 (November 15, 1895),
        5.

FLY, JOSEPH (Sioux)
    681N "A Kind Grandfather: A Reminiscence of Sitting Bull's
        Grandson," Talks and Thoughts, 15 (January, 1902),
        1, 3. Relates an anecdote about Sitting Bull.

FLYINGEARTH, EVA (Standing Rock Sioux)
    682M "Legend of the Seven White Pigeons," Word Carrier of San-
        Normal Training School, 43 (July-August, 1914), 16.

FOBB, RHODA (Choctaw)
    683A "Salutatory," Carlisle 1917. Carlisle, PA: U.S. Indian
        School, 1917, pp. 7-9.

FOLSOM, DANIEL (Choctaw)
   684N "Prospectus for the Choctaw Telegraph," Indian Advocate,
          3 (November, 1848), 1. Presents the newspaper's objec-
          tives.

FOLSOM, DAVID (Choctaw)
   685L Letter, Missionary Herald, 19 (February, 1823), 46. Con-
          cerns the death of Mrs. Cyrus Kingsbury.

FOLSOM, DON JUAN (Choctaw)
   686L "The Gubernatorial Election," Indian Citizen, June 7, 1890.
          Concerns the race of Smallwood against Jones.

FOLSOM, ISRAEL (Choctaw)
   687L "For the Intelligencer," Choctaw Intelligencer, August 20,
          1851. Describes the Choctaw court.
  See also 1981 Biobibliography, 1257-1259.

FOLSOM, J. T. (Choctaw)
   688L "For the Arkansas Intelligencer," Arkansas Intelligencer,
          July 19, 1845. Vindicates Indian character.
   689L "From the Arkansas Intelligencer," Cherokee Advocate,
          July 31, 1845. Vindicates Indian character.

FOLSOM, JACOB (Choctaw)
   690L "From the Choctaw Telegraph," Indian Advocate, 3 (Feb-
          ruary, 1849), 3. Concerns the Indian Territory west of
          the Mississippi.

FOLSOM, L. S. W. (Choctaw)
   691L "Okchamali Kaunti," Indian Citizen, August 10, 1889. De-
          scribes events at federal court.

FOLSOM, PETER (Choctaw)
   692L "Remonstrance to the Hon. Thompson McKenney's Circular,"
          Choctaw Intelligencer, September 11, 1850. Concerns
          Choctaw national affairs.

FOLSOM, S. (Choctaw)
   693L "For the Intelligencer," Choctaw Intelligencer, June 11,
          1851. Concerns the tomb of Pushmataha in Washington.

FONTAINE, PETER (Blackfeet)
   694N "Glacier National Park," Chemawa American, 15 (May, 1913),
          19-20. Describes legends about the place names.
   695N "Kindness to Animals," Chemawa American, 16 (November,
          1913), 23. Describes his experiences with a horse.

FOREMAN, JOHNSON (Cherokee)
   696L Letter, Cherokee Advocate, August 21, 1845. Concerns a
          fight.

FOREMAN, STEPHEN (Cherokee)
    697N   "Cherokee Bible Society. Annual Meeting," Cherokee Ad-
            vocate, October 26, 1844. Records of activities at the
            meeting.
    698N   "Proceedings of the Cherokee Bible Society," Cherokee Ad-
            vocate, November 19, 1846.
    699N   "Proceedings of the Cherokee Bible Society," Cherokee Ad-
            vocate, November 5, 1850.
    700N   "Report," Cherokee Advocate, November 18, 1851. Reports
            on the Cherokee Bible Society.
    See also 1981 Biobibliography, 1264-1266.

FOSTER, SAM (Creek)
    701N   "The Horse," Creek Boys' and Girls' Monthly, December,
            1870. Concerns uses of the horse.

FRASS, ROSA (Cheyenne)
    702N   "Darning a Sock," Indian Leader, May 10, 1901.

FRAZIER, DAVID (Santee Sioux)
    703N   "Haying for the Church," Word Carrier of Santee Normal
            Training School, 43 (May-June, 1914), 12. Describes
            hay harvest on church property.

FRAZIER, FRANCIS (Santee Sioux)
    704A   "Address by Rev. Francis Frazier," Word Carrier of Santee
            Normal Training School, 45 (May-June, 1916), 10. Praises
            the work of A. L. Riggs among the Dakotas.

FRAZIER, FRANCIS PHILIP (Santee Sioux)
    705L   "From Our Indian Pastor's Son," Word Carrier of Santee
            Normal Training School, 48 (July-August, 1919), 15.
            Reports his war experience and lists Santee graduates
            in the army.

FRAZIER, GEORGE J. (Santee Sioux)
    706N   "Hampton Indian Y.P.S.C.E.," Talks and Thoughts, 11
            (July, 1895), 1. Concerns Indian Christian Endeavor
            Society.

FRAZIER, HOWARD E. (Santee Sioux)
    707N   "The Santee Indians," Word Carrier of Santee Normal Train-
            ing School, 33 (March-April, 1904), 6. Describes condi-
            tions among the Santee.
    708L   Letter, Word Carrier of Santee Normal Training School, 34
            (March-April, 1905), 6. Reports on his experiences at
            Hampton Institute.

FRAZIER, JESSIE H. (Sioux)
    709N   With Grace Olive Eastman. "Our Last Year's Class," Word

Carrier of Santee Normal Training School, 34 (September-
October, 1905), 17. Describes their experiences at Oxford, Ohio.

FRAZIER, STELLA M. (Santee Sioux)
    710L "Former Pupils' Letters," Word Carrier of Santee Normal
          Training School, 42 (March-April, 1913), 8. Describes
          her school experiences at St. Johnsbury, Vermont.

FREEMONT, HENRIETTA R. (Omaha)
    711A "That the Negro Is Superior to the Indian," Red Man, 12
          (January-February, 1894), 4. Argues the affirmative
          side.
  See also 1981 Biobibliography, 1271.

FRENCH, DORA (Chippewa)
    712N "Work and Play," Peace Pipe, June 19, 1914. Argues for
          balance of the two.

FRENCH, GRACE (Chippewa)
    713N "Salutatory," Peace Pipe, July 2, 1915. Encourages stu-
          dents to strive.

FRENIER, JAMES (Sioux)
    714N "History," Iapi Oaye, 1 (April, 1884), 3. Defines "his-
          tory."

FRIDAY, MOSES L. (Northern Arapaho)
    715M "Arapaho Tradition of Creation," Carlisle Arrow, September
          16, 1910.
    716N "General George Armstrong Custer," Carlisle Arrow, Octo-
          ber 21, 1910. Concerns the Battle of the Little Big Horn
          and the unveiling of a statue at Monroe, Michigan.
    717M "The Morning and Evening Star," Carlisle Arrow, December
          16, 1910. Arapaho legend about the origin of the stars.
    718N "Ancient Customs of the Arapahoes," Carlisle Arrow, June
          2, 1911. Touches on dances, war parties, Sun Dance,
          and assimilation.
  See also 1981 Biobibliography, 1273-1275.

FRIDAY, ROBERT (Northern Arapaho)
    719A "The Progress of the Northern Cheyennes," Arrow, Decem-
          ber 21, 1906.

FRITTS, JOHN (Klamath)
    720N "My Trip to Gettysburg," Chemawa American, 15 (March,
          1913), 13-14. Describes his travels.

FRYE, CHARLES OLIVER (Cherokee)
    721N "Favors the Treaty," Stilwell Standard, August 1, 1902.
          Supports the Cherokee Agreement of 1902.

FRYE, LEONA (Creek)
    722N "Religious Conditions Among the Indian People," Word Car-
        rier of Santee Normal Training School, 43 (January-
        February, 1914), 4. Concerns Creeks.

GABRIEL, CHRISTIANA (Serrano)
    723F "Stories of the Serrano," Carlisle Arrow, November 4, 1910.
        Animal stories.
    724N "The Fiestas of the Serrano Indians," Carlisle Arrow, Jan-
        uary 27, 1911.
    See also 1981 Biobibliography, 1281-1282.

GADDY, VIRGINIA (Delaware)
    725N "The Adoption Dance," Carlisle Arrow, September 23, 1910.
        Describes the Shawnee dance.
    See also 1981 Biobibliography, 1283.

GANSWORTH, HOWARD EDWARD (Tuscarora)
    726A "Application of His Life to Ours," Red Man, 13 (November-
        December, 1895), 6. Eulogy for Herbert Littlehawk.
    See also 1981 Biobibliography, 1284-1287.

GANSWORTH, WILLARD N. (Tuscarora)
    727M "The Battle," Red Man, 15 (February, 1900), 6. Legend
        of the bear and skunk.

GARCIA, NAZARIA (Mission)
    728L "Yes, Santa Claus Visits Banning, Too," Mission Indian,
        1 (December 15, 1895), 5.

GARDNER, LUCIE (Sioux)
    729N "Value of Domestic Training," Indian Leader, July 4, 1902.

GARFIELD, EVA (Sioux)
    730N "Indian Hunting Life," Word Carrier, 26 (March, 1897), 9.
        Describes old hunting life.

GARGIE, LEWIS (Creek)
    731N "Play," Creek Boys' and Girls' Monthly, December, 1870.
        Argues that work and study are necessary.
    732N "Work," Creek Boys' and Girls' Monthly, December, 1870.
        Concerns diligence.

GARGIE, WASHINGTON (Creek)
    733N "Water," Creek Boys' and Girls' Monthly, December, 1870.
        Stresses its importance.

GARLOW, WILLIAM (Tuscarora)
    734A "Development," Carlisle Arrow, November 12, 1909. Con-
        cerns mental, moral, and physical development in boys.

735N   "Bridging the Chasm," <u>Carlisle Arrow</u>, June 9, 1911. Advocates education, a trade, and return to the reservation to lead others.

736N   "Learn to Obey Orders," <u>Carlisle Arrow</u>, March 28, 1913. Stresses discipline.

See also 1981 Biobibliography, 1291.

GARLOW, WINIFRED (Tuscarora)

737N   "Religious Life Among Our People," <u>Word Carrier of Santee Normal Training School</u>, 42 (November–December, 1913), 24. Concerns the Tuscaroras.

GARNETTE, RICHARD (Sioux)

738N   "Habits and Manners," <u>Ogalalla Light</u>, 1 (May 1, 1900), 4. Urges politeness.

GARRETT, ROBERT BRUCE (Cherokee)

739A   "Valedictory--Hamlet," <u>Tahlequah Arrow</u>, June 1, 1901. Presents Hamlet's story as a moral lesson.

GARVIE, JAMES (Santee Sioux)

740N   "The Jane E. Waldron Case," <u>Word Carrier</u>, 20 (December, 1891), 40. Concerns litigation that went against the mixed bloods.

741N   "The Indian Problem from an Indian Standpoint," <u>Word Carrier</u>, 24 (January, 1895), 4. Concerns education and misconceptions about Indians.

742N   "Our Ponca Mission," <u>Word Carrier</u>, 25 (October, 1896), 32. Describes mission work, conditions, and schools among the Poncas in Nebraska.

743N   "The Race Problem," <u>Word Carrier</u>, 25 (November–December, 1896), 36. Stresses the failure of the U.S. to keep its agreements with the Sioux.

744N   "The Race Problem," <u>Word Carrier</u>, 26 (January, 1897), 1. Espouses Christian education for the Indian.

745N   "From a Christian Stand Point," <u>Word Carrier</u>, 26 (February, 1897), 5. Appeals to American society to aid in Christianizing the Indian.

746N   "Progress of the Santee Sioux Indians," <u>Word Carrier</u>, 27 (March, 1898), 9. Emphasizes the Santees' tendency toward education and Christianity.

747N   "In Memory of My Child Dwight Raymond," <u>Word Carrier</u>, 28 (March, 1899), 10. Eulogy for his three-year-old.

748N   "My Impression of Boston," <u>Word Carrier</u>, 28 (May, 1899), 19. Describes his experiences at the annual meeting of the American Missionary Association.

749N   "An Indian Right Gained," <u>Word Carrier</u>, 28 (June–July, 1899), 23. Appeals for Indian equality under the law.

750N   Untitled, <u>Word Carrier</u>, 29 (May–July, 1900), 20. Concerns Indian citizenship and judicial jurisdiction.

751N   "The Race Problem," Word Carrier, 19 (August-October, 1900), 21. Urges adaptation to changing ways and acquisition of Christian education.

GATES, JOSEPHINE (Sioux)
  752N   "Housekeeping," Carlisle Arrow, April 16, 1909. Praises training in the outing system at Carlisle.

GATES, NAKWALETZOMA (Hopi)
  753N   "A Hopi Indian Girl," Word Carrier of Santee Normal Training-School, 43 (May-June, 1914), 12. Describes life on the Hopi mesas.

GEFFE, EUGENE C. (Alaska Native)
  754N   "Some Alaskan Customs," Arrow, March 27, 1908. Concerns the potlach.

GEISDORF, LOUISE (Crow)
  755A   "America," Red Man, 13 (January, 1896), 6. Discusses the political goals of Americans.

GEORGE, HAL B. (Quileute)
  756N   "Language Lesson," Quileute Independent, January 21, 1909. Concerns horseback riding.

GEORGE, LEWIS (Klamath)
  757M   "Tradition of the Crows," Carlisle Arrow, April 1, 1910. Legend telling why the birds are black.
See also 1981 Biobibliography, 1297-1299.

GEORGE, SAMUEL (Cattaraugus Seneca)
  758N   "Indian Machinists," Talks and Thoughts, 11 (March, 1896), 2.
  759N   "A Trip to Washington," Talks and Thoughts, 12 (August, 1896), 1. Describes his travels.
  760N   "The People of the Skillful Hands," Talks and Thoughts, 13 (June, 1897), 2-3. Concerns the Six Nations.

GHANGRAW, FRANCES A. (Wallawalla)
  761N   "My Work in the Normal," Arrow, December 15, 1905. Describes her experiences in teaching.
  762N   "Housekeeping," Arrow, April 5, 1907. Stresses the need for housekeeping skills.

GIBEAU, MARY (Flathead)
  763N   "Education," Indian News, 13 (May-June, 1911), 6-8.

GIBSON, CHARLES (Creek)
  764N   "The Indian's First Drink," Tahlequah Arrow, April 2, 1898. Accuses Columbus.
  765N   "The Creek Situation," Tahlequah Arrow, February 2, 1901.

Concerns Creek Snake faction. Reprinted from South McAlester Daily Capital.

766N   "Indian Festivities," Red Man and Helper, July 26, 1901. Describes Creek activities in the summer. Reprinted from Indian Journal.

767N   "The Josh Billings of the Indians," Red Man and Helper, October 4, 1901. Concerns Creek schools and Indian education.

768N   "The Indian's Future," Osage Journal, June 26, 1902.

769N   "The Indian--His Present," Osage Journal, June 26, 1902.

770N   "Indian Cure for Snake Bite," Tahlequah Arrow, August 23, 1902. Presents a recipe.

771N   "Lye Bread," Red Man and Helper, August 29, 1902. Describes how the Creeks made it.

772L   "An Indian Advises the Indian," Red Man and Helper, September 19, 1902. Autobiographical statement, encouraging students to stay in school.

773F   "The Indian's Rumination," Red Man and Helper, November 14, 1902. Story of an Indian, reminiscing about old times. Reprinted from Indian Journal.

774F   "The Indian's Rumination," Osage Journal, December 4, 1902. Story of an Indian, reminiscing about old times. Reprinted from Indian Journal.

775N   "Sententious Sayings of a Creek Writer About His People," Jones Academy Herald, 1 (December 18, 1902), 5. Aphorisms, often humorous, about Creek character. Reprinted from Indian Journal.

776N   "Then and Now," Red Man and Helper, June 12, 1903. Compares Creek life-styles in 1903 to that of decades past.

777N   "The Medicine Fire," Indian Leader, March 18, 1904. Concerns Creek fire keepers. Reprinted from Indian Journal.

778N   "Lion Tammers for Snakes," Tahlequah Arrow, May 6, 1905. Concerns attempts to enroll Creek fullboods.

779N   "Early Customs of Indians," Tahlequah Arrow, December 23, 1905. Describes Creek eating habits. Reprinted from Indian Journal.

See also 1981 Biobibliography, 1301-1584.

GIBSON, JOHN (Pima)

780N   "Education," Sherman Bulletin, March 11, 1914. Reprinted from Carlisle Arrow.

GIBSON, JULIA (Pima)

781M   "A Pima Legend," Sherman Bulletin, April 10, 1912. Concerns the deluge.

GILBERT, ISAAC (Sioux)

782N   "Education of the Sioux," Indian Herald, 1 (July, 1903), 16.

GILLIS, ALFRED C. (Wintu)
- 783P "The Bird with the Wounded Wing," California Indian Herald, 1 (April, 1923), 10. Wintu legend put into verse.
- 784N "Dinner at the States Restaurant," California Indian Herald, 1 (April, 1923), 10. Reports on a meeting of the Indian Board of Co-Operation.
- 785N "Trip Through Sonoma, Mendocino and Lake Counties," California Indian Herald, 1 (April, 1923), 15. Describes conditions of the Indians and his work for the Indian Board of Co-Operation.
- 786P "An Indian Cradle Song," California Indian Herald, 1 (July, 1923), 10.
- 787N "The Story of Sid-di-pou-i-wi-ta as Told by Alfred C. Gillis, a Wintun Indian and Recorded by George Wharton James," California Indian Herald, 1 (July, 1923), 13, 14, 15.
- 788P "The Shasta Lily, Den-Hu-Luly," California Indian Herald, 1 (December, 1923), 3.
- 789N "The Passing of George Wharton James," California Indian Herald, 1 (December, 1923), 4. Reviews James's work in behalf of Indians. Reprinted from Pasadena Star-News.
- 790P "The California Indians," California Indian Herald, 2 (January, 1924), 13-14.
- 791P "To the Wenem Mame River," California Indian Herald, 2 (February, 1924), 10.
- 792P "The Sacramento River," California Indian Herald, 2 (April, 1924), 3.
- 793P "The Klamath Girl," California Indian Herald, 2 (July, 1924), 14.

GIVEN, JOSHUA H. (Kiowa)
- 794M "Indian Story," School News, 3 (February, 1883), 1. Kiowa folklore.
- 795A "Saturday Night Speech," Red Man, 8 (April, 1888), 7. Defends Carlisle and nonreservation schools.
See also 1981 Biobibliography, 1586.

GOFF, ROSE (Assiniboin)
- 796N "Abraham Lincoln," Peace Pipe, 5 (February, 1916), 7-8.

GOLSH, MARY (Mission)
- 797A "Valedictory," Sherman Bulletin, May 22, 1912. Encourages students to strive.

GOLSH, ROSA (Mission)
- 798A "Valedictory," Sherman Bulletin, May 25, 1910. Encourages students to strive.

GONZALEZ, FELIX (Mission)
- 799L "It Is Well to Have a Home," Mission Indian, 1 (January 15, 1896), 3. Presents the benefits of the Banning Mission School.

GOODBOY, BESSIE (Sioux)
800N   "Indian Women's Missionary Society," <u>Word Carrier of San-</u>
       <u>tee Normal Training School</u>, 37 (May-June, 1908), 9.
       Reports on a meeting at Long Hollow, South Dakota.

GOODBOY, SARA (Sioux)
801F   "Blue Earring--An Indian Tale," <u>Word Carrier of Santee</u>
       <u>Normal Training School</u>, 42 (January-February, 1913), 4.

GOODCLOUD, FRANK (Standing Rock Sioux)
802L   Letter, <u>Word Carrier of Santee Normal Training School</u>,
       36 (May-June, 1907), 12. Denounces liquor as the bar-
       rier to Indian "civilization."
803L   "A Letter," <u>Word Carrier of Santee Normal Training School</u>,
       37 (March-April, 1908), 8. Argues that Standing Rock
       delegates to Washington should work for the tribe, not
       themselves.

GOODE, ANDREW (Mono, i.e., Monache)
804N   "Scientific Farming," <u>Sherman Bulletin</u>, May 29, 1919.

GOODEAGLE, CHARLES (Quapaw)
805A   "The Development of the Farm," <u>Indian Leader</u>, June 29,
       1906. Concerns the Indian and farming.

GOODEAGLE, FANNIE (Quapaw)
806N   "Indian Festival," <u>Indian Leader</u>, May 6, 1910. Describes
       Green Corn feast.

GOULD, ISAAC R. (Alaska Native)
807N   "Hunting the Land Otter," <u>Carlisle Arrow</u>, January 13,
       1911.
808N   "Customs of the Alaskans," <u>Carlisle Arrow</u>, October 6, 1911.
       Describes their homes.

GOWDY, APIS (Yakima)
809M   "Yakima Legend of the Coyote," <u>Indian Leader</u>, March 17,
       1911. Reprinted from <u>Chemawa American</u>.

GOYITNEY, ANNIE (Pueblo)
810A   "Pottery," <u>Arrow</u>, March 23, 1906. Describes how Pueblo
       pottery is made.
811A   "Housekeeping," <u>Arrow</u>, December 14, 1906. Stresses the
       need for good housekeeping.
See also 1981 Biobibliography, 1609.

GRANDE, ENCARNATION (Mission)
812L   "How Sad to Be Motherless," <u>Mission Indian</u>, 1 (November
       15, 1895), 5. Concerns praying for the dead.

GRAYSON, GEORGE WASHINGTON (Creek)
813N   "Grand Council Resolutions in Regard to the International

Fair," Our Monthly, 4 (June, 1875), 4. Concerns the Indian International Fair at Muskogee, Creek Nation.

814N "Memorial," Our Monthly, 4 (June, 1875), 2-3. Calls for repeal of concessions to railroads in the 1866 treaty.

815A "Speech of G. W. Grayson, of the Creek Nation," Council Fire, 9 (March, 1886), 46-47. Opposes territorial status for the Indian Territory.

816N "An Indian Editor Travels with the Secretary of the Interior," Red Man and Helper, May 22, 1903. Describes a train ride from Okmulgee to Muskogee, Creek Nation. Reprinted from Indian Journal.

See also 1981 Biobibliography, 1611-1621.

GREENBRIER, ADELINE (Menominee)

817M "The Legend of the Pond Lilies," Carlisle Arrow, March 25, 1910. Legend about their origin.

818N "Rudyard Kipling," Carlisle Arrow, April 8, 1910.

See also 1981 Biobibliography, 1626.

GREENBRIER, CARLYSLE (Menominee)

819M "The Beaver Medicine," Carlisle Arrow, September 17, 1909. Legend of Api-Kunni.

820M "The Flying Canoe," Carlisle Arrow, February 11, 1910. A Menominee legend.

821N "Trades and Occupations," Carlisle Arrow, April 8, 1910. Concerns what Carlisle does for the Indian.

See also 1981 Biobibliography, 1627-1629.

GREENWOOD, T. C. (Sioux)

822A "Address by Greenwood," Southern Workman and Hampton School Record, 16 (January, 1887), 9.

GREY CLOUD, DAVID (Santee Sioux)

823N "Protest Against the Grass Dance," Iapi Oaye, 7 (August, 1878), 4. Denounces it as pagan debauchery.

824T "Odowan Sigsice," Iapi Oaye, 9 (December, 1880), 94. Interlinear translation of a Dakota fable.

825T "Dakota Myths," Iapi Oaye, 10 (April, 1881), 30, and (May, 1881), 40. Interlinear translation.

GREYBEARD, SALLIE (Eastern Band Cherokee)

826N "The Art of Weaving," Carlisle 1917. Carlisle, PA: U.S. Indian School, 1917, p. 45.

GUNTER, KEE KEE (Cherokee)

827L "Another View," Indian Arrow, April 4, 1889. Concerns Cherokee affairs.

GURULE, RALPH E. (Pueblo)

828N "Blacksmithing--Horseshoeing," Indian Leader, July 13, 1906. Describes the trade.

GUTIERREZ, CARLOTTA (Navajo)
    829N   "An Indian Girl's Trip from Albuquerque to Nacimiento,"
           Talks and Thoughts, 17 (August-September, 1903), 7.
           Describes her travels.
    830N   "The Blanket Weaving," Talks and Thoughts, 19 (May,
           1906), 1.

GUY, JAMES HARRIS (Chickasaw)
    831P   "The White Man Wants the Indian's Home," Council Fire,
           1 (July, 1878), 110.
    832L   Letter, Council Fire, 1 (July, 1878), 110. Calls for equal-
           ity for Indians.
    833L   Letter, Council Fire, 2 (January, 1879), 15. Concerns the
           persecution of Indians.
    834L   "A Chickasaw Gives the Facts in the Case," Council Fire
           and Arbitrator, 8 (January, 1885), 14.
    See also 1981 Biobibliography, 1664-1665.

HAMILTON, ROBERT J. (Piegan)
    835N   "Give Me a Vote, Says the Indian," Indian Advance, 1
           (April 1, 1900), 2.
    836L   Letter, Red Man and Helper, April 11, 1902. Reports con-
           ditions among his people.
    See also 1981 Biobibliography, 1668-1669.

HAMLIN, GEORGE (White Earth Chippewa)
    837N   "June the Fourteenth," Talks and Thoughts, 15 (August-
           September, 1901), 5-6. Describes events at White Earth,
           Minnesota.
    838N   "The Wild Rice Industry Among the Chippewas," Talks and
           Thoughts, 16 (May, 1902), 1, 4.
    839N   "Along New Trails," Talks and Thoughts, 17 (October,
           1903), 4. Argues for Indian education.
    840N   "Along New Trails," Chippeway Herald, 3 (February, 1904),
           2. Argues for Indian education.
    See also 1981 Biobibliography, 1670.

HAMLIN, LOUIS C. (White Earth Chippewa)
    841N   "Chippeways," Talks and Thoughts, 17 (August-September,
           1903), 4.

HANCOCK, BENJAMIN (Choctaw)
    842L   "From a Full Blood Choctaw," Star-Vindicator, January 27,
           1877. Argues for education in English.

HANCOCK, SIMON (Choctaw)
    843N   "Absolutely True," Bacone Chief. Bacone, OK: Bacone
           College, 1915, pp. 35-37.

HAND, HARRY (Crow Creek Sioux)
    844F   "A Story of a Horse," Talks and Thoughts, 5 (June, 1891), 4.

845F   "A Fox and a Wolf," Talks and Thoughts, 5 (July, 1891), 1, 3-4. A fable.

846M   "The Brave War-Chief and the Ghost," Talks and Thoughts, 6 (March, 1892), 4. A legend.

847F   "A Buffalo Hunt," Talks and Thoughts, 6 (April, 1892), 1, 4. A story.

848M   "The Adventures of a Strange Family: An Old Sioux Legend," Talks and Thoughts, 7 (April, 1893), 1, 7.

HANKS, ROBERT T. (Cherokee)

849L   Letter, Cherokee Advocate, March 31, 1882. Signed "Black Fox" and concerns Cherokee citizenship.

HANSKAKAGAPI, JOSEPH (Sioux)

850N   "Resist Temptation," Word Carrier of Santee Normal Training School, 37 (May-June, 1908), 11. Presents a Christian exhortation.

HARE, DAVID (Yankton Sioux)

851N   "The Yankton Indians," Word Carrier of Santee Normal Training School, 41 (March-April, 1912), 9. Describes their history and present conditions.

852N   "Dakota Child Training," Word Carrier of Santee Normal Training School, 41 (May-June, 1912), 12. Describes current practices.

HARE, DE WITT (Sioux)

853L   "Former Pupils' Letters, II," Word Carrier, 32 (January-February, 1903), 2. Urges students to stay in school.

854L   "From Former Pupils," Word Carrier of Santee Normal Training School, 34 (September-October, 1905), 17. Relates his ambitions to study law.

See also 1981 Biobibliography, 1676.

HARJO, HENRY M. (Creek)

855A   "The Light of the Nation," Indian Missionary, 2 (March, 1886), 2. Advocates Christian education.

HARJO, IDA (Creek)

856N   "Cooking Potatoes," Indian Leader, June 24, 1904.

HARKINS, GEORGE W. (Chickasaw)

857N   "To the American People," Niles' Register, 41 (February 25, 1832), 480. Concerns Choctaw removal.

858L   "To the People of Pucksnubbee District," Choctaw Intelligencer, January 7, 1852. Concerns acts pending before the Choctaw National Council.

859A   "Speech of Col. G. W. Harkins of the Chickasaws," Council Fire, 9 (February, 1886), 23. Concerns Indian rights.

See also 1981 Biobibliography, 1677-1679.

HARLIN, NONA P. (Cherokee)
860N "Woman's Influence," Indian Missionary, 2 (June, 1886), 3.
Concerns the women behind great men.

HARPER, ALFRED (Cherokee)
861M "The Origin of the White Man,"Indian Leader, September
27, 1912.
862M "The Origin of the White Man," Indian's Friend, 25 (December, 1912), 10.

HARRIS, COLONEL JOHNSON (Cherokee)
863N "Cherokees and Osages," Tahlequah Arrow, January 27,
1906. Concerns early hostilities in the West.
See also 1981 Biobibliography, 1681-1700.

HARRIS, EDITH (Catawba)
864N "My Visit to the Shoe Shop," Carlisle Arrow, November 6,
1908. Describes what goes on in the shop at Carlisle.
865N "Signs of Spring," Carlisle Arrow, April 30, 1909.

HARRIS, HARVEY (Eel River)
866N "The Modern Indian," Sherman Bulletin, May 12, 1909.

HARRIS, HENRY E. (Pyramid Lake Ute)
867L "From a Ute Indian," Red Man, 8 (June, 1888), 7. Autobiographical statement.

HART, JOSEPH C. (Umatilla)
868N "The Umatilla Indians," Indian Leader, September 4, 1908.
Concerns "progress" among the Umatillas.

HASHOLY, NANCY (Sioux)
869N "Something of My Life," Carlisle Arrow, June 11, 1909.
Autobiographical statement.

HASTINGS, CATHERINE (Cherokee)
870N "The Algebra Sum Soliloquy," Cherokee Rose Buds, August
2, 1854. Signed "Na-li" and describes how to work a
problem.
871A "An Address to the Females of the Cherokee Nation," Cherokee Rose Buds, August 2, 1854. Signed "Na-li" and
argues that it is no disgrace to be a full-blood.
872N "Two Scenes in Cherokee Land: Scene I," Wreath of Cherokee Rose Buds, August 1, 1855. Signed "Na-li" and describes the natural scene.
873N "The Seed," A Wreath of Cherokee Rose Buds, August 11,
1855. Signed "Na-li" and concerns nature.

HASTINGS, WILLIAM WIRT (Cherokee)
874A "Speech of W. W. Hastings," Vinita Leader, July 10, 1902.

Concerns the condition of the Cherokees and the decline of the nation.
See also 1981 Biobibliography, 1709-1716.

HATCH, AGNES (Chippewa)
875P   With Mary Wilmet. "Our Cottage," Carlisle 1917. Carlisle, PA: U.S. Indian School, 1917, p. 40. Concerning Model Home, a cottage at Carlisle.

HATCH, NICK (Aleut)
876N   "Tailoring--Demonstration," Chemawa American, 15 (June, 1913), 17-19.

HAUSER, ANNA (Southern Cheyenne)
877N   "A 'Sane' Fourth," Carlisle Arrow, July 4, 1912. Opposes use of fireworks.
See also 1981 Biobibliography, 1717-1721.

HAUSER, MARY (Southern Cheyenne)
878N   "Have a Purpose," Indian Leader, April 26, 1901. Encourages students to strive.
879N   "Two Phases of Education," Indian Leader, June 26, 1903.

HAUSER, PETER (Southern Cheyenne)
880N   "Christmas at Home," Carlisle Arrow, December 31, 1909. Describes activities there.
881N   With Joseph Libby. "Practical Business Education," Carlisle Arrow, April 8, 1910. Discusses the Carlisle program and what they expect to do with their training.

HAWK, BERTHA B. (Sioux)
822N   "What I Have Learned at Carlisle," Carlisle Arrow, June 18, 1909. Presents the value of the outing system.

HAWKINS, DIANA (Southern Cheyenne)
883M   "A Pawnee Legend," Indian School Journal, 19 (December, 1918), 145-146. Concerns the adventures of Red Wing.

HAYES, AXTELL (Nez Percé)
884N   "Experience at Carlisle," Arrow, January 31, 1908. Autobiographical statement.

HEBRON, ELSIE (Paiute)
885M   "The Beginning of the World," Sherman Bulletin, December 29, 1909. A Coyote Man legend.

HEMLOCK, JULIA (Seneca)
886N   "The Hen," Carlisle Arrow, October 23, 1908.
887N   "Abraham Lincoln," Carlisle Arrow, February 26, 1909. Biographical sketch.

HENRY, LEVI J. (Cherokee)
888L "The Mother," Cherokee Advocate, May 9, 1884.

HENTOH (Wyandot)
See WALKER, BERTRAND N. O.

HERMAN, JAMES (Rosebud Sioux)
889N "Indian Farming," Word Carrier of Santee Normal Training School, 43 (July-August, 1914), 16. Concerns farming on Rosebud Reservation.

HERROD, MARY LEWIS (Creek)
890L Letter, Indian Missionary, 4 (April, 1888), 1. Describes Wewogufkee Town, Creek Nation. Reprinted from Indian Journal.
See also 1981 Biobibliography, 1738.

HESCHINYA, MARY H. (Pueblo)
891N "Spring," Red Man, 9 (April, 1889), 3. Describes the season.

HEWITT, JOHN NAPOLEON BRINTON (Tuscarora)
892N "Teaching of Ethnology in Indian Schools," Indian Leader, May 30, 1913.
See also 1981 Biobibliography, 1739-1755.

HEYL, RICHARD D. (Apache)
893L "To the Thinking Boys and Girls of Carlisle," Red Man and Helper, May 31, 1901. Urges hard work.
894L "A Live Indian's View of the Situation," Red Man and Helper, September 27, 1901. Concerns the death of William McKinley.
895L "From a Spirited and Citizenized Apache," Red Man and Helper, November 29, 1901. Advocates education of Indians.
896L "From Richard D. Heyl, Our Apache Friend," Red Man and Helper, May 2, 1902. Advocates education for citizenship.
897L "The Getting a Start Is of Paramount Importance," Red Man and Helper, October 3, 1902. Advocates education and choosing a vocation wisely.
See also 1981 Biobibliography, 1756-1758.

HICKS, AARON (Cherokee)
898L Letter, Fort Smith Herald, October 10, 1849. Reports on Old Settler Cherokee affairs.

HICKS, ED D. (Cherokee)
899L "That Gillis Matter," Indian Chieftain, May 28, 1885. Concerns Cherokee affairs.

HICKS, ELIJAH (Cherokee)
- 900L   "Mission to the Comanches and Others," Cherokee Advocate, July 2, 1846. Describes the mission.
- 901L   "To My Friends and Constituents," Cherokee Advocate, October 28, 1847. Concerns the Cherokee national debt.
- 902L   "To the Editor of the Cherokee Advocate," Cherokee Advocate, November 6, 1848. Concerns Cherokee affairs.
- 903A   "Address of Judge E. Hicks on the Occasion of Laying the Corner Stone of the Seminary for a High School Near Tahlequah, by Request of the Principal Chief," Cherokee Advocate, April 1, 1851. Concerns Cherokee education.

See also 1981 Biobibliography, 1760-1765.

HICKS, GEORGE WASHINGTON (Cherokee)
- 904L   Letter, Indian Missionary, 1 (January, 1885), 3. Concerns two Choctaw boys at the Indian University at Tahlequah.
- 905L   "From Tahlequah," Indian Missionary, 1 (February, 1885), 2. Describes activities at the Tahlequah Baptist Church.
- 906N   "The Psi Delta Society of Indian University," Indian Missionary, 1 (April, 1885), 2. Concerns the social and literary society.
- 907L   "A Newsy Letter," Indian Missionary, 1 (May, 1885), 1. Reports events at Tahlequah Baptist Church and Indian University.
- 908L   Letter, Indian Missionary, 2 (December, 1885), 1. Describes Rochester Theological Seminary.
- 909S   "A Called Ministry," Indian Missionary, 2 (May, 1886), 4-5.
- 910L   "Theological Seminary," Indian Missionary, 3 (February, 1887), 2. Reports events at Rochester Theological Seminary.
- 911L   Letter, Indian Missionary, 3 (August, 1887), 1. Reports his trip to Wichita Agency and initial mission efforts there.
- 912L   Letter, Indian Missionary, 3 (September, 1887), 1. Describes events at Kiowa, Comanche, and Wichita Agency.
- 913L   "From Anadarko," Indian Missionary, 3 (November, 1887), 1. Reports on events and people at Kiowa, Comanche, and Wichita Agency.
- 914L   Letter, Indian Missionary, 4 (February, 1888), 7. Reports events at the Wichita Baptist Church.
- 915L   Letter, Indian Missionary, 4 (April, 1888), 2. Reports events at Anadarko Mission.
- 916L   Letter, Indian Missionary, 4 (September, 1888), 1. Sums up his year in missionary service at Anadarko Agency.
- 917L   Letter, Indian Missionary, 5 (January, 1889), 2. Reports activities at Wichita Mission.
- 918L   Letter, Indian Missionary, 5 (April, 1889), 2. Concerns construction of a school at Wichita Agency.
- 919L   Letter, Indian Missionary, 5 (May, 1889), 1. Appeals for help in building his school.
- 920L   Letter, Indian Missionary, 5 (October, 1889), 1. Concerns building the mission school at Anadarko.

921L   Letter, Indian Missionary, 5 (October, 1889), 1. Reports
       events at Anadarko.
922L   Letter, Indian Missionary, 7 (February, 1891), 1. Reports
       Ghost Dance among Caddo, Kiowa, and Comanches.
923L   Letter, Indian Missionary, 7 (March, 1891), 2. Reports
       on the Ghost Dance.
924L   Letter, Indian Missionary, 7 (July, 1891), 2. Concerns
       the Muskogee, Seminole, and Wichita Baptist Association.
925L   Letter, Indian Missionary, 7 (August, 1891), supplement.
       Reports on Ghost Dance.

HICKS, VICTORIA SUSAN (Cherokee)
926N   "An Osage Wedding," Cherokee Rose Buds, August 2, 1854.
       By "Ka-ya-kun-stah" and attributed to Hicks by her
       sister Mrs. O. C. Waite.

HICKS, WILLIAM (Cherokee)
927L   Letter, Niles' Register, 36 (August 1, 1829), 370-371. Con-
       cerns Indian removal. Reprinted from Cherokee Phoenix.
See also 1981 Biobibliography, 1766-1767.

HIGHEAGLE, ROBERT PLACIDUS (Standing Rock Sioux)
928N   "A Trip to Norfolk," Talks and Thoughts, 6 (January,
       1892), 4. Describes his travels.
929N   "The Mock Trial Given by the Wigwam Literary Society,"
       Talks and Thoughts, 7 (January, 1893), 6-7. Concerns
       the literary society at Hampton Institute.
930F   "The Brave Deaf and Dumb Boy," Talks and Thoughts, 7
       (March, 1893), 2. A tale.
931N   "Tipi-iyokihe," Talks and Thoughts, 9 (January, 1895), 6.
       Concerns the Sioux custom of tipiiyokihe.
932M   "The Legend of Owl River," Talks and Thoughts, 11 (July, 1895
       1895), 3. 7. A Sioux legend.
933N   "Report: The Returned Students and Progressive Indian
       Association. In Session," Talks and Thoughts, 11 (May,
       1896), 4, and 12 (June-July, 1896), 8. Reports on Lower
       Brule Returned Students Association.
See also 1981 Biobibliography, 1768.

HIGHTOWER, JOSHUA (Chickasaw)
934L   "The Chickasaw School Law," Atoka Independent, March
       29, 1878.

HILDEBRAND, ORAGONIA B. (Osage)
935A   "Valedictory," Sherman Bulletin, May 27, 1914. Encourages
       students to strive.

HILDEBRAND, SUSAN C. (Osage)
936A   "Valedictory," Sherman Bulletin, May 28, 1913. Encourages
       students to strive.

937N   "Our Y.W. and Y.M.C. A.," Sherman Bulletin, May 28, 1913. Concerns Sherman Institute.

HILL, DAVID RUSSELL (Oneida)
938N   Article about Self-Control Alliance, Talks and Thoughts, 11 (March, 1896), 7.
939N   "The Education We Need," Talks and Thoughts, 16 (August-September, 1902), 3.

HILL, ISRAEL (Oneida)
940N   "Oneida, Wisconsin," Talks and Thoughts, 5 (May, 1891), 1. Describes the community.
941F   "The Woman and Her Son: An Indian Fable," Talks and Thoughts, 6 (September, 1891), 4.

HILL, JESSE (Seneca)
942N   "Celebration of Lincoln's Birthday," Talks and Thoughts, 12 (March, 1897), 6-7. Reports events on the Hampton Institute Campus.
943F   "The Iroquois Runners," Talks and Thoughts, 13 (April, 1898), 4. A tale.
See also 1981 Biobibliography, 1769.

HILL, JOSEPHINE (Oneida)
944M   "The Witch Owl," Talks and Thoughts, 18 (June, 1904), 4. A legend.
945N   "Indian Corn Bread," Talks and Thoughts, 18 (August, 1904), 4.
946M   "The Witch Owl," Indian Leader, October 7, 1904. A legend. Reprinted from Talks and Thoughts.

HILL, MARIE (Onondaga)
947N   "A Country Experience," Carlisle Arrow, March 19, 1909. Describes her work as an outing student.

HILL, MINA (Klamath)
948N   "Consumption," Sherman Bulletin, November 13, 1907.
949P   "Class Poem," Sherman Bulletin, June 10, 1908. Concerns Sherman Institute students.

HILLMAN, LEVI (Oneida)
950N   "The Building Trades," Carlisle Arrow, April 8, 1910. Describes the Carlisle program.
951M   "A Seneca Story," Carlisle Arrow, May 27, 1910. Concerns the end of the world.
952N   "A-yent-wa-ta--Planting Festival," Carlisle Arrow, June 11, 1909. Concerns the Iroquois.
953N   "The Walking Purchase," Carlisle Arrow, November 19, 1909. Historical sketch of the Delawares.
954A   "Desirable Objects of Attainment," Carlisle Arrow, December 17, 1909. Espouses independence and humility.

955N "Our Christmas Customs," Carlisle Arrow, January 7, 1910. Describes activities on the Onondaga Reservation.

HITCHCOCK, RAYMOND (Hupa)
956P "The Webs of Life," Carlisle Arrow, April 8, 1910. Inspirational poem about gaining knowledge.

HODJKISS, WILLIAM D. (Cheyenne River Sioux)
957P "Song of the Storm-Swept Plain," Indian's Friend, 25 (May, 1913), 10.
See also 1981 Biobibliography, 1777.

HOFFMANN, JOHANNA E. (Red Lake Chippewa)
958N "The Influence of the Home School and Community Upon the Education of a Child," Chemawa American, 15 (June, 1913), 1-4.

HOLT, LITTLE BEAR H., JR. (Sioux)
959N "A Plea for Indian Education," American Indian Advocate, 3 (Summer-Autumn, 1922), 5-7.

HOLT, R. D. (Yakima)
960L "Worthy of Attention," Chemawa American, 15 (October, 1912), 4-5. Comments on conditions of U.S.-Yakima relations, concerning water rights.

HOMEHOYOMA, NORA (Hopi)
961N "Sewing," Sherman Bulletin, January 24, 1912.
962M "Jus-Wa-Kep-La," Sherman Bulletin, January 31, 1912. Legend of Oraibi.
963M "Jus-Wa-Kep-La," Indian Leader, January 31, 1913. Legend of Oraibi. Reprinted from Sherman Bulletin.

HOMER, MARY (Choctaw)
964A "The True Americans," Baconian, 9 (March, 1906), 5-8. Argues that the Indian's greatest weakness is a taste for strong drink.

HONYOUST, WILLIAM (Oneida)
965N "Pagan Dances in New York. Are They Carried on, and How Can They Be Stopped?" Talks and Thoughts, 8 (March, 1894), 7.
966N "Our Main School Building," Talks and Thoughts, 8 (April, 1894), 1-2. Concerning Hampton Institute.
967L Letter, Talks and Thoughts, 9 (August, 1894), 3-4. Concerns a legend about a cane.

HOOD, TENA M. (Klamath)
968N "The Klamath River," Carlisle Arrow, November 20, 1908. Describes the river.

HOPPER, RICHARD (Cherokee)
  969A "Mechanical and Industrial Accomplishments," Indian Leader,
        17 (June, 1913), 19-20. Concerns Haskell Institute and
        its work.

HOXIE, SARA G. (Nomlaki)
  970M "Origin of the Medicine Pipe," Carlisle Arrow, May 28, 1909.
  971F "Story of Two Indian Boys," Carlisle Arrow, September 24,
        1909. Tale of Mantee and Manchese.
  972N "A Happy Vacation," Carlisle Arrow, October 1, 1909. De-
        scribes a visit to Ocean City, New Jersey.
  973N "The American Indian," Carlisle Arrow, December 10, 1909.
        Concerns how the Indian has changed since contact.
  974N "The Art of Teaching," Carlisle Arrow, April 8, 1910.

HUBBARD, CHESTER (Oklahoma Seneca)
  975N "A Brief History of a 'Gob,'" Indian School Journal, 19
        (June, 1919), 45-46. Relates his navy experiences.

HUFF, MORRIS (Seneca)
  976N "The Heating System at Carlisle," Carlisle Arrow, June 4,
        1909. Describes the works.

HUNT, ALFRED (Acoma Pueblo)
  977N "Religious Conditions Among the Indian People," Word Car-
        rier of Santee Normal Training School, 43 (January-
        February, 1914), 4. Concerns Acoma.

HUNT, IRVING (Pueblo)
  978N "An Indian Thanksgiving," Indian Leader, November 26,
        1909. Describes activities among the Pueblos.
  979N "A Christmas Celebration Among the Indians," Indian Leader,
        December 24, 1909. Describes activities among the Pueb-
        los.

HUNTER, FLORENCE D. (Fort Totten Sioux)
  980N "Sequoyah," Arrow, January 10, 1908. Biographical sketch.

HUNTER, LUCY E. (Winnebago)
  981L "Santee Graduates' Letters," Word Carrier of Santee Normal
        Training School, 39 (July-August, 1910), 16. Describes
        her return home from school.
  982L "Former Pupils' Letters," Word Carrier of Santee Normal
        Training School, 42 (March-April, 1913), 8. Describes
        her experiences at Hampton Institute.
  983A "The Nebraska Winnebagoes," Word Carrier of Santee Normal
        Training School, 42 (May-June, 1913), 12. Describes
        their present conditions.
  984N "Higher Academic Training for the Indian," Word Carrier
        of Santee Normal Training School, 44 (March-April, 1915),
        8. Argues for higher education.
  See also 1981 Biobibliography, 1787-1789.

HUSS, JOHN (Cherokee)
    985L   Letter, Cherokee Advocate, April 3, 1845. Concerns the
        whiskey trade.

IKE, LUCINDA (Klamath)
    986N   "A Memory Sketch," Sherman Bulletin, February 7, 1912.
        Concerns the Klamath.

INGALLS, SADIE M. (Sac and Fox)
    987N   "Field Observations," Carlisle Arrow, December 1, 1911.
        Report on nature observed on a field trip.
    988N   "Independence Day," Carlisle Arrow, July 4, 1912. Urges
        patriotism.
    See also 1981 Biobibliography, 1792-1794.

IRON, ERNEST (Crow)
    989N   "How Crow Indians Celebrate Christmas," Carlisle Arrow,
        January 21, 1910.

IRON CROW, AMELIA (Sioux)
    990N   Untitled, Ogalalla Light, 1 (July 2, 1900), 4. Describes
        the cube.

IRONROAD, IGNATIUS (Sioux)
    991N   "Northfield," Red Man and Helper, July 15, 1904. De-
        scribes a trip to Northfield, Connecticut.

IRVING, JAMES (Yankton Sioux)
    992M   "A Legend. The Spider Tribe," Peace Pipe, May 9, 1913.
    993N   "Discipline in Indian Schools," Peace Pipe, June 20, 1913.
        Reprinted from Indian School Journal.
    994N   "Girls and Athletics," Peace Pipe, June 20, 1913.
    995N   "The Famous Pipestone Quarry," Peace Pipe, April 10,
        1914. Discusses lore about the quarry.

IRVING, JOHN W. (Yankton Sioux)
    996N   "The Sioux Reservations," Indian Leader, April 26, 1907.

ISHAM, WILLIAM J. (Lac Courte Oreilles Chippewa)
    997N   "Home Conditions," Arrow, October 20, 1905. Describes
        life at Reserve, Wisconsin.

IVEY, AUGUSTUS E. (Cherokee)
    998L   "A Letter from Ivey," Tahlequah Arrow, December 19,
        1896. Concerns his dispute with the Cherokee Nation.
    999N   "The National Council," Stilwell Standard, November 29,
        1901. Reports events there.
    1000N "Webbers Falls," Stilwell Standard, June 6, 1902. De-
        scribes the town.
    1001N "Texanna," Stilwell Standard, June 6, 1902. Describes
        the town in the Cherokee Nation.

1002N "National Council Notes Written by A.E. Ivey," Sallisaw
       Star, November 28, 1902. Reports on National Council.
1003N "National Council Notes Written by A.E. Ivey," Sallisaw
       Star, December 5, 1902. Reports on National Council.
1004N "How I Stand," New Era, July 28, 1906. Announces his
       political stand as a Democratic editor.
1005L "An Open Letter by Augustus E. Ivey," Standard-Sentinel,
       December 11, 1913. Urges protection of the Indians
       from grafters.
See also 1981 Biobibliography, 1797-1798.

JACK, NORA (Maidu)
1006F "The Bear and the Deer," Sherman Bulletin, February 22,
       1911. A tale.
1007N "Valedictory," Sherman Bulletin, June 2, 1915. Encourages
       students to strive.

JACKSON, JONAS (Eastern Band Cherokee)
1008A "What Has the Outing System Accomplished?" Arrow,
       April 5, 1907.

JACKSON, JULIA (Crow)
1009N "Country Experiences," Arrow, December 6, 1907. Praises
       the outing system.
1010M "Legend of the Stars," Arrow, December 27, 1907.

JACKSON, STELLA (Chippewa)
1011N "Sunshine and Shadow," Peace Pipe, July 2, 1915. Con-
       cerns balance in life.

JAGO, FRANK (Pima)
1012A "Valedictory," Sherman Bulletin, May 24, 1916. Encourages
       students to strive.

JAMES, HATTIE (Winnebago)
1013L "Indian Girls' Games," Talks and Thoughts, 4 (April,
       1890), 4. Reports games at Winnebago, Nebraska.
1014N "Going North," Talks and Thoughts, 8 (October, 1892), 3.
       Describes her travels.
1015L "From Nebraska," Talks and Thoughts, 7 (March, 1893),
       3. Concerns sweet corn.

JANIS, ELLEN (Sioux)
1016N "Items from Classrooms," Oglala Light, 20 (December 1,
       1919), 3. Reports classroom activities at the Oglala
       Boarding School.
1017N "Items from Classrooms," Oglala Light, 20 (December 15,
       1919), 3. Reports classroom activities at the Oglala
       Boarding School.
1018N "Items from Classrooms," Oglala Light, 20 (January 1,

1920), 3. Reports classroom activities at the Oglala
Boarding School.

JEFFERSON, THOMAS (Mohave)
    1019F   "Hiawatha," Red Man, 14 (May-June, 1897), 7. Prose
             rendition of the Hiawatha story.

JEMISON, IRENE (Cattaraugus Seneca)
    1020N   "Horse Hair Snakes," Talks and Thoughts, 7 (February,
             1892), 4.
    1021N   "How Indian Citizenship Day Was Observed," Talks and
             Thoughts, 7 (March, 1893), 6.

JEROME, ELMIRA C. (Chippewa)
    1022N   "Biography of Susan Longworth," Arrow, March 22, 1907.
    1023N   "The Munsee Indians," Carlisle Arrow, November 6, 1908.
             Historical sketch.
    1024M   "A Pottawatomie Tradition," Carlisle Arrow, January 22,
             1909. Legend of Mondamin.
    1025N   "Weaving, Basketry, and Pottery," Carlisle Arrow, April
             9, 1909.
    See also 1981 Biobibliography, 1815-1816.

JIMERSON, MARY (Onondaga)
    1026N   "The Laundry," Carlisle Arrow, March 12, 1909. De-
             scribes what goes on in the Carlisle laundry.

JOHN, ANDREW (Seneca)
    1027A   "A Speech by a Seneca Indian," Council Fire, 9 (April,
             1886), 63-64. Opposes a bill to allot the Seneca Reser-
             vation in New York.

JOHNSON, A. ELLA (Seneca)
    1028N   "The Medicine Man," Carlisle Arrow, January 19, 1912.
             Concerns Iroquois attitudes toward the medicine man.
    1029N   "My Trip to Boston," Carlisle Arrow, April 19, 1912. De-
             scribes her travel.
    See also 1981 Biobibliography, 1823.

JOHNSON, ADDISON E. (Eastern Band Cherokee)
    1030N   "The Redman and the Gospel," Arrow, February 15, 1907.
             Advocates Christianity for the Indian.

JOHNSON, EDNA M. (Pit River)
    1031N   "Class History," Sherman Bulletin, June 2, 1915. Concerns
             students at Sherman Institute.

JOHNSON, FRANK (Alaska Native)
    1032A   "Valedictory," Chemawa American, 15 (June, 1913), 4-6.
             Advocates hard work.

JOHNSON, FRANK L. (Winnebago)
1033N "How the Winnebago Indians Celebrate Christmas," Carlisle Arrow, February 4, 1910.

JOHNSON, JOHN (Ottawa)
See ENMEGAHBOWH

JOHNSON, JOHN (Seminole)
1034N "Closing Days at Camp Pike," Indian School Journal, 19
(June, 1919), 28-29. Describes his experiences.

JOHNSON, JOHN P. (Winnebago)
1035F "Class Prophecy," Sherman Bulletin, May 10, 1911. Fantasy, concerning Sherman Institute students.

JOHNSON, VICTOR H. (Dalles)
1036P "The Brook," Arrow, July 12, 1907. Reprinted from Dartmouth Magazine.
See also 1981 Biobibliography, 1828-1830.

JONES, FLORA E. (Seneca)
1037N "Chief Red Jacket," Arrow, December 27, 1907. Biographical sketch.
1038N "The Carlisle Indian School," Carlisle Arrow, January 22,
1909. Describes its location, background, and present
work. Reprinted from the Buffalo Sunday Courier.
See also 1981 Biobibliography, 1833, in which she is identified as
Munsee.

JONES, HENRY CLAY (Sac and Fox)
1039N "A Good Word for the Kickapoos," Red Man and Helper,
October 5, 1900. Concerns "progress" of the Oklahoma
Kickapoos.
1040N "Some Views of an Indian," Red Man and Helper, July 5,
1901. Describes his visit to Carlisle and praises Indian
education.

JONES, LUCY N. (Tuscarora)
1041L "A Berkshire Letter," Talks and Thoughts, 11 (October,
1895), 3-4. Reports on life in Richmond, Massachusetts.
1042N "The Progress of the Tuscarora Indians," Talks and
Thoughts, 12 (June-July, 1896), 6-7.

JONES, PENNINAH (Sioux)
1043F "An Indian Ghost Story," Word Carrier of Santee Normal
Training School, 43 (May-June, 1914), 12. Story of
two schoolmates.

JONES, SIMON (Rosebud Sioux)
1044N "A Tribe of Loafers," Word Carrier of Santee Normal

Training School, 43 (May-June, 1914), 12. Criticizes
the Indians at Pine Ridge.

JONES, STEPHEN S. (Santee Sioux)
    1045N   "Y.M.C.A. Work Among the Sioux," Talks and Thoughts,
          15 (May, 1900), 3-4.
    1046N   "A Pupil's Tribute," Word Carrier of Santee Normal Train-
          ing School, 35 (May-June, 1906), 11. Praises a former
          teacher, Sarah Elizabeth Voorhees.
    1047N   "Y.M.C.A. Conference," Word Carrier of Santee Normal
          Training School, 35 (May-June, 1906), 12. Reports a
          meeting at Santee, Nebraska.
    1048N   "An Indian Student's Essay on the Bible," Word Carrier
          of Santee Normal Training School, 37 (July-August,
          1908), 13. Advocates the Bible as a guide for great
          men's lives.
    1049N   "A Mission in India," Word Carrier of Santee Normal Train-
          ing School, 42 (March-April, 1913), 7. Concerns the
          Indian Y.M.C.A. and its support for Y.M.C.A. in India.
    1050A   "Reservation Leaders--The Good and the Bad," Indian
          Leader, 19 (October, 1915), 10-11.
    1051N   "The Indian Y.M.C.A.," Word Carrier of Santee Normal
          Training School, 52 (September-October, 1923), 19. His-
          torical sketch. Reprinted from Sioux Falls Argus-Leader.
    See also 1981 Biobibliography, 1837-1838.

JONES, WILLIAM (Sac and Fox)
    1052F   "Anoska Nimiwina," Indian Leader, March 9, 1900. A
          short story.
    See also 1981 Biobibliography, 1839-1862.

JONES, WILSON N. (Choctaw)
    1053A   "Gov. Jones' Message," Indian Citizen, October 18, 1890.
          Concerns Choctaw national affairs.

JORDAN, HENRY M. (Mohawk)
    1054M   "Legend of the Small Dipper," Carlisle Arrow, April 30,
          1909.

JORDAN, JOHN W. (Cherokee)
    1055L   Letter, Cherokee Telephone, March 31, 1892. Concerns
          the Cherokee Strip.
    See also 1981 Biobibliography, 1863-1864.

JORDAN, PETER JOSEPH (Chippewa)
    1056N   "White Earth Reservation," Arrow, May 29, 1908. Concerns
          "progress" of the White Earth Chippewas.
    See also 1981 Biobibliography, 1865-1867.

JOSE, MAGELA (Papago)
    1057N   "Papago Girl Tells of Hopi Snake Dance," Word Carrier

of Santee Normal Training School, 40 (January-February, 1911), 1. Describes the ceremony.
See also 1981 Biobibliography, 1868-1869.

JUMPER, JOHN (Seminole)
1058L   Letter, Council Fire, 1 (April, 1878), 53-54. Seeks spiritual help for Indians.

KACHIKUM, LOUISE (Menominee)
1059F   "The Apple Tree's Story," Carlisle Arrow, April 19, 1912. Fantasy concerning the Carlisle campus.

KADASHON, MARY R. (Alaska Native)
1060N   "A Glimpse of Alaskan Life," Arrow, March 23, 1905.

KAUBOODLE, CHARLES (Kiowa)
1061L   "What Charles Kauboodle, Kiowa, Writes to His Cousin Laura," School News, 1 (May, 1881), 1. Encourages others to attend Carlisle.

KAY, SUSIE (Creek)
1062N   "Fields," Creek Boys' and Girls' Monthly, December, 1870. Concerns agriculture.

KEALEAR, CHARLES H. (Yankton Sioux)
1063L   Letter, Talks and Thoughts, 2 (March, 1887), 4. Concerns his early life.
1064L   "Mount Hermon School," Talks and Thoughts, 2 (July, 1888), 1. Describes his travels to Mount Hermon, Massachusetts.
1065N   "Sharp Eyes," Talks and Thoughts, 4 (August, 1889), 1. Concerns what students face in going back to the West.
1066N   "Vacation in the Dictionary," Talks and Thoughts, 4 (August, 1889), 4. Concerns language study.
See also 1981 Biobibliography, 1877-1881.

KEEL, WILLIAM (Chickasaw)
1067N   "What the Training Camp Has Done for the Indian," Indian School Journal, 19 (June, 1919), 22-23.

KENDALL, HENRY J. (Isleta Pueblo)
1068N   "Shall the Indians Be Admitted to Citizenship?" Morning Star, 6 (May, 1886), 8. Argues the positive side.
See also 1981 Biobibliography, 1886.

KENNEDY, ALVIN W. (Seneca)
1069N   "The Green Corn Dance," Carlisle Arrow, May 27, 1910. Describes the celebration.
1070N   "Poultry Raising," Carlisle Arrow, September 23, 1910.
1071M   "The Keepers of the West Door of the Lodge," Carlisle

Arrow, December 23, 1910. Legend concerning the location of the Five Nations.

1072N   "The Coming of the New Year," Carlisle Arrow, March 10,
1911. Describes the Seneca New Year celebration.

1073N   "How I Spent My Vacation," Carlisle Arrow, September 29,
1911. Describes his work on the railroad.

See also 1981 Biobibliography, 1888-1891.

KENNEY, HELENA (Klamath)

1074F   "A Story of Ten Brothers," Sherman Bulletin, February 15,
15, 1911. A tale.

KENNEY, LOUISA (Klamath)

1075M   "The Legend of the Fire," Arrow, December 20, 1907.

1076N   "How to Acquire Success," Carlisle Arrow, November 6,
1908. Advocates honesty, hard work.

1077F   "Lorenzo, the Little Pueblo," Carlisle Arrow, December 24,
1909. A short story.

1078N   "Indian New Year," Carlisle Arrow, February 18, 1910.
Describes the Klamath pick-ya-wish celebration.

1079F   "Why the Rabbit Is Timid," Carlisle Arrow, March 25,
1910. A tale.

1080N   "Greeting and Farewell," Carlisle Arrow, April 8, 1910.
Praises Carlisle's work for the Indian.

See also 1981 Biobibliography, 1892-1893.

KEOKUK, FANNIE (Sac and Fox)

1081N   "The Croatan Indians," Carlisle Arrow, October 29, 1909.
Discusses their status in 1909.

1082N   "How I Spent the Summer," Carlisle Arrow, November 5,
1909. Describes her outing experiences at Sea Island,
New Jersey.

1083N   "The Medicine Dance," Carlisle Arrow, March 11, 1910.
Describes the dance among the Sac and Fox.

1084N   "Chief Keokuk," Carlisle Arrow, April 8, 1910. Biographical sketch.

1085N   "Choctaw Traditions," Carlisle Arrow, May 14, 1909. Describes the beginnings of the tribe.

See also 1981 Biobibliography, 1894-1897.

KESHENA, ELIZA (Menominee)

1086F   "The Wonderful Gift," Carlisle Arrow, June 17, 1910.
Menominee story of a fasting dream vision.

1087F   "The Catfish," Carlisle Arrow, December 2, 1910. A Menominee story.

1088F   "How the Hunter Punished the Snow," Carlisle Arrow,
May 19, 1911. A tale.

See also 1981 Biobibliography, 1902-1903.

KESHOITEWA, CLARA TALAVENSKA (Hopi)

1089F   "Saquavicha, the Fox-Girl," Indian Leader, March 3, 1911.
A story of Oraibi. Reprinted from Native American.

See also 1981 Biobibliography, 3795-3797.

KEYES, JAMES M. (Cherokee)
1090L   Letter, Cherokee Advocate, April 7, 1882. Concerns law
         and order in the Cherokee Nation.

KEYS, RILEY (Cherokee)
1091L   Letter, Cherokee Advocate, April 18, 1874. Concerns lo-
         cation of the Cherokee Orphan Asylum.

KILLED, LOUIS (Standing Rock Sioux)
1092N   "About Eskimo Dogs," Talks and Thoughts, 7 (March,
         1893), 3.

KIMMEL, HELEN (Sioux)
1093N   "My Work in the Club Kitchen," Carlisle Arrow, April 29,
         1910. Concerns her approaching summer outing.

KINGMAN, HARRY (Cheyenne River Sioux)
1094N   "One Boy's Story," Talks and Thoughts, 4 (May, 1890),
         4. Describes his early educational experiences.

KINGSLEY, EBENEZER (Winnebago)
1095N   "A Winter Campaign," Talks and Thoughts, 7 (March,
         1893), 5-6. Reports on a tour by the Hampton Quartet.
1096L   "A Graduate's Christmas," Talks and Thoughts, 11 (Feb-
         ruary, 1896), 6. Describes Christmas at the Cheyenne
         School.

KINGSLEY, NETTIE MARY (Winnebago)
1097N   "My First Christmas," Carlisle Arrow, January 12, 1912.
         Describes her school experiences at Tomah, Wisconsin.
See also 1981 Biobibliography, 1914-1915.

KINNINOOK, PAUL (Tlingit)
1098N   "Recollections of My Past and Aspirations for My Future,"
         Chemawa American, 15 (June, 1913), 7-10.
1099M   "Indian Legend--The Crow and His Servants," Chemawa
         American, 15 (May, 1913), 17. Legend of Crow and
         Salmon, set on Nass River.
1100N   "The Need and Opportunity of Studying," Chemawa Amer-
         ican, 16 (May, 1914), 40-41.

KIRK, SIMON J. (Sioux)
1101N   "Who Will Teach Us How to Farm," Word Carrier of Santee
         Normal Training School, 34 (March-April, 1905), 6. Ad-
         vocates industrial and agricultural training for Indians.
1102N   "An Indian's Opinion of the Qualifications of a Pastor,"
         Word Carrier of Santee Normal Training School, 37 (July-
         August, 1908), 13.

KNOX, STEPHEN W. (Pima)
1103N   "Kindness to Animals," Sherman Bulletin, February 15,
         1911.

1104A   "Salutatory," Sherman Bulletin, May 10, 1911. Encourages
        students to strive.

KOHPAY, HARRY (Osage)
1105L   "To My Osage Brothers," Osage Journal, February 13,
        1902. Advocates education for the Indian.
1106L   Letter, Red Man and Helper, March 21, 1902. Advocates
        education and Christianity for the Indians. Reprinted
        from Osage Journal.
1107L   "Kohpay Replies," Osage Journal, August 14, 1902. Re-
        lates his experiences and conditions of the Osages.
See also 1981 Biobibliography, 1920.

KONKITAH, ROBERT HARRIS (Alaska Native)
1108M   With B. K. Wilbur. "How They Found That the Sun Was
        on Fire," North Star, 7 (March, 1896), 3. A legend.
1109M   With B. K. Wilbur. "A Legend of Sitka," North Star, 7
        (July, 1896), 3.

KUDNOK, FRED THOMAS (Eskimo)
1110N   "Enupeak Ahtick (Eskimo Name)," Eskimo, 2 (June, 1918),
        8. Argues that Eskimos should keep native names.

KUTOOK, CHARLES (Eskimo)
1111N   "Some Reasons for Sending Children to School," Eskimo,
        1 (May, 1917), 7.

LACIE, ADAM L. (Cherokee)
1112L   Letter, Indian Missionary, 1 (August, 1885), 4. Concerns
        his life and activities as a preacher.

LACK, BERRYMAN (Hupa)
1113A   "Salutatory," Sherman Bulletin, May 25, 1910. Encourages
        students to strive.

LACK, HIRAM (Hupa)
1114M   "Why an Eel Has No Bones," Sherman Bulletin, December
        15, 1909. A legend.

LA CROIX, KATIE (Yankton Sioux)
1115L   Letter, School News, 1 (March, 1881), 4. Encourages
        students to attend school.

LA FLESCHE, FRANCIS (Omaha)
1116N   "The Curing of Corn," Albuquerque Indian, 1 (December,
        1905), 19.
See also 1981 Biobibliography, 1911-1946.

LA FLESCHE, MARGUERITE (Omaha)
1117N   "Our Work," Talks and Thoughts, 1 (June, 1886), 4.
        Concerns letter writing.

1118N   Untitled, Talks and Thoughts, 2 (May, 1887), 4. Reminisces about her school days.

1119L   Letter, Ten Years' Work for Indians at Hampton Institute. Hampton, VA: Hampton Institute, 1888, pp. 51-55. Concerns Hampton's work for Indians and returned students.

LA FLESCHE, SUSAN (Omaha)
See PICOTTE, SUSAN LA FLESCHE

LA FLEUR, MITCHELL (Colville)
1120N   "An Ideal Christmas," Carlisle Arrow, January 12, 1912. Concerns the giving of gifts.

LA FROMBOISE, JULIA (Sioux)
1121M   "Dakota Myths: II: Unktomi--the Spider," Iapi Oaye, 12 (July-August, 1883), 56.

1122T   "Dakota Myths III. The Orphan Boy," Iapi Oaye, 12 (September, 1883), 72.

1123T   "Dakota Myths V: Canktewin the Ill-Fated Woman, Part I," Iapi Oaye, 12 (April, 1884), 4.

LA FROMBOISE, JUSTINE AMELIA (Sisseton Sioux)
1124L   "An Open Letter," Iapi Oaye, 11 (January, 1882), 8. Describes Carlisle.

1125N   "Description of the Journey to Carlisle," School News, 3 (June, 1882), 1, 4.

LA HAY, JOSEPH M. (Cherokee)
1126P   "Consolation," Tahlequah Arrow, August 26, 1905. Political verse about graft.

LAMBERT, BAPTISTE P. (Yankton Sioux)
1127N   "Indian Folk-lore," Talks and Thoughts, 3 (June, 1889), 1, 4. Relates an anecdote about Brave Bear, the Cheyenne.

1128N   "What Lambert Thinks," Talks and Thoughts, 4 (July, 1889), 3. Discusses conditions at Hampton Institute.

LAMBERT, JESSE B. (Eastern Band Cherokee)
1129N   "Some Native Industries," Talks and Thoughts, 11 (March, 1896), 1-3. Discusses blankets, canoes, and pottery.

1130N   "Indian Citizenship Day," Talks and Thoughts, 12 (March, 1897), 2. Describes ceremonies on campus.

LAMBERTON, MAMIE (Klamath)
1131N   "Home Training," Sherman Bulletin, May 29, 1919.

LAMOUREAUX, LOUISE G. (Sioux)
1132N   "Class History," Sherman Bulletin, May 28, 1913. Concerns Sherman Institute students.

1133N "A Sketch of the Domestic Service Class," Sherman Bulletin,
       May 28, 1913.

LANE, HELEN F. (Lummi)
  1134M "Iroquois Legend of the Three Sisters," Carlisle Arrow,
       March 19, 1909. Concerns the sister spirits of beans,
       corn, and squash.
  See also 1981 Biobibliography, 1958.

LA POINTE, PIERRE (Sioux)
  1135N "An Indian's Opinion of 'The Wild West Show,'" Word Car-
       rier, 20 (April, 1891), 14. Argues for Indian education.

LA POINTE, ROSE (Sioux)
  1136N "Our Indian Camp Meeting," Word Carrier of Santee Normal
       Training School, 42 (May-June, 1914), 12. Describes
       events at the annual meeting.

LA POINTE, SAMUEL (Rosebud Sioux)
  1137L "Some of Our Expeditionary Soldiers," Word Carrier of
       Santee Normal Training School, 48 (March-April, 1919),
       5. Describes his army experiences.
  1138L "One of Our Expeditionary Soldiers," Word Carrier of San-
       tee Normal Training School, 48 (July-August, 1919), 16.
       Autobiographical sketch, describing his war experiences.

LA POINTE, SAMUEL O. (Rosebud Sioux)
  1139A "Our Progress," Word Carrier, 27 (June-July, 1898), 22.
       Praises Christian education for Indians.

LARGE, ROY (Shoshoni)
  1140F "How One Boy Passed His Examination," Carlisle Arrow,
       September 25, 1908. Story about a boy who cleans the
       schoolroom to get in school.
  1141F "The Coyote," Carlisle Arrow, June 25, 1909. A Coyote
       tale in which Coyote outsmarts Cowboy.

LA ROQUE, DAVID (Sioux)
  1142N "Cutting and Fitting Harness," Indian Leader, May 10, 1901.

LASHEN, DAN M. (Oto)
  1143P "A Poem Written by Dan M. Lashen, an Otoe Indian Boy,
       Ten Years of Age," Indian's Friend, 13 (May, 1901),
       12. Concerns Jesus and salvation.

LA VATTA, EMMA (Fort Hall Shoshoni)
  1144F "The Story of the Deerskin," Carlisle Arrow, June 3, 1910.
       A tale about the skin over the door of the wigwam.
  1145F "Why the Snake's Head Became Flat," Carlisle Arrow, De-
       cember 16, 1910. A tale.
  1146N With William Owl. "History of the Class of 1911," Carlisle
       Arrow, April 21 1911. Describes the Carlisle experience.

See also 1981 Biobibliography, 1963-1964, where she is identified
as Bannock.

LA VATTA, GEORGE (Fort Hall Shoshoni)
1147N "About the Soils," Carlisle Arrow, February 12, 1909.
Describes kinds of soils.
See also 1981 Biobibliography, 1965.

LA VATTA, PHILIP (Fort Hall Shoshoni)
1148A "That the Negro Is Superior to the Indian," Red Man, 12
(January-February, 1894), 4. Argues the negative side.
See also 1981 Biobibliography, 1967.

LAWRENCE, P. M. (Sioux)
1149N "An Indian's Opinion," Word Carrier of Santee Normal
Training School, 37 (March-April, 1908), 8. Concerns
legal marriages.

LAY, BLANCHE (Seneca)
1150N "Laundrying," Arrow, March 30, 1906. Describes the
process.

LAZELLE, DELLA (Citizens' Band Potawatomi)
1151N "Business Methods in the Home," Indian Leader, June 14,
1912.

LAZELLE, RUTH (Citizens' Band Potawatomi)
1152N "'By Their Clothes Ye Shall Know Them,'" Indian School
Journal, 19 (December, 1918), 143-145. Discusses proper
dress and attire for women.

LEACH, JOHN R. (Cherokee)
1153L "Defense of the Fullblood," Tahlequah Arrow, September
28, 1899. Defends the Keetoowah Society.

LEE, ALONZO (Eastern Band Cherokee)
1154N "Indian Folk-Lore," Talks and Thoughts, 12 (November,
1896), 4. Argues that modern civilization is destroying
it.
1155N "An Indian Naturalist," Talks and Thoughts, 12 (February,
1897), 2-3. Presents Cherokee nature lore.
1156N "Transition Scenes," Talks and Thoughts, 14 (March,
1899), 3. Describes changes among the Cherokees in
North Carolina.

LEE, WILLIAM (Sioux)
1157N "A Change in Mourning," Word Carrier of Santee Normal
Training School, 37 (March-April, 1908), 8. Concerns
proper conduct during mourning period.
1158N "Indian Mourning Customs," Word Carrier of Santee Normal
Training School, 37 (May-June, 1908), 10. Concerns
old customs versus new ways.

LE FLORE, CARRIE (Choctaw)
    1159N "My Native People," Indian Advocate, 3 (July, 1891), 11.
        Concerns the Choctaws.
    1160N "The New Brotherhood," Indian Advocate, 3 (October,
        1891), 14. Concerns an organization in France.
    1161N "Leaving the Yazoo," Indian Advocate, 7 (July, 1895),
        69-74. Concerns Pushmataha.
    1162F "An Indian Tale," Indian Advocate, 8 (April, 1896), 37-
        39. A short story.

LEMIEUX, AGNES (Chippewa)
    1163N "Prohibition," Peace Pipe, March 26, 1915.
    1164N "Valedictory," Peace Pipe, July 2, 1915. Encourages
        students to strive.

LEVERING, LEVI (Omaha)
    1165L "He Wants to Be Serviceable," Red Man and Helper, De-
        cember 20, 1901. Advocates Christian education for
        Indians.
See also 1981 Biobibliography, 1979-1981.

LEWIS, DOTY (Bannock)
    1166F "The Coyote," Sherman Bulletin, March 15, 1911. A
        Coyote tale.

LEWIS, MARIE (Cherokee)
    1167N "How I Spent Christmas," Carlisle Arrow, December 31,
        1909. Describes her activities.

LEWIS, WALLACE (Narragansett)
    1168N "The City of Buffalo," Carlisle Arrow, February 5, 1909.
        Describes the city.

LIBBY, JOSEPH (Chippewa)
    1169N "Christmas with the Chippewas," Carlisle Arrow, February
        10, 1910. Describes Christmas programs at the school
        houses.
    1170N With Peter Hauser. "Practical Business Education,"
        Carlisle Arrow, April 8, 1910. Describes what they
        expect to do with their Carlisle training.

LITTLE CHIEF, LUCY (Pawnee)
    1171N "How Pawnees Celebrate Christmas," Indian Leader, Decem-
        ber 20, 1907.

LITTLE MOON, SARAH (Sioux)
    1172N "Citizenship," Oglala Light, 15 (April, 1914), 11-14.

LITTLE WOLF, FELIX (Sioux)
    1173N "About H. W. Longfellow," Ogalalla Light, 1 (July 2, 1900),
        4. Concerns the poet.

LOCUST, PETER (Cherokee)
   1174N "Toys or Play Things," Carlisle Arrow, January 8, 1909.

LOCUST, WILLIAM (Cherokee)
   1175N "Examples of Nations," Indian Missionary, 5 (July, 1889),
         6. Espouses patriotism.

LOLORIAS, JOHN M. (Papago)
   1176N "The Indians of Mexico," Talks and Thoughts, 15 (May,
         1900), 1.
   1177M "The Last Great War," Talks and Thoughts, 14 (January,
         1901), 1. A legend.
   1178N "The Rain and the Wind," Talks and Thoughts, 14 (Feb-
         ruary, 1901), 4, and (March, 1901), 1, 4.
   1179M "The Last Great War--Legend of Brown Condor," Indian
         Advance, 2 (April 12, 1901), 4.
   1180N "The Red and the White Man," Talks and Thoughts, 14
         (April, 1901), 3-4.
   1181N "Music in Nature," Talks and Thoughts, 14 (May, 1901),
         4.
   1182N "Christmas Among the Papagoes," Talks and Thoughts, 15
         (December, 1901), 1. Reprinted from Work at Home.
   See also 1981 Biobibliography, 1993.

LOMOVITU, OTTO (Hopi)
   1183L "Full-Blood Calls Indian Snake Dance a Fake," Word Car-
         rier of Santee Normal Training School, 52 (September-
         October, 1923), 20. Denounces the dance as degrading.
         Reprinted from Flagstaff Coconino Sun.

LONG, SYLVESTER (Catawba-Cherokee)
   1184M "Origin of Names Among the Cherokees," Carlisle Arrow,
         November 11, 1910. Concerns naming children after
         animals.
   1185N "Virginia Dare or the White Fawn," Carlisle Arrow, Feb-
         ruary 9, 1912.
   1186N "The White Man Follows the Indian's Example," Carlisle
         Arrow, February 16, 1912. Discusses the willow basket
         industry in Grant, Michigan.
   1187N "Salutatory," Carlisle Arrow, April 19, 1912. Concerns
         Carlisle ideals.
   1188N "Indians of the Northwest and West Canada," Mentor, 12
         (March, 1924), 1-40. Signed "Chief Buffalo Child Long
         Lance."
   1189N "Story of Carlisle Indian Military School," Mentor, 12 (Sep-
         tember, 1924), 56-58. Signed "Chief Buffalo Child Long
         Lance."
   See also 1981 Biobibliography, 1998.

LONG, WILL WEST (Eastern Band Cherokee)
   1190N "Indians as Voters and Tax-Payers," Talks and Thoughts,
         12 (April, 1897), 2-3.

LONG LANCE, CHIEF BUFFALO CHILD (Catawba-Cherokee)
See LONG, SYLVESTER

LORENTZ, HENRY (Wichita)
1191N "A Visit to the Printing Office," Carlisle Arrow, February
25, 1910. Describes what goes on there.

LOTT, HARRISON (Nez Percé)
1192N "The Sewing Room," Carlisle Arrow, January 1, 1909. Describes what goes on there.
1193N "Experiments in Germination," Carlisle Arrow, January 15,
1909. Concerns germinating wheat.

LOWE, ADELIA (Sioux)
1194A "Ceylon," Red Man, 13 (January, 1896), 5. Describes
life there.

LOWREY, GEORGE (Cherokee)
1195A "Message of the Acting Principal Chief," Cherokee Advocate, October 9, 1848. Concerns Cherokee national affairs.
See also 1981 Biobibliography, 2000.

LOWRY, MAUDE (Washo)
1196A "Breadmaking," Chemawa American, 15 (June, 1913), 10-
14.
1197P "The Purple and the White," Chemawa American, 15 (June,
1913), 28. Concerns school spirit.

LUCE, MAXIE (Nisenan)
1198N "Steam Engineering," Carlisle Arrow, October 23, 1908.
Discusses steam engineering as an occupation.

LUDWICK, LENA (Oneida)
1199M "Origins of the Violets," Talks and Thoughts, 19 (September-October, 1905), 1. A legend.
1200F "The Wise Sachem's Gift," Talks and Thoughts, 19 (September-October, 1905), 1, 4. A story.
1201N "The Oneidas of Today," Word Carrier of Santee Normal
Training School, 39 (January-February, 1910), 1. Describes their present conditions. Reprinted from Southern Workman.

LUGO, ASSIDRO (Mission)
1202L "Bravo Boys," Mission Indian, 1 (October 15, 1895), 5.
Concerns baseball.

LUGO, FRANK (Mission)
1203L "I Am Pleased," Mission Indian, 1 (December 15, 1895),
5. Concerns the importance of religion.

LUJAN, MATTIE (Pueblo)
 1204N "The Story of Silk," Sherman Bulletin, May 29, 1919.

LYDICK, HENRY (Chippewa)
 1205N "Engineering Department," Arrow, January 3, 1908. De-
    scribes the department at Carlisle.

LYMAN, HENRY (Yankton Sioux)
 1206N "Indian Picnic," Talks and Thoughts, 2 (June, 1887), 1.

LYONS, JAMES F. (Onondaga)
 1207N "The Grove," Carlisle Arrow, April 19, 1912. Describes
    woods on the Carlisle campus.

Mac ARTHUR, LINDA (White Earth Chippewa)
 1208N "How We Make Dresses," Indian Leader, May 10, 1901.

Mc ARTHUR, ROSABELLE (Umpqua)
 1209N "The History of Our Cattle," Carlisle Arrow, November
    27, 1908. Concerns the evolution of cattle.

McCARTHY, JOSEPHINE (Standing Rock Sioux)
 1210L Letter, Talks and Thoughts, 2 (March, 1887), 3. Con-
    cerns her people and the legend of the Standing Rock.

McCAULEY, DORA (Chippewa)
 1211A "Results in the Realm of the Household," Indian Leader,
    14 (June, 1913), 21-23. Discusses the study of domes-
    tic arts.

McCAULEY, ELLA (Winnebago)
 1212M "The Legend of the Fireballs," Indian Leader, December
    16, 1904. A Winnebago legend.
 1213F "An Indian Story," Indian Leader, January 13, 1905.
    A tale about Mr. Sleeping Buffalo.

McCLELLAN, WILLIAM A. (Cherokee)
 1214A "Gen. Stan Watie," Tahlequah Arrow, June 4, 1904.

McCOY, JAMES (Pawnee)
 1215L Letter, Talks and Thoughts, 1 (February, 1887), 2-3.
    Autobiographical statement.

McCULLY, ELLA JULIA (Kake, i.e., Tlingit)
 1216N "Facts About the Panama Canal," Chemawa American, 16
    (October, 1913), 32-33.
 1217N "Some Insect Friends," Chemawa American, 16 (June,
    1914), 14-15.

McCURTAIN, EDMOND (Choctaw)
 1218A "Inaugural Address of Edmond McCurtain, Principal Chief,

Choctaw Nation," Indian Missionary, 1 (November, 1884),
1. Expresses his desire to uplift the Choctaws.
See also 1981 Biobibliography, 2022-2025.

McCURTAIN, GREEN (Choctaw)
1219A "McCurtain's Message," Fort Smith Elevator, October 21,
1898. Surveys Choctaw national affairs.
1220A "Questions of Citizenship," Fort Smith Elevator, March
24, 1899. Concerns claimants to citizenship in the
Choctaw Nation.
1221L "Hon. Green M'Curtain," Fort Smith Elevator, July 20,
1900. Expresses opposition to G.W. Dukes.
1222A "McCurtain's Message," Fort Smith Elevator, December 12,
1902. Surveys Choctaw affairs.
1223A "M'Curtain's Message," Fort Smith Elevator, October 16,
1903. Surveys Choctaw affairs.
1224A "Gov. McCurtain's Message," Adair Ledger, October 6,
1905. Surveys Choctaw affairs.
See also 1981 Biobibliography, 2026-2052.

McDONALD, CHARLES F. (Chippewa)
1225N "My Experience in a Railroad Camp," Carlisle Arrow, April
19, 1912.

McDONALD, CLAUDIA E. (Chippewa)
1226N "Enthusiasm," Arrow, March 27, 1908. Stresses its importance.
1227A "Vocational Education," Indian Leader, June 24, 1910.

McDONALD, FLORA (Spokan)
1228N "The Pilgrims and the Indians," Carlisle Arrow, October
9, 1908. Concerns Samoset, Squanto, and Thanksgiving.

McDRID, CHARLES (Ukiah, i.e., Pomo)
1229N "Misrepresenting the Indian," Indian Leader, 17 (November, 1913), 18. Criticizes moving pictures.

McDRID, SAVANNAH (Ukiah, i.e., Pomo)
1230N "Indian Superstitions," Indian Leader, 17 (January, 1914),
16.

McGAA, ALBERT D. (Sioux)
1231N Untitled, Ogalalla Light, 1 (July 2, 1900), 4. Describes
the bee.

McINNIS, JOHN (Washo)
1232M "The Sheldrake Duck," Carlisle Arrow, January 6, 1911.
Legend concerning its origin.
See also 1981 Biobibliography, 2073-2074.

McINTOSH, DONALD (San Carlos Apache)
  1233M "How Fire Was Secured," Red Man, 15 (January, 1900),
       6. Legend of Beaver and Coyote.

McINTOSH, ROLLIE (Creek)
  1234A "Message of the Chief," Daily Chieftain, November 26,
       1898. Concerns Creek national affairs.

McINTOSH, SADIE (Creek)
  1235F "Buffalo Heena--A Creek Legend," Indian Leader, August
       25, 1911.

McKENZIE, MINNIE (Cherokee)
  1236P "An Ode to the Juniors," Indian School Journal, 18 (June,
       1918), 56. Humorous verse, a parody of "A Psalm of
       Life."
  1237P "Doings at Chilocco," Indian School Journal, 18 (June,
       1918), 61. Occasional poem.
  1238P "Nineteen," Indian School Journal, 19 (June, 1919), 47.
       Poem about graduation.
  1239P "To Our Teachers," Indian School Journal, 19 (June,
       1919), 27. Poem of thanks.
  1240N "Valedictory--'Service,'" Indian School Journal, 19 (June,
       1919), 41-42. Concerning the duties of Indian grad-
       uates.
  1241P "What's in a Name," Indian School Journal, 19 (June, 1919),
       48. Occasional verse.

McKESSON, ISABELLE (Apache)
  1242N "A Heroic Goat," Sherman Bulletin, December 30, 1914.
       Autobiographical statement.

McKINNEY, HENRY (Potawatomi)
  1243N "A Trade Makes Every Man Equal," Indian School Journal,
       19 (December, 1918), 142-143. Lauds vocational educa-
       tion.

McKINNEY, THOMPSON (Choctaw)
  1244L "To the Citizens of the Choctaw Nation," Choctaw Intelli-
       gencer, August 21, 1850. Concerns Choctaw govern-
       ment.
  1245L "Letter from the Choctaw Nation," Fort Smith Times, June
       9, 1858. Explains Choctaw disagreements over a new
       constitution.
  See also 1981 Biobibliography, 2093-2094.

McLEAN, DINAH (Hopi)
  1246F "Kachinnas," Sherman Bulletin, April 5, 1911. A tale.
  1247F "Why We Hate the Snake," Sherman Bulletin, April 26,
       1911. A tale.

McLEAN, SAMUEL J. (Rosebud Sioux)
  1248N "Indian Christmas," Arrow, January 3, 1908. Describes
         celebrations at Rosebud Reservation.
  1249N "Feathers," Arrow, June 12, 1908. Discusses Indians'
         use of feathers.
  See also 1981 Biobibliography, 2096.

MacLEOD, MICHAEL (Kenai, i.e., Tanaina)
  1250N "My Trip from Alaska to Chemawa," Chemawa American,
         15 (April, 1913), 11-12. Describes his trip.
  1251N "Injurious Insects," Chemawa American, 16 (April, 1914),
         23-24. Concerns San José scale, codling moth, plum
         curculio, and peach borer.
  1252N "Injurious Insects," Chemawa American, 16 (May, 1914),
         28-29. Concerns the cabbage worm, chinch bug, Hes-
         sian fly, and squash bug.
  1253N "Class History," Chemawa American, 16 (June, 1914),
         6-9. Concerns Chemawa students.
  1254N "Graduation," Chemawa American, 16 (June, 1914), 20.
         Encourages students to strive.

MACHUKAY, MARTIN (Apache)
  1255N "The Apaches as Workers," Arrow, March 23, 1905.

MACK, JOHN A. (Pima)
  1256F "An Old Football," Sherman Bulletin, February 10, 1909.
         Fantasy.
  1257F "The Fox and the Coyote," Sherman Bulletin, March 1,
         1911. A tale.

MACK, MINNIE (Pima)
  1258M "A Pima Legend," Sherman Bulletin, March 13, 1912.
         Concerns the bluebird.
  1259M "Pima Legend of the Bluebird," Indian Leader, September
         27, 1912. Reprinted from Sherman Bulletin.

MADISON, LYMAN B. (Mashpee)
  1260N "A New England Light-Station," Carlisle 1917. Carlisle,
         PA: U.S. Indian School, 1917, p. 44. Describes one.

MADRID, CARLOS (Pueblo)
  1261F "Class Prophecy," Sherman Bulletin, May 25, 1910, supple-
         ment. Fantasy concerning Sherman Institute students.

MAGASKAWIN, THERESA (Sioux)
  1262L Letter, Sina Sapa Wocekiye Taeyanpaha, August, 1892.
         Urges others to attend school.

MAIN, LIZZIE E. (Blackfeet)
  1263N "Class History," Indian News, 13 (May-June, 1911), 11-
         13. Concerns Genoa Indian School students.

MAKESITLONG, JOHN (Sioux)
    1264L   "An Indian Elder to His Brother Elders," <u>Word Carrier of Santee Normal Training School</u>, 43 (January-February, 1914), 3. Urges them to persevere in Christian endeavors.

MANDAN, ARTHUR (Mandan)
    1265A   "Painting," <u>Arrow</u>, April 5, 1907. Discusses painting as an occupation.

MANITOWA, BERTHA (Sac and Fox)
    1266M   "Indian Legend," <u>Indian Leader</u>, January 22, 1909. Sac and Fox legend about the origin of Indians.

MANRIQUEZ, JUANITA (Mission)
    1267L   "The Dead Not Forgotten," <u>Mission Indian</u>, 1 (January 15, 1896), 4. Autobiographical statement.

MANSFIELD, FRANCIS (Fort Apache Apache)
    1268N   "My Visit to a Cave," <u>Indian Leader</u>, February 28, 1902. Describes a cave near the Fort Apache Agency.

MANSUR, SARAH (Ousakie, i.e., Sauk)
    1269N   "How the Laundering Is Done at Carlisle," <u>Carlisle Arrow</u>, December 18, 1908.

MANTEL, JAMES (Bois Fort Chippewa)
    1270N   "Religious Life Among Our People," <u>Word Carrier of Santee Normal Training School</u>, 42 (November-December, 1913), 24. Concerns the Bois Fort Chippewa.

MARMON, ALICE (Pueblo)
    1271N   "A Practical Domestic Training," <u>Indian Leader</u>, July 7, 1905. Advocates it.

MARMON, BELLE (Laguna Pueblo)
    1272N   "More Wonderful Than Fairyland," <u>Indian Leader</u>, March 16, 1900. Concerns the wonders of nature.
    1273N   "Story of the Pueblo Indians," <u>Indian Leader</u>, June 28, 1901. Delineates their history and character.

MARMON, FRANK (Laguna Pueblo)
    1274N   "How Steam Is Made and Used," <u>Sherman Bulletin</u>, December 17, 1913.
    1275A   "Salutatory," <u>Sherman Bulletin</u>, June 2, 1915. Encourages students to strive.

MARMON, HENRY C. (Laguna Pueblo)
    1276A   "Salutatory," <u>Sherman Bulletin</u>, May 22, 1912. Encourages students.

MARMON, KENNETH A. (Laguna Pueblo)
  1277F "An Indian Story," Sherman Bulletin, December 28, 1910.
      A tale.
  1278A "Valedictory," Sherman Bulletin, May 10, 1911. Encourages
      students to strive.
  1279T "El Jaboli y la Zorra (The Wild Boar and the Fox),"
      Sherman Bulletin, May 28, 1913. A poem.
  1280A "Degrees of Accuracy Required in Engineering Work,"
      Sherman Bulletin, October 17, 1917.
  1281L "From Kenneth Marmon," Sherman Bulletin, February 6,
      1919. Concerns Germany and World War I.

MARMON, ROBERT (Laguna Pueblo)
  1282N "The Pueblo of New Mexico," Indian Leader, July 15, 1899.
      Describes life and customs of the Pueblo.

MARSDEN, EDWARD (Tsimshian)
  1283L Letter, North Star, 1 (June, 1888), 2. Concerns removal
      of his people from Metlakatla, British Columbia, to
      Alaska.
  1284N "A Day in the Mission at Sitka," North Star, 3 (March,
      1890), 110-111. Describes activities there.
  1285N "A Trip to Yakutat," North Star, 3 (October, 1890), 140.
      Describes his trip.
  1286N "A Trip to Marietta, Ohio," North Star, 4 (June, 1891),
      170; (July, 1891), 175; (August, 1891), 177; (September,
      1891), 182-183; and (October, 1891), 185, 188. De-
      scribes the trip.
  1287M "A Tsimpshean Legend," Red Man, 12 (July-August, 1893),
      7. Concerns the origin of nationalities.
  1288N "Needs of Alaska. 6--Health," North Star, 8 (November,
      1897), 4.
  1289N "Needs of Alaska. 7--Workers," North Star, 8 (December,
      1897), 1, 4.
  1290N "Edward Marsden at Work," Home Mission Monthly, 13
      (June, 1899), 181. Concerns his missionary efforts at
      Saxman, Alaska.
  1291N "Saxman," Home Mission Monthly, 15 (June, 1901), 181.
      Reports on mission efforts there.
  1292N "A Victory Over Old Customs," Home Mission Monthly, 19
      (June, 1905), 175-177. Concerns missionary efforts
      among the Tongas and Cape Fox tribes.
See also 1981 Biobibliography, 2109-2125.

MARSHALL, ERNEST (Klamath)
  1293F "Why the Coyote Has a Thin Face," Sherman Bulletin, De-
      cember 10, 1913. A tale.

MARTIN, BERTHA (Osage)
  1294N "Class History," Sherman Bulletin, May 27, 1914. Con-
      cerns Sherman Institute students.

MARTIN, DANIEL (Assiniboin)
    1295N "Christmas on the Fort Peck Reservation," Sherman Bulle-
            tin, December 24, 1913.
    1296N "A Year in the Print Shop," Sherman Bulletin, May 27,
            1914.
    1297N "A Paper Read at Chapel," Sherman Bulletin, March 31,
            1915. Concerns understanding ourselves and our ani-
            mal servants.

MARTIN, EDNA I. (Citizens' Band Potawatomi)
    1298P "Class of '18," Indian School Journal, 18 (June, 1918),
            58. Occasional verse.

MARTIN, JOSEPH LYNCH (Cherokee)
    1299L Letter, South-West Independent, March 18, 1856. Signed
            "Green Brier," concerns sale of Neutral Lands and dis-
            tribution of funds.
    1300L Letter, Council Fire, 1 (August, 1878), 123-124. Signed
            "Joe Degar-noo-li," concerns the "civilization" level of
            the Cherokees.
    1301L Letter, Council Fire, 4 (June, 1881), 90. Praises Council
            Fire and stresses its value.
    See also 1981 Biobibliography, 2128-2145.

MARTIN, MAUDE (Chippewa)
    1302F "Indian Story of Cinderella," Indian Leader, October 16,
            1908. Recast of the fairy tale.

MATHEWS, JOHN JOSEPH (Osage)
    1303N "A Hamlet Dilemma in Modern Guise," University of Okla-
            homa Magazine, 8 (December, 1919), 8, 12-13. Humor,
            concerns modern dance fads.
    1304L "Ye Greeks: Distinctive Marks of Modern Classicists,"
            University of Oklahoma Magazine, 8 (March, 1920), 8.
            Humor, concerns college fraternity life.

MATILTON, JOHN (Hupa)
    1305N "What the Indian Most Needs," Sherman Bulletin, June
            10, 1908. Concerns education.
    1306N "Wise Words by an Indian Writer," Quileute Independent,
            December 17, 1908. Argues that education and Chris-
            tianity will lead to citizenship. Reprinted from Indian's
            Friend.

MATT, STEVENS (Flathead)
    1307N "Religious Life Among Our People," Word Carrier of San-
            tee Normal Training School, 42 (November-December,
            1913), 24. Concerns the Flatheads.

MAYBE, LILA (Seneca)
    1308N "The Teeth and Their Care," Carlisle Arrow, June 9, 1911.

MAYES, SOGGIE (Cherokee)
    1309A "The Curse of Idleness," Tahlequah Arrow, July 2, 1904.

MEDICINE BULL, SAMUEL (Lower Brule Sioux)
    1310L "To Show Our Success," Talks and Thoughts, 1 (May,
           1886), 4. Concerns "civilization" of the Indians.

MEDICINE EAGLE, BEN (Rosebud Sioux)
    1311N "What I Am to Do When I Leave School," Red Man and
           Helper, July 5, 1901. Relates his plans to farm.

MEEK, RILLA (Sac and Fox)
    1312N "Religious Conditions Among the Indian People," Word
           Carrier of Santee Normal Training School, 43 (March-
           April, 1914), 8. Concerns the Sac and Fox.

MELOVIDOV, ALEX (Aleut, i.e., Chugach Eskimo)
    1313N "The Fur Seal of the Pribiloff Islands," Chemawa Amer-
           ican, March 14, 1911. Discusses the history of seal
           hunting and habits of seals.
    1314N "Story of an Arewe," Chemawa American, 15 (February,
           1913), 22. Describes the bird from the Bering Sea.
    1315N "A Visit Home," Chemawa American, 15 (May, 1913), 28-
           29. Describes the visit of three Alaskan students to
           their homes.

MELTON, ANNA (Cherokee)
    1316F "The Legend of Black-Snake," Carlisle Arrow, November
           17, 1911. Tale of an Oklahoma Cherokee named Black-
           Snake.
    1317N "The Campus Beautiful," Carlisle Arrow, April 19, 1912.
           Describes Carlisle.
    See also 1981 Biobibliography, 2171.

MELTON, CLARA (Cherokee)
    1318F "Class Prophecy," Carlisle Arrow, April 19, 1912. Fan-
           tasy, concerns Carlisle students.

MENADALOOK, CHARLES (Eskimo)
    1319N "The Story of the Diomedes," Eskimo, 1 (December, 1916),
           11. Concerns Diomedes Islands and the natives there.
    1320N "'Enupeak' or a Real Human Being," Eskimo, 2 (April-
           May, 1918), 1. Concerns the name the Eskimos give
           themselves.

MENAUL, JOHN (Laguna Pueblo)
    1321N "We Not All Go Up Some Bad People Go Down," School
           News, 2 (August, 1881), 4. Concerns heaven and hell.
    1322L "From a Boy Who Does Not Go Through the World with
           His Eyes Shut," School News, 3 (February, 1883), 4.
           Describes his life on a farm as an outing student.

MENTZ, JOSEPH (Standing Rock Sioux)
　　1323N　"The Onondaga New Year's Feast," Talks and Thoughts, 18
　　　　　　(April, 1905), 1, 3. Relates events as told by Charles
　　　　　　Doxon.

MERRILL, GEORGE (Chippewa)
　　1324P　"Class Song," Carlisle 1917. Carlisle, PA: U.S. Indian
　　　　　　School, 1917, p. 7. Poem about school spirit.

MESKET, ANDERSON (Hupa)
　　1325N　"The American Indian," Sherman Bulletin, June 2, 1915.
　　　　　　"Progress" of the Indians.

METOXEN, IVY E. (Oneida)
　　1326N　"My Country Home," Carlisle Arrow, September 25, 1908.
　　　　　　Describes her life on a farm as an outing student.
　　1327N　"The Fourth of July on My Reservation," Carlisle Arrow,
　　　　　　July 4, 1912. Describes activities.
　　See also 1981 Biobibliography, 2180.

METOXEN, JOSEPH (Oneida)
　　1328N　"New Year's Day in Wisconsin," Indian Leader, December
　　　　　　28, 1906. Describes activities among the Oneidas.
　　See also 1981 Biobibliography, 2181.

MEZA, THECKLA (Mission)
　　1329N　"Class History," Sherman Bulletin, May 24, 1916. Con-
　　　　　　cerns Sherman Institute students.

MIGUEL, JEFFERSON (Yuma)
　　1330N　"Yuma Advancing," Arrow, December 13, 1907. Describes
　　　　　　recent changes in Yuma life-style.

MILES, THOMAS J. (Sac and Fox)
　　1331N　"Anniversary," Talks and Thoughts, 2 (June, 1887), 2-
　　　　　　3. Concerns graduation at Hampton Instiute.
　　See also 1981 Biobibliography, 2184-2186.

MILLER, EDWIN (Miami)
　　1332N　"Lacrosse," Carlisle 1917. Carlisle, PA: U.S. Indian
　　　　　　School, 1917, pp. 91, 93. Concerns the sport at Car-
　　　　　　lisle.
　　1333N　"Basketball," Carlisle 1917. Carlisle, PA: U.S. Indian
　　　　　　School, 1917, p. 93. Concerns the sport at Carlisle.

MILLER, FLORENCE (Stockbridge)
　　1334A　"That the Negro Is Superior to the Indian," Red Man, 12
　　　　　　(January-February, 1894), 4. Argues the affirmative.

MILLER, IVA M. (Cherokee)
　　1335N　"A Trip to Harrisburg," Carlisle Arrow, December 22,
　　　　　　1911. Describes her trip.

1336F   "Robin Red Breast," Carlisle Arrow, February 23, 1912.
        A tale.
1337N   "Room No. 14," Carlisle Arrow, April 19, 1912. Describes
        activities there.
See also 1981 Biobibliography, 2188.

MILLER, MARY (Chippewa)
1338A   "The American Girl," Red Man, 13 (January, 1896), 6-7.
        Examines her qualities.
See also 1981 Biobibliography, 2189.

MILLS, EMMA (Sioux)
1339N   "Items from Classrooms," Oglala Light, 20 (December 1,
        1919), 3. Reports classroom activities at the Oglala
        Boarding School.
1340N   "Items from Classrooms," Oglala Light, 20 (December 15,
        1919), 3. Reports classroom activities at the Oglala
        Boarding School.
1341N   "Items from Classrooms," Oglala Light, 20 (January 1,
        1920), 3. Reports classroom activities at the Oglala
        Boarding School.

MINTHORN, AARON (Cayuse)
1342N   "My Home People," Carlisle Arrow, November 27, 1908.
        Describes Cayuse life-style and relation to the Nez
        Percé.
See also 1981 Biobibliography, 2193.

MINTHORN, ANNA E. (Cayuse)
1343N   "Thoughts from Miss Collins' Talk," Arrow, March 9, 1906.
        Advocates assimilationist education.

MITCHELL, CHARLES (Assiniboin)
1344N   "Wampum," Arrow, June 12, 1908. Describes its origin
        and use.
1345M   "Our Prairies," Arrow, June 19, 1908. Legend of their
        origin.
1346N   "My Summer's Outing," Carlisle Arrow, October 2, 1908.
        Describes his work in a woodworking shop.
1347N   "Caddo Indians," Carlisle Arrow, October 23, 1908. His-
        torical sketch.
1348N   "Uto Aztecan Indian," Carlisle Arrow, October 23, 1908.
        Describes the tribes belonging to the linguistic group.
1349N   "About Indian Totems," Carlisle Arrow, February 19, 1909.
        Describes totem practices.
1350N   "Corn Culture," Carlisle Arrow, March 19, 1909. Dis-
        cusses soils, yields, and varieties.
1351N   "Chief Cornstalk," Carlisle Arrow, March 26, 1909. Bio-
        graphical sketch of the Shawnee.
1352N   "Ambition Must Be Directed Honestly," Carlisle Arrow,
        April 9, 1909.

1353N   "Making of Wagons and Carriages," <u>Carlisle Arrow</u>, April
        9, 1909. Describes activities at Carlisle.
See also 1981 Biobibliography, 2194-2196.

MITCHELL, HORACE (Ponca)
    1354F   "Indian Story," <u>Indian Leader</u>, March 15, 1912. A Ponca
        bear story.

MITCHELL, LAWRENCE J. (Penobscot, i.e., Eastern Abenaki)
    1355L   Letter, <u>Arrow</u>, November 3, 1905. Describes his trip to
        the Philippines.

MODESTO, LOUISA (Mission)
    1356L   "I Am So Happy," <u>Mission Indian</u>, 1 (December 15, 1895),
        5. Concerns boarding school life.

MONCHAMP, CHARLES (Chippewa)
    1357N   "A Non-Reservation Indian Christmas," <u>Carlisle Arrow</u>,
        January 28, 1910. Describes the celebration.

MONROE, LYDIA (Sac and Fox)
    1358N   "Our Journey to Hampton," <u>Talks and Thoughts</u>, 1 (De-
        cember, 1886), 3-4. Describes her trip.

MONROE, MABEL (Blackfeet)
    1359N   "Religious Conditions Among the Indian People," <u>Word</u>
        <u>Carrier of Santee Normal Training School</u>, 43 (March-
        April, 1914), 8. Concerns the Blackfeet.

MONTEZUMA, CARLOS (Yavapai)
    1360L   "An Apache Indian's Estimate of the Occasion," <u>Red Man</u>,
        14 (January, 1897), 3. Outlines the positive aspects
        of the Carlisle football team and band.
    1361N   "The Future of the Indian," <u>State Herald</u>, March 22, 1905.
    1363N   "He Laughs," <u>Wassaja</u>, 2 (August, 1917), 3. Belittles the
        idea that Apaches are savages.
    1364N   "Started Right, But Derailed," <u>Wassaja</u>, 2 (August, 1917),
        2. Concerns the condition of the Indians.
    1365N   "In the Fight," <u>Wassaja</u>, 5 (December, 1920), 3. Concerns
        how Indian agents dislike <u>Wassaja</u>.
    1366N   "An Indian Can Accomplish Anything," <u>Wassaja</u>, 5 (Decem-
        ber, 1920), 2-3. Urges Indian self-sufficiency.
    1367N   "Indian Freedom and Citizenship and Not Indian Shows,"
        <u>Wassaja</u>, 5 (December, 1920), 4. Argues that shows
        belittle Indians.
    1368N   "W--W--Well, You Know," <u>Wassaja</u>, 5 (December, 1920),
        1-2. Advocates public school for Indians, not segre-
        gated schools.
    1369N   "Who Would Like It?" <u>Wassaja</u>, 5 (December, 1920), 2.
        Attacks the reservation system.
    1370N   "Defending the Indian Bureau," <u>Wassaja</u>, 5 (February,

1921), 3-4. Criticizes William M. Robertson, former interpreter at Sisseton.

1371N   "An Indian for the Commissioner of Indian Affairs," Wassaja, 5 (February, 1921), 2. Urges nomination of an Indian.

1372N   "Citizenship for Everybody But Indians," Wassaja, 5 (March, 1921), 4.

1373N   "Conference of the Indians of California," Wassaja, 5 (March, 1921), 4. Advocates organization of all tribes.

1374N   "Indian Commissionership," Wassaja, 5 (March, 1921), 3. Urges it.

1375N   "Indian Has No Rights Whatsoever," Wassaja, 5 (March, 1921), 1-2.

1376N   "Indian Organizations," Wassaja, 5 (March, 1921), 2. Advocates them on reservations.

1377N   "Commissioner of Indian Affairs," Wassaja, 6 (July, 1921), 2. Advocates abolishing the office.

1378N   "Indians vs. Indian Bureauism," Wassaja, 6 (July, 1921), 4.

1379N   "President Harding," Wassaja, 6 (July, 1921), 4. Complains of the failure to appoint an Indian as Commissioner of Indian Affairs.

1380N   "The S.A.I. Is Not Dead," Wassaja, 7 (October, 1921), 1-2. Attacks the Bureau of Indian Affairs.

1381N   "Aim--Fire! Shoot Straight!" Wassaja, 7 (October, 1921), 1-2. Attacks the Bureau of Indian Affairs.

1382N   "Death of James Murie," Wassaja, 8 (March, 1922), 3. Biographical sketch.

1383N   "Evils of Indian Bureau System," Wassaja, 8 (March, 1922), 1-2. Concerns Fort McDowell Indians.

1384N   "Friends of Indians, Do You Know," Wassaja, 8 (March, 1922), 2-3. Concerns the economic conditions of the Indians.

1385N   "Another Indian Land Case," Wassaja, 8 (August, 1922), 2. Concerns the White Earth Chippewas.

1386N   "Capt. Parker's Conference in Chicago," Wassaja, 8 (August, 1922), 4. Concerns factionalism in the Society of American Indians.

1387N   "Conference of the Society of American Indians," Wassaja, 8 (August, 1922), 3-4. Wonders if the Society is working for the Bureau of Indian Affairs.

1388N   "For 'Congress to Respond,'" Indian, Unnumbered (November, 1922), 12-13. Attacks the Bureau of Indian Affairs. Reprinted from Wassaja.

See also 1981 Biobibliography, 2199-2554.

MOORE, FRANK (Pine Ridge Sioux)
1389N   "The Value of a Trade to a Reservation Indian," Indian Leader, June 26, 1903.

MOORE, JOHN (Creek)
1390N   "An Opossum Hunt," Creek Boys' and Girls' Monthly, December, 1870. Recounts a hunt.

MOORE, WILLIAM (Sac and Fox)
    1391N "Oklahoma To-day," Talks and Thoughts, 7 (June, 1892), 4.

MOORE, WILSON D. (Pawnee)
    1392N "Stories of the Pawnees," Talks and Thoughts, 4 (April, 1890), 4. Concerns the old days.

MOOSE, JOSEPH (Citizens' Band Potawatomi)
    1393N "Dom Bede Negahnquet, O.S.B., First Benedictine Indian Monk in America," Indian Advocate, 8 (January, 1896), 8-13.
  See also 1981 Biobibliography, 2559-2561.

MORAGO, EDITH J. (Pima)
    1394N "Domestic Science," Sherman Bulletin, September 22, 1909.

MORAGO, JAY ROE (Pima)
    1395N "My Tribe," Sherman Bulletin, September 14, 1910. Concerns the Pimas.

MORALES, NANCY A. (Mission)
    1396L "Indeed, I Am Pleased," Mission Indian, 1 (January 15, 1896), 3. Concerns the benefits of the Banning Mission School.

MORGAN, GIDEON (Cherokee)
    1397L "Mr. Morgan Writes on Allotment," Cherokee Telephone, May 12, 1892.
    1398N "Allotment," Fort Smith Elevator, July 29, 1892.
    1399N "An Indian About Indians," Tahlequah Arrow, October 14, 1905. Concerns conditions in the Indian Territory. Reprinted from New York Outlook.
  See also 1981 Biobibliography, 2562-2563.

MORGAN, JACOB CASIMERA (Navajo)
    1400N "The Life of the Navajoes," Talks and Thoughts, 15 (June, 1899), 1, 4.
    1401F "Navajoe Children's Story," Talks and Thoughts, 16 (July, 1900), 1, 3. A tale.
    1402N "Out in the Southwest," Talks and Thoughts, 15 (January, 1902), 3-4, and (February, 1902), 1. Describes events at agency schools.
    1403N "The Navajos at Home," Talks and Thoughts, 15 (May, 1902), 1, 3-4.
    1404F "Navaho Story," Talks and Thoughts, 16 (June, 1902), 1, 4. A Coyote tale.
    1405N "From Hampton to Bloomfield," Talks and Thoughts, 16 (July, 1902), 3-4. Describes a trip to Bloomfield, Connecticut to attend school.

1406N   "The Huntington Memorial Library," Talks and Thoughts, 16 (December, 1902), 1. Concerns the history of the library at Hampton Institute.

1407N   "In and About Isleta," Talks and Thoughts, 16 (February, 1903), 1, 4.

MORRIS, L. PEARL (Cherokee)
1408P   "A Reverie," Sherman Bulletin, February 2, 1910. Poem on carpe diem theme.

MORSEA, CHARLES ROY (Lower Brule Sioux)
1409N   "The Indian and the Present Crisis," Word Carrier of Santee Normal Training School, 46 (March-April, 1918), 7. Discusses Indians and World War I.

MORTON, ANNIE M. (Laguna Pueblo)
1410N   "Spring," Red Man, 9 (April, 1889), 3.
See also 1981 Biobibliography, 2570.

MOSELY, GARNETT (Chickasaw)
1411N   "Why I Am a Printer," Indian School Journal, 18 (June, 1918), 38-39. Concerns printing as an occupation.

MOSES, HENRY (Washo)
1412N   "Indian Doctoring," New Indian, 2 (Summer, 1905), 5. Argues that medicine men are outmoded.

MT. PLEASANT, EDISON (Tuscarora)
1413M   "The Great Spirit and the Monstrous Mosquito," Carlisle Arrow, January 6, 1911. A Tuscarora legend.

1414N   "Tuscarora and Mohawk Contest," Carlisle Arrow, May 5, 1911. Describes a ball game.
See also 1981 Biobibliography, 2573-2576.

MOUNTAIN SHEEP, BERTHA (Crow)
1415M   "A Crow Legend," Talks and Thoughts, 17 (November, 1903), 1, 3.

1416N   "From a New Student," Talks and Thoughts, 17 (December, 1903), 4. Autobiographical statement.

1417M   "The Big Dipper," Indian Leader, September 21, 1906. A legend.

MOUSSEAU, JULIA (Sioux)
1418L   Letter, Ogalalla Light, 1 (June 1, 1900), 4. Urges others to attend the Oglala Boarding School.

MUMBLEHEAD, JAMES W. (Eastern Band Cherokee)
1419N   "Biography of Sequoyah," Arrow, December 28, 1906.

1420N   "Spare Moments," Carlisle Arrow, May 13, 1920. Discusses Indians who used them to do great things.

1421M   "A Legend of the Cherokee Rose," Carlisle Arrow, Feb-
        ruary 10, 1911. Concerns the origin of the wildflower.
1422M   "A Legend of the Cherokee Rose," Peace Pipe, February
        9, 1912. Concerns the origin of the flower. Reprinted
        from Indian's Friend.
See also 1981 Biobibliography, 2580-2582.

MURRAY, LAURA (Sioux)
    1423N   "An Indian Superstition," Indian Leader, 17 (October,
          1913), 18-19. Concerns thunder and lightning.

MURRAY, WALLACE (Sioux)
    1424N   "The Indian Sun Dance," Word Carrier of Santee Normal
          Training School, 43 (July-August, 1914), 16. Describes
          the dance as told him by his grandfather.

MUSKRAT, RUTH MARGARET (Cherokee)
    1425P   "Songs of the Spavinaw," University of Oklahoma Maga-
          zine, 8 (February, 1920), 4. Narrative poem.
    1426N   "The Cane and Swagger Stick Class," University of Okla-
          homa Magazine, 8 (April, 1920), 15, 19. Concerns the
          graduating class of 1920.
    1427P   "My Warrior," University of Oklahoma Magazine, 8 (April,
          1920), 4. Love poem.
    1428P   "The House by the Ferry," University of Oklahoma Maga-
          zine, 9 (November, 1920), 10. Descriptive poem.
    1429N   "Relapse of 'Cowboy Poet' into Prof," University of Okla-
          homa Magazine, 9 (November, 1920), 13, 20. Concerns
          Edward Everett Dale.
    1430P   "The Road to Arden," University of Oklahoma Magazine,
          9 (December, 1920), 17. Lyric poem about love.
    1431P   "The Jar Flies," University of Oklahoma Magazine, 9 (Feb-
          ruary, 1921), 16. Lyric poem about cicadas.
    1432P   "The Shady Deep," University of Oklahoma Magazine, 9
          (April, 1921), 4. Lyric poem about nature.
    1433L   "A Cherokee Invading Apache Soil," University of Okla-
          homa Magazine, 10 (October, 1921), 9-10, 20. Concerns
          her summer experiences as Y.M.C.A. secretary among
          the Apaches.
    1434P   "The Hunter's Wooing," University of Oklahoma Magazine,
          10 (October, 1921), 4. Descriptive poem on nature.
    1435P   "My House of Dreams," University of Oklahoma Magazine,
          10 (November, 1921), 4. Didactic lyric poem.
    1436P   "An Indian Lullaby," University of Oklahoma Magazine,
          10 (December, 1921), 13. Lyric poem.
    1437P   "Walleah," University of Oklahoma Magazine, 10 (Decem-
          ber, 1921), 12. Lyric poem on love with an Indian mo-
          tif.
    1438P   "Nunih Waiyah," University of Oklahoma Magazine, 10
          (January, 1922), 5. Lyric poem about the legend of
          Nunih Waiyah.

1439P   "Sonnets from the Cherokee (May Mrs. Browning Pardon Me)," University of Oklahoma Magazine, 10 (January, 1922), 11. Sequence of four sonnets on a love theme.

1440P   "The Warriors' Dance," University of Oklahoma Magazine, 10 (January, 1922), 23. Descriptive lyric poem.

1441P   "A Welcome to the New Year," University of Oklahoma Magazine, 10 (January, 1922), 4. Topical poem.

1442P   "The Apache Reservation," University of Oklahoma Magazine, 10 (February, 1922), 15. Descriptive poem.

1443P   "The Trail of Tears," University of Oklahoma Magazine, 10 (February, 1922), 14. Lyric poem.

1444L   "Wait, I'll Tell You 'Bout China," University of Oklahoma Magazine, 11 (November, 1922), 12, 22-24. Describes her experiences in China.

1445L   "Letters That Ruth Muskrat Wrote," Tahlequah Leader, December 28, 1922. Describes shipboard activities on her way to China.

1446L   "Third Letter from Ruth Muskrat," Tahlequah Leader, January 4, 1923. Describes her trip to Hawaii.

1447L   "Letters from Ruth Margaret Muskrat (Letter No. 4)," Tahlequah Leader, February 15, 1923. Describes life in Japan.

1448P   "If You Knew," University of Oklahoma Magazine, 11 (April, 1923), 4. Love lyrics.

1449N   "The Homecoming of Katherine Kanoy," University of Oklahoma Magazine, 12 (Winter, 1924), 11-12. Concerns a student from Haskell Institute.

See also 1981 Biobibliography, 2598.

NAGOZRUK, ARTHUR (Eskimo)

1450N   "Youth Teaching Age," Eskimo, 1 (August, 1917), 3. Argues that educated youth should show respect for the elderly and serve as models.

NAIL, ROBERT W. (Choctaw)

1451L   "For the Intelligencer," Choctaw Intelligencer, June 11, 1851. Describes a trip through the Choctaw Nation.

NAMEQUA, JOSIE (Comanche)

1452N   "Prevention of Tuberculosis," Indian Leader, 17 (January, 1914), 12.

1453N   "Religious Conditions Among the Indian People," Word Carrier of Santee Normal Training School, 43 (January-February, 1914), 4. Concerns the Comanches.

NARCHA, PABLO (Papago)

1454N   "Home-Building," Indian Leader, 17 (September, 1913), 12-15. Describes what he will do on his allotment.

1455N   "The Papagoes," Word Carrier of Santee Normal Training

School, 43 (May-June, 1914), 10. Concerns conditions
and "progress" of the tribe.

See also 1981 Biobibliography, 2600-2603, where he is listed as
Narcho.

NASH, AUGUSTA M. (Winnebago)
1456M   "The Old Witch," Red Man, 15 (January, 1900), 8. A
        legend.

NATONI, PAULINE (Navajo)
1457P   "Class Prophecy," Purple and Gold. Riverside, CA:
        Sherman Institute, 1923, p. 29.

NAVARRE, PETER (Prairie Band Potawatomi)
1458N   "The Industrial Department," Indian Leader, June 28, 1901.
        Concerns Haskell Institute.

NECKAR, ZELIA (Crow)
1459F   "The Worm's Story," Word Carrier, 28 (January, 1899),
        4. Fantasy concerning the life cycle of a worm.

NELSON, ALMA (Aleut)
1460N   "My Experience with the Volcano," Chemawa American,
        15 (March, 1913), 17. Describes her trip from Alaska
        to Washington.

NELSON, WILLIAM (Pima)
1461N   "Sitting Bull," Arrow, December 6, 1907. Biographical
        sketch.
1462N   "Home Life," Arrow, January 3, 1908. Describes the
        games he played as a child.
1463N   "Hog Raising," Arrow, February 28, 1908. Discusses
        breeds, origin, classification, and production.
1464N   "Blacksmithing," Carlisle Arrow, May 14, 1909. Concerns
        blacksmithing at Carlisle.
1465F   "The Fast Runners--a Pawnee Story," Carlisle Arrow,
        June 4, 1909. A tale about the deer and antelope.
1466N   "How I Spent the Summer," Carlisle Arrow, October 8,
        1909. Describes his work in the paint shop at Carlisle.
1467A   "A Good Name," Carlisle Arrow, November 26, 1909. Con-
        cerns the need for a good reputation.
1468N   With Enos Johnson. "School Athletics, 1910," Carlisle Ar-
        row, April 8, 1910. Argues that athletics develop sound
        bodies and minds.

NEPHEW, EDITH L. (Seneca)
1469N   "Our Garden," Carlisle Arrow, May 21, 1909. Describes
        the garden at Carlisle.

NEWASHE, EMMA M. (Sac and Fox)
1470N   "Chief Tecumseh," Arrow, May 15, 1908. Biographical sketch.

1471N   "My Summer Outing," <u>Carlisle Arrow</u>, February 16, 1912.
        Describes little trips she took in New Jersey.

1472F   "The Merman's Prophecy," <u>Carlisle Arrow</u>, April 5, 1912.
        A tale about a prophecy of Sac destiny.

1473P   "Limericks," <u>Carlisle Arrow</u>, April 19, 1912. Concerns
        the senior class members.

1474F   "The Merman's Prophecy," <u>Indian's Friend</u>, 25 (January,
        1913), 10. A tale about a prophecy of Sac destiny.
        Reprinted from <u>Carlisle Arrow</u>,

See also 1981 Biobibliography, 2622.

NEWASHE, WILLIAM (Sac and Fox)
1475N   "In Washington," <u>Carlisle Arrow</u>, December 17, 1909.
        Describes the city.

NEWBEAR, EVA (Crow)
1476F   "Original Story," <u>Sherman Bulletin</u>, June 10, 1908. A
        story about a child going to government boarding school.

NEWMAN, WALLACE (Mission)
1477A   "The Service Flag," <u>Sherman Bulletin</u>, April 10, 1918.
        Urges patriotism.

1478N   "Valedictory," <u>Sherman Bulletin</u>, May 29, 1919. Encour-
        ages students to strive.

NOMBRIE, LORENZO (Mission)
1479M   "The Sun and the Wind," <u>Sherman Bulletin</u>, May 4, 1910.

NORRIS, ELLEN L. (Klamath)
1480N   "Why Every Girl Should Have a Knowledge of Sewing,"
        <u>Sherman Bulletin</u>, May 29, 1919.

1481N   "School Days of an Indian Girl," <u>California Indian Herald</u>,
        1 (January, 1923), 8, 9. Describes her stay at Sherman
        Institute.

NORRIS, SADIE C. (Chippewa)
1482N   "Valedictory," <u>Peace Pipe</u>, June 20, 1913. Encourages
        students to strive.

NORTH, MARY (Arapaho)
1483L   Letter, <u>School News</u>, 1 (March, 1881), 3. Encourages
        others to attend school.

NORTHRUP, JOHN (Chippewa)
1484M   "Indian Legends," <u>Arrow</u>, May 22, 1908. Concerns medic-
        inal plants.

NUNEZ, OCTAVIANO (Papago)
1485L   "A Lovely Feast," <u>Mission Indian</u>, 1 (January 15, 1896),
        4. Concerns the celebration of the feast of St. Francis
        Xavier.

OAKES, FANNIE (Choctaw)
    1486L   Letter, Indian Missionary, 1 (November, 1884), 2. De-
            scribes efforts to organize a Sunday school.

OCCOM, SAMSON (Mohegan)
    1487S   A Sermon, Preached at the Execution of Moses Paul, an
            Indian, Who Was Executed at New-Haven, on the 2d of
            September 1772, for the Murder, of Mr. Moses Cook,
            Late of Waterbury on the 7th of December 1771. Preached
            at the Desire of Said Paul. Hartford, CT: Ebenezer
            Watson, 1773.
    1488S   A Sermon, Preached at the Execution of Moses Paul, an
            Indian, Who Was Executed at New-Haven, on the 2d of
            Sept. 1772. For the Murder of Mr. Moses Cook, Late
            of Waterbury, on the Seventh of December, 1771.
            Preached at the Desire of Said Paul. Salem, MA: S.
            and E. Hall, 1773.
    1489E   A Choice Collection of Hymns and Spiritual Songs Intended
            for the Edification of Sincere Christians, of All Denomi-
            nations. 3rd. ed. Hudson, MA: Ashbel Stoddard, 1787.
    1490N   "An Account of the Montauk Indians, on Long Island,"
            Collections of the Massachusetts Historical Society, 10
            (1809), 106-111. Reprinted, Johnson Reprint Corpora-
            tion, 1968.
    See also 1981 Biobibliography, 2630-2645.

OEQUA, VIRGINIA (Kiowa)
    1491L   "Virginia (Kiowa) Writes from Her Farm Home, Where She
            Has Gone to Stay a Few Weeks," School News, 2 (July,
            1881), 1. Concerns her experience as an outing student.

OFFIELD, FITSIMONS (Klamath)
    1492N   "The Stick Game," Sherman Bulletin, December 20, 1911.

OHMERT, ROSE (Delaware)
    1493N   "The Industry of Blacksmithing," Carlisle Arrow, March
            19, 1909. Stresses its importance as a course of study
            at Carlisle.

OJIBWAY, FRANCIS (Chippewa)
    1494N   "Track, Relay, Hurdles, Sprinting," Carlisle 1917. Car-
            lisle, PA: U.S. Indian School, 1917, pp. 89-91. Dis-
            cusses sports at Carlisle.

OKILLOOK, ABRAHAM (Eskimo)
    1495N   "Make Your Things. Do Not Buy Them," Eskimo, 1 (May,
            1917), 3. Admonishes people not to waste their money.
    1496N   "Reindeer Notes," Eskimo, 1 (May, 1917), 6. Concerns
            herding and care of deer.

ONEBULL, C. (Standing Rock Sioux)
    1497L   "A Pupil's Letter," Word Carrier of Santee Normal School,

37 (March-April, 1908), 7. Relates family history and
school experiences.

ONEROAD, AMOS (Sisseton Sioux)
    1498N "A Beautiful Christmas," Indian Leader, December 29,
          1905. Describes events at Riggs's Tawacinwaste Church
          in South Dakota.
    1499N "Thanksgiving at Home," Indian Leader, November 25,
          1910.

ONLIAY, WARREN (Zuni)
    1500F "The Story of the Flood," Indian Leader, September 30,
          1910. A Zuni tale.

OQUILLUK, CUDLUK (Eskimo)
    1501N "Cudlook Oquillok Will Tell You About Reindeer," Eskimo,
          1 (November, 1916), 1.

OREALUK, JAMES (Eskimo)
    1502N "Tanning Reindeer Leather," Eskimo, 2 (October, 1917),
          7. Describes the process.

OSHKENENY, MITCHELL (Menominee)
    1503N "The Influence of Civilization," Talks and Thoughts, 1
          (December, 1886), 3-4.

OSKISON, JOHN MILTON (Cherokee)
    1504N "A Carlisle Commencement as Seen by Collier's Weekly,"
          Carlisle Arrow, June 24, 1910.
  See also 1981 Biobibliography, 2658-2728.

OTTLEY, RALPH (Klamath)
    1505N "The Benefits of Civilization," Sherman Bulletin, April 7,
          1909.
    1506N "Making the Woodwork of a Wagon," Sherman Bulletin, May
          19, 1909, supplement.

OVERTON, BENJAMIN FRANKLIN (Chickasaw)
    1507L Letter, Oklahoma Star, June 25, 1875. Concerns noncit-
          izens who buy livestock.
    1508A "To the Honorable Members of the Chickasaw Legislature,"
          Oklahoma Star, September 17, 1875. Concerns Chicka-
          saw national affairs.
    1509A "Overton's Message," Oklahoma Star, September 28, 1876.
          Discusses the state of affairs in the Chickasaw Nation.
  See also 1981 Biobibliography, 2729-2733.

OWEN, ROBERT LATHAM (Cherokee)
    1510L "A Very Sensible and Interesting Letter on a Vital Sub-
          ject," Cherokee Telephone, October 15, 1891. Concerns
          Cherokee land title and the Cherokee Outlet.

1511N   "Oklahoma, the Land of Opportunity," Oklahoma Magazine,
        4 (March, 1912), 5. Promotes the state's image.
See also 1981 Biobibliography, 1736-2839.

OWL, HENRY M. (Eastern Band Cherokee)
  1512N   "Indian Leaders," Indian News, 19 (March, 1918), 6.
        Concerns Susan Picotte, Angel DeCora, and Henry Roe
        Cloud. Reprinted from Southern Workman.
  1513N   "The Indian in the War," Word Carrier of Santee Normal
        Training School, 46 (July-September, 1918), 15. Con-
        cerns World War I.
See also 1981 Biobibliography, 2843-2845.

OWL, WILLIAM J. (Eastern Band Cherokee)
  1514M   "The Beautiful Bird," Carlisle Arrow, December 30, 1910.
        Cherokee legend on the origin of the turkey buzzard.
  1515N   With Emma La Vatta. "History of the Class of 1911,"
        Carlisle Arrow, April 21, 1911. Concerns the Carlisle
        experience.
  1516F   "The Way the Opossum Derived His Name," Carlisle Arrow,
        June 7, 1912. A tale.
See also 1981 Biobibliography, 2849-2850.

PADIA, ONOFRE (Pueblo)
  1517N   "Mining in Colorado," Indian Leader, June 15, 1899.
  1518N   "The Jemez Pueblos," Indian Leader, June 15, 1900. Dis-
        cusses life and customs.

PADILLA, POLITA (Pueblo)
  1519N   "Santa Fe," Indian Leader, November 16, 1900. Describes
        interesting sites.
  1520N   "Mexico," Indian Leader, March 15, 1901. Describes cus-
        toms and sights.
  1521N   "Domestic Art," Indian Leader, June 26, 1903.
  1522N   "Self-Discipline," Indian Leader, June 3, 1904.
See also 1981 Biobibliography, 2852.

PAISANO, MABLE (Pueblo)
  1523N   "An Indian Thanksgiving," Indian Leader, December 6,
        1907. Concerns customs in the Pueblos of New Mexico.
  1524N   "The Model Kitchen," Indian Leader, June 14, 1912.

PALMER, JOHN (Skokomish)
  1525P   "Yes, Sister, I Do Allways Remember You," Council Fire,
        3 (March, 1880), 48.

PARKER, ARTHUR CASWELL (Seneca)
  1526N   "Making New Americans from Old," Word Carrier of Santee
        Normal Training School, 40 (September-October, 1911),

20. Appeals for Indian self-help as a way to American-
ize Indians. Reprinted from Assembly Herald.

1527L   "The Society of American Indians," Word Carrier of Santee Normal Training School, 41 (January-February, 1912),
1. Answers Word Carrier's criticism of the Society.

1528N   "Progress of the Indian," Word Carrier of Santee Normal
Training School, 42 (January-February, 1913), 2-3.
Argues for assimilation but retention of racial identity.
Reprinted from Southern Workman.

1529N   "Needed Changes in Indian Affairs," Word Carrier of Santee Normal Training School, 41 (November-December,
1913), 22. Argues for doing away with the reservations.
Reprinted from Week.

1530N   "Third Annual Conference of American Indians," Oglala
Light, 15 (December, 1913), 11-13. Reports on the
meeting.

1531N   "The Red Man Is Not a Tanned Mongolian," Weekly Review,
January 30, 1915. Argues against stereotypes of American Indians.

1532N   "Awakened American Indian," Chemawa American, 17 (January, 1915), 6-11. Discusses a memorial to President
Wilson concerning defining the legal status of Indians.

1533N   "The Red Man Is Not a Tanned Mongolian," Chemawa American, 17 (February, 1915), 21-22. Argues against stereotypes of the Indians.

1534N   "The Red Man Is Not a Tanned Mongolian," Word Carrier
of Santee Normal Training School, 44 (May-June, 1915),
9. Argues against stereotypes of the Indians.

1535N   "An Indian Conference for Progress," Peace Pipe, 5 (November, 1915), 7-13. Reports on a Society of American
Indians meeting in Lawrence, Kansas.

1536N   "Indians for Progress," Chemawa American, 18 (November,
1915), 1-6. Reports on a Society of American Indians
meeting in Lawrence, Kansas.

1537N   "Why the Red Man Fights for Democracy," Chemawa American, November 21, 1917. Concerns Indians' role in
World War I.

1538N   "Why the Red Man Fights for Democracy," Sherman Bulletin,
December 19, 1917. Concerns Indians' role in World War
I. Reprinted from American Indian Y.M.C.A. Bulletin.

1539L   "Defining Our Indian Policy," Word Carrier of Santee Normal Training School, 53 (January-February, 1924), 1.
Reports the views of the Committee of 100 on Indian affairs.

See also 1981 Biobibliography, 2856-2939.

PARKER, GABRIEL E. (Choctaw)
1540A   "Address of Hon. Gabe Parker at Lake Mohonk," Indian
Leader, (September, 1913), 8-11. Concerns the condition of Indians under allotment.

1541A   "The Indian--Personal vs. Property," Oglala Light, 15
(January-February, 1914), 5-14.

1542L   Letter, Chemawa American, 17 (October, 1914), 2-3.
          Concerns Indian fairs.
See also 1981 Biobibliography, 2947-2956.

PARKER, LENA (Seneca)
1543N   "A Reading from Homer," Carlisle 1917. Carlisle, PA:
          U.S. Indian School, 1917, p. 60.

PARKER, MATTIE E. (Cayuga)
1544M   "The Creation," Red Man, 15 (February, 1900), 6. Leg-
          end about creation of whites, Indians, and blacks.

PASCHAL, SARAH (Cherokee)
1545L   "The Cherokees," Arkansas Gazette, January 15, 1840.
          Concerns the Cherokee feud and attacks John Ross.

PATONE, EDGAR (Zuni)
1546F   "Zuni Folk Tale," Indian Leader, September 30, 1910.
          Tale about a mouse and a hawk.

PATTEE, JOHN (Crow Creek Sioux)
1547N   "John Pattee in Washington," Talks and Thoughts, 5
          (March, 1891), 3-4.

PATTERSON, SPENCER (Seneca)
1548M   "The Bear Star," Carlisle Arrow, September 23, 1910.
          A Seneca legend.
See also 1981 Biobibliography, 2964.

PATTON, ALONZO A. (Alaska Native)
1549N   "Mercy Is Sometimes Better Than Justice," Carlisle Arrow,
          November 27, 1908.
1550N   "Status of the Indian," Carlisle Arrow, December 25,
          1908. Compares Indians to blacks.
1551N   "The Pipe of Peace," Carlisle Arrow, January 8, 1909.
          Discusses history, uses, and rituals related to the calu-
          met. Reprinted from Indian Craftsman. Reprinted in
          the Baltimore Sunday Sun.
1552M   "A Chickasaw Tradition," Carlisle Arrow, March 5, 1909.
          Legend about their origin.
1553N   "The American Indian To-day," Carlisle Arrow, April 9,
          1909. Argues that the Indian must work for an equal
          chance.
1554N   "The Carlisle Indian School," Carlisle Arrow, April 9,
          1909. Historical sketch.
See also 1981 Biobibliography, 2965-2966.

PATTON, MINNIE (Pima)
1555N   "The Desert Plants," Sherman Bulletin, December 31, 1913.

PATTON, SARAH (Pima)
1556N   "The Stone Game," Sherman Bulletin, December 27, 1911.

1557F   "The Story of My Life," Sherman Bulletin, November 25,
       1914. Fantasy, pretends she is a turkey.

PAUL, EDWARD (Nez Percé)
  1558N   "Lesson from the Tailor Shop," Carlisle Arrow, February
       19, 1909. Describes what goes on in the Carlisle shop.

PAUL, LOUIS F. (Tlingit)
  1559N   "Thoughts from Miss Collins' Talk," Arrow, March 9, 1906.
       Defends assimilationist education.
  1560N   "The Indian Problem in Alaska," Chemawa American, 16
       (February, 1914), 21-22.
  1561N   "General R.H. Pratt," Alaskan Fisherman, 1 (June, 1924),
       2. Eulogy for Pratt.
  1562N   "Statesmanship," Alaskan Fisherman, 1 (July, 1924), 5.
       Discusses politics and fishing controversy.
  1563N   "Trap Shots," Alaskan Fisherman, 2 (October, 1924), 17.
       Summarizes news relating to fishing districts and fish
       traps.
  1564N   "Who's to Blame," Alaskan Fisherman, 2 (October, 1924),
       7. Concerns the closing of Lynn Canal fishing district.

PAUL, MATILDA K. (Tlingit)
  1565N   "Marriage Customs Among the Alaskans," Home Mission
       Monthly, 10 (March, 1896), 102-103.
  1566M   "The Old Metlakahtlan's Legend," North Star, 7 (May,
       1896), 2.
  See also 1981 Biobibliography, 2969.

PAUL, PAULINE (Chitimacha)
  1567N   "The Wagon Shop," Carlisle Arrow, November 20, 1908.
       Describes what goes on in the Carlisle shop.

PAUL, SAMUEL (Chickasaw)
  1568L   "From a Chickasaw Indian," Council Fire and Arbitrator,
       8 (April, 1885), 62-63. Describes conditions in the
       Chickasaw Nation.

PAUL, WILLIAM L. (Tlingit)
  1569N   "William L. Paul Files," Alaskan Fisherman, 1 (February,
       1924), 7. Supports home rule and control of utilities
       and opposes fish hatchery.
  1570N   "The Answer," Alaskan Fisherman, 1 (March, 1924), 6-7.
       Reviews his life, defends his candidacy for territorial
       representative.
  1571N   "The Race Problem in Alaska," Alaskan Fisherman, 1
       (June, 1924), 6. Argues that race is not a problem in
       his candidacy.
  1572N   "Ketchikan: The First City," Alaskan Fisherman, 1 (Sep-
       tember, 1924), 6. Description of the city.
  1573N   "A Letter and an Answer," Alaskan Fisherman, 2 (October,

1924), 4. Supports John Rutgard for Attorney General
of Alaska.

1574N "Platform of William L. Paul," Alaskan Fisherman, 2 (October, 1924), 2-3. Opposes fish traps and stabilized fishing industry, home rule, and development of resources.
See also 1981 Biobibliography, 2970.

PAXON, AL (Choctaw)
1575N "Macbeth," Jones Academy Herald, 1 (June, 1903), 6-7.

PAYNE, JAMES M. (Cherokee)
1576N "The Old Settler Council," Cherokee Advocate, February
4, 1851. Reports on the Old Settler affairs.

PEAKE, GEORGE C. (Chippewa)
1577N "My Tribe," Indian Leader, June 14, 1907. Concerns
Chippewa customs.

PEAWO, WILBUR A. (Comanche)
1578N "Harness Making," Arrow, March 30, 1906. Describes the
process.

PEAZZONI, ELI M. (Nisenan)
1579A "Steam Fitting," Arrow, April 5, 1907. Describes what
he learned in the course.

PECK, MARY I. (Pine Ridge Sioux)
1580N "The Necessity of Domestic Training," Indian News, 15
(May, 1913), 2-3.

PEDRO, FRANCISCO (Mission)
1581L "Address: Mission Indian, Banning, Cal.," Mission Indian,
1 (December 15, 1895), 5. Concerns boarding school
life.

PENISKA, BELLE (Ponca)
1582N "The First Spinners," Carlisle 1917. Carlisle, PA: U.S.
Indian School, 1917, p. 61.

PENN, WILLIAM (Quileute)
1583N "Beginning of the Indian Wars," Quileute Independent,
January 21, 1909. Concerns Makah history.

PENNY, ELIZABETH (Nez Percé)
1584A "The Nez Percés," Arrow, April 4, 1908. Describes old
customs of the Nez Percé.

PERRY, SAMUEL (Shawnee)
1585N "Tecumseh the Shawnee," Talks and Thoughts, 3 (April,
1889), 4.

1586M   "Indian Folk Lore," Talks and Thoughts, 3 (April, 1889),
        4. Legends.
1587M   "Indian Folk Lore," Talks and Thoughts, 3 (May, 1889),
        1. Legend about duck hunting and about taboo foods.

PERRYMAN, DANIEL (Creek)
  1588L   Letter, Council Fire, 1 (August, 1878), 116-117. Con-
        cerns growth of Christianity in the Creek Nation.

PERRYMAN, PHOEBE A. (Creek)
  1589N   "Idleness," Creek Boys' and Girls' Monthly, December,
        1870. Concerns the evils of idleness.
  1590N   "Mountains," Creek Boys' and Girls' Monthly, December,
        1870. Describes mountain scenery.

PERRYMAN, SUSIE (Creek)
  1591N   "Going Home," Creek Boys' and Girls' Monthly, December,
        1870. Concerns going to heaven.

PETERS, MARGARET (Ottawa)
  1592N   "My Visit to the Tailor Shop," Carlisle Arrow, January 22,
        1909. Describes what goes on in the Carlisle shop.

PETERS, MYRTLE (Stockbridge)
  1593N   "Some Names of Indian Origin in the State of Pennsylvania,"
        Carlisle Arrow, March 12, 1909.
  See also 1981 Biobibliography, 2988-2989.

PETERS, NELLIE H. (Stockbridge)
  1594N   "The Stockbridge Reservation in Wisconsin," Talks and
        Thoughts, 11 (October, 1895), 3. Describes conditions
        there.

PETERS, ROSINA (Tonawanda Seneca)
  1595N   "The Tonawanda Reservation," Arrow, January 3, 1908.
        Describes the life-style on the reservation.

PETERS, WILLIAM (Pima)
  1596A   "The Medicine Man and the Christian Religion," Word Car-
        rier of Santee Normal Training School, 43 (September-
        October, 1914), 20. Argues for the latter.
  See also 1981 Biobibliography, 2990-2992.

PETERSON, EDWARD W. (Klamath)
  1597A   Address, Red Man, 14 (January, 1897), 6. Argues that
        the reservation system does not make independent citi-
        zens.

PHELPS, GIDEON (Sisseton Sioux)
  1598N   "How the Indians Lived," Word Carrier, 26 (May, 1897),

20. Concerns the domestic life of the Sioux in earlier days.

1599N   "How the Indians Lived," Talks and Thoughts, 13 (June, 1897), 7. Concerns the domestic life of the Sioux in earlier days.

PHILBRICK, MARY (Sioux)
1600N   Untitled, Iapi Oaye, 1 (May, 1884), 2. Describes a puppy.

PHILIPS, DANIEL (Standing Rock Sioux)
1601N   "Christmas in South Dakota," Carlisle Arrow, January 28, 1910. Describes activities on the Standing Rock Reservation.

PHILLIPS, ALICE (Klamath)
1602M   "Legend of the Cricket," Indian Leader, January 9, 1903. Reprinted from Twin Territories.

PHILLIPS, LUKE (Nez Percé)
1603A   "An Original Speech," School News, 3 (November, 1881), 4. Argues how good "civilization" is for Indians.

PICARD, CHARLES (Chippewa)
1604N   "Carpentry," Indian Leader, July 15, 1899. Argues that it contributes to "progress."

PICARD, JOSEPH (Chippewa)
1605N   "The Chippewas," Arrow, June 5, 1908. Concerns contact, enemies, and lands.

PICKET PIN, EVA (Sioux)
1606L   "Letter, Ogalalla Light, 1 (June 1, 1900), 4. Argues the benefits of education.

PICOTTE, CHARLES F., JR   (Yankton Sioux)
1607N   "Indian Dances," Talks and Thoughts, 1 (December, 1886), 1.
See also 1981 Biobibliography, 2996-2997.

PICOTTE, SUSAN LA FLESCHE (Omaha)
1608L   "Courage," Talks and Thoughts, 1 (July, 1886), 4. Inspirational statement.
1609N   "Fourth of July," Talks and Thoughts, 2 (August, 1887), 2-3. Describes events on campus.
1610L   Letter, Ten Years' Work for Indians at Hampton Institute. Hampton, VA: Hampton Institute, 1888, pp. 55-57. Praises Hampton's work for Indians and returned students.
1611L   "Letter from Dr. La Flesche," Indian's Friend, 3 (February, 1891), 3. Concerns condition of the Omahas.

1612L   "Another Appeal," Indian's Friend, 12 (March, 1900), 8-
      9. Advocates suppression of the liquor trade.
See also 1981 Biobibliography, 3002-3005.

PIERCE, BEMUS (Seneca)
  1613A   "Personnel of the Carlisle Indian Team," Red Man, 14
      (January, 1898), 6. Concerns football.

PIERCE, EVELYN (Seneca)
  1614N   "Tuberculosis," Carlisle Arrow, April 30, 1909. Describes
      symptoms and precautions.
  1615N   "Colds and Their Causes," Carlisle Arrow, April 30, 1909.
  1616N   "My Summer's Outing," Carlisle Arrow, October 1, 1909.
      Describes her work at Glenolden, Pennsylvania.
  1617M   "A Seneca Tradition," Carlisle Arrow, November 12, 1909.
      Concerns their origin.
  1618N   "Seneca Christmas Observances," Carlisle Arrow, January
      28, 1910.
  1619N   "The Susans' Portrait Gallery," Carlisle Arrow, April 8,
      1910. Sketches of Susan Longstreth, Susan Anthony,
      Frances Willard, and Elizabeth Fry.
  1620N   "Doing One's Duty," Carlisle Arrow, April 8, 1910.
  1621N   "A Seneca Superstition," Carlisle Arrow, October 14, 1910.
      Concerns witchcraft.
See also 1981 Biobibliography, 3007-3011.

PILCHER, ETTA M. (Omaha)
  1622N   "Christmas Holidays," Talks and Thoughts, 4 (January,
      1890), 2. Describes events on campus.
  1623N   "Indian Citizenship Day," Talks and Thoughts, 4 (March,
      1890), 2-3. Describes ceremonies at Hampton Institute.
  1624N   "Washington's Birthday," Talks and Thoughts, 4 (April,
      1890), 2. Describes events at Hampton.
  1625L   "Letter from Our Late Editor," Talks and Thoughts, 5
      (September, 1890), 4. Describes trip to the Omaha
      Reservation and events there.

PITCHLYNN, PETER PERKINS (Choctaw)
  1626N   "Remonstrance of Col. Peter Pitchlynn, Choctaw Delegate,
      Against the Passage of the Bill to Unite Under One
      Government the Several Indian Tribes West of the Mis-
      sissippi River," Cherokee Advocate, June 4, 1849.
See also 1981 Biobibliography, 3019-3039.

PLENTY HOLES, EUNICE (Sioux)
  1627N   "Items from Classrooms," Oglala Light, 20 (December 1,
      1919), 3. Reports classroom activities at the Oglala
      Boarding School.

PLENTY HORSES, GUY (Sioux)
  1628N   "A Christmas Story," Carlisle Arrow, January 1, 1909.

Relates his experiences at Christmas in a Catholic mission school.

1629N   "An Indian Christmas in Dakota," Carlisle Arrow, January 14, 1910.

POKAGON, JULIA (Potawatomi)
1630N   "The Camel," Indian Leader, 1 (February, 1898), 4.

POKAGON, SIMON (Pokaguns Potawatomi)
1631L   "A Grateful Friend," Indian's Friend, 10 (June, 1898), 8. Reports the loss of his home by fire and assistance in rebuilding.
1632N   "An Indian's Plea for Prohibition," Indian's Friend, 11 (October, 1898), 10-11. Reprinted from New Time.
See also 1981 Biobibliography, 3041-3055.

POO, LAH (Hopi)
1633N   "The Burro," Indian Leader, September 15, 1898. Describes Hopi use of the animal.

POODRY, FANNIE C. (Tonawanda Seneca)
1634N   "Opportunities for Self-Support," Talks and Thoughts, 15 (April, 1902), 4. Discusses what various reservations offer.

POOR BEAR, PETER (Sioux)
1635N   "Items from the Class Rooms," Oglala Light, 20 (April 1, 1920), 3. Reports classroom activities at Oglala Boarding School.
1636N   "Items from the Class Rooms," Oglala Light, 20 (April 15, 1920), 3. Reports classroom activities at the Oglala Boarding School.

PORTER, JOSE (Navajo)
1637N   "What Christmas Means to Me," Carlisle Arrow, December 31, 1909.

PORTER, NANCY (Creek)
1638N   "Passing Away," Creek Boys' and Girls' Monthly, December, 1870. Concerns passage of time.

PORTER, PLEASANT (Creek)
1639N   "Explanation of Origin of Tribal Tax," Muskogee Phoenix, June 7, 1905.
See also 1981 Biobibliography, 3057-3071.

PORTER, SUSIE (Chippewa)
1640N   "Vacation at School," Carlisle Arrow, September 25, 1908. Describes her work at the school during summer.
1641N   "Wheat," Carlisle Arrow, January 8, 1909. Discusses its growth and use.

POSEY, ALEXANDER LAWRENCE (Creek)
1642F   "Chinnubbie Scalps the Squaws," B.I.U. Instructor, May
      20, 1893. A tale.
1643P   "To a Morning Warbler," Indian's Friend, 13 (April, 1901),
      12. Signed "Chinnubbie Harjo."
1644P   "The Decree," Indian's Friend, 14 (September, 1901), 12.
      Signed "Chinnubbie Harjo."
1645P   "Arkansas," Tahlequah Arrow, June 29, 1907. Verse,
      signed "Fus Fixico."
1646P   "The Comet's Tale," Indian Leader, November 4, 1910.
      Reprinted from B.I.U. Instructor.
1647P   "Eyes of Blue and Brown," Indian Orphan, 7 (February,
      1911), 3. Signed "Chinnubbie Harjo."
1648P   "Red Man's Pledge of Peace," Indian Orphan, 9 (June,
      1912), 5.
1649P   "Pity," Indian's Friend, 25 (April, 1913), 10.
See also 1981 Biobibliography, 3072-3256.

POSEYSEVA, JOHN (Hopi)
1650F   "How the Turkey and Coyote Became Enemies," Sherman
      Bulletin, March 30, 1910. A tale.

POSTOAK, NANCY (Creek)
1651N   "Birds," Creek Boys' and Girls' Monthly, December, 1870.

POWERS, EDITH (Paiute)
1652N   "Wool," Sherman Bulletin, March 6, 1919. Describes its
      uses.

POWLESS, ALFRED (Oneida)
1653N   "Logging in Wisconsin," Talks and Thoughts, 11 (May,
      1896), 1.

POWLESS, DENNISON (Oneida)
1654N   "Indian Christmas Celebration," Indian Leader, December
      21, 1906. Describes celebration among the Nebraska
      Winnebagoes.

POWLESS, ELLA (Oneida)
1655N   "Indian Women in the Homes," Talks and Thoughts, 8
      (March, 1894), 2-3. Concerns women's roles in earlier
      days.

POWLESS, GRACE (Oneida)
1656N   "Religious Conditions Among the Indian People," Word Car-
      rier of Santee Normal Training School, 43 (January-
      February, 1914), 4. Concerns the Oneidas.

POWLESS, LYMAN (Oneida)
1657N   "My Visit to the Onondaga Reservation," Talks and
      Thoughts, 4 (November, 1889), 3. Describes his visit.

POWLESS, RICHARD S. (Oneida)
    1658L   Letter, Talks and Thoughts, 3 (September, 1888), 4.
            Reports on Oneida affairs.
    See also 1981 Biobibliography, 3257.

PRADT, EDWIN (Pueblo)
    1659A   "Our Flag," Sherman Bulletin, March 27, 1918. Urges
            patriotism.

PRADT, ELIZABETH (Laguna Pueblo)
    1660F   "A Pueblo Student," Sherman Bulletin, May 19, 1909. A
            story.

PRADT, GEORGE H. (Laguna Pueblo)
    1661N   "Our Saturday Evening Meetings," Red Man and Helper,
            October 25, 1901. Reports on English-speaking meetings
            at Carlisle.

PRADT, LAURA (Pueblo)
    1662F   "Why Rabbits Can Jump," Sherman Bulletin, April 19,
            1911. A tale.

PRIMEAU, LULU (Sioux)
    1663N   "The Rooster and the Little Puppy," Iapi Oaye, 1 (May,
            1884), 2.

PROPHET, EDNA (Chippewa)
    1664F   "Class Prophecy," Indian School Journal, 19 (June, 1919),
            24, 27. Fantasy concerning Chilocco students.
    1665P   "Class Song," Indian School Journal, 19 (June, 1919), 42.

PROPHET, WILLIAM (Shawnee)
    1666N   "Dairying," Indian Leader, May 18, 1906.

PUGH, WILLIAM G. (Sioux)
    1667N   "Salutatory," Sherman Bulletin, May 28, 1913. Encourages
            students to strive.
    1668N   "Social Life at School," Sherman Bulletin, May 28, 1913.
    1669N   "Salutatory," Sherman Bulletin, May 27, 1914. Presents
            his opening editorial for Martin Messenger, Martin,
            South Dakota. Reprinted from the Messenger.

QUICK BEAR, REUBEN (Rosebud Sioux)
    1670N   "How a Little Sioux Boy, 13 Years Old, Feels About Talk-
            ing English," School News, 2 (December, 1881), 1.
            Urges his fellow students to try to speak only English.

QUINLAN, DELIA (White Earth Chippewa)
    1671N   "A Chippewa Girl," Arrow, June 19, 1908. Autobiograph-
            ical statement.

QUINN, RENA (Hupa)
    1672N   "Hoopa Indian School," Sherman Bulletin, December 27,
         1911. Describes the school.

QUITAC, LORETTA (Mission)
    1673F   "A Boy and an Eagle," Sherman Bulletin, March 8, 1911.
         A tale.

RABBIT, ELSIE M. (Chippewa)
    1674N   "Christmas at an Indian Boarding School," Carlisle Arrow,
         January 28, 1910. Describes exercises at a school in
         Minnesota.

RAFAEL, HARRY E. (Papago)
    1675N   An Indian Festival," Indian Leader, December 3, 1909.
         Describes the festival among the Francisco Indians.
    1676N   "A Christmas Celebration Among the Papago Indians,"
         Indian Leader, December 24, 1909.
    1677N   "A Christmas Feast Among the Papago Indians," Indian
         Leader, December 23, 1910.

RAMSEY, JOHN (Nez Percé)
    1678N   "My Home in Idaho," Carlisle Arrow, September 25, 1908.
         Describes life among the Nez Percé.
    See also 1981 Biobibliography, 3268.

RANDOLPH, GEORGE EDDY (Chippewa)
    1679N   "Electricity," Indian School Journal, 18 (June, 1918), 25-
         27. Concerns its history, use, and control.

RAVEN, ANNA (Arapaho)
    1680N   "Description of a Trip to Philadelphia," School News, 1
         (October, 1880), 4.

RAY, LEWIS J. (Pueblo)
    1681N   "The Plumbing Trade," Carlisle Arrow, February 12, 1909.
         Concerns the advantages of the course at Carlisle.
    1682N   "Visit to the Sewing Room," Carlisle Arrow, March 19,
         1909. Describes what goes on there.

REBOIN, ALLEN (Nez Percé)
    1683N   "A Nez Percé Christmas," Carlisle Arrow, January 7,
         1910.

RED FOX (Blackfeet)
    See SKIUHUSHU

REDBIRD, NED (Cherokee)
    1684L   "Born in a Cherokee Log Cabin," Word Carrier of Santee
         Normal Training School, 50 (November-December, 1921),
         22. Autobiographical statement.

REDDIE, WILLIE (Haida)
    1685N   "A Famous Double Bass, 1648," Chemawa American, 16
          (May, 1914), 28. Concerns a musical instrument made
          in Holland.
    1686N   "Breeds of Chickens," Chemawa American, 16 (June,
          1914), 18-20.

REDEYE, ROSA (Seneca)
    1687N   "Porto Ricans," Carlisle Arrow, February 12, 1909. De-
          scribes their life-style.

REDTHUNDER, MARY M. (Sisseton Sioux)
    1688N   "My Summer Vacation," Carlisle Arrow, October 22, 1909.
          Describes her outing work at Sea Island, New Jersey.
    1689N   "An Indian Story," Carlisle Arrow, February 25, 1910.
          Concerns Sioux medicine men.
    1690N   "At the Shore," Carlisle Arrow, April 8, 1910. Describes
          her experiences at the Atlantic shore.

REED, KATIE (Crow)
    1691N   "Death of an Indian Chief," Indian Leader, October 22,
          1909. Describes burial customs.
    1692M   "The Origin of Stones--An Indian Legend," Indian Leader,
          April 29, 1910.
    1693M   "Why the Crows Like Dogs," Indian Leader, February 2,
          1912.

REID, NETTIE (Washo)
    1694N   "How the Washoe Indians Keep Their New Year," Indian
          Leader, January 17, 1908.

REINKEN, OLGA (Alaska Native)
    1695N   "Adobes," Arrow, June 19, 1908. Describes how they are
          made and used.
    1696N   "Pottery," Carlisle Arrow, December 25, 1908. Concerns
          its production by American Indians.
    1697M   "A Chickasaw Tradition," Carlisle Arrow, February 26,
          1909. Legend about their origin.
    1698N   "Chitamache," Carlisle Arrow, April 9, 1909. Describes
          the life-style of the Chitimachas.
    See also 1981 Biobibliography, 3323-3324.

RENVILLE, GABRIEL (Sisseton Sioux)
    1699L   "Lake Traverse Sioux Reservation--Enoch Mahpiyahdinape's
          Case," Progress, April 14, 1888.
    See also 1981 Biobibliography, 3326.

RICE, SAMUEL J. (Mission)
    1700N   "The American Indian," Indian, Unnumbered (January,
          1922), 9. Appeals for liberty and justice.
    1701N   "Guidance, Duty of Counselor," Indian, Unnumbered

(January, 1922), 9. Lauds the growth of the Mission Indian Federation.

1702N   "Indians--Notice," Indian, Unnumbered (January, 1922), 9, 14. Appeals for support for Indian.

1703N   "The Gleams of the Past," Indian, Unnumbered (February, 1922), 10, and (March, 1922), 10-11. Reminiscences of an old Temecula, Joseph Lonegan Weaver.

1704N   "The Meaning of Our Co-Operation," Indian, Unnumbered (February, 1922), 10-11. Lauds the Mission Indian Federation.

1705N   "Inspiration of the Mission Indian Federation," Indian, Unnumbered (March, 1922), 10.

1706P   "Courage," Indian, Unnumbered (March, 1922), 11.

1707N   "The April Convention," Indian, Unnumbered (April, 1922), 10. Reports on a meeting of the Mission Indian Federation.

1708N   "Our Foundation as a Light to Justice," Indian, Unnumbered (April, 1922), 11, 18. Concerns the Mission Indian Federation.

1709P   "Courage," Indian, Unnumbered (October, 1922), front cover. Praises Mission Indian Federation.

1710N   "The Convention," Indian, Unnumbered (November, 1922), 7-8. Reports on a meeting of the Mission Indian Federation.

1711N   "The Octopus and What," Indian, Unnumbered (November, 1922), 8-9. Compares the Office of Indian Affairs to an octopus.

See also 1981 Biobibliography, 3332.

RICHARDSON, IDA (Klamath)
1712F   "Why Bears Have Small Ears," Sherman Bulletin, April 12, 1911. A tale.

RIDGE, JOHN (Cherokee)
1713L   Letter, Niles' Register, 40 (April 9, 1831), 96. To the people of Pennsylvania, concerning treatment of the Cherokees. Reprinted from American Daily Advertiser.

1714L   Letter, Niles' Register, 40 (June 18, 1831), 286. Concerns the Cherokee delegation's interview with President Jackson. Reprinted from Cherokee Phoenix.

See also 1981 Biobibliography, 3335-3342.

RIDGE, JOHN ROLLIN (Cherokee)
1715L   Letter, Fort Smith Herald, March 1, 1848. Signed "Yellow Bird," discusses the treatment of Cherokees who visited England.

1716P   "A Pleasant Morn in June," Fort Smith Herald, August 23, 1848. Signed "Yellow Bird."

1717L   Letter, Fort Smith Herald, January 24 and 31, 1851. Describes his journey overland to California.

1718P   "A June Morning," Daily Bee, June 5, 1857. Signed "Yellow Bird." Reprinted from Southwest Independent.

1719P   "Sunday in the Woods: Impromptu, Addressed to L----," Daily Bee, June 15, 1857. Signed "Yellow Bird."

1720N   "A True Sketch of 'Si Bolla,' a Digger Indian," Daily Bee, June 24, 1857.

1721N   "Valedictory," Daily Bee, July 25, 1857. Concerns his leaving the editorship.

1722P   "The Arkansas Root Doctor," Weekly California Express, November 28, 1857. Signed "Yellow Bird."

1723P   "The Gold Seekers," Weekly California Express, January 23, 1858. Signed "Yellow Bird."

1724P   "On Mount Shasta, Seen from a Distance," Weekly California Express, May 22, 1858. Composed in 1852.

1725P   "To a Mockingbird Singing in a Tree," Hutchings' California Magazine, 4 (August, 1859), 65.

1726P   "California," Daily Alta California, September 10, 1859.

1727P   "California," Hesperian, 3 (October, 1859), 345-347. Delivered at the celebration of the ninth anniversary of the admission of California to the Union.

1728P   "The Unknown Lover," Hutchings' California Magazine, 4 (November, 1859), 227.

1729P   "Humboldt River," Hesperian, 4 (March, 1860), 21-22. Reprinted from Shasta Courier.

1730P   "Humboldt River," Hesperian, 4 (April, 1860), 82-83. Corrected version of poem published in March issue.

1731P   "The Rainy Season in California," Hesperian, 4 (May, 1860), 103-104.

1732P   "Poem Delivered at Marysville Fair," Daily Union, September 8, 1860.

1733P   "Eyes," Hesperian, 6 (June, 1861), 209-210.

1734P   "Poem Written for Fourth of July Celebration, 1861," Daily Alta California, July 6, 1861.

1735P   "Poem Delivered at Metropolitan Theater, San Francisco, July 4, 1861," Golden Era, July 7, 1861.

1736N   "Valedictory," San Francisco Herald, September 24, 1861. Discusses his giving up the editorship.

1737P   "A Bright Summery Morning on the Sea Coast," Hesperian, 7 (November, 1861), 451.

1738N   "The North American Indians," Hesperian, 8 (March, 1862), 5-18, (April, 1862), 51-60, and (May, 1862), 99-109. Concerns their history and condition.

1739P   "A Scene--the Feather River Slough," Pacific Monthly, 11 (April, 1864), 544-546.

See also 1981 Biobibliography, 3343-3364.

RIGGS, ROLLA LYNN (Cherokee)

1740N   "Poems of the Month," University of Oklahoma Magazine, 10 (December, 1921), 17. Critical commentary on poems.

1741N   "Poems of the Month," University of Oklahoma Magazine, 10 (January, 1922), 18. Critical commentary on poems.

1742N   "Poems of the Month," University of Oklahoma Magazine, 10 (February, 1922), 16. Critical commentary on poems.

1743F   "The Dishwasher," University of Oklahoma Magazine, 10 (March, 1922), 16. Short story.

1744N   "Poems of the Month," University of Oklahoma Magazine, 10 (May, 1922), 18. Critical commentary on poems.

1745N   "Poems of the Month," University of Oklahoma Magazine, 11 (October, 1922), 12. Critical commentary on poems.

1746N   "Poems of the Month," University of Oklahoma Magazine, 11 (November, 1922), 10. Critical commentary on poems.

1747N   "Call Number 39 Quick," University of Oklahoma Magazine, 11 (November, 1922), 19. Humorous anecdote concerning vacation experience.

1748N   "Poems of the Month," University of Oklahoma Magazine, 11 (December, 1922), 12. Critical commentary on poems.

1749N   "The Lyric Art of B.A. Botkin," University of Oklahoma Magazine, 11 (January, 1923), 14.

1750N   "Winifred Johnston: Narrative Lyricist," University of Oklahoma Magazine, 11 (February, 1923), 14.

1751P   "I Would Not Be Free," University of Oklahoma Magazine, 11 (March, 1923), 15. A sonnet.

1752P   "Anthony," University of Oklahoma Magazine, 11 (March, 1923), 14. Lyric poem.

1753P   "The Cow That Smiled," University of Oklahoma Magazine, 11 (March, 1923), 14. Humorous lyric poem.

1754P   "The Deacon," University of Oklahoma Magazine, 11 (March, 1923), 14. A lyric poem. Reprinted from Smart Set.

1755P   "The Jester," University of Oklahoma Magazine, 11 (March, 1923), 14. A lyric poem. Reprinted from Smart Set.

1756P   "A Song of People," University of Oklahoma Magazine, 11 (March, 1923), 14. A lyric poem.

1757P   "Two Women," University of Oklahoma Magazine, 11 (March, 1923), 14. Humorous lyric poem.

1758P   "The Werwolf (A Roman Legend)," University of Oklahoma Magazine, 11 (March, 1923), 14, 22. A lyric poem.

1759N   "An Interpreter of Life," University of Oklahoma Magazine, 11 (April, 1923), 12. Concerns Violet McDougal's poetry.

1760D   "The Queen's Illness (A Burlesque on Lord Dunsany)," University of Oklahoma Magazine, 11 (May, 1923), 11, 24. A one-act play.

See also 1981 Biobibliography, 3365-3370.

RILEY, AGNES H. (Southern Cheyenne)

1761N   "The Value of Music," Indian School Journal, 18 (June, 1918), 34, 37.

1762N   "Dear School," Indian School Journal, 18 (June, 1918), 59. Concerns Chilocco Indian School.

RILEY, MINNIE (Shawnee)

1763N   "The Returned Student," Indian Leader, July 1, 1899.

RIOS, VICENTE STANISLAUS (Papago)
1764L "Very Good and Pleasing: Write Again," Mission Indian,
November 15, 1895. Concerns life at San Xavier School,
Arizona.

ROBARDS, CHRISTOPHER C. (Cherokee)
1765L "Cherokee Affairs," Afton News, March 15, 1895.

ROBERTS, ETHEL (Smith River, i.e., Tolowa)
1766M "An Indian Legend--The First Fire," Chemawa American,
15 (March, 1913), 15. A Klamath legend.
1767M "The First Fire," Indian's Friend, 25 (April, 1913), 10.
A Klamath legend.

ROBERTS, HENRY E. (Pawnee)
1768N "The Indian Story," Indian Leader, January 9, 1903.
Concerns his father's reminiscences about life in Nebraska.

ROBERTS, MAE A. (Pima)
1769N "Home and the Home Maker," Sherman Bulletin, May 29,
1919.

ROBERTSON, BERTHA (Santee Sioux)
1770N "Mission and Government Schools," Word Carrier of Santee
Normal Training School," 43 (May-June, 1914), 12. Defends her preference for the former.

ROBERTSON, EMILY (Sioux)
1771N "How the Indians Keep Thanksgiving Day," Indian Leader,
November 26, 1909. Concerns the Sioux.
1772N "Some Customs Among the Sioux Indians," Indian Leader,
August 21, 1908.

ROBERTSON, FLORENCE (Sioux)
1773N "A Thought for Other People," Word Carrier of Santee
Normal Training School, 43 (May-June, 1914), 12. Argues that Christianity has freed the Indian.

ROBINETTE, PAUL (Santee Sioux)
1774N "Thanksgiving at Santee," Indian Leader, December 12,
1902. Describes Thanksgiving, 1901.

ROBINSON, WILLIAM (Chippewa)
1775N "Silkworm Culture," Carlisle Arrow, October 27, 1911.
Describes the culture in China.

ROCQUE, LEO (Sioux)
1776N "An Ideal Dwelling House," Indian Leader, June 14, 1912.

RODGERS, THOMAS L. (Cherokee)
1777N "The Old Settlers' Money," Cherokee Advocate, July 29,

1851. Concerns Old Settler Cherokee claims.
See also 1981 Biobibliography, 3379.

ROE CLOUD, HENRY (Winnebago)
See CLOUD, HENRY C. ROE

ROGERS, EDWARD L. (Chippewa)
1778A   "Getting the Right Start," Red Man, 14 (February, 1897),
         7. Advocates hard work and patience.
See also 1981 Biobibliography, 3382-3384.

ROGERS, WILLIAM CHARLES (Cherokee)
1779L   "Chief's Wise Talk," Talequah Democratic Arrow, August
         1, 1908. Warns Cherokees not to mortgage their land.
See also 1981 Biobibliography, 3507-3512.

ROMAN NOSE, HENRY CARUTHERS (Southern Cheyenne)
1780N   "Roman Nose Goes to Indian Territory," School News, 1
         (October, 1880), 3. Describes a recruiting trip for
         Carlisle.

ROMERO, ESTHER (Acomita Pueblo)
1781A   "Demonstration," Sherman Bulletin, May 27, 1914. Con-
         cerns a well-balanced meal.

ROOKS, GEORGE (Sioux)
1782N   "Items from Classrooms," Oglala Light, 20 (December 1,
         1919), 3. Reports classroom activities at the Oglala
         Boarding School.
1783N   "Items from Classrooms," Oglala Light, 20 (December 25,
         1919), 3. Reports classroom activities at the Oglala
         Boarding School.
1784N   "Items from Classrooms," Oglala Light, 20 (January 1,
         1920), 3. Reports classroom activities at the Oglala
         Boarding School.

ROOT, CLARA (Northern Arapaho)
1785N   "Domestic Science in the Indian Home," Indian School
         Journal, 18 (June, 1918), 32-34. Argues that it will
         raise the standard of living for Indians.
See also 1981 Biobibliography, 3516.

ROSS, A. FRANK (Choctaw)
1786N   "Christianity and Civilization," Indian Missionary, 1 (Sep-
         tember, 1884), 1.
1787N   "The Dying Indian Boy," Indian Missionary, 1 (September,
         1884), 3. Narrative about a Christian conversion.
1788N   "A Converted Membership," Indian Missionary, 1 (October,
         1884), 1. Concerns Baptist churches in Indian Terri-
         tory.
1789N   "The Wild Indians," Indian Missionary, 1 (October, 1884), 1.

1790N   "Choctaw and Chickasaw Association," Indian Missionary,
        1 (October, 1884), 2. Concerns the Baptist church
        organization.

1791N   "Indian Burials of Ancient Times," Indian Missionary, 1
        (November, 1884), 2.

1792N   "Dr. T. A. Bland's Visit to the Territory," Indian Mis-
        sionary, 1 (November, 1884), 2.

1793N   "Notes from the Field," Indian Missionary, 1 (January,
        1885), 1. Concerns Baptist mission activities.

1794N   "Little Lillian Blake Is Dead," Indian Missionary, 1 (Jan-
        uary, 1885), 1.

1795N   "Choctaw Teachers," Indian Missionary, 1 (January, 1885),
        1.

1796N   "An Indian's Indurance," Indian Missionary, 1 (January,
        1885), 1. Concerns the Reverend Wesley Smith.

1797N   "A Wild Indian Speech," Indian Missionary, 1 (January,
        1885), 2.

1798N   "Christmas Among the Indians," Indian Missionary, 1 (Jan-
        uary, 1885), 3. Concerns Indian Territory.

1799N   "Choctaw Baptist in Mississippi," Indian Missionary, 1
        (January, 1885), 5.

1800N   "Full-Blood Indian Membership," Indian Missionary, 1
        (February, 1885), 1. Concerns the Baptist church in
        the Indian Territory.

1801N   "High Hill Church Again," Indian Missionary, 1 (February,
        1885), 1. Concerns Baptist church activities.

1802N   "Treaties with the Indians," Indian Missionary, 1 (Feb-
        ruary, 1885), 1.

1803N   "Encouragement," Indian Missionary, 2 (February, 1886),
        1. Appeals to Indian Missionary supporters.

1804N   "A Good Deacon Gone," Indian Missionary, 2 (February,
        1886), 4. Concerns W. D. King.

1805N   "Ordination of a Preacher and Deacon," Indian Missionary,
        2 (March, 1886), 1. Concerns W. D. King.

1806N   "Young Men's Prayer Meeting," Indian Missionary, 2 (March,
        1886), 3. Concerns a meeting at South Canadian, Choc-
        taw Nation.

1807N   "An Honest Boy," Indian Missionary, 2 (March, 1886), 5.
        Narrative about a boy who returns a pocketbook.

1808N   "Choctaw Academy," Indian Missionary, 2 (April, 1886) 3.

1809N   "Observations and Organizations," Indian Missionary, 2
        (July, 1886), 4. Concerns Baptist church activities in
        Indian Territory.

1810N   "Ministerial Discouragement," Indian Missionary, 2 (August,
        1886), 1. Concerns difficulties faced by preachers in
        the Indian Territory.

1811N   "Duties of Church Members," Indian Missionary, 2 (August,
        1886), 4.

1812N   "Choctaw Chief or Governor," Indian Missionary, 3 (Sep-
        tember, 1886), 1. Concerns the recent election.

1813N   "Ministerial Disappointments," Indian Missionary, 3 (September, 1886), 3.

1814N   "Eufaula Colored Baptist Church," Indian Missionary, 3 (December, 1886), 3. Concerns its establishment.

1815N   "Hays and Thrasher," Indian Missionary, 3 (December, 1886), 3. Relates church activities of William Hays and M. V. Thrasher of Oklahoma Territory.

1816N   "Valedictory," Indian Missionary, 3 (December, 1886), 4. Relates his reasons for giving up the editorship.

1817L   "International Council of the Indian Territory," Indian Missionary, 3 (July, 1887), 6. Describes events at a meeting in Eufaula.

1818L   "Canadian Revivals," Indian Missionary, 3 (August, 1887), 1. Concerns revivals at South Canadian, Choctaw Nation.

1819L   "The Banner Meeting of the Season," Indian Missionary, 5 (September, 1889), 3. Concerns a camp meeting at Scipio, Indian Territory.

1820L   "Baptist Churches Commune Together," Indian Missionary, 5 (September, 1889), 4. Calls for unity.

1821L   "Missionary Cordell," Indian Missionary, 6 (May, 1890), 2. Concerns H. H. Cordell.

1822N   "Christian Teachers," Indian Missionary, 6 (May, 1890), 5.

1823N   "Choats Prairie Church," Indian Missionary, 6 (August, 1890), 1. Concerns the church's decline.

1824P   "Our Prayer," Indian Missionary, 6 (November, 1890), 5. Concerns the Reverend J. S. Murrow.

1825L   Letter, Indian Missionary, 7 (August, 1891), 2. Concerns a church at Rock Creek, Indian Territory.

ROSS, DANIEL H. (Cherokee)

1826N   "Annual Meeting of the Cherokee Temperance Society," Cherokee Advocate, October 29, 1850. Reports on the meeting.

1827N   "Meeting of the Cherokee Temperance Society," Cherokee Advocate, November 4, 1851. Reports on the meeting.

1828N   "Report," Cherokee Advocate, November 4, 1851. Reports on meeting of the Cherokee Temperance Society.

1829N   "Annual Report," Cherokee Advocate, November 24, 1852. Reports on the Cherokee Temperance Society.

1830A   "Address Delivered by D. H. Ross, by Request of Caney Division, of a Celebration of the Order of Sons of Temperance, at Caney School House, C.N., April 30th, 1853," Cherokee Advocate, June 1, 1853.

See also 1981 Biobibliography, 3518-3546.

ROSS, JOHN (Cherokee)

1831A   "Message of the Principal Chief of the Cherokee Nation, Submitted Before the National Committee and Council, in Joint Committee of the Whole, Wednesday, October 14, 1829," Niles' Register, 37 (November 14, 1829), 189-190.

Concerns Cherokee lands. Reprinted from Cherokee Phoenix.

1832A   "Message of the Principal Chief to the General Council of the Cherokee Nation," Niles' Register, 38 (August 7, 1830), 423. Concerns Georgia's extension of her laws over the Cherokee Nation. Reprinted from Nashville Republican.

1833N   Proclamation, Niles' Register, 42 (August 18, 1832), 441. Announces a day of fasting.

1834L   "To the Committee and Council, in General Council Convened," Niles' Register, 45 (October 19, 1833), 121-122.

1835L   "Letter from John Ross, Principal Chief of the Cherokee Nation, in Answer to Inquiries from a Friend, Regarding Cherokee Affairs with the United States," Niles' Weekly Register, 51 (October 6, 1836), 90-91. Reprinted from New York American.

1836A   "Message of the Principal Chief," Cherokee Advocate, November 28, 1844. Concerns Cherokee national affairs.

1837A   "To the National Council," Cherokee Advocate, November 19, 1846. Concerns the Treaty of 1846.

1838N   "Proclamation," Cherokee Advocate, December 3, 1846. Announces Thanksgiving.

1839L   Letter, Cherokee Advocate, April 29, 1847. Concerns Cherokee contributions for relief of the poor in Scotland.

1840A   "Message to the National Committee and Council, in National Council Convened," Cherokee Advocate, October 14, 1851. Concerns Cherokee national affairs.

1841A   "Message of the Principal Chief," Cherokee Advocate, October 27, 1852. Concerns Cherokee national affairs.

1842A   "Message of the Principal Chief," Cherokee Advocate, 7 (December, 1852), 1. Concerns Cherokee affairs.

1843A   "The Hon. John Ross's Message to the Cherokee Nation," Van Buren Press, October 14, 1859. Reviews Cherokee affairs.

1844A   "Message of the Principal Chief of the Cherokee Nation," Van Buren Press, November 9, 1860. Concerns conditions, growing sectionalism, and the slavery question.

1845L   "Letter from Hon. John Ross," Van Buren Press, February 8, 1861. Answers charges that the Cherokees will attack Arkansas in event of civil war.

1846N   "Proclamation to the Cherokee People," Van Buren Press, July 10, 1861. Reminds the Cherokees of their neutral position in the developing sectional conflict.

See also 1981 Biobibliography, 3548-3574.

ROSS, JOSHUA (Cherokee)

1847P   "Sequoyah," Sequoyah Memorial, July 31, 1856. Signed "The Wanderer."

1848P   "The Wanderer," Sequoyah Memorial, July 31, 1856. Signed "The Wanderer."

1849P   "On a Lady's Eyes," <u>Arkansian</u>, March 12, 1859. Signed
        "The Wanderer."
1850L   Letter, <u>Oklahoma Star</u>, November 13, 1874. Concerns the
        Indian International Fair.
See also 1981 Biobibliography, 3576-3577.

ROSS, OLIVER C. (Pine Ridge Sioux)
  1851N   "The Ghost Dance," <u>Talks and Thoughts</u>, 17 (October,
          1903), 1.

ROSS, ROSA L. (Cherokee-Creek)
  1852L   "The Girl's Mistake in Time," <u>School News</u>, 2 (October,
          1881), 1. Anecdote about going to York, Pennsylvania,
          fair.
  1853N   "English Speaking Wight," <u>School News</u>, 2 (December,
          1881), 2. Urges students not to worry about mistakes
          in language.

ROSS, S. W. (Cherokee)
  1854N   "A Scottish-Indian Family," <u>Tahlequah Arrow</u>, December
          23, 1905. Concerns the Ross family. Reprinted from
          <u>Scottish-American</u>.
See also 1981 Biobibliography, 3582-3584.

ROSS, WILLIAM POTTER (Cherokee)
  1855N   "Prospectus for the Cherokee Advocate," <u>Cherokee Advo-
          cate</u>, September 26, 1844.
  1856N   "The Rumored Indian War a Humbug," <u>Cherokee Advocate</u>,
          February 27, 1845. Concerns rumored war between
          Creeks and Osages.
  1857L   "To Capt. S. Wood, U.S.A.," <u>Cherokee Advocate</u>, May
          15, 1845. Concerns violence at Fort Gibson.
  1858N   "The Convention," <u>Cherokee Advocate</u>, April 29, 1847.
          Concerns the nominating convention for chief.
  1859N   "Change of Editors," <u>Cherokee Advocate</u>, November 13,
          1848.
  1860L   "For the Cherokee Advocate," <u>Cherokee Advocate</u>, June
          3, 1851. Concerns the per capita payment.
  1861A   "Address Delivered by William P. Ross, before Cherokee
          Division of Sons of Temperance, December 25, 1852,"
          <u>Cherokee Advocate</u>, January 12, 1853.
See also 1981 Biobibliography, 3586-3603.

ROUILLARD, ALEX (Santee Sioux)
  1862N   "Whittier's 'Snow-Bound,' a Paraphrase," <u>Talks and
          Thoughts</u>, 11 (February, 1896), 1.
  1863N   "Whittier's Bare Foot Boy," <u>Talks and Thoughts</u>, 11
          (March, 1896), 6. A paraphrase.

ROUILLARD, DAVID (Santee Sioux)
  1864M   "The One Legged Giant," <u>Talks and Thoughts</u>, 9 (April,
          1895), 1-2, and 10 (May, 1895), 1. A legend.

ROUILLARD, EUGENE (Santee Sioux)
1865L "Some of Our Expeditionary Soldiers," Word Carrier of
Santee Normal Training School, (March-April, 1919),
5. Relates his army experiences.

ROUILLARD, LUCY (Santee Sioux)
1866N "School and Home," Word Carrier of Santee Normal Training School, 43 (May-June, 1914), 12. Describes life at
Santee and praises the normal school.

ROUILLARD, THOMAS J. (Santee Sioux)
1867F "Onktoni. Story Told by an Old Wahpekute or Santee Indian," Talks and Thoughts, 11 (December, 1895), 1-2.
A tale.

ROWLAND, EMMA J. (Northern Cheyenne)
1868M "Legend of the Opeche," Carlisle Arrow, March 25, 1910.
Legend of Robin Red Breast.
See also 1981 Biobibliography, 3605.

ROY, MARY (Ponca)
1869N "Child Study," Indian Leader, June 28, 1901.

RUIZ, EMMA (Nisenan)
1870N "The Grass Game," Sherman Bulletin, January 3, 1912.
1871A "Adulteration of Foods," Sherman Bulletin, May 28, 1913.

RULO, CORA A. (Ponca)
1872L Letter, Talks and Thoughts, 1 (October, 1886), 3. Concerns attending off-reservation schools.

RULO, LOUIS (Oto)
1873N "John Greenleaf Whittier," Indian Leader, January 22,
1904. Biographical sketch.
See also 1981 Biobibliography, 3606-3607.

RUNNELS, LOUIS H. (Sanpoil)
1874L "Lew Runnels in Washington," Arrow, August 30, 1907.
Describes his trip from Carlisle to Keller, Washington.
1875N "Toloman Mountain," Carlisle Arrow, June 10, 1910. Describes the mountain in Washington.
1876F "Plenty and Famine," Carlisle Arrow, January 22, 1911.
Story of an Indian's struggle to find game.
1877M "The Struggle Against Darkness," Carlisle Arrow, March
31, 1911. Legend concerning the origin of light.
See also 1981 Biobibliography, 3611-3612.

RUNNELS, MARY E. (Sanpoil)
1878N "Dressmaking," Arrow, March 30, 1906.

RYAN, CHARLES (Pokanoket, i.e., Wampanoag)
1879N "Lobster Fishing," Carlisle Arrow, December 18, 1908.

SAGE, ALEXANDER W. (Arickara)
 1880N "Worship of the Arickarees," Arrow, January 10, 1908.

ST. PIERRE, MARY (Chippewa)
 1881N "The Relation of the School and the Home," Indian Leader,
  June 22, 1900.

SAKEASTEWA, VICTOR (Hopi)
 1882F "Why the Coyote Is Shy," Sherman Bulletin, April 12,
  1911. A tale.

SANDERS, SAMUEL STEPHEN (Cherokee)
 1883L "In Reply to Mr. R. T. Walker," Fort Smith Elevator,
  April 22, 1898. Argues against Indian emigration to
  Mexico.
 1884L "Emigration Scheme," Indian Sentinel, April 29, 1898.
  Argues against Indian emigration to Mexico. Reprinted
  from Fort Smith Elevator.

SANDS, ROBERT (Kansa)
 1885N "Evils of Intemperance," Osage Journal, September 4,
  1902.

SANGO (Eskimo)
 1886N "Good Advice," Eskimo, 1 (November, 1916), 3. Advises
  Eskimos to try to be like whites.

SANGSTER, MARGARET (Navajo)
 1887N "Organizations," Purple and Gold. Riverside, CA: Sherman Institute, 1923, pp. 12-14, 16. Describes organizations at Sherman Institute.

SAUL, THOMAS T. (Crow Creek Sioux)
 1888N "My Reservation," Carlisle Arrow, April 9, 1909. Concerns
  the Crow Creek Reservation.

SAUNOOKE, NAN E. (Eastern Band Cherokee)
 1889M "Why Corn Is Cultivated," Carlisle Arrow, May 20, 1910.
  A Cherokee legend.
 1890M "How Medicine Originated Among the Cherokees," Carlisle
  Arrow, September 30, 1910. A legend.
 1891M "Why the Turkey Is Bald," Carlisle Arrow, March 10,
  1911. A legend.
 1892N "Home Making," Carlisle Arrow, April 21, 1911. Describes
  it as woman's work.

SCHANANDOAH, CHAPMAN (Oneida)
 1893F "How the Bear Lost His Tail: an Old Indian Story,"
  Talks and Thoughts, 7 (February, 1893), 1.
 1894M "The Sand Story," Talks and Thoughts, 8 (April, 1894),
  3. Legend about creation.

1895L   "A Letter from Cuba," Talks and Thoughts, 14 (December, 1898), 3. Describes what he saw.

1896L   Letter, Talks and Thoughts, 17 (April, 1904), 3-4.

SCHOOLCRAFT, JANE JOHNSTON (Ojibwa)

1897L   "Character of Aboriginal Historical Tradition," Literary Voyager, No. 1, December, 1826. Concerns her source of knowledge of Chippewa traditions. Reprinted in Philip P. Mason, ed., Literary Voyager or Muzzeniegun (East Lansing: Michigan State University Press, 1962), 5-7. Original is in the Library of Congress.

1898P   "To Sisters on a Walk in the Garden, After a Shower," Literary Voyager, No. 1, December, 1826. Reprinted in Philip P. Mason, ed., Literary Voyager or Muzzeniegun (East Lansing: Michigan State University Press, 1962), 8. Original is in the Library of Congress.

1899P   "Resignation," Literary Voyager, No. 2, December, 1826. Reprinted in Philip P. Mason, ed., Literary Voyager or Muzzeniegun (East Lansing: Michigan State University Press, 1962), 26-27. Original is in the Library of Congress.

1900M   "The Origin of the Robin, an Oral Allegory," Literary Voyager, No. 3, January, 1827. Reprinted in Philip P. Mason, ed., Literary Voyager or Muzzeniegun (East Lansing: Michigan State University Press, 1962), 37-38. Original is in the Library of Congress.

1901M   "Moowis, the Indian Coquette: A Chippewa Legend," Literary Voyager, No. 4, January 12, 1827. Reprinted in Philip P. Mason, ed., Literary Voyager or Muzzeniegun (East Lansing: Michigan State University Press, 1962), 56-57. Original is in the Library of Congress.

1902P   "Lines to a Friend Asleep," Literary Voyager, No. 5, January, 1827. Reprinted in Philip P. Mason, ed., Literary Voyager or Muzzeniegun (East Lansing: Michigan State University Press, 1962), 71. Original is in the Library of Congress.

1903M   "Mishosha, or the Magician and His Daughters: A Chippewa Tale or Legend," Literary Voyager, No. 5, January, 1827. Reprinted in Philip P. Mason, ed., Literary Voyager or Muzzeniegun (East Lansing: Michigan State University Press, 1962), 64-71. Original is in the Library of Congress.

1904P   "Lines Written Under Affliction," Literary Voyager, No. 7, February, 1827. Reprinted in Philip P. Mason, ed., Literary Voyager or Muzzeniegun (East Lansing: Michigan State University Press, 1962), 84-85. Original is in the Library of Congress.

1905M   "The Forsaken Brother, A Chippewa Tale," Literary Voyager, No. 8, February 13, 1827. Reprinted in Philip P. Mason, ed., Literary Voyager or Muzzeniegun (East

Lansing: Michigan State University Press, 1962), 93-
96. Original is in the Library of Congress.

1906P   "Lines Written Under Severe Pain and Sickness," Literary
Voyager, No. 8, February 13, 1827. Reprinted in Philip
P. Mason, ed., Literary Voyager or Muzzeniegun (East
Lansing: Michigan State University Press, 1962), 97.
Original is in the Library of Congress.

1907M   "Origin of the Miscoded or the Maid of Toquimenon," Lit-
erary Voyager, No. 11, February, 1827. A legend.
Reprinted in Philip P. Mason, ed., Literary Voyager or
Muzzeniegun (East Lansing: Michigan State University
Press, 1962), 122-124. Original is in the Library of
Congress.

1908P   "Otagamiad," Literary Voyager, No. 13, March 10, 1827.
Concerns her grandfather Waub Ojeeg. Reprinted in
Philip P. Mason, ed., Literary Voyager or Muzzeniegun
(East Lansing: Michigan State University Press, 1962),
138-142. Original is in the Library of Congress.

1909P   "Invocation to My Maternal Grandfather on Hearing His
Descent from Chippewa Ancestors Misrepresented," Lit-
erary Voyager, No. 13, March 10, 1827. Reprinted in
Philip P. Mason, ed., Literary Voyager or Muzzeniegun
(East Lansing: Michigan State University Press, 1962),
142-143. Original is in the Library of Congress.

1910P   "To My Ever Beloved and Lamented Son William Henry,"
Literary Voyager, No. 14, March 28, 1827. Reprinted
in Philip P. Mason, ed., Literary Voyager or Muzzeniegun
(East Lansing: Michigan State University Press, 1962),
157-158. Original is in the Library of Congress.

1911P   "Say Dearest Friend, When Light Your Bark," Literary
Voyager, No. 14, March 28, 1827. Poem to her husband.
Reprinted in Philip P. Mason, ed., Literary Voyager or
Muzzeniegun (East Lansing: Michigan State University
Press, 1962), 156. Original is in the Library of Con-
gress.

1912P   "Sonnet," Literary Voyager, No. 14, March 28, 1827.
Concerns the death of her child. Reprinted in Philip
P. Mason, ed., Literary Voyager or Muzzeniegun (East
Lansing: Michigan State University Press, 1962), 153.
Original is in the Library of Congress.

SCHRAM, GRACE (Chippewa)
1913N   "Education," Peace Pipe, 5 (June, 1916), 9.

SCOTT, COLBY (Creek)
1914N   "Spring," Creek Boys' and Girls' Monthly, December, 1870.
Concerns the characteristics of spring in the Indian Territory.

SCREAMER, ALBERT MANUS (Eastern Band Cherokee)
1915N   "Indian Band Entertained," Arrow, September 27, 1907.
Describes their appearance and reception at Long Branch.

1916N   "What Carlisle Has Done for the North Carolina Cherokees,"
        Arrow, September 27, 1907.

SEARS, LEE ALLEN (Sioux)
   1917N   "Class History," Peace Pipe, June 20, 1913. Biographical
           sketches of students at Pipestone Indian School.

SEARS, ROSALIND (Assiniboin)
   1918N   "Found! a Gold Mine!" Indian School Journal, 18 (June,
           1918), 21-22. Concerns literature.

SEATTLE, MATTHEW (Puyallup)
   1919A   "Matthew Seattle's Address," Indian Leader, March 15,
           1899. Concerns education and patriotism.
   1920A   Address, Indian Leader, August 1, 1899. Concerns the
           meaning of the name "Tacoma."

SEDICK, EUDOCIA M. (Alaska Native)
   1921N   "What I Am Going to Do When I Leave School," Red Man
           and Helper, June 7, 1901. Describes her desire to be
           a dressmaker or a music teacher.

SEKONIK, JOE (Eskimo)
   1922F   "The Adventures of Iki-ya-yuk-tua-look," Eskimo, 2 (Jan-
           uary, 1918), 1-8. A folktale of a famous Eskimo hero.
   1923F   "The Story of Apukeena," Eskimo, 2 (February, 1918), 4-6.
           A strange tale of Point Hope.

SELKIRK, CHARLES (White Earth Chippewa)
   1924L   "Give the Indian a Chance," American Indian Advocate,
              3 (Summer-Autumn, 1922), 2. Reprinted from the Min-
              neapolis Journal.
   See also 1981 Biobibliography, 3633-3634.

SERVICE, ROBERT (Clatsop)
   1925N   "The Apple Tree--Planting and Pruning," Chemawa Amer-
              ican, 16 (June, 1914), 16-17.
   1926L   "Writes from Omaha," Chemawa American, December 12,
              1917. Concerns Indians in the Army and army life.

SEVECK, CHESTER (Eskimo)
   1927N   "About the Good Sled Deer," Eskimo, 2 (July-August,
              1918), 2. Describes how to break in a sled deer.

SHAMBOW, MARY (Chippewa)
   1928N   "Valedictory," Peace Pipe, June 19, 1914. Encourages
           students to strive.

SHANGREAU, MARY (Pine Ridge Sioux)
   1929N   Untitled, Ogalalla Light, 1 (July 1, 1900), 4. Concerns
           Abraham Lincoln.

SHANGREAU, WILLIAM (Sioux)

1930N   "Items from Classrooms," <u>Oglala Light</u>, 20 (December 1, 1919), 3. Reports classroom activities at the Oglala Boarding School.

1931N   "Items from the Classrooms," <u>Oglala Light</u>, 20 (December 15, 1919), 3. Reports classroom activities at the Oglala Boarding School.

1932N   "Items from Classrooms," <u>Oglala Light</u>, 20 (January 1, 1920), 3. Reports classroom activities at the Oglala Boarding School.

1933N   "Items from Classrooms," <u>Oglala Light</u>, 20 (January 15, 1920), 3. Reports classroom activities at the Oglala Boarding School.

1934N   "Items from the Class Rooms," <u>Oglala Light</u>, 20 (February 15, 1920), 3. Reports classroom activities at the Oglala Boarding School.

1935N   "Story of George Washington," <u>Oglala Light</u>, 20 (March 15, 1920), 3. Concerns facts and fiction surrounding Washington.

1936N   "Items from the Class Rooms," <u>Oglala Light</u>, 20 (March 15, 1920), 3. Reports classroom activities at the Oglala Boarding School.

1937N   "Items from the Class Rooms," <u>Oglala Light</u>, 20 (April 1, 1920), 3. Reports classroom activities at the Oglala Boarding School.

1938N   "Items from the Class Rooms," <u>Oglala Light</u>, 20 (April 15, 1920), 3. Reports classroom activities at the Oglala Boarding School.

SHAW, EVALYN CALLAHAN (Creek)

1939P   "October," <u>Muskogee Phoenix</u>, November 1, 1900. Reprinted from <u>Wagoner Sayings</u>.

SHAWNEE, GEORGE (Shawnee)

1940N   "Liberty," <u>Indian Leader</u>, 1 (April, 1897), 4. Concerns slavery versus liberty.

SHEEHAN, JOSEPH (Alaska Native)

1941N   "How the Arrow Is Printed," <u>Arrow</u>, January 4, 1907. Describes printing activities at Carlisle.

SHEPHERD, MASON (Sioux)

1942N   "The Sioux Indians," <u>Indian Leader</u>, April 18, 1902. Concerns "progress" and Christian influence.

SHEPPARD, GRACE (Sisseton Sioux)

1943N   "Punctuality," <u>Peace Pipe</u>, 5 (September, 1915), 3.

SHERIDAN, RACHEL (Omaha)

1944N   "A Buffalo Hunt," <u>Talks and Thoughts</u>, 17 (December, 1903), 4. Describes a hunt.

1945N   "My Summer Home," Talks and Thoughts, 19 (September-October, 1905), 4. Describes her summer job as an outing student.

1946N   "Pow Wow," Talks and Thoughts, 19 (November, 1905), 1. Concerns the Omahas.

1947N   "Christmas on the Reservation," Talks and Thoughts, 19 (January, 1906), 1.

1948N   "A Childish Wish," Talks and Thoughts, 20 (July-August, 1906), 3-4.

SHEYAHSHE, GEORGE (Caddo)

1949N   "With the Colors at Camp Travis," Indian School Journal, 19 (June, 1919), 17. Describes his army experiences.

SHIELD, DAWSON (Sioux)

1950N   "Items from Classrooms," Oglala Light, 20 (January 15, 1920), 3. Reports classroom activities at the Oglala Boarding School.

1951N   "Items from the Class Rooms," Oglala Light, 20 (February 15, 1920), 3. Reports classroom activities at the Oglala Boarding School.

SHIELDS, F. H. (Sioux)

1952L   Letter, Word Carrier of Santee Normal Training School, 36 (May-June, 1907), 12. Urges a revival to counter church dissension and dancing.

SHIELDS, MARY (Sioux)

1953N   "Items from Classrooms," Oglala Light, 20 (December 1, 1919), 3. Reports classroom activities at the Oglala Boarding School.

1954N   "Items from Classrooms," Oglala Light, 20 (December 15, 1919), 3. Reports classroom activities at the Oglala Boarding School.

1955N   "Items from Classrooms," Oglala Light, 20 (January 1, 1920), 3. Reports classroom activities at the Oglala Boarding School.

SHIPSHE, ROSA (Potawatomi)

1956N   "The Green Corn Dance," Indian Leader, April 5, 1907. Describes activities at the dance.

SHOTLEY, EVA (Chippewa)

1957N   "Perseverence," Peace Pipe, 4 (July 2, 1915), 7.

SIFTSOFF, LUBOVA (Alaska Native)

1958N   "A Seed Tester," Chemawa American, 16 (May, 1914), 32. Describes how to make one.

SILK, CARL E. (Gros Ventre)

1959N   "Some Customs of My People," Arrow, April 5, 1907. Describes Christianity, dances, and celebrations.

SILOOK, PAUL (Eskimo)
  1960M "The Creation of Sivookak (St. Lawrence Island)," Eskimo,
      1 (June, 1917), 5. A legend.

SILVAS, CARMELITA (Tule River, i.e. Yokuts)
  1961N "Three Things Necessary to Good Sewing," Sherman Bul-
      letin, May 29, 1919.

SILVAS, MARTINA (Mission)
  1962L "How Nice," Mission Indian, 1 (December 15, 1895), 5.
      Concerns boarding school life.

SILVERHEELS, FLORENCE W. (Cattaraugus Seneca)
  1963N "New York Indians," Native American, March 26, 1904.
  1964N "New York Indians," Talks and Thoughts, 17 (March,
      1904), 4.
  1965N "A Visit to Richmond," Talks and Thoughts, 19 (June,
      1905), 3. Describes a trip to the educational exhibition
      of the Eastern Public Education Association.
  1966N "A Visit to Richmond," Chippeway Herald, 4 (June, 1905),
      8. Describes a trip to the educational exhibition of the
      Eastern Public Education Association.

SIMPSON, ALBERT H. (Arickara)
  1967L "From Albert Simpson," Arrow, May 31, 1907. Describes
      the people and his work at Fort Defiance.

SIMPSON, ELLA (Nisenan)
  1968M "How the Rivers and Ditches Were Made," Sherman Bulletin,
      April 20, 1910. A legend.

SIMPSON, PETER (Tlingit)
  1969L "A Letter from Port Gravina," North Star, 5 (November,
      1892), 2. Concerns the sawmills there.
  1970N "The Native Viewpoint on Citizenship," Word Carrier of
      Santee Normal Training School, 40 (July-August, 1911),
      16. Advocates citizenship for Indians.
  See also 1981 Biobibliography, 3651.

SIXKILLER, JULIA A. (Cherokee)
  1971A "Gleams Through the Darkness," Indian Missionary, 1
      (January, 1885), 2. Advocates hope through Christian-
      ity.

SKENANDORE, AMELIA (Oneida)
  1972L "A Letter from a Returned Student," Talks and Thoughts,
      5 (June, 1891), 4. Relates news from Oneida, Wiscon-
      sin.

SKENANDORE, ELI (Oneida)
  1973N "The Oneidas," Talks and Thoughts, 14 (May, 1901), 1.

SKENANDORE, JOEL W. (Oneida)
  1974T "How the Prince Was Scared, an Old Story as Told Among
         the Oneida Indians," Talks and Thoughts, 11 (Novem-
         ber, 1895), 2-3.
  1975F "The Boy That Had Never Been in the Open Air," Talks
         and Thoughts, 16 (August-September, 1902), 6-7. A
         story.

SKENANDORE, WILSON (Oneida)
  1976N "Some Facts About the Oneidas," Talks and Thoughts, 4
         (April, 1890), 1.

SKIUHUSHU (Blackfeet)
  1977P "Spirit of Cooperation," Indian, Unnumbered (January,
         1922), 1.
  1978L "Letter to Hayden," American Indian Advocate, 3 (Grass
         Moon, 1922), 24-25. Responds to the Senator's speech
         on Indian affairs.
  1979N "Sunrise," American Indian Advocate, 3 (Summer-Autumn,
         1922), 8. Concerns a religious theme.
  See also 1981 Biobibliography, 3660-3664.

SKYE, ESTELLA (Peoria)
  1980M "Ojibwa Tradition," Carlisle Arrow, May 7, 1909. Con-
         cerns Nanahbozhoo.

SKYE, GLADYS (Peoria)
  1981N "Alcohol and My Future," Indian Leader, 17 (October,
         1915), 12-13.

SKYE, MAZIE L. (Seneca)
  1982N "The Medicine Dance," Carlisle Arrow, June 3, 1910.
         Concerns the Seneca dance.
  1983M "The Seven Stars," Carlisle Arrow, January 6, 1911. A
         Seneca legend of the Seven Sisters.
  1984A "Character," Carlisle Arrow, February 3, 1911.
  1985N "The Green Corn," Carlisle Arrow, February 17, 1911.
         Concerns the origin of corn.
  1986N "The Value of Accuracy," Carlisle Arrow, May 12, 1911.
  See also 1981 Biobibliography, 3668-3670.

SLOAN, THOMAS (Omaha)
  1987N "The Lend-a-Hand Club," Talks and Thoughts, 1 (Novem-
         ber, 1886), 2-3. Relates the history of the club.
  1988N "Indian Christmas at Hampton," Talks and Thoughts, 1
         (January, 1887), 1-2.
  1989N "The Day We Celebrate," Talks and Thoughts, 2 (March,
         1887), 2-3. Concerns the Dawes Act.
  1990N "A Missionary Trip," Talks and Thoughts, 2 (June, 1887),
         3-4. Describes the trip.
  1991N "Citizenship Class," Talks and Thoughts, 2 (March-April,
         1888), 1. Describes a visit to Hampton city officials.

1992N   "Sale of Indian Lands," Talks and Thoughts, 3 (September, 1888), 1. Argues for legal rights for Indians.

1993N   Untitled, Talks and Thoughts, 4 (July, 1889), 2. Concerns discipline and conditions at Hampton.

1994L   "Indian Light Bearers," Talks and Thoughts, 4 (February, 1890), 3. Reports formation of a club at the Omaha Agency.

1995N   "Indian Base Ball Players," Talks and Thoughts, 5 (July, 1890), 3-4. Discusses decline of native sports and rise of baseball at Indian schools. Reprinted from Wide Awake.

1996N   "Settle Tribal Claims," American Indian Magazine, 4 (April-June, 1916), 146-149.

1997N   "The New Administration in the Affairs of the American Indians," American Indian Tepee, 2 (Indian Summer, 1921), 7-8. Argues that Indians will not do any better under the present administration.

1998N   "The Indian Runner," American Indian Tepee, 2 (Indian Summer, 1921), 5-6. Concerns the Indian Bureau and rights of Fort McDowell Indians.

1999N   "Showing Up an Indian Agent," American Indian Tepee, 2 (Indian Summer, 1921), 8-9. Concerns fraud and unfair treatment of Indians by agents.

See also 1981 Biobibliography, 3674.

SMALLWOOD, BENJAMIN FRANKLIN (Choctaw)

2000A   "The Governor's Message," Indian Citizen, October 11, 1890. Concerns Choctaw national affairs.

See also 1981 Biobibliography, 3676-3677.

SMITH, AMY (Little Lake, i.e., Pomo)

2001N   "The Radish," Carlisle Arrow, June 4, 1909. Describes how to grow and prepare it.

SMITH, BURNHAM (Konkow)

2002N   "General Blacksmithing," Sherman Bulletin, June 10, 1908.

SMITH, CHARLES H. (Chemehuevi)

2003N   "The Silo," Sherman Bulletin, May 29, 1919.

SMITH, CLARENCE (Arapaho)

2004M   "The Great Dipper," Carlisle Arrow, December 18, 1918. An Arapaho legend.

See also 1981 Biobibliography, 3690.

SMITH, FRANK (Chippewa)

2005N   "Every Man Is the Architect of His Own Fortune," Peace Pipe, June 19, 1914.

SMITH, HARRISON B. (Oneida)

2006N   "The Fourth of July on My Reservation," Carlisle Arrow,

July 4, 1912. Describes the holiday at Oneida, Wisconsin.
See also 1981 Biobibliography, 3695.

SMITH, JAMES (Warm Springs, i.e., Shasta)
    2007A "Twenty-Nine Years of Progress," Indian Leader, 17 (June, 1913), 24-26.
    2008N "Education and Progress: Salvation of the Red Man," Indian Leader, 17 (December, 1913), 7-8.
See also 1981 Biobibliography, 3699-3700.

SMITH, JEFFERSON B. (Gros Ventre)
    2009N "My Trip to Washington," Carlisle Arrow, June 10, 1910. Describes his trip.
    2010M "The Separation of the Crows and Gros Ventres," Carlisle Arrow, November 18, 1910. A legend.
    2011N "Some Early Beliefs of Indians," Carlisle Arrow, May 5, 1911. Concerns medicine, thunder, and child rearing.
See also 1981 Biobibliography, 3701.

SMITH, LOTTIE (Eastern Band Cherokee)
    2012N "Cherokee," Talks and Thoughts, 4 (December, 1889), 1. Concerns the Cherokees of North Carolina.

SOUCEA, HUGH (Pueblo)
    2013L Letter, Carlisle Arrow, January 26, 1912. Encourages students to work and to persist.
See also 1981 Biobibliography, 3714-3715.

SPATZ, LEE (Hupa)
    2014N "Care of Farm Implements," Sherman Bulletin, May 29, 1919.

SPICER, ALEX (Oklahoma Seneca)
    2015N "From a Seneca Indian," Indian Moccasin, 1 (November, 1893), 1. Concerns the lost continent of Atlantis.

SPLITLOG, JOHN (Cayuga)
    2016N "History of the Christmas Tree," Indian Leader, January 12, 1900.

SPOTTED CROW, LIZZIE (Sioux)
    2017N "Items from Classrooms," Oglala Light, 20 (December 15, 1919), 3. Reports classroom activities at the Oglala Boarding School.
    2018N "Items from Classrooms," Oglala Light, 20 (January 1, 1920), 3. Reports classroom activities at the Oglala Boarding School.
    2019N "Items from Classrooms," Oglala Light, 20 (January 15, 1920), 3. Reports classroom activities at the Oglala Boarding School.

2020N   "Items from the Class Rooms," Oglala Light, 20 (March 1, 1920), 3. Reports classroom activities at the Oglala Boarding School.

2021N   "Items from the Class Rooms," Oglala Light, 20 (April 1, 1920), 3. Reports classroom activities at the Oglala Boarding School.

2022N   "Items from the Class Rooms," Oglala Light, 20 (April 15, 1920), 3. Reports on classroom activities at the Oglala Boarding School.

SPOTTEDBEAR, RUSSEL (Sioux)

2023N   "Growth of the Church," Word Carrier of Santee Normal Training School, 36 (November-December, 1907), 23. Concerns laxity in the church.

SPOTTEDHORSE, CLARA (Crow)

2024N   "Conditions at My Home," Arrow, December 20, 1907. Describes conditions, changes, and life-style.

2025N   "Our Spare Moments," Carlisle Arrow, March 11, 1910. Urges students to use them to get ahead.

SPRADLING, ORA V. (Cherokee)

2026N   "Drifting with the Tide," Indian Missionary, 3 (July, 1887), 4. Urges Christian endeavor.

STABLER, ROY DORSEY (Omaha)

2027N   "The Dawes Bill," Talks and Thoughts, 8 (March, 1894), 3, 7.

2028N   "Indian Chivalry," Talks and Thoughts, 8 (April, 1894), 2. Relates an anecdote about Cadahoun.

2029N   "Hampton Roads," Talks and Thoughts, 11 (January, 1896), 1. Describes the town.

STANDING BEAR, LUTHER (Pine Ridge Sioux)

2030L   Letter, School News, 1 (March, 1881), 4. Urges others to attend school.

STANDING ELK, BESSIE (Cheyenne)

2031N   "The Tools of the Animals," Carlisle Arrow, March 19, 1909. Concerns animals' use of their bodies to get food.

STANLEY, ARNOLD (Choctaw)

2032N   "The Ideal Teacher," Jones Academy Herald, 1 (June, 1903), 5-6.

STANLEY, GRACE B. (Chippewa)

2033A   "Domestic Art--The Tailor-Made Suit," Indian Leader, July 17, 1906. Describes how to make a suit.

STARR, EMMET (Cherokee)

2034N   "Historic Rogers County," Osage Magazine, 1 (March, 1910), 14-16.

2035N   "Beaver County Had Varied History Under Old and New
World Governments," <u>Daily Oklahoman</u>, May 7, 1922.
See also 1981 Biobibliography, 3722-3730.

STARR, JOHN CALEB (Cherokee)
2036N   "Burning the White Dog," <u>Afton News</u>, January 11, 1895.
Concerns the Seneca White Dog sacrifice.
2037N   "Work of enrollment," <u>Tahlequah Arrow</u>, August 11, 1900.
2038N   "Changed Conditions," <u>Tahlequah Arrow</u>, August 23, 1902.
Concerns ratification of Cherokee Agreement of 1902.
See also 1981 Biobibliography, 3735-3739.

STEPHENS SPENCER SEAGO (Cherokee)
2039L   "The Indian Problem," <u>Indian Sentinel</u>, April 8, 1898.
Reviews Indian-white relations.

STEVENS, ADDIE (Winnegabo)
2040N   "Indian Day," <u>Talks and Thoughts</u>, 6 (March, 1892), 1,
4. Describes events at Hampton Institute.
2041N   "Thoughts from the Sermon," <u>Talks and Thoughts</u>, 6
(April, 1892), 3. Analyzes and comments on a sermon.

STEVENS, BERTHA (Klamath)
2042N   "How I Spent the Summer," <u>Carlisle Arrow</u>, October 22,
1909. Describes her outing experience.

STEWART, ROBERT W. (Creek)
2043N   "We All Hope That President Garfield Will Get Well,"
<u>School News</u>, 2 (July, 1881), 2.
2044L   "A Letter from One of Our Creek Boys," <u>School News</u>,
2 (October, 1881), 4. Relates news of Carlisle.

STIDHAM, LEONIDAS (Creek)
2045N   "Betting," <u>Creek Boys' and Girls' Monthly</u>, December,
1870. Concerns the evils of gambling.

STRIKE AXE, BENJAMIN E. (Osage)
2046L   "Mescal Bean Habit," <u>Osage Journal</u>, May 21, 1903. Opposes use of mescal.

STUART, MARION (Piegan)
2047N   "The Round-Up," <u>Chemawa American</u>, 16 (April, 1914),
22-23. Describes the cattle roundup on the Blackfeet
Reservation.

STYLES, LOTTIE (Arickara)
2048M   "A Sun Story," <u>Talks and Thoughts</u>, 17 (August-September,
1903), 4-5. A legend.
2049N   "Students' Industrial Training," <u>Arrow</u>, March 27, 1908.
Stresses the need for training.

SUNDOWN, REUBEN (Seneca)
2050A "The Men to Make a Society," Carlisle Arrow, February
11, 1910. Describes their characteristics.

SUTTON, MYRTLE (Seneca)
2051N "Henry Cloud's Speech," Carlisle Arrow, September 9,
1910. Reports on a speech made by Cloud at Carlisle.

SWALLOW, IDA (Sioux)
2052M "The Fox and the Geese," Red Man, 15 (January, 1900),
8. A legend.

SWAYNEY, ARIZONA (Eastern Band Cherokee)
2053N "Basket Making," Talks and Thoughts, 16 (June, 1902),
1.

SWIMMER, GEORGE (Cherokee)
2054L Letter, Council Fire, 1 (August, 1878), 116. Presents
Christian testimonial.
2055L Letter, Indian Missionary, 1 (September, 1884), 2. Concerns his preaching.

TAHAMONT, ROBERT J. (Abenaki)
2056M "The Grasshopper War," Carlisle Arrow, May 13, 1910. A
Susquehannock legend.
2057N "How the Term 'Fire Water' Originated," Carlisle Arrow,
June 14, 1910.
2058N "Chief Teedyuscung," Carlisle Arrow, October 7, 1910.
Historical sketch.
2059N "Christmas at Carlisle," Carlisle Arrow, January 6, 1911.
Describes events there.
2060M "The Story of the Magic Arrow," Carlisle Arrow, September 22, 1911. A tale.
2061N "My First Experience on a Farm," Carlisle Arrow, September 29, 1911. Describes his outing at New Kingston,
Pennsylvania.
See also 1981 Biobibliography, 3791-3794.

TALKAHPEUR, EUGENE (Comanche)
2062N "From One of Our Comanche Boys at Oak Grove, N.J.,"
School News, 3 (March, 1883), 3. Describes his experiences as an outing student.

TALL CHIEF, EVES (Osage)
2063N "The Customs and Character of the Osages," Indian Leader,
April 20, 1900.
2064N "Life of Eves Tall Chief," Indian Leader, November 1,
1901. Autobiographical sketch.

TALLCHIEF, MARY (Seneca)
2065N "Dried Fruit and Jelly," Carlisle Arrow, October 23, 1908. Describes their uses and the drying process.

TALLCRANE, FRED (Sioux)
2066N "My Visit to the Laundry," Carlisle Arrow, February 26, 1909. Describes what goes on in the Carlisle laundry.

TARBELL, JOE F. (Mohawk)
2067M "Indian Legend," Carlisle Arrow, October 23, 1908. Concerns Tekakwith.

TAUTUK, THOMAS (Eskimo)
2068N "Chief Tautuk's Talk to Herders," Eskimo, 1 (October, 1916), 3. Gives advice concerning reindeer herding.
2069N "Reindeer Hardships in the Old Days," Eskimo, 2 (September, 1917), 2. Describes problems when the first deer were brought to Alaska.

TAYLOR, CLIFFORD (Pawnee)
2070N "The Buffalo Chase," Carlisle Arrow, March 15, 1912. Describes how the Indians enjoyed it.
2071N "Four Arbor Days," Carlisle Arrow, April 19, 1912. Concerns trees planted on campus by his class.

TEHEE, HOUSTON BENGE (Cherokee)
2072N "Pioneer President of the W.C.T.U.--Mrs. L. Jane Stapler," Tahlequah Arrow, May 31, 1902. Biographical sketch.
2073N "To the Democratic Voters of Cherokee County," Tahlequah Arrow, July 18, 1912. Announces his candidacy.
See also 1981 Biobibliography, 3807-3810.

TERRY, LIDDY (Sioux)
2074L Letter, Sina Sapa Wocekiye Taeyanpaha, April, 1894. Urges others to attend school.

THOMAS, DANIEL N. (Pima)
2075N "The Value of Trade," Sherman Bulletin, May 10, 1911.
2076N "Yesterday and To-Day with My Tribe the Pima Indians," Sherman Bulletin, May 24, 1916. Historical sketch.
2077N "Yesterday and Today with My Tribe, the Pima Indians," Chemawa American, 18 (June, 1916), 1-4. Historical sketch.
2078N "Yesterday and Today with My Tribe, the Pima Indians," Word Carrier of Santee Normal Training School, 45 (September-October, 1916), 20. Historical sketch.
See also 1981 Biobibliography, 3818-3819.

THOMAS, FRED (Eskimo)
2079N "'Wake the Old Ipanee Man,'" Eskimo, 1 (August, 1917), 7. Gives advice to reindeer herding apprentices.

THOMPSON, EMMA (Sioux)
    2080N "This Picture is About the Rooster and Puppy," Iapi Oaye,
          1 (May, 1884), 2.

THOMPSON, NOBLE A. (Pueblo)
    2081N "The Tailor Shop," Carlisle Arrow, November 27, 1908.
          Describes work going on in the Carlisle shop.

THOMPSON, WILLIAM ABBOTT (Cherokee)
    2082P "You Can Always Tell," Arrow, July 5, 1895. Political
          verse.

THORPE, JAMES F. (Sac and Fox)
    2083N "Co-fa-che-qui," Carlisle Arrow, October 23, 1908. Re-
          tells the story about De Soto's arrival at her village.

THREE STARS, CLARENCE (Pine Ridge Sioux)
    2084M "Sioux Indian Legends, The Spider and the Fat Ducks,"
          Oglala Light, 10 (March, 1909), 24-26.
See also 1981 Biobibliography, 3827-3828.

THUNDER BEAR, JULIA (Sioux)
    2085N Untitled, Oglalla Light, 1 (July 2, 1900), 4. Describes
          ducks.

THUNDER HAWK, MAGGIE (Sioux)
    2086L Letter, Sina Sapa Wocekiye Taeyanpaha, August, 1892.
          Urges others to attend school.

TIAOKASIN, JOHN (Standing Rock Sioux)
    2087A "Another Education War Path," Talks and Thoughts, 1
          (June, 1886), 2-3. Concerns education of the Indians.
    2088A "Last Temperance Meeting," Talks and Thoughts, 1 (Au-
          gust, 1886), 3. Concerns the dangers of whiskey.
See also 1981 Biobibliography, 3829.

TIBBETTS, ARTHUR T. (Sioux)
    2089N "The Indians and Their Problems," Indian Leader, October
          12, 1900. Concerns the aims and efforts of the Y.M.C.A.
    2090N "How Should Young Men Who Graduate Use Their Educa-
          tion," Word Carrier of Santee Normal Training School,
          36 (March-April, 1907), 5. Espouses Christian educa-
          tion, care of family, and helping others.

TIBBETTS, GEORGE (Chippewa)
    2091N "Football," Carlisle 1917. Carlisle, PA: U.S. Indian
          School, 1917, p. 89. Concerns football at Carlisle.

TIBBETTS, JESSE J. (Chippewa)
    2092N "The Indian and His Struggle for Civilization," Peace Pipe,
          June 20, 1913.
See also 1981 Biobibliography, 3830.

TIBBETTS, LUZENIA E. (Leech Lake Chippewa)
2093M   "The Origin of Thunder," Red Man, 15 (January, 1900),
      8. A legend.
2094M   "A Legend of the Chippewas," Red Man, 15 (January,
      1900), 8. Legend concerning Wa-na-boo-sho.

TINKER, GEORGE EDWARD (Osage)
2095N   With Curtis J. Phillips. "The Osage: A Historical Sketch,"
      Osage Magazine, 1 (November, 1909), 7-11. Concerns
      early Osage history.
2096N   With Curtis J. Phillips. "The Osage," Osage Magazine,
      1 (December, 1909), 17-27. Concerns early Osage his-
      tory.
2097N   With Curtis J. Phillips. "The Osage," Osage Magazine, 1
      (January, 1910), 13-24. Concerns history of the Os-
      ages.
2098N   With Curtis J. Phillips. "The Osage," Osage Magazine, 1
      (March, 1910), 17-28. Concerns history of the Osages.
2099N   "Shall Osage Mineral Rights Be Alotted," Osage Magazine,
      1 (February, 1910), 11-13.
2100N   "Who Gets the Oil? And Who Is Responsible for Clouded
      Land Titles?" Osage Magazine, 1 (May, 1910), 53-60.
2101N   With Curtis J. Phillips. "The Osage," Osage Magazine,
      1 (May, 1910), 63-71. Concerns history of the Osages.
2102N   With Curtis J. Phillips. "The Osage: Treaty with the
      Confederate States," Osage Magazine, 2 (June, 1910),
      29-37.
2103N   With Curtis J. Phillips. "Osage History: The Loyal Os-
      age," Osage Magazine, 2 (July-August, 1910), 31-34.
      Concerns the pro-Union Osages.

TOMEY, JOSEPHINE (Prairie Band Potawatomi)
2104N   "Religious Conditions Among the Indian People," Word
      Carrier of Santee Normal Training School, 43 (January-
      February, 1914). Concerns the Potawatomis in Kansas.

TOO-QUA-STEE (Cherokee)
See DUNCAN, DeWITT CLINTON.

TOURTILLOTTE, EDITH (Menominee)
2105N   "A Fish Story," Indian Leader, May 3, 1901. Relates a
      personal adventure in fishing.

TOWNS, IDA (Crow)
2106A   "Cheerfulness," Carlisle Arrow, November 12, 1909.

TREPANIA, CLARA (Chippewa)
2107N   "Make Every Day Count," Carlisle Arrow, June 11, 1909.
      Urges work.

TRIPP, DORA (Klamath)
2108N   "Ways of the Klamath Indians," Indian Leader, September

18, 1903). Describes the life-style of the Klamaths.
See also 1981 Biobibliography, 3847.

TROTTERCHAUD, LIZZIE D. (Chippewa)
2109A "The Old and the New," Indian News, 13 (May-June, 1911),
13-14. Encourages students to strive.

TRUCHOT, LOUISE (Shoshoni)
2110N "Class History," Sherman Bulletin, May 29, 1919. Concerns
students at Sherman Institute.

TRUDELL, LUCY (Santee Sioux)
2111F "The Vain Young Man: An Indian Story," Talks and
Thoughts, 6 (February, 1892), 1, 4.

TUBBS, LAURA (Cherokee)
2112N "Physiology," Carlisle Arrow, February 19, 1909. Concerns care of the teeth.

TUCKER, GEORGE (Cherokee)
2113L "Will Vote with Democrats," Tahlequah Arrow, August 18,
1906. Reprinted from the Tulsa Democrat.

TUNGOT, LESTER (Eskimo)
2114F "The Raven, the Fox and the Old Woman," Eskimo, 1
(July, 1917), 3. A fable.

TUPPER, HOBSON (Choctaw)
2115F "Class Prophecy," Carlisle 1917. Carlisle, PA: U.S. Indian School, 1917, 61-63. Fantasy concerning Carlisle
students.

TURNER, HATTIE (Choctaw)
2116N "Religious Life Among Our People," Word Carrier of Santee Normal Training School, 42 (November-December,
1913), 24. Concerns the Choctaws.

TURRISH, BLANCHE (Chippewa)
2117N "An Indian Festival," Indian Leader, December 10, 1909.
Describes a celebration of the hunt.

TWISS, FRANK W. (Pine Ridge Sioux)
2118L Letter, School News, 1 (March, 1881), 4. Urges others
to attend school.
See also 1981 Biobibliography, 3853.

TWOGUNS, EVELYN R. (Seneca)
2119N "What My Mother Taught Me," Talks and Thoughts, 20
(November, 1906), 3.
See also 1981 Biobibliography, 3854.

TWOGUNS, SELINA (Seneca)
2120N "New York State," Carlisle Arrow, April 2, 1909. Concerns the geography of New York.
2121F "Iniskim, or Buffalo Rock," Carlisle Arrow, June 4, 1909.
A Blackfeet story.
2122N "My Vacation," Carlisle Arrow, September 24, 1909. Concerns her work at Carlisle during the summer.
2123F "A Story of Two Indian Boys, Manteo and Manchese,
Chapter III," Carlisle Arrow, October 8, 1909. Story
concerning early white contact.
2124N "Christmas on Seneca Reservation," Carlisle Arrow, January 7, 1910. Describes activities on the Cattaraugus
Reservation.
2125N "Iroquois Burial Customs," Carlisle Arrow, March 4, 1910.
2126N "Senior Class History," Carlisle Arrow, April 8, 1910.
Concerns the goals and tribal makeup of the class.
See also 1981 Biobibliography, 3855.

TYNDALL, VICTORIA A. (Oneida)
2127F "Senior Class Prophecy," Indian News, 13 (May-June,
1911), 3-6. Fantasy concerning students at Genoa
Indian School.

TYNER, JOHN (Shawnee)
2128N "The Western Cherokees," Talks and Thoughts, 18 (January, 1905).

TYNER, RACHEL K. (Shawnee)
2129N "An Indian Game," Talks and Thoughts, 19 (December,
1905), 1. Concerns the ball game.
2130N "Gardening of Indian Women," Talks and Thoughts, 19
(April, 1906), 1.

UN-A-QUA (Menominee)
2131N "The White Elephant of the Menominees," Indian Observer,
1 (January, 1911), 1. Concerns waste and fraud in the
Menominee timber industry.
2132N "What Indians Get and What They Don't Get," Indian Observer, 1 (January, 1911), 1. Concerns the present
status of the Indians.
2133N "Notes from Riggs Institute," Peace Pipe, December 19,
1913.

UNGAROOK, ANDY (Eskimo)
2134N "Deer or Dogs," Eskimo, 2 (March, 1918), 7. Debates
which is better for pulling sleds in winter.

UPHAM, ALEXANDER B. (Crow)
2135A "His Social Life," Red Man, 13 (November-December,
1895), 6. Eulogy for Herbert Littlehawk.

2136A   Address, Red Man, 14 (January, 1897), 7. Argues that
         the reservation system makes independent citizens.
See also 1981 Biobibliography, 3856.

UPHAM, MYRTLE S. (Blackfeet)
2137N   "Valedictory," Indian News, 13 (May-June, 1911), 15-16.
         Encourages students to strive.

VALENSKI, CHAY SHERMAN (Navajo)
2138N   "About Tobacco," Carlisle Arrow, February 26, 1909.
         Argues against the use of tobacco and chewing gum.
2139N   "Some Tools the Navajo Uses," Carlisle Arrow, April 2,
         1909. Discusses the spinning wheel, hand card, press,
         and level.
2140N   "Two Roads--Heathen and Christian," Word Carrier of San-
         tee Normal Training School, 44 (March-April, 1915), 6.
         Autobiographical statement full of Christian testimonial.

VALENZUELA, THOMAS (Pima)
2141M   "The Legend of the Coyote," Indian Leader, April 12, 1912.
         Reprinted from Native American.
See also 1981 Biobibliography, 3861-3863.

VANN, CLEMENT NEELEY (Cherokee)
2142A   "Oration," Arkansas Intelligencer, July 21, 1849. Flowery
         praise of American freedom.
2143L   "For the Van Buren Press," Van Buren Press, October 7,
         1859. Recounts the case of Thomas F. Brewer, accused
         of killing a white man.
See also 1981 Biobibliography, 3864-3865.

VANN, DAVID (Cherokee)
2144L   Letter, Niles' Register, 40 (July 16, 1831), 357-358. Re-
         counts his arrest by the Georgia guards. Reprinted
         from Cherokee Phoenix.
2145N   "The Past, Present, and Future," Cherokee Advocate,
         March 2, 1852. Reprinted from Christian Advocate and
         Journal.
See also 1981 Biobibliography, 3870.

VANN, JAMES SHEPHERD (Cherokee)
2146A   "An Address, Delivered by James S. Vann, Before Chero-
         kee Lodge No. 21, A.Y.M., at Tahlequah, C. N., on
         the 24th June, 1853," Cherokee Advocate, July 13, 1853.
         Concerns Masonry and its benefits.

VEIX, BESSIE L. (Munsee)
2147N   "A Loaf of Bread," Indian Leader, June 10, 1904. Con-
         cerns baking process and food value.

2148N   "A Journey in Imagination," Indian Leader, January 12, 1900. Reminisces about life back home.

2149N   "Home-making," Indian Leader, February 23, 1906.

VEIX, CORA E. (Munsee)
2150N   "First Lesson in Cooking," Indian Leader, November 19, 1909.

VEIX, KATIE (Munsee)
2151N   "To a Water Fowl--A Paraphrase," Indian Leader, June 1, 1899.

2152N   "The Munsee Indians," Indian Leader, June 28, 1901. Concerns their history and character.

VEIX, ROSE (Munsee)
2153N   "Haskell Girl's Idea of Planning a Home for Indians," Indian Leader, 17 (December, 1913), 5-6.

VENNE, ALFRED MICHAEL (Chippewa)
2154N   "The Band to Rherersburg," Red Man and Helper, May 15, 1903. Describes experiences during a trip.

2155N   "Gymnastics at Carlisle," Arrow, December 22, 1905. Describes the program at Carlisle.

See also 1981 Biobibliography, 3872.

VENNE, ERNESTINE (Chippewa)
2156N   "Facts about the Chippewas," Carlisle Arrow, November 17, 1911. Contains a tale about marriage customs.

2157N   "History of the Class of 1912," Carlisle Arrow, April 19, 1912. Discusses what Carlisle has done for the graduates.

2158N   "My Last Outing at Carlisle," Carlisle Arrow, May 3, 1912. Concerns the outing system and her work.

See also 1981 Biobibliography, 3873.

VERIGAN, FRANCIS L. (Tlingit)
2159N   "Indian Fishermen of the North," Indian School Journal, 22 (December, 1922), 72-74. Reprinted from Southern Workman.

See also 1981 Biobibliography, 3874-3880.

VERNEY, PATRICK (Tsimshian)
2160N   "Learning the Printing Trade," Carlisle Arrow, April 16, 1909. Describes the processes at Carlisle.

WACKER, VICTOR (Alaska Native)
2161N   "Why America Should Prohibit Immigration for Five Years," Alaska Fisherman, 1 (March, 1924), 12.

WAGGONER, RAMONA (Standing Rock Sioux)
2162N   "Christmas in North Dakota," Indian Leader, December

29, 1905. Describes activities at the Standing Rock
Agency.

WAGNER, FRED (Wasco)
2163N "Building a House," Indian Leader, June 28, 1907.

WAGNER, VERA (Alaska Native)
2164N "Farming," Arrow, December 13, 1907. Concerns the
kinds of work in farming and the value of the occupation.
2165N "The Carlisle Graduate," Arrow, March 27, 1908. Praises
her education and moral training at Carlisle.
2166N "Something about Alaska," Carlisle Arrow, January 1,
1909. Discusses farming, fishing, native industry, and
basketry.

WAITE, AGNES V. (Serrano)
2167M "The Legend of the Tacquish," Carlisle Arrow, November
10, 1911. Concerns an evil spirit in the San Bernardino
Mountains.
2168N "Pueblo de Taos," Carlisle Arrow, March 22, 1912. Describes the Pueblo.
2169N "Practical Laundering," Carlisle Arrow, May 3, 1912.
Concerns the outing system.
See also 1981 Biobibliography, 3881-3883.

WALKER, BERTRAND N. O. (Wyandot)
2170P "A Wyandotte Cradle Song," Oglala Light, 12 (June, 1911),
34.
2171P "Song of the Navaho Weaver," Oglala Light, 12 (November,
1911), 39.
2172F "Old Fox Goes Fishing," American Indian Advocate, 3
(Grass Moon, 1922), 15-16. A Wyandot tale.
See also 1981 Biobibliography, 3884-3909.

WALKER, JOHN B. (Miami)
2173A "After School--What?" Indian Leader, June 29, 1906.

WALKER, JOHN GREEN (Navajo)
2174N "My People--The Navajoes," Talks and Thoughts, 12 (November, 1896), 1-2.
2175N "News from the Navajo Reservation," Talks and Thoughts,
15 (August-September, 1901), 4-5.
2176N "Navaho 'Chicken Pull,'" Talks and Thoughts, 16 (November, 1902), 1, 4. Describes the game.
See also 1981 Biobibliography, 3912-3915.

WALKER, TULIE (Navajo)
2177N "Fort Defiance," Talks and Thoughts, 17 (August-September,
1903), 1, 2-3.

WALKINGSTICK, SIMON RALPH, JR. (Cherokee)
2178N "The Pueblo and Citizenship," American Indian YMCA Bulletin, 9 (October, 1921), 1, 4. Argues that none of the charm of the Pueblos will be lost with citizenship.
See also 1981 Biobibliography, 3918-3920.

WARD, JIM (Quileute)
2179N "About the Indian," Quileute Chieftain, January 26, 1910. Argues that Indians are as capable as the white man.

WARREN, EUGENE J. (Chippewa)
2180M "Wa-na-boo-sho," Red Man, 15 (January, 1900), 8. Legend set in Minnesota.

WARRINGTON, GEORGE (Menominee)
2181A "Valedictory," Carlisle 1917. Carlisle, PA: U.S. Indian School, 1917, pp. 67, 69. Encourages students to strive.

WARRINGTON, JENNIE (Menominee)
2182N "Our Visit to the Tailor Shop," Carlisle Arrow, November 20, 1908. Describes what goes on in the Carlisle shop.
2183N "Geography," Carlisle Arrow, February 26, 1909. Concerns New England.

WASHINGTON, CHARLES (Oto)
2184N "Summer Pleasants," Talks and Thoughts, 5 (August, 1890), 4. Describes pleasures enjoyed in summer.
2185N "Thoughts on the Season," Talks and Thoughts, 4 (February, 1890), 4. Concerns life on the farm in each season.

WATERMAN, LEILA (Seneca)
2186N "My First Fourth at Carlisle," Carlisle Arrow, July 4, 1912. Describes activities there.
See also 1981 Biobibliography, 3936-3939.

WATIE, STAND (Cherokee)
2187L With John A. Bell. Letter, Arkansas Gazette, August 21, 1839. Gives an account of the Ridge-Boudinot assassinations.
2188L With John A. Bell. Letter, Arkansas Gazette, August 21, 1839. Attacks John Ross.

WATKINS, BEN (Choctaw)
2189L Letter, Oklahoma Star, September 17, 1875. Describes the valley of the Nuni Hatchi.

WATTA, VENTURA (Mission)
2190N "Advantages of Business Education," Sherman Bulletin, January 31, 1912.
See also 1981 Biobibliography, 3943.

WAWA CHAW (Luiseño)
    2191P   "The Trial of the Mission Indian," <u>Indian</u>, Unnumbered
           (January, 1922), 1, 14.
    2192P   "The Indian Cry," <u>Indian</u>, Unnumbered (February, 1922),
           9. Poem of protest.
    2193P   "The Indians' Spirits," <u>Indian</u>, Unnumbered (May, 1922),
           8.
    2194P   "The Indian Game," <u>Indian</u>, Unnumbered (August, 1922),
           1.
    2195P   "Haunted Brains," <u>Indian</u>, Unnumbered (September, 1922),
           1.

WEATHERSTONE, ROBERT (Sioux)
    2196N   "Our Visit to the Sewing Room," <u>Carlisle Arrow</u>, March
           11, 1910. Describes what goes on there.

WEAVER, HENRY (Chippewa)
    2197N   "Advanced Tailoring," <u>Peace Pipe</u>, 5 (June, 1916), 12.

WEBSTER, ISAAC N. (Oneida)
    2198N   "Oneidas of Wisconsin," <u>Talks and Thoughts</u>, 15 (March,
           1902), 1, 3-4. Concerns their condition.

WEEKS, WILLIAM H. (Gros Ventre)
    2199N   "Adobes," <u>Carlisle Arrow</u>, October 9, 1908. Describes
           processes and uses.

WELCH, GUSTAVUS (Chippewa)
    2200A   "Quitter," <u>Carlisle Arrow</u>, December 17, 1909. Criticizes
           those who quit.
    2201N   "Opportunity," <u>Carlisle Arrow</u>, April 19, 1912. Urges
           work and capitalizing on opportunities.
    2202N   "Blacksmithing," <u>Carlisle Arrow</u>, May 3, 1912. Discusses
           the trade taught at Carlisle.

WELLINGTON, JAMES (Maricopa)
    2203M   "One of the Traditions of My People," <u>Word Carrier of</u>
           <u>Santee Normal Training School</u>, 43 (September, October,
           1914), 20. Legend about the Maricopa captive among
           the Yumas and Apaches. Reprinted from <u>Indians of</u>
           <u>the Southwest</u>.

WELLS, ALFRED (Oneida)
    2204A   "Salutatory," <u>Sherman Bulletin</u>, May 29, 1919. Encourages
           students to strive.

WELLS, FLORENCE (Alaska Native)
    2205A   "That the Negro Is Superior to the Indian," <u>Red Man</u>, 12
           (January-February, 1894), 6. Argues the affirmative
           side.

WELSH, HERBERT (Standing Rock Sioux)
2206N "Old Time Education," Talks and Thoughts, 5 (January, 4). Describes how Indian youth were educated.

WEMARK, GRANT (Eskimo)
2207N "Grant Wemark's Instructions to Herders. Pinned Up in His Cabin," Eskimo, 1 (October, 1916), 5. Concerns reindeer herding.

WHEELER, JOHN CALDWELL (Cherokee)
2208L "Editorial Correspondence," Western Independent, October 9, 1873. Four letters, describing Jenny Lind, James Fork, Hartford Township, and Salem Township, Arkansas.
2209N "A Card," Western Independent, June 25, 1874. Concerns Arkansas elections.
2210N "Our Trip," Western Independent, August 28, 1875. Signed "Junior," describes Sebastian County, Arkansas.
2211L "Rosebank Nurseries, Nashville, Tennessee," Western Independent, October 11, 1876. Describes varieties of trees and shrubs available there.
2212N "A Letter from the Junior at Excelsior," Wheeler's Western Independent, May 8, 1878. Signed "Junior," describes Excelsior School at Salem, Arkansas, and backwoods Arkansas politics.

WHEELOCK, JOEL (Oneida)
2213N "A Trip to Washington," Carlisle Arrow, November 26, 1909. Describes the trip.

WHEELOCK, LEHIGH (Oneida)
2214N "My Hampton Summer," Talks and Thoughts, 4 (November, 1889), 4.
2215N "New Year's Customs at Oneida," Talks and Thoughts, 4 (February, 1890), 1.

WHEELOCK, PERCY MAE (Oneida)
2216N "Chickens on the Farm," Carlisle Arrow, May 3, 1912. Concerns how to raise them.

WHITE, HUGH (Nisenan)
2217N "Agriculture," Carlisle Arrow, December 18, 1908. Describes a field trip.

WHITE, JEFFERSON (Sioux)
2218N "Items from the Class Rooms," Oglala Light, 20 (April 15, 1920), 3. Reports classroom activities at the Oglala Boarding School.

WHITE, JOHN (Mohawk)
2219 "A Trip to Gettysburg," Arrow, May 4, 1906. Describes his trip.

2220N   "Class Pride," Arrow, March 13, 1908. Concerns what
       Carlisle will give in return for work.

2221N   "Picture Writing--Sign Language," Carlisle Arrow, Jan-
       uary 1, 1909.

2222M   "An Osage Tradition," Carlisle Arrow, February 19, 1909.
       Legend about the origin of the tribe.

See also 1981 Biobibliography, 3969-3970.

WHITE, MELVINA K. (Blackfeet)
  2223N   "The Educated Indian," Indian News, 13 (May-June, 1911),
        9-10.

WHITE, MINNIE O. (Mohawk)
  2224M   "Mohawk Legend," Carlisle Arrow, June 17, 1910. Con-
        cerns the Great Turtle.

  2225N   "Good Manners," Carlisle Arrow, April 28, 1911. Stresses
        the need for them.

See also 1981 Biobibliography, 3971.

WHITE, RALPH (Standing Rock Sioux)
  2226N   "Obstacles to Our Progress," Word Carrier of Santee
        Normal Training School, 32 (November-December, 1903),
        22. Criticizes the Sioux tendency to want to remain
        as they are.

  2227N   "The Standing Rock Indians," Word Carrier of Santee
        Normal Training School, 33 (March-April, 1904), 6.
        Describes their conditions, advantages, and needed
        improvements.

  2228N   "The Standing Rock," Talks and Thoughts, 18 (March,
        1905), 4. Concerns the legends and history of the
        Standing Rock.

  2229L   Letter, Word Carrier of Santee Normal Training School,
        34 (September-October, 1905), 17. Relates his exper-
        iences at Hampton Institute.

  2230L   "Former Pupils," Word Carrier of Santee Normal Training
        School, 35 (May-June, 1906), 11. Relates his exper-
        iences at Hampton Institute.

  2231N   "Progress of the Indian," Arrow, March 22, 1907. Re-
        printed from Talks and Thoughts,

  2232N   "Progress of the Indian," Talks and Thoughts, 20 (March,
        1907), 1, 4.

WHITE BULL, LEVI (Sioux)
  2233N   "Items from the Class Rooms," Oglala Light, 20 (February
        15, 1920), 3. Reports classroom activities at the Oglala
        Boarding School.

WHITECROW, GERTRUDE (Oklahoma Seneca)
  2234N   "Religious Conditions Among the Indian People," Word Car-
        rier of Santee Normal Training School, 43 (March-April,
        1914), 8. Concerns the Oklahoma Seneca.

WHITETREE, JESSE WILLIS (Oklahoma Seneca)
2235N "The Value of Horticulture to the Farmer," Indian School
Journal, 19 (June, 1919), 29-30. Concerns the extra
profit to be gained.

WHITTAKER, HORACE (Pima)
2236F "Rabbit's Narrow Escape," Sherman Bulletin, February
8, 1911. A tale of Rabbit and Coyote.

WILBUR, EARNEY E. (Menominee)
2237A "Industry and Independence," Red Man and Helper, February 20-27, 1903. Argues that industry leads to tribal
independence.

WILBUR, LAVINA CHRISTINA (Klikitat)
2238N "Laundering," Chemawa American, 16 (June, 1914), 4-6.
Describes the process.

WILLIAMS, JAMES P. (Ponca)
2239N "My Trip to Washington and Oklahoma," Talks and Thoughts,
14 (June, 1898), 4. Concerns the Poncas.
2240F "Inctincete and the Coyote," Talks and Thoughts, 14 (February, 1899), 4, and (March, 1899), 4. A tale.
2241N "My Trip to Washington," Talks and Thoughts, 14 (April,
1899), 1, 4.
See also 1981 Biobibliography, 3982.

WILLIAMS, NATHAN (Navajo)
2242N "The Navajo Indians," Talks and Thoughts, 14 (January,
1901), 1, 4.

WILLIAMS, SPENCER F. (Seneca)
2243N "Great Men as Life's Teachers," Arrow, March 23, 1905.
2244N "Progress of the Indian," Carlisle Arrow, June 11, 1909.
Argues that Indians should "progress" but not lose re-
lationship with nature.
See also 1981 Biobibliography, 3986-3987.

WILLIS, PERRY M. (Choctaw)
2245N "Editorial," Jones Academy Herald, 1 (June, 1903), 11.
Outlines the history of the Herald.

WILSON, ALFRETTA (Nisenan)
2246N "Infection," Sherman Bulletin, October 28, 1908.
2247N "Vaccination," Sherman Bulletin, May 26, 1909.
2248N "California's Big Trees," Sherman Bulletin, March 3, 1909.

WILSON, ETHEL (Columbia River Tribe)
2249N "Class History," Chemawa American, 15 (June, 1913), 20-
22. Concerns students at Chemawa Indian School.

WILSON, SOPHIA (Nisenan)
2250M "The Sun and the Mole," Sherman Bulletin, May 18, 1910.

WINSLETT, KIZZIE (Creek)
2251N "Woods," Creek Boys' and Girls' Monthly, December, 1870.
Concerns the beauty of the forest.

WINSLETT, NANCY JANE (Creek)
2252N "The Farmer," Creek Boys' and Girls' Monthly, December,
1870. Concerns farming as a pleasant and rewarding
occupation.

WISACOBY, JOSEPH (Menominee)
2253L Letter, School News, 1 (March, 1881), 4. Urges others
to attend school.

WOLF, FLORA A. (Crow)
2254P "Academic Class Poem," Sherman Bulletin, May 19, 1909,
supplement.

WOLFE, EDWARD (Eastern Band Cherokee)
2255N "My Race," Arrow, April 24, 1908. Argues for assimilation of the Cherokees.

WOLFE, KATHERINE E. (Eastern Band Cherokee)
2256N "My Summer Experience," Carlisle Arrow, September 24,
1909. Concerns her outing at Ocean City, New Jersey.
2257N "The Chinookan Family," Carlisle Arrow, November 19,
1909. Describes characteristics of the family.
2258N "Christmas at a Cherokee School," Carlisle Arrow, February 4, 1910. Describes activities at her home in
North Carolina.
2259N "Abraham Lincoln," Carlisle Arrow, April 1, 1910. Emphasizes the characteristics that caused him to suc-
ceed.
2260N "A Cherokee Indian Ball Game," Carlisle Arrow, May 6,
1910. Describes the game as played in 1910.
See also 1981 Biobibliography, 4005-4007.

WOOD, ISAAC (Quileute)
2261N "My Trip," Quileute Independent, February 4, 1909. Describes his personal experience.

WOODFACE, HARRY (Cheyenne River Sioux)
2262F "Sacred Bow," Talks and Thoughts, 2 (August, 1888), 1.
A tale.

WOOTHTAKEWAHBITTY, OWEN (Comanche)
2263A "Salutatory," Indian School Journal, 19 (June, 1919), 15.
Encourages students to strive.

WRIGHT, ALLEN (Choctaw)
    2264L   Letter, Oklahoma Star, November 16, 1875. Describes
               events at the Choctaw National Council.
    2265L   "A Visit to the Mansion of the Chickasaw Governor,"
               Oklahoma Star, May 23, 1876. Concerns B. F. Overton.
    See also 1981 Biobibliography, 4022-4028.

WRIGHT, DAVID (Pawnee)
    2266N   "Athletics," Indian School Journal, 19 (June, 1919), 39-40.
               Concerns the history and value of athletics.

WYLY, PERCY (Cherokee)
    2267L   "Ratify the Treaty," Tahlequah Arrow, April 27, 1901.

YELLOW BOY, ROSA (Sioux)
    2268N   "Items from Classrooms," Oglala Light, 20 (January 15,
               1920), 3. Reports classroom activities at the Oglala
               Boarding School.
    2269N   "Items from Class Rooms," Oglala Light, 20 (February 15,
               1920), 3. Reports classroom activities at the Oglala
               Boarding School.
    2270N   "Items from the Class Rooms," Oglala Light, 20 (March 1,
               1920), 3. Reports classroom activities at the Oglala
               Boarding School.

YELLOW ROBE, CHAUNCEY (Yanktonai Sioux)
    2271A   "The Menace of the Wild West Show," Word Carrier of San-
               tee Normal Training School, 44 (January-February, 1915),
               4.
    2272A   "Wild West Shows," Chemawa American, 17 (February,
               1915), 5-6. Criticizes the shows. Reprinted from
               Quarterly Journal of the Society of American Indians.
    2273N   "Booze and the Indian," Indian News, 18 (January, 1916),
               6-7. Urges temperance. Reprinted from Rapid City
               Beacon Light.
    See also 1981 Biobibliography, 4034-4041.

YELLOWBIRD, EDWARD (Yankton Sioux)
    2274L   Letter, Talks and Thoughts, 2 (May, 1887), 1. Reports
               what he saw upon his return to the reservation.
    2275L   "Education," Talks and Thoughts, 1 (August, 1886), 1.

YELLOWFISH, ADA (Comanche)
    2276F   "How a Boy Got to the Land of the Spirits," Indian Leader,
               September 2, 1910. A tale.

YELLOWFISH, BESSIE (Comanche)
    2277F   "Class Prophecy," Indian School Journal, 18 (June, 1918),
               28-32. Fantasy, concerning students at Chilocco Indian
               School.

YELLOWTAIL, ROBERT (Crow)
  2278N   "Why the Crow Indian Reservation Should Not Be Opened,"
          Sherman Bulletin, May 10, 1916. Reprinted from Red
          Man.
  See also 1981 Biobibliography, 4042-4043.

YOUNG MAN, FRANK (Sioux)
  2279L   Letter, Ogalalla Light, 1 (July 2, 1900), 4. Urges others
          to attend school.

YUDA, MONTREVILLE (Oneida)
  2280N   "How Christmas Is Celebrated in New Orleans," Carlisle
          Arrow, December 23, 1910.

YUKKATANACHE, DOCK G. (Mohave)
  2281N   "Printing," Arrow, March 30, 1906. Describes the proc-
          ess.

ZANE, OLIVE (Wyandot)
  2282N   "How to Dress in the Home," Indian Leader, June 14, 1912.

ZEIGLER, CORA (New River Tribe, i.e., Ipai)
  2283F   "Class Prophecy," Chemawa American, 16 (June, 1914),
          9-12. Fantasy concerning students at Chemawa Indian
          School.

ZITKALA-SA (Yankton Sioux)
  See BONNIN, GERTRUDE SIMMONS

PART II

A BIBLIOGRAPHY OF NATIVE AMERICAN WRITERS
KNOWN ONLY BY PEN NAMES

BLACK FOX (Cherokee)
    2284N "Reflections of an Old Indian Minstrel," <u>Indian's Friend</u>,
        22 (August, 1910), 12. Reprinted from <u>Indian Home</u>
        <u>and Farm</u>. The writer might be Robert T. Hanks (q.v.),
        who wrote under the pen name in earlier days.

CANE BREAK ORATOR (Cherokee)
    2285N "Mellowhorn Reviewed," <u>Cherokee Advocate</u>, October 15,
        1849.
    2286N "Mellowhorn Reviewed, No. 2," <u>Cherokee Advocate</u>, Octo-
        ber 22, 1849.
    2287N "Mellowhorn Reviewed, No. 3," <u>Cherokee Advocate</u>, Octo-
        ber 29, 1849.
    2288N "Mellowhorn Reviewed, No. 4," <u>Cherokee Advocate</u>, Novem-
        ber 5, 1849.
    2289N "Mellowhorn Reviewed, No. 5," <u>Cherokee Advocate</u>, Novem-
        ber 19, 1849.

CATHARINE (Mission)
    2290L "Ask Santa Claus Next Christmas Where He Lives," <u>Mis-</u>
        <u>sion Indian</u>, 1 (November 15, 1895), 5.

CHEROKEE (Cherokee)
    2291N "Our Nation and Its Origin," <u>Cherokee Advocate</u>, Feb-
        ruary 4, 1851.
    2292N "For the Cherokee Advocate," <u>Cherokee Advocate</u>, April
        8, 1851. Concerns Christianity in the New World.
    2293N "Evening Thoughts," <u>Cherokee Advocate</u>, August 19, 1851.
        Concerns moral improvement.
    2294L "For the Cherokee Advocate," <u>Cherokee Advocate</u>, Octo-
        ber 28, 1851. Concerns national finances.
    2295L Letter, <u>Cherokee Advocate</u>, April 20, 1852. Concerns the
        per capita payment.

CHEROKEE (Cherokee)
    2296N "John Howard Payne Among the Cherokees," <u>Council Fire</u>,
        3 (July 1, 1880), 106-107.

CHEROKEE (Cherokee)
    2297L "An Interesting Letter," <u>Cherokee Telephone</u>, December

17, 1891. Concerns the sale of the Cherokee Outlet.

CHEROKEE (Cherokee)
2298N "Indians Should Be Democrats," Stilwell Standard, January 3, 1902.

A CHEROKEE (Cherokee)
2299L "For the Cherokee Advocate," Cherokee Advocate, November 25, 1851. Concerns repair of Riley's Chapel.

CHICKASAW (Chickasaw)
2300L "From the Chickasaw Nation," Western Independent, October 13, 1875. Concerns whites in the Chickasaw Nation, alleged profligacy of Indians, and poverty.

CHOON-STOO-TEE (Cherokee)
2301L "Choon-stoo-tee's Letter," Arrow, June 13, 1896. Concerns citizenship.
See also 1981 Biobibliography, 4128-4140.

CHUN-CHESTEE (Cherokee)
2302L "Chunchestee Writes," Adair Ledger, June 17, 1904. Concerns education.

CHUNULOSKY (Cherokee)
2303L "Chunulosky's Letter," Cherokee Telephone, January 22,
1891.
See also 1981 Biobibliography, 4124-4127.

GOING SNAKE (Cherokee)
2304L Letter, Western Frontier Whig, January 28, 1845. Relates
affairs at a recent Cherokee Council and includes some
humor.

AN INDIAN (Cherokee)
2305P "The Indian's Farewell," Indian Advocate, 3 (November,
1848), 3. According to H. F. Buckner, the Indian is
the elder Bushyhead, who composed the poem just before he removed to the West.

JACOB FAITHFUL (Cherokee)
2306N "Two Days at the Cherokee Male Seminary," Cherokee Advocate, February 24, 1852.
2307N "Closing Exercises of the Cherokee Female Seminary,"
Cherokee Advocate, February 24, 1852.

KE-TOO-WHA (Cherokee)
2308L "Letter from the Cherokee Nation," Van Buren Press,
September 20, 1859. Recounts a trial in the Cherokee
Nation.

LOGAN (Cherokee)
    2309L "Letter from the Cherokee Nation," Van Buren Press,
            April 3, 1861. Urges the Cherokees to remain loyal to
            the United States.

MISSYSAGANGUN (Chippewa)
    2310M "Weniboshu, an Indian Legend," Indian Advocate, 7 (Oc-
            tober, 1895), 86-87. The writer is identified as a Chip-
            pewa girl. Reprinted from the Chicago Inter-Ocean.

NER-NO-HA-DA-HI (Cherokee)
    2311N "Courage," Sequoyah Memorial, July 31, 1856.
    2312N "Gambling," Sequoyah Memorial, July 31, 1856. Presents
            sentiments against gambling.

OLD SETTLER (Cherokee)
    2313L "For the Cherokee Advocate," Cherokee Advocate, July
            8, 1851. Concerns the Old Settler claims.

OO-LAW-NAH-STEE-SKY (Cherokee)
    2314L "Where Is Coo-nul-lun-sky?" Afton News, March 1, 1895.
            Concerns Cherokee politics.

PATRIOT (Cherokee)
    2315L "Letter from the Cherokee Nation," Van Buren Press,
            April 10, 1861. Praises Abraham Lincoln and criticizes
            Jefferson Davis.

ROSALIA (Mission)
    2316L "Truly a Sacred Spot," Mission Indian, 1 (November 15,
            1895), 6. Concerns the first church built by Junipero
            Serra.

ROSENDA (Mission)
    2317L "Ask Papa," Mission Indian, 1 (December 15, 1895), 5.
            Concerns parental advice.

SI-TU-A-KEE, JR. (Cherokee)
    2318P "To the Tahlequah Gals," Cherokee Advocate, November
            5, 1850.

TE-CON-EES-KEE (Cherokee)
    2319P "Suggested by the Report, in the Advocate, of the Lay-
            ing of the cornerstone of the Pocahontas Female Seminary,
            Cherokee Nation," Cherokee Advocate, May 15, 1848.
    2320P "Though Far from Thee Georgia in Exile I Roam," Chero-
            kee Advocate, July 3, 1848.

TICE-ER-LAW-DI (Cherokee)
    2321N "Beauties of Nature," Sequoyah Memorial, July 31, 1856.

TOOSTOO   (Cherokee)
   2322L   "Toostoo at the Picnic," <u>Adair Ledger</u>, July 29, 1904.
           Concerns Fourth of July celebration.
   2323L   "Too-stoo Writes," <u>Adair Ledger</u>, August 18, 1905. Con-
           cerns Democrats versus Republicans.

TSOO-LE-OH-WOH   (Cherokee)
   2324P   "A Red Man's Thoughts," <u>Cherokee Advocate</u>, May 25,
           1853. Poem suggested by the number of applicants for
           jobs as Indian superintendents or agents.
   2325P   "What an Indian Thought When He Saw the Comet," <u>Chero-</u>
           <u>kee Advocate</u>, September 28, 1853.

TUSHKA   (Choctaw)
   2326L   "For the Intelligencer," <u>Choctaw Intelligencer</u>, March 19,
           1851. Concerns the weather.

WA-CAH-AH-KE-NAH   (Cherokee)
   2327N   "The Reason Why We Are Great," <u>Sequoyah Memorial</u>,
           July 31, 1856.

WAH-LO-SU-GLAH-WAH   (Cherokee)
   2328N   "How Became the Western Continent Inhabited?" <u>Cherokee</u>
           <u>Advocate</u>, March 25, 1847. Concerns the origin of In-
           dians.

WESTERN EXILE   (Cherokee)
   2329L   California Letter from a Cherokee, <u>Cherokee Advocate</u>,
           March 2, 1879. Describes conditions there.

WHITE EAGLE   (Sioux)
   2330P   "Indian Maid Up-to-Date," <u>American Indian Advocate</u>, 6
           (Winter, 1925), 5.

WHITE HORSE   (Cherokee)
   2331L   "For the Cherokee Advocate," <u>Cherokee Advocate</u>, Novem-
           ber 10, 1880. Concerns the history of Tahlequah.
   See also 1981 Biobibliography, 4344-4362.

PART III

BIOGRAPHICAL NOTES

ADAIR, BRICE MARTIN (Cherokee)

Brice Martin Adair was born in the Eastern Cherokee Nation, the son of George Washington and Martha (Martin) Adair. He married Sarah McNair and lived in Saline District in the western Cherokee Nation. He died in 1861. Cherrie Adair Moore, "William Penn Adair," Chronicles of Oklahoma, 19 (Spring, 1951), 32, 36; Emmet Starr, History of the Cherokee Indians and Their Legends and Folk Lore (Oklahoma City: The Warden Company, 1921), 404, 406.

ADAIR, WALTER SCOTT (Cherokee)

Walter Scott Adair was born on January 28, 1791, the son of Edward and Elizabeth Adair. He was a prominent public figure in the Eastern Cherokee Nation and served on a commission appointed by Chief John Ross (q.v.) to locate the townsite of New Echota. Adair married Nancy Harris. After removal, he lived at Flint, Cherokee Nation, where he was the first postmaster in 1846. Adair died on September 26, 1854. Emmet Starr, History of the Cherokee Indians and Their Legends and Folk Lore (Oklahoma City: The Warden Company, 1921), 403-404, 474; "First Post Offices in What Is Now the State of Oklahoma," Chronicles of Oklahoma, 4 (June, 1926), 203; "Notes and Documents," Chronicles of Oklahoma, 34 (Summer, 1956), 229.

ADAIR, WILLIAM PENN (Cherokee)

William Penn Adair was born in the Cherokee Nation in Georgia on April 15, 1830, the son of George Washington and Martha Martin Adair. He was educated in the Cherokee National schools and studied law. He was a Mason, and during the Civil War he served in the Confederate army. He was twice married, to Sarah Ann Adair and to Susannah McIntosh Drew, and made his home on Grand River, east of present-day Adair, Oklahoma. A prominent public figure, he served in various capacities in the Cherokee Nation: senator, justice of the Supreme Court, delegate to Washington, and assistant principal chief. He died on October 23, 1880. Cherrie Adair Moore, "William Penn Adair," Chronicles of Oklahoma, 29 (Spring, 1951), 32-41; "Indians Weeping," Cherokee Advocate, October 27, 1880; "William Penn Adair," Chronicles of Oklahoma, 29 (Spring, 1951), 32-41.

ADAMS, JOHN F. (Siletz)

John F. Adams was a student at Carlisle Indian Industrial School in 1894.

ADAMS, JOSEPH E. (Sioux)
Joseph E. Adams was a student at the Oglala Boarding School in 1900.

ADAMS, SUSIE (Sioux)
Susie Adams was a student at the Oglala Boarding School in 1900.

AITSAN, LUCIAN BEN (Kiowa)
Lucian Ben Aitsan, the son of Mokeen, was born about 1864 and attended school on Cache Creek Indian Territory. In 1878 he entered the school at Fort Sill and then spent three years at the Carlisle Indian Industrial School. After graduation he entered the Army at Fort Sill and later served as district farmer and interpreter at the Kiowa Agency. In 1912, he was ordained. He and his wife Mabel lived at Saddle Mountain in the Kiowa Reservation, where he was pastor. Aitsan died on October 31, 1918. Indian Education, 15 (January-February, 1919), 1; Hugh D. Corwin, "Protestant Missionary Work Among the Comanches and Kiowas," Chronicles of Oklahoma, 41 (Spring, 1968), 50, 51.

ALFORD, PIERREPONT (Absentee Shawnee)
Pierrepont Alford, from Shawnee, Indian Territory, was the son of Thomas Wildcat Alford (q.v.). He was a student at Hampton Institute from 1901 through 1903. He later served as farmer at the Shawnee Agency and laborer at the Shawnee Sanitorium. Oklahoma Historical Society, Archives Division, Pawnee-Hampton Institute, July 23 and October 10, 1904; Shawnee--Employees, June 30, 1914; Shawnee --Doctors, April 30, 1925.

ALFORD, REESE (Absentee Shawnee)
Reese Alford attended Hampton Institute.

ALFORD, THOMAS WILDCAT (Absentee Shawnee)
Thomas Wildcat Alford, born about 1860 near present-day Sasakwa, Oklahoma, was the son of George Wildcat Alford and Way-lah-skse. He attended school at the Shawnee Mission School near the Sac and Fox Agency and entered Hampton Institute in 1879, graduating in 1882. From 1882 through 1884 he taught at the Potawatomi School, was a freighter in 1889, Sac and Fox Agency farmer in 1893, and clerk in 1905. Alford married Mary Grinnell. He retired from public life and wrote a traditional history of his people, published under the title of Civilization. Oklahoma Historical Society, Archives Division, Sac and Fox--Potawatomi School, December 12, 1882, and April 5, 1884; Sac and Fox--Freight and Transportation, June 4, 1889; Sac and Fox--Farmers, November 21, 1893; Shawnee--Buildings, August 11, 1905; Some Results of Hampton's Work (Hampton: The Institute Press, 1915), 8; 52 Congress, 1 Session, Senate Executive Document 31, 15; Indian-Pioneer History (Oklahoma Historical Society, Archives Division), 77: 14; Thomas Wildcat Alford, Civilization and the Story of the Absentee Shawnees as told to Florence Drake (Norman: University of Oklahoma Press, 1936).

ALFORD, WEBSTER (Absentee Shawnee)
Webster Alford, who was from Oklahoma, graduated from Haskell Institute in 1914. Indian Leader, 17 (June, 1914), 25.

ALLEN, DOROTHEA (Klamath)
Dorothea Allen was a student at Sherman Institute.

ALLMAN, PANSY (Sioux)
Pansy Allman was a student at the Oglala Boarding School in 1920.

AMAGO, SORTERO (Mission)
No information is available.

ANAKARTUK, JOHN (Eskimo)
No information is available.

ANDERSON, PHENIA (Konkow)
Phenia Anderson, from California, was born about 1893 and attended Carlisle. She later lived at Covela, California.

ANNEBUCK
See BUCK, ANNE

ANOWOLUKWUK, ANDREW G. (Eskimo)
Andrew G. Anowolukwuk lived at Kotzebue, Alaska.

ANTONIO, CALLISTRO (Mission)
Callistro Antonio was a student at the Banning Mission School in 1895.

APES, WILLIAM (Pequot)
William Apes was born near Colrain, Massachusetts, on January 31, 1798, of Pequot parents. Because of harsh treatment by his parents, he was taken and reared by whites. He ran away at an early age and joined the Army. After his military experience, he became a Methodist preacher. He became a missionary to and leader of the Cape Cod Indians, whose tribe he joined. He was their active spokesman for a number of years. Kim McQuaid, "William Apes, Pequot: An Indian Reformer in the Jackson Era," New England Quarterly, 50 (December, 1977), 605-625; Ernest Sutherland Bates, "William Apes," in Allen Johnson, ed., Dictionary of American Biography (New York: Charles Scribner's Sons, 1928), 1: 323.

APPLE, JENNIE (Sioux)
In 1900, Jennie Apple was a student at the Oglala Boarding School.

ARCASA, ALEXANDER (Colville)
Alexander Arcasa was born on the Colville Reservation in Washington about 1890. He entered Carlisle in 1906 and graduated from

that school in 1912. After graduation he went to work in the boiler shops at Altoona, Pennsylvania.

ARCHER, ADA (Cherokee)
Ada Archer was born in the Cherokee Nation on March 16, 1860, the daughter of Edwin F. and Mary (Vann) Archer. Her father was from New York, and her mother was the daughter of the well-known Cherokee official Joseph Vann. Ada Archer was educated in Cherokee public schools and Kirkwood (Missouri) Seminary, from which she graduated in 1882. She married Daniel Vincent Jones. Mrs. Jones was a school teacher in Mayes County after Oklahoma became a state in 1907. Emmet Starr, History of the Cherokee Indians and Their Legends and Folk Lore (Oklahoma City: The Warden Company, 1921), 629.

ARKEKETAH, MARY (Oto)
From Oklahoma, Mary Arkeketah graduated from Haskell Institute in 1906. She worked as assistant matron at Tomah, Wisconsin, for several years before being transferred to Stewart, Nevada. She married a man named Thompson.

ARMELL, JOSEPHINE (Winnebago)
Josephine Armell was a student at Hampton Institute in 1897.

ARMELL, LOUIS H. (Winnebago)
Louis H. Armell was a student at Hampton Institute in 1897.

ARPAN, AMELIA (Cheyenne River Sioux)
Amelia Arpan was born in 1895 and lived at Whitehorse on the Cheyenne River Reservation. She was a student at the Oahe Mission School in 1907.

ARTESHAW, MARIE (Bad River Chippewa)
Marie Arteshaw, who was from Wisconsin, attended Carlisle from 1907 to 1910.

ATKINS, LOU (Creek)
Lou Atkins was a student at Tullahassee Mission in 1870.

ATKINS, MARY (Creek)
Mary Atkins, who was from Oklahoma, was a student at Haskell Institute in 1913.

ATKINS, MINNIE (Creek)
Minnie Atkins was from the Indian Territory and attended Carlisle Indian Industrial School in 1882.

AZULE, ESTHER (Pima)
Esther Azule was from Sacaton, Arizona, and graduated from Sherman Institute in 1923.

BAGNELL, AMY T. (Rogue River, i.e., Shasta)
Amy Bagnell, from Oregon, attended the Chemawa Indian School and then spent a year in Oklahoma. She graduated from the Phoenix Indian School in 1902 and then attended Hampton Institute.

BAHR, SUSAN WAMBDISUS (Santee Sioux)
Mrs. Susan Bahr, who lived about twelve miles from the Santee Agency, graduated from the Santee Normal Training School in 1895 and was a graduate of Hampton Institute. Iapi Oaye, 49 (June–July, 1920), 23.

BAIRD, ELIZABETH J. (Oneida)
Elizabeth Baird, from Wisconsin, was a 1908 graduate of Carlisle Indian Industrial School. In 1914 she was a nurse in Philadelphia. Arrow, April 3, 1908; Red Man, 7 (December, 1914), 146.

BALDWIN, MARIE L. BOTTINEAU (Chippewa)
Marie L. Bottineau Baldwin was born about 1864, the daughter of John B. Bottineau, a Chippewa lawyer who fought for Chippewa rights. Mrs. Baldwin graduated from the Washington School of Law in 1914. She worked in the Education Division of the Indian Office while she was in school and continued there after graduation. In 1915 she was in charge of the railroad transportation department of the Indian Office and that year toured the Indian schools and reservations.

BALENTI, MICHAEL R. (Southern Cheyenne)
Michael R. Balenti was born at Darlington Agency, Indian Territory. He was the son of Mike Balenti and Cheyenne Belle. Balenti, a soldier at Fort Reno, became a tailor at the Indian school. Belle was the daughter of Charlie Rath, the founder of Dodge City, and Roadmaker, a Cheyenne woman, and served as interpreter for General Sheridan during the Stone Calf uprising of 1885. Michael Balenti graduated from Carlisle in 1909. He distinguished himself in sports, and after graduation played shortstop for the St. Louis Browns. At the close of the American League season in 1913, Balenti became assistant football coach at St. Louis University. Balenti also briefly attended Texas Agricultural and Mechanical College. Muriel H. Wright, "A Cheyenne Peace Pipe Smoked and Betrayed by Custer," Chronicles of Oklahoma 36 (Spring, 1958), 92; Oklahoma Historical Society, Archives Division, Cheyenne and Arapaho--Carlisle Indian School, May 8, 1905, and March 16, 1906; Red Man, 6 (September, 1913), 40.

BALL, JOSEPH (Klamath)
Joseph Ball was born at Fort Klamath, Oregon, in 1885. At the age of eight, he was sent to the reservation school and then attended the public schools for three or four years. After attending Carlisle for a year, Ball entered the Phoenix Indian School from which he graduated in 1903. He became a prosperous livestock farmer.

BALMER, JAMES (Chippewa)
James Balmer was a student at Haskell Institute in 1899. In 1912 he lived at Mt. Pleasant, Michigan. Indian Leader, March 1, 1912.

BALMER, WILLIAM (Chippewa)
William Balmer, who was from Minnesota, graduated from Haskell Institute and became assistant disciplinarian at the school in 1900. He was later assistant clerk at Chilocco and held positions at other schools including Pine Ridge and Crow Agency. Red Man and Helper, August 10, 1900.

BANKS, JESSIE (Crow Creek Sioux)
Jessie Banks, or Red Legs, was the daughter of George Banks. She entered Hampton Institute in 1884 at age 16. She remained until 1887 and then went to the Crow Creek government school for two years. She attended Hampton again from 1889 to 1891. 52 Congress, 1 Session, Senate Executive Document 31, 8, 32-33, 36-37.

BANKS, MARY (Mission)
Mary Banks attended the Banning Mission School.

BANKS, SARAH (Mission)
Sarah Banks attended the Banning Mission School.

BARADA, LOTTIE (Omaha)
Lottie Barada attended Haskell Institute.

BARBY, GRACE (Sioux)
Grace Barby was a student at Holy Rosary School in 1894.

BARKER, ALFRED H. (Santee Sioux)
Alfred H. Barker (or Hepan) was the son of John Barker and entered Hampton Institute in 1890 at age 20. 51 Congress, 1 Session, Senate Executive Document 31, 50-51.

BARLETT, EDITH (Bannock)
Edith Barlett, who was from Idaho, graduated from Carlisle Indian Industrial School in 1905. She married Titus Whitecrow and lived at Fort Hall, Idaho. Arrow, September 20, 1907; Red Man, 6 (January, 1914), 206.

BARNABY, JOSEPHINE E. (Omaha)
Josephine Barnaby was born in Nebraska about 1863, the daughter of William Barnaby. She entered Hampton Institute in 1884 and graduated in 1887. She attended school for nurses at New Haven, Connecticut. She then entered mission work at Standing Rock and in 1890 was placed in charge of the hospital there. She returned to the Omaha Agency where she married. She and her husband lived at Hermon, Nebraska. 52 Congress, 1 Session, Senate Executive Document 31, 8; Twenty-Two Years' Work of the Hampton Normal

and Agricultural Institute (Hampton: Normal School Press, 1891), 55-56.

BARRETT, EMMA (Yankton Sioux)
Emma Barrett graduated from Haskell Institute in 1907. She worked at Haskell and at schools in Montana and South Dakota before marrying Frank Lambert and settling down at Lake Andes, South Dakota.

BARTON, INEZ M. (Navajo)
Inez Barton was from Leupp, Arizona. She graduated from Sherman Institute in 1923.

BASKIN, EUNICE KITTO (Santee Sioux)
A graduate of Rockford College, Eunice Baskin was the daughter of Mrs. Ellen Kitto. She and her husband, Samuel Baskin (q.v.), lived at Santee, Nebraska, where she worked at the Santee Normal Training School. Red Man and Helper, December 7, 1900.

BASKIN, SAMUEL (Santee Sioux)
Samuel Baskin, the son of James Baskin, was from Santee, Nebraska. He entered Hampton Institute in 1890 at age 20 and graduated in 1895. In 1896 he attended Kimball Academy at Meriden, New Hampshire. He married Eunice Kitto (q.v.). 52 Congress, 1 Session, Senate Executive Document 31, 50-51; Talks and Thoughts, November, 1896; Red Man and Helper, December 7, 1900.

BASTIAN, JOHN (Puyallup)
John Bastian, from Washington, graduated from Carlisle in 1910, after which he followed his trade as a carpenter at Tacoma.

BATTICE, C. WALTER (Sac and Fox)
C. Walter Battice (Paminathuskuk) was born about 1863 near Topeka, Kansas. He attended the Sac and Fox school in Indian Territory before entering Hampton Institute in 1882. While he was at Hampton, he edited the student monthly Talks and Thoughts. After graduation in 1887, he returned to the Indian Territory and taught one year at the Sac and Fox school. He then entered normal school in Bridgewater, Massachusetts, graduating in 1889. Battice returned to Indian Territory and taught two more years. He then entered a partnership in a store at Econtuchka. While conducting his business as a trader, he served as secretary of the Sac and Fox Nation and as clerk at the agency. In 1896 he took business courses at Haskell Institute. In 1906-1909 and in 1912, he served as Sac and Fox delegate to Washington and in 1909 and 1910, he was agency clerk. Battice married the daughter of principal chief Mahkoshtoe. Oklahoma Historical Society, Archives Division, Sac and Fox--Sac and Fox School, July 28, 1887, and September 23, 1890; Sac and Fox--Freight and Transportation, November 1, 1890, and November 8, 1894; Sac and Fox and Shawnee--Surveys, July 23, 1891; Sac and Fox--Farmers, March 19, 1909, and August 16, 1910; Sac and Fox--Per Capita Payment,

January 30, 1906, and January 20, 1912; 52 Congress, 1 Session, Senate Executive Document 31, 19-20.

BAYHYLLE, LOUIS (Skeedee Band Pawnee)
Louis Bayhylle attended the Carlisle Indian Industrial School. In 1902 he worked at the First National Bank in Pawnee, Oklahoma. In 1916 he was Pawnee delegate to Washington and in 1923 he was a member of the Business Committee of the Skeedee Band. Oklahoma Historical Society, Archives Division, Volume Pawnee 7, February 17, 1892, p. 395; Pawnee-Federal Relations, February 28, 1916; Pawnee-- Indian Council, February 26, 1923.

BEAR, JOSEPH L. (Sioux)
Joseph L. Bear was a student at Carlisle Indian Industrial School in 1910.

BEAR, SAMSON (Santee Sioux)
Samson Bear attended the Santee Normal Training School at Santee, Nebraska, from which he graduated in 1907. In 1910, he was a printer at the Goodwell Mission in South Dakota. He later farmed at Winnebago, Nebraska. Word Carrier, 39 (March-April, 1910), 7; Iapi Oaye, 49 (June-July, 1920), 23.

BEAR, STELLA VANESSA (Arickara)
Stella V. Bear, from the Fort Berthold Reservation in North Dakota, was born about 1883. She attended Hampton Institute and then in 1903 entered Carlisle Indian Industrial School, from which she graduated in 1910. After graduation, she became field matron at the Cheyenne and Arapaho Agency at Cantonment, Oklahoma. In 1913 she was boys' matron at the Standing Rock school in North Dakota, and in 1916 she was seamstress in the boarding school at El- bowoods, North Dakota. Thirty-Fifth Annual Catalogue of the Hamp- ton Normal and Agricultural Institute (Hampton: Hampton Institute Press, 1903), 111; Red Man and Helper, August 28, 1903.

BEARSKIN, GLADYS (Wyandot)
Gladys Bearskin attended Sherman Institute at Riverside, Cal- ifornia, from which she graduated in 1915. In 1916, she lived at Pawhuska, Oklahoma. Sherman Bulletin, May 24, 1916.

BEAUDOIN, WILLIAM (Chippewa)
William Beaudoin, from Michigan, was a student at Carlisle in 1909.

BEAULIEU, C. H. (White Earth Chippewa)
The identity of this man is uncertain. Three members of the same family bore these initials: Clement H. Beaulieu and his two sons, C. H., who was later superintendent of logging at Bena, and the Reverend C. H., who later lived at Wasceca, Minnesota.

BEAULIEU, GUSTAVE H. (White Earth Chippewa)
Gustave H. Beaulieu, of the White Earth Reservation, was born

at Crow Wing, Minnesota, on June 12, 1852, the son of Clement H. Beaulieu, who founded Crow Wing. He moved to White Earth in 1869. Gustave Beaulieu was founder and editor of the White Earth Tomahawk, which he edited until his death at Barrows, Minnesota, on August 8, 1917. He married Ella Holmes. Chippeway Herald, 2 (March, 1903), 5; American Indian Magazine, 5 (April–June, 1917), 180.

BEAULIEU, PAUL H. (White Earth Chippewa)
No information is available.

BEAULIEU, T. B. H. (Leech Lake Chippewa)
No information is available.

BEAULIEU, THEODORE H. (White Earth Chippewa)
Theodore H. Beaulieu was born near Kaukauna, Wisconsin, on September 4, 1850, the son of Bazil and Mary (Saulliard) Beaulieu. He was twelve years a printer and then entered the International Marine Service between Philadelphia and Liverpool. In 1879 he entered the U.S. service in various capacities among the Chippewas and as U.S. land examiner, having charge of the land department on the White Earth Reservation, of which he was a member. In 1887 he established the first aboriginal newspaper in the Chippewa country, forming the nucleus for the Tomahawk, published at White Earth in the early years of this century. For fifteen years before his death, he was in the real estate business. He was always involved in Chippewa affairs, served on the Chippewa council, and wrote in their behalf, publishing in various newspapers. Beaulieu died on May 13, 1923. Tomahawk, April 6 and 30, 1903.

BEBEAU, GENEVIEVE (Chippewa)
Genevieve Bebeau, from Minnesota, was a student at Carlisle Indian Industrial School in 1911.

BEBEAU, MATILDA (Sioux)
Matilda Bebeau was born at St. Paul, Minnesota, on June 3, 1899. She attended public schools there before entering the Pipestone Indian School in 1910. She graduated in 1916. Peace Pipe, 5 (June, 1916), 9.

BECK, SAVANNAH (Cherokee)
In 1908, Savannah Beck was a student at Carlisle Indian Industrial School.

BECK, STACEY (Eastern Band Cherokee)
Stacey Beck was a 1910 graduate of Carlisle and after graduation held jobs at the Oto Indian Training School in Oklahoma and in the Indian school at Albuquerque. She married Alfred Hardy. Red Man, 4 (September, 1911), 41.

BELLANGER, CLEMENT (Leech Lake Chippewa)
Clement Bellanger, from Leech Lake Reservation, Minnesota, graduated from the Indian school at Genoa, Nebraska, in 1913.

BEMO, DOUGLAS (Creek)

Douglas Bemo attended Tullahassee Mission School and then taught in the Creek schools. In 1877, he was prosecuting attorney of Muskogee District. Oklahoma Historical Society, Archives Division, Creek--Tullahassee Mission, April 4, 1872, No. 36812-A; Creek--Schools, Neighborhood, January 31, 1875, No. 38161; Creek--National Council, October 30, 1877, No. 32562.

BEMO, ONIE (Creek)

Onie Bemo was a student at the Tullahassee Mission School in 1870.

BEMO, SONIA (Creek)

Sonia Bemo was a student at the Tullahassee Mission School in 1870.

BENCHLER, SARAH (Paiute)

Sarah Benchler was a student at Carlisle Indian Industrial School in 1909.

BENDER, ANNA (White Earth Chippewa)

Anna Bender attended Hampton Institute. From 1908 to 1911, she was a clerk at the Chemawa Indian School at Salem, Oregon, where she died on September 29, 1911, at age 26. She married Reuben Sanders. Thirty-Fifth Annual Catalogue of the Hampton Normal and Agricultural Institute (Hampton: Hampton Institute Press, 1903), 111; Weekly Chemawa American, October 6, 1911.

BENDER, ELIZABETH G. (Bad River Chippewa)

Elizabeth Bender was a member of the Bad River Band in Minnesota. She graduated from Hampton Institute in 1907 and did post-graduate work for a year before becoming a teacher among the Blackfeet. In 1914 she returned to Hampton to do some special work in practice teaching and then became a teacher at Carlisle, where she remained until her marriage to Henry Roe Cloud (q.v.) in 1916. She worked with Cloud at the American Indian Institute in Wichita, Kansas. In her later years, she was active in club work and in programs aimed at developing Indian leadership.

BENDER, TIFFANY (Washo)

Tiffany Bender, from Nevada, graduated from Carlisle Indian Industrial School in 1904. Red Man and Helper, February 26-March 4, 1904.

BENGE, SAMUEL HOUSTON (Cherokee)

Samuel Houston Benge was born in the Eastern Cherokee Nation on January 28, 1832, the son of Martin and Eliza Lowry Benge. During the Civil War he served in the Union army. He held public office for thirty-five years, during which time he held every national office except Supreme Judge and Principal Chief. Benge was married to Lucy Blaire and to Nancy Brewster. He died at Fort Gibson,

Oklahoma, on October 23, 1902. Purcell Register, November 7, 1902; Emmet Starr, History of the Cherokee Indians and Their Legends and Folk Lore (Oklahoma City: The Warden Company, 1921), 630; D. C. Gideon, Indian Territory (New York: The Lewis Publishing Company, 1901), 376-378.

BENOIST, ELSIE (Cheyenne River Sioux)
    Elsie Benoist, from the Cheyenne River Reservation, South Dakota, graduated from the Indian school at Genoa, Nebraska.

BENOIST, LAURA L. (Sioux)
    Laura Benoist, born in 1893, was from Sioux Falls, South Dakota. She attended the Indian schools at Flandreau, South Dakota, and Genoa, Nebraska. She entered the latter in 1904 and graduated in 1907.

BENSON, DANIEL (Alaska Native)
    Daniel Benson was a native wood-carver from Sitka.

BENT, JULIA (Cheyenne)
    Julia Bent was a student at the Carlisle Indian Industrial School in 1881.

BIG HORSE, LOUIS (Osage)
    Louis Big Horse, who was from the Indian Territory, was a student at Carlisle Indian Industrial School in 1883.

BIG JIM DRIVER, GOLIATH (Eastern Band Cherokee)
    Goliath Big Jim Driver was a student at Carlisle Indian Industrial School in 1907.

BIGWALKER, LELIA (Sac and Fox)
    Lelia Bigwalker, from Oklahoma, attended Haskell Institute, from which she graduated in 1906, and then became a teacher at the Sac and Fox school. Oklahoma Historical Society, Archives Division, Chilocco--Haskell Institute, June 29, 1904; Sac and Fox--Employees, April 11, 1912, and May 31, 1915.

BILLY, LUCINDA (Choctaw)
    Lucinda Billy, who was from Talihina, Oklahoma, graduated from Chilocco Indian Agricultural School in 1919.

BIRD, ETTA R. CRAWFORD (Sisseton Sioux)
    Etta C. Bird attended the Santee Normal Training School at Santee, Nebraska, graduating in 1895. She resided at Sisseton, South Dakota. Iapi Oaye, 49, (June-July, 1920), 23.

BIRD, LULU (Maricopa)
    In 1912, Lulu Bird was a student at the Maricopa Day School on the Salt River Reservation, Arizona.

BIRDNECKLACE, ANNIE (Sioux)
Annie Birdnecklace, from North Dakota, was born on December 1, 1894. She attended the Oahe Mission School before she entered Haskell Institute. Indian Leader, 19 (June, 1916), 4.

BISHOP, LUCIUS (Seneca)
Lucius Bishop, from New York, was a student at Hampton Institute in 1897.

BISHOP, THOMAS G. (Chimakum, i.e., Skokomish)
Thomas G. Bishop was secretary of the Society of American Indians in 1922.

BISHOP, WILLIAM C. (Cayuga)
William C. Bishop was born about 1893; he attended Carlisle, graduating in 1912.

BISSIONETTE, LEONARD (Sioux)
Leonard Bissionette was a student at the Oglala Boarding School in 1920.

BISSIONETTE, RICHARD (Sioux)
Richard Bissionette was a student at the Oglala Boarding School in 1919 and 1920.

BLACK, THOMPSON (Quileute)
No information is available.

BLACK BEAR, THOMAS (Pine Ridge Sioux)
Thomas Black Bear, an Oglala from the Pine Ridge Reservation in South Dakota, graduated from Carlisle in 1894. After graduation, he returned to South Dakota and became a farmer and stock raiser at Porcupine. In 1902 he was associated with his brother Joseph in a general store and restaurant at the same location. Red Man and Helper, April 11, 1902.

BLACK HAWK, MINNIE (Sioux)
Minnie Black Hawk attended Carlisle Indian Industrial School.

BLACK HORSE, WILLIAM (Sioux)
William Black Horse attended the Oglala Boarding School in 1900.

BLACKHAWK, JOSEPH (Winnebago)
Joseph Blackhawk, from Nebraska, was a student at Hampton Institute in 1902-1903 and at Carlisle Indian Industrial School from 1903 to 1908. Thirty-Fifth Annual Catalogue of the Hampton Normal and Agricultural Institute (Hampton: Hampton Institute Press, 1903), 112.

BLACKHOOP, BENEDICT (Standing Rock Sioux)
A native missionary, Benedict Blackhoop lived at Cannon Ball, North Dakota. Iapi Oaye, 50 (May, 1922), 18.

BLACKHOOP, FRANK (Standing Rock Sioux)
The son of Benedict Blackhoop (q.v.) of Cannon Ball, North Dakota, Frank Blackhoop attended Santee Normal Training School at Santee, Nebraska. Word Carrier, 44 (May-June, 1915), 9; 46 (March-April, 1917), 7.

BLACKWATER, EMMA (Pima)
Emma Blackwater was from Arizona. She attended Sherman Institute at Riverside, California.

BLACKWATER, JOSEPH (Pima)
Joseph Blackwater was a 1920 graduate of Sherman Institute.

BLACKWOOD, MARGARET O. (Chippewa)
Margaret Blackwood attended Carlisle.

BLAINE, JOHN C. (Sioux)
John C. Blaine was from North Dakota and graduated from the Carlisle Indian Industrial School in 1901.

BLANDIN, LENORA (Potawatomi)
Lenora Blandin was a student at Haskell Institute in 1908.

BLUEEYES, DORA (Cheyenne River Sioux)
Dora Blueeyes, who was from Cherry Creek, South Dakota, attended Oahe Mission School.

BOHANAN, SILAS D. (Choctaw)
Silas D. Bohanan was from Oklahoma and in 1915 attended Haskell Institute. He lived at Octavia, Oklahoma.

BOND, GEORGE M. (Choctaw)
George M. Bond taught school and was a judge of Tobucksy County, Choctaw Nation. Frank E. Park, aided by J. W. LeFlore, "Some of Our Choctaw Neighborhood Schools," Chronicles of Oklahoma, 4 (June, 1926), 151; A. D. Hefley, "Tobucksy County Courthouse," Chronicles of Oklahoma, 48 (Spring, 1970), 27.

BOND, THOMAS J. (Choctaw)
Thomas J. Bond was born in the Choctaw Nation in Mississippi on June 16, 1829. Because he lost his father at an early age, he attended Choctaw boarding schools and attended medical school in Kentucky at Choctaw expense. In 1854 he returned to his nation to practice medicine, one of the first of his tribe to do so. During the Civil War he served as surgeon for the First Regiment of Choctaw and Chickasaw Confederate Volunteers. After the war he was twice national treasurer, twice national superintendent of schools, and once senator from Atoka County. He married the daughter of Israel Folsom (q.v.). Bond died on March 31, 1878, at Atoka. Bernice Norman Crockett, "Health Conditions in Indian Territory 1830 to the Civil War," Chronicles of Oklahoma, 35 (Spring, 1957), 90.

BONGA, CECELIA (White Earth Chippewa)
Cecelia Bonga was born near Walker, Minnesota. She lived near Bena and attended school at Morris before entering the Pipestone Indian School at Pipestone. Peace Pipe, 5 (May, 1916), 11.

BONGA, JULIA (Chippewa)
Julia Bonga attended Haskell Institute.

BONNIN, EDNA (Sioux)
Edna Bonnin was a student at Haskell Institute in 1909.

BONNIN, GERTRUDE (Sioux)
Gertrude Simmons Bonnin, or Zitkala-Sa (Red Bird), was a Yankton, born on February 22, 1875, on the Pine Ridge Reservation in South Dakota, the daughter of John Haysting and Ellen Taté Iyohi-win Simmons. She received her early education on the reservation and then was sent to the Quaker missionary school at Wabash, Indiana. After three years there, she returned to the reservation, where she remained four years before returning to school. She graduated from Earlham College at Richmond, Indiana, and became a teacher at Carlisle. She later entered government service as a teacher in the West, where she married. She then moved to Washington, D.C., where she was involved in the activities of the Society of American Indians and in 1919 became editor of its quarterly, The American Indian Magazine. She spent the remainder of her life lecturing and otherwise working on behalf of Indian reform and other Indian causes. She died in 1938. Frederick J. Dockstader, Great North American Indians (New York: Van Nostrand Reinhold Company, 1977), 41-42.

BONSER, CLARA (Sioux)
Clara Bonser attended Carlisle Indian Industrial School.

BOSIN, JOHN (Kiowa)
John Bosin, who was from Oklahoma, attended Haskell Institute.

BOSWELL, CHRISTINE (Alaska Native)
Christine Boswell was from Cordova, Alaska, and attended Chemawa Indian School.

BOUDINOT, ELIAS (Cherokee)
Elias Boudinot was born in the Eastern Cherokee Nation about 1802, the son of Oo-watie. He studied at Cornwall, Connecticut, under the sponsorship of the Philadelphia philanthropist whose name he took. He married Harriet Gold, a Cornwall native. Upon his return to the Cherokee Nation, Boudinot became editor of the Cherokee Phoenix. After his first wife's death, he married Delight Sargeant, who cared for his children after he was assassinated on June 22, 1839, for having signed the Cherokee removal treaty at New Echota in 1835. Ralph Henry Gabriel, Elias Boudinot, Cherokee, and His America (Norman: University of Oklahoma Press, 1941), passim; David Y. Thomas, "Elias Boudinot," in Allen Johnson, ed., Dictionary

of American Biography (New York: Charles Scribner's Sons, 1929),
2:   748-749.

BOUDINOT, ELIAS CORNELIUS (Cherokee)
    Elias Cornelius Boudinot was born at New Echota in the Eastern
Cherokee Nation in 1835, the son of Elias (q.v.) and Harriet Gold
Boudinot. When his father was assassinated in 1839 for having signed
the removal treaty, his stepmother, Delight Sargeant Boudinot, took
Elias and his brothers to New England. He was educated at Manches-
ter, Vermont, and at the age of seventeen began working for an Ohio
railway company. He then went to Fayetteville, Arkansas, where he
studied law in the office of A. M. Wilson, earning admission to the
Arkansas bar in 1856. He was also admitted to the bar of the U.S.
Court for the Western District of Arkansas. He edited the Fayetteville weekly Arkansian and before the Civil War, the Little Rock True
Democrat. In 1860 he was chairman of the Arkansas Democratic State
Central Committee, and in 1861 he was secretary of the state's seces-
sion convention. During the war he served in the regiment of Cherokee volunteers under the command of his uncle Stand Watie and reached
the rank of major in the Confederate army. In 1863 he was chosen
as the Cherokee delegate to the Confederate Congress in Richmond.
After the war he strongly advocated the dissolution of the tribal governments and allotment of lands. Because of his stand on those is-
sues, he was not generally well liked in the Cherokee Nation. Although he maintained his Cherokee citizenship, he made his home in
Fort Smith, Arkansas, where he died on September 27, 1890. Boudinot wrote under the pen name "Sebastian." Edward Everett Dale,
"Letters of the Two Boudinots," Chronicles of Oklahoma, 6 (September,
1928), 328-347; Lois Elizabeth Forde, "Elias Cornelius Boudinot," Ph.D.
dissertation, Columbia University, 1951; Fort Smith Weekly New Era,
June 9, 1875; Muriel H. Wright, "Notes on Colonel Elias C. Boudinot,"
Chronicles of Oklahoma, 41 (Winter, 1963-1964), 382-407; H. F.
O'Beirne and E. S. O'Beirne, The Indian Territory (St. Louis: C.
B. Woodward Company, 1892), 115-116; David Y. Thomas, "Elias Cor-
nelius Boudinot," in Allen Johnson, ed., Dictionary of American Biography (New York: Charles Scribner's Sons, 1929), 2:   179.

BOUDINOT, FRANKLIN JOSIAH (Cherokee)
    Franklin Josiah (Frank) Boudinot was born on August 20, 1866,
the son of William Penn (q.v.) and Caroline Fields Boudinot. He
graduated from the Indian Baptist University, then from high school
in Flint, Michigan. He returned to the Cherokee Nation where he
was executive secretary to the principal chief, was placed in charge
of the Cherokee Advocate, which was edited by his father, and
served as clerk of the senate. In 1894 he entered the law school
of Michigan State University and was later admitted to the bar. In
1896 he served as attorney for the Cherokee Nation and later for the
Keetoowah Society. Boudinot made his home at Fort Gibson. He
married Anna S. Meigs. D. C. Gideon, Indian Territory (New York:
The Lewis Publishing Company, 1901), 854.

BOUDINOT, WILLIAM PENN (Cherokee)

William Penn Boudinot was born in the Eastern Cherokee Nation in 1830, the son of Elias (q.v.) and Harriet Gold Boudinot. When his father was assassinated in 1839 for having signed the removal treaty, his stepmother, Delight Sargeant Boudinot, took William and his brothers to New England. Boudinot was educated in Vermont and Connecticut. Then he learned the trade of ornamental jewelry engraving in Philadelphia. During the Civil War, he served in the Confederate forces under the command of his uncle Stand Watie (q.v.). Following the Civil War, Boudinot was a leader of the National Party, he was twice editor of the Cherokee Advocate, and he served as executive secretary to Chief Dennis Bushyhead (q.v.) and as Cherokee delegate to Washington. In the spring of 1898, Boudinot went to Kansas City to obtain treatment for a morphine habit and disappeared. That summer, it was thought that he either jumped or fell from a steamer on Lake Michigan between Chicago and Milwaukee. H. F. O'Beirne and E. S. O'Beirne, The Indian Territory (St. Louis: C. B. Woodward Company, 1892), 266-268; Tahlequah Arrow, April 30 and June 25, 1898.

BOURASSA, PETER B. (Citizen Band Potawatomi)

Peter B. Bourassa, from Oklahoma, attended Chilocco Indian Agricultural School, and in 1915 and 1916, served as a member of the Potawatomi Council and the Potawatomi Business Committee. Oklahoma Historical Society, Archives Division, Chilocco--Enrollments, January 14, 1905; Sac and Fox--Potawatomi Indians, October 29 and December 20, 1915, and August 11, 1916.

BOURASSA, SHERMAN (Prairie Band Potawatomi)

Sherman Bourassa was the son of Mrs. Mary Bourassa of Maple Hill, Kansas. He attended Chilocco Indian Agricultural School and Haskell Institute. Oklahoma Historical Society, Archives Division, Chilocco--Haskell, August 16, 1902.

BOYD, OSCAR (Blackfeet)

Oscar Boyd, from Montana, was a student at Carlisle Indian Industrial School.

BRAVE, BENJAMIN (Lower Brule Sioux)

Benjamin Brave (Ohitika), from the Lower Brule Reservation, was born about 1865, the son of Long Feather. He was taken in by the Rev. Luke C. Walker, a missionary. In 1881 he was sent to Hampton Institute. He returned to the Lower Brule as a teacher and lay reader. Then he worked at the Rosebud and other agencies. He was associated with several missionaries and traveled, giving lectures. In 1897 he went on an extended lecture tour of the North. In 1918, he was head of the tribal council and in 1920 was postmaster at the Lower Brule agency. Brave married Ida Rencontre. 52 Congress, 1 Session, Senate Executive Document 31, 18, 40-41; "Ben Brave," Red Man, 13 (June, 1895), 7-8; Tomahawk, May 24, 1917; American Indian Magazine, 4 (October-December, 1916), 351-352;

Marion E. Gridley, Indians of Today (Chicago: The Lakeside Press, 1936), 21-22.

BREAST, SILA (Sioux)
    Silas Breast was a student at the Oglala Boarding School in 1900.

BREWER, ELLA L. (Puyallup)
    Ella L. Brewer graduated from the Chemawa Indian School in Oregon.

BREWER, OLIVER P. (Cherokee)
    Oliver P. Brewer was a well-known figure in the Cherokee Nation, having served as Cherokee Senator. He was appointed principal chief of the Cherokees by the president and served only one day, May 26, 1931. Gaston L. Litton, "The Principal Chiefs of the Cherokee Nation," Chronicles of Oklahoma, 15 (September, 1937), 270.

BRINGSTHEARROW, JULIA (Sioux)
    Julia Bringsthearrow was born about 1895 and attended Oahe Mission School in South Dakota.

BROKER, CLAUDIA G. (Chippewa)
    Claudia Broker was a student at Hampton Institute in 1918.

BROKER, JOSEPH HENRY (Chippewa)
    In 1912, Joseph Henry Broker was a student at Carlisle Indian Industrial School.

BROOKS, CHARLES LONEDOG (Sioux)
    Charles Lonedog Brooks graduated from Santee Normal Training School in 1907. He then graduated from Haskell Institute and entered Indian Service, holding several positions. In 1922, he lived at Pine Ridge, South Dakota. Word Carrier, 39 (March-April, 1910), 7, and 51 (September-December, 1922), 20; Iapi Oaye, 49 (June-July, 1920), 23.

BROOKS, EMILY (Seneca)
    Emily Brooks attended Hampton Institute at Hampton, Virginia, in 1895 and the next year attended high school at Pittsfield, Massachusetts. Talks and Thoughts, November, 1896.

BROWN, CATHARINE (Cherokee)
    Catharine Brown was educated at the Brainerd Mission between 1817 and 1821, when she became a teacher at Creek Path, Cherokee Nation. She died on July 18, 1823. Her life was later popularized in Rufus Anderson's Memoir of Catharine Brown, A Christian Indian of the Cherokee Nation. Missionary Herald, 17 (February, 1821), 46; 19 (October, 1823), 336.

BROWN, DAVID (Cherokee)
    David Brown was educated at Brainerd Mission and the Foreign

Mission School at Cornwall, Connecticut. He married Rachel Lowrey, the daughter of George Lowrey (q.v.). Missionary Herald, 17 (February, 1821), 44; Emmet Starr, History of the Cherokee Indians and Their Legends and Folk Lore (Oklahoma City: The Warden Company, 1921), 367.

BROWN, FANNIE (Little Lakes, i.e., Pomo)
Fannie Brown, from California, graduated from the domestic science department at Haskell Institute in 1914. Indian Leader, 17 (June, 1914), 25.

BROWN, INEZ (Sioux)
Inez Brown graduated from the Carlisle Indian Industrial School in 1910. In 1912 and 1913 she served in the Indian Service at the Jicarilla Apache Agency and at Fort Totten, North Dakota. Red Man, 5 (September, 1912), 42; (February, 1913), 264.

BROWN, IRENE M. (Sioux)
Irene M. Brown was a 1909 graduate of Carlisle. She was a teacher at Pine Point, Minnesota, and later a general merchant at the Sisseton Agency.

BROWN, THOMAS (Yankton Sioux)
Thomas Brown was born on March 6, 1901, at Granite Falls, Minnesota. He attended public schools before entering the Pipestone Indian School, from which he graduated in 1916. Peace Pipe, 5 (June, 1916), 9.

BRUCE, HAROLD E. (Winnebago)
Harold E. Bruce was educated in public schools in Washington, D.C., and at Carlisle Indian Industrial School, from which he graduated in 1913. He entered the Indian Service and worked as a stenographer and clerk for several years. He also served as superintendent of the Potawatomi Agency at Mayetta, Kansas. Marion E. Gridley, Indians of Today (Chicago: The Lakeside Press, 1936), 24.

BRUNETTE, CECILIA (Menominee)
Cecilia Brunette was born in 1897 on the Menominee Reservation in Wisconsin, the daughter of Mrs. Mary Ann Brunette. She attended Haskell Institute, graduating from the business department in 1919. She worked in government service as assistant clerk at the Indian schools at Chemawa, Oregon, and White River, Arizona. At the latter place in 1922, she married Arthur K. Knoop.

BRUNETTE, FRANCES (White Earth Chippewa)
Frances Brunette was born in White Earth, Minnesota, on November 9, 1900. She entered the Pipestone Indian School in 1914.

BRUNETTE, JOSEPH M. (Menominee)
Joseph M. Brunette, from Wisconsin, attended Haskell Institute at Lawrence, Kansas, in 1913.

BRUSHEL, SAMUEL J. (Stockbridge)
Samuel J. Brushel, from Wisconsin, was a 1903 graduate of the Carlisle Indian Industrial School. Red Man and Helper, February 20-27, 1907.

BRUYIER, JOHN (Crow Creek Sioux)
John Bruyier, born about 1866, attended Hampton Institute at Hampton, Virginia, from 1886 to 1890, when he graduated. He then entered college preparatory study at Meriden, New Hampshire. 52 Congress, 1 Session, Senate Executive Document 31, 27, 46-47; Twenty-Two Years' Work of the Hampton Normal and Agricultural Institute (Hampton: Normal School Press, 1891), 56.

BRYANT, MICHAEL (Yuma)
Michael Bryant attended Sherman Institute at Riverside, California, from which he graduated in 1913.

BUCK, ANNE (Eskimo)
Anne Buck was from Deering, Alaska. She attended Carlisle Indian Industrial School from 1900 to August, 1906. In 1911, she was employed at Sherman Institute at Riverside, California, and in 1914 lived in Los Angeles, where she was known as Aneva Buck. Carlisle Arrow, December 15, 1911; Red Man, 6 (February, 1914), 240.

BUFFINGTON, THOMAS MITCHELL (Cherokee)
Thomas Mitchell Buffington was born in Going Snake District, Cherokee Nation, on October 19, 1855. He attended tribal schools and began farming, settling in 1887 in the Delaware District. In 1889 he became judge of the district and in 1891 its senator. As president of the Senate, he served briefly as principal chief when Joel Bryan Mayes died in office in 1891. Buffington also served as mayor of Vinita and was elected principal chief of the Cherokees in 1899. John Bartlett Meserve, "Chief Thomas Mitchell Buffington and Chief William Charles Rogers," Chronicles of Oklahoma, 17 (June, 1939), 135-140.

BULL BEAR, JOCK (Northern Arapaho)
Jock Bull Bear attended the Indian school at Genoa, Nebraska, before he entered Carlisle Indian Industrial School, which he attended for three years. After he returned to the reservation, he worked at the agency as a scout, farmer, carpenter, and policeman. Red Man, 10 (June, 1890), 3.

BULLEATER, ALBERT (Rosebud Sioux)
Albert Bulleater attended the Santee Normal Training School at Santee, Nebraska.

BULLIS, Lon S. (San Carlos Apache)
Born in 1882, Lon S. Bullis, or Dajida, was the son of Chief Chequito. He went to East Fork Mission on the San Carlos Reservation

in 1923 and worked as an interpreter. He died at Phoenix on July
11, 1924. Apache Scout, 2 (August, 1924), 8, and 8 (April, 1930),
7; Apache Lutheran, 58 (December, 1980), 5.

BURNEY, BENJAMIN CROOKS (Chickasaw)
Benjamin Crooks Burney was born at Shreveport, Louisiana,
during his parents' journey from Mississippi to the western Chickasaw country. They settled near present-day Burneyville, Love County,
Oklahoma, but died when Burney was quite young. Thus he was
educated at the Chickasaw Orphans School at Tishomingo. During
the Civil War he served as a private in Shocoe's Chickasaw Battalion
of Mounted Volunteers (Confederate), and after the war settled down
to farming and stock raising in present-day Marshall County, Oklahoma. He served one term as national treasurer and one as governor,
elected in 1878. After his governorship, he went back to farming.
He died on November 25, 1892. John Bartlett Meserve, "Governor
Benjamin Franklin Overton and Governor Benjamin Crooks Burney,"
Chronicles of Oklahoma, 16 (June, 1938), 221-223.

BURNS, MICHAEL (San Carlos Apache)
Michael Burns entered Carlisle Indian Industrial School in 1880
and remained until 1882. In 1885 he served as a scout for the U.S.
Army against Geronimo's Apaches. He then returned to the San
Carlos Reservation where he worked as a commissary clerk at the
agency. Red Man, 8 (July-August, 1888), 8 and 10 (June, 1890),
3; Red Man, 4 (June, 1912), 485-486.

BURSON, RACHEL (Ute)
Rachael Burson attended Haskell Institute at Lawrence, Kansas.

BUSCH, ELMER (Pomo)
Born in California in 1890, Elmer Busch graduated from Carlisle Indian Industrial School in 1913. Carlisle Arrow, December 20,
1912.

BUSHOTTER, GEORGE (Yankton Sioux)
George Bushotter, born in 1864, was from the Yankton Reser-
vation. Bushotter (his Indian name was Oterhê) entered Hampton
Institute in 1878 and remained until 1881. After teaching a year at
the government school on the Lower Brule Reservation, he reentered
Hampton in 1882 and remained until 1885. After studying at Alex-
andria, Virginia, in the Theological Seminary there, he assisted the
Bureau of American Ethnology in collecting Teton Sioux materials.
He married Evalina Hull and lived on her farm at Hedgeville, West
Virginia, where he died on February 2, 1892. Raymond J. DeMallis,
"George Bushotter: The First Lakota Ethnographer," in Margot Lib-
erty, ed., American Indian Intellectuals (St. Paul: West Publishing
Co., 1978), 91-102; 52 Congress, 1 Session, Senate Executive Docu-
ment 31, 13, 38-39, 42-43; S. C. Armstrong, The Indian Question
(Hampton: Normal School Steam Press, 1883), 29.

BUSHYHEAD, DENNIS WOLFE (Cherokee)

Dennis Wolfe Bushyhead was born near present-day Cleveland, Tennessee, on March 18, 1826, son of the Reverend Jesse and Elizabeth Wilkinson Bushyhead. He attended mission schools in the eastern and western Cherokee Nations. From 1841 through 1844 he attended school at Lawrenceville, New Jersey, and was enrolled briefly at Princeton before returning to the Indian Territory, where he was a clerk in a merchantile establishment. In 1847 he became clerk of the Cherokee National Committee. In 1849 he went to the gold fields of California and did not return to the Cherokee Nation until 1868. In 1871, he became national treasurer, and from 1879 through 1887 he served as principal chief. Bushyhead was married to Elizabeth Alabama Schrimscher Adair. He died on February 4, 1898. H. Craig Miner, "Dennis Bushyhead," in R. David Edmunds, ed., American Indian Leaders: Studies in Diversity (Lincoln: University of Nebraska Press, 1920), 192-205; Harold Keith, "Problems of a Cherokee Principal Chief," Chronicles of Oklahoma, 17 (September, 1939), 296-308; John Bartlett Meserve, "Chief Dennis Wolfe Bushyhead," Chronicles of Oklahoma, 14 (September, 1936), 349-359; H. F. O'Beirne and E. S. O'Beirne, The Indian Territory (St. Louis: C. B. Woodward Company, 1892), 117-120.

BUTLER, BESSIE (Stockbridge)

Bessie Butler was a student at Haskell Institute in 1901.

BUTLER, CHARLES W. (Cattaraugus Seneca)

Charles W. Butler, who was from the Cattaraugus Reservation in New York, attended Lincoln University in 1897-1898. In the latter year he entered the Navy. In 1903 he lived eight miles southwest of Buffalo, New York.

BYANUABA, ELENA (Pueblo)

Elena Byanuaba was born at Galisto, New Mexico and attended Haskell Institute. She married S. B. Lincoln and taught at the Fort Defiance School in Arizona.

CABRILLAS, MARIANA (Mission)

Mariana Cabrillas was a student at St. Anthony's Industrial School, San Diego, in 1895.

CAJUNE, FRANK (Chippewa)

Frank Cajune was from the White Earth Reservation. He attended Carlisle and then worked as a day laborer and lived at Mahnomen, Minnesota. In 1907 he was elected justice of the peace and for several years after 1908 he was a deputy sheriff. He was defeated in the election for sheriff in 1910. Cajune also served as clerk of the local school board and as a delegate to the general council of Minnesota Chippewas. In 1922 he became subagent for the White Earth Chippewas at Bena.

CALAC, JOSEPH (Mission)

Joseph Calac was a student at Sherman Institute in 1914.

CALLSEN, MINNIE J. (Alaska Native)
    From Sitka, Alaska, Minnie J. Callsen graduated from Carlisle Indian Industrial School in 1903. Red Man and Helper, February 20-27, 1903.

CAMPBELL, IRENE (Santee Sioux)
    Mrs. Irene Campbell Beaulieu was born in 1888 on the Santee Reservation. In 1916 she lived at Pawhuska, Oklahoma, and wrote under the name of Wenonah.

CAMPBELL, JAMES (Sioux)
    James Campbell attended Carlisle Indian Industrial School in 1909.

CANUP, WILLIAM T. (Eastern Band Cherokee)
    William T. Canup was born on February 17, 1866, in Cherokee County, North Carolina. Of Cherokee descent, Canup migrated to the Indian Territory, where he worked for The Telephone at Tahlequah, Cherokee Nation, and was special correspondent for a number of newspapers in Texas, Ohio, New York, Kansas, and Georgia. In 1890 and 1891 he was owner of the Indian Sentinel at Webbers Falls and Tahlequah. H. F. O'Beirne and E. S. O'Beirne, The Indian Territory (St. Louis: C. B. Woodward Company, 1892), 430.

CARDIN, FRED WILLIAM (Quapaw)
    Fred William Cardin (or Pejawa) from Oklahoma, attended St. Mary's School on the Quapaw lands in Oklahoma and Carlisle Indian Industrial School. In 1914-1915 he studied at Dana Musical Institute, Warren, Ohio. After serving in World War I, he became a composer and an authority in music. He served as instructor of music at the University of Nebraska and studied at the Curtis School of Music in Philadelphia. In 1926, he received a scholarship to study at the Conservatoire Americaine. He was a conductor and director of music at Reading High School, Reading, Pennsylvania, from 1930 to 1957. Velma Nieberding, "St. Mary's of the Quapaws, 1894-1927," Chronicles of Oklahoma, 31 (Spring, 1953), 12; Red Man, 6 (January, 1914), 204, and 7 (February, 1915), 218; Marion E. Gridley, Indians of Today (Chicago: Towertown Press, 1960), 57-58.

CARLOW, ANNA (Sioux)
    Anna Carlow was a student at Haskell Institute, Lawrence, Kansas, in 1908.

CARPENTER, LINDA L. (Chippewa)
    Linda Carpenter graduated from the Pipestone Indian School at Pipestone, Minnesota.

CARR, VIOLA (Navajo)
    Viola Carr graduated from Sherman Institute in 1921.

CARTER, BENJAMIN WINSOR (Cherokee)
    Benjamin Winsor Carter was born on January 5, 1837, in the

Cherokee Nation, the son of David and Jennie Riley Carter. David
Carter was justice and chief justice of the Cherokee Supreme Court
and edited The Cherokee Advocate. Benjamin graduated from the
Cherokee Male Seminary in 1856. He served in the First Cherokee
Regiment during the Civil War. In 1886, he married Serena Josephine
Guy, sister of Governor William M. Guy of the Chickasaws. In 1882
he took charge of the Chickasaw Manual Labor Academy and served
over three years. He held serveral public offices in the Chickasaw
Nation. Emmet Starr, History of the Cherokee Indians and Their
Legends and Folk Lore (Oklahoma City: The Warden Company, 1921),
402, 474, 666; Carolyn Thomas Foreman, "Chickasaw Manual Labor
Academy," Chronicles of Oklahoma, 23 (Winter, 1945-1946), 354; D.
C. Gideon, Indian Territory (New York: The Lewis Publishing Company, 1901), 417; H. F. O'Beirne, Leaders and Leading Men of the
Indian Territory (Chicago: American Publishers' Association, 1891),
249.

CARTER, CALEB W. (Nez Percé)
    Caleb Carter was born about 1887. He attended Haskell Insti-
tute before going to Carlisle, from which he graduated in 1912. After graduation he worked briefly at the Kickapoo Agency at Horton,
Kansas, returning to his home in Kamiah, Idaho, in early 1913. He
married Mary Amera. Red Man, 6 (September, 1913), 41-42.

CARY, NELLIE (Apache)
    Nellie Cary was a student at the Carlisle Indian Industrial
School in 1881. Eadle Keatah Toh, 1 (April, 1881), 4.

CASH, A. WARREN (Sioux)
    In 1922 A. Warren Cash was High Chief of the Minneapolis
Council and Great Sentinel of the American Indian Association.

CASTRO, FELICITA (Mission)
    Felicita Castro was a student at St. Anthony's Industrial School,
San Diego, in 1895.

CASTRO, MARIE AGNES (Klamath)
    Marie Agnes Castro was a senior at Sherman Institute in 1911.

CASWELL, BENJAMIN (Chippewa)
    Benjamin Caswell, from Minnesota, entered Carlisle in 1889 and
graduated valedictorian of his class in 1892. He was sent into the
Indian Service as a teacher at Fort Belknap, Montana. In 1902 he
was superintendent of the Cass Lake Indian School, at which post
he remained for a number of years. In 1916 he sought but failed
to be appointed superintendent of one of the Minnesota reservations
under an amendment to an appropriations bill giving Indians preference
in such jobs. In 1919 he was a leader of a group who opposed the
duly elected officials of the Minnesota Chippewas and tried to establish a separate council. Caswell married Leila Cornelius (q.v.), an
Oneida. Red Man and Helper, February 20-27, 1903.

CAYOU, FRANK (Omaha)
Frank Cayou graduated from Carlisle Indian Industrial School in 1896 and taught athletics at Washington University in St. Louis. He later attended Illinois State University. He then worked for the Spalding Sporting Company of Chicago. Red Man, 13 (March, 1896), 1; Red Man and Helper, June 27, 1902.

CEDARTREE, CLARA (Southern Arapaho)
Clara Cedartree attended Haskell Institute.

CEERLEY, ELIZABETH (Navajo)
Elizabeth Ceerley attended school at Fort Defiance and Ganado, Arizona, before entering the Charles H. Cook Bible School at Phoenix, where she was a student in 1917.

CENTER, NANCY (Sioux)
Nancy Center was a student at the Oglala Boarding School in 1920.

CETAN SAPA (Sioux)
Publishers identified Cetan Sapa as a Sioux. This may have been Cetan Sapa from the Fort Berthold Reservation. He attended Hampton Institute during the 1880's and could read and write in Dakota.

CHAPMAN, ARTHUR (White Earth Chippewa)
No information is available.

CHARGING EAGLE, AGNES (Standing Rock Sioux)
Agnes Charging Eagle attended the Standing Rock Agricultural Boarding School.

CHARGING WOLF, LIZZIE (Pine Ridge Sioux)
Lizzie Charging Wolf, or Wacinwapi, attended Hampton Institute in 1902 and 1903. Thirty-Fifth Annual Catalogue of the Hampton Normal and Agricultural Institute (Hampton: Hampton Institute Press, 1903), 111.

CHARLES, JOSEPHINE S. (Oneida)
Josephine Charles was from Wisconsin. She entered Carlisle Indian Industrial School in 1897 and graduated in 1908. In 1912 she was employed in the Indian Service at Hoopa, California. Arrow, April 3, 1908; Red Man, 5 (October, 1912), 86.

CHARLES, REUBEN (Tonawanda Seneca)
Reuben Charles was from the Tonawanda Reservation and attended the Carlisle Indian Industrial School.

CHARLEY, BESSIE M. (Peoria)
Bessie Charley was from Oklahoma and attended Carlisle Indian Industrial School in 1907 and 1908.

CHARLEY, FANNIE (Peoria)
Fannie Charley attended Carlisle Indian Industrial School. Carlisle Arrow, December 8, 1911.

CHECOTE, SAMUEL (Creek)
Samuel Checote was born on the Chattahooche River in Alabama in 1819, a full-blood Creek of the McIntosh faction. At the age of nine he entered Asbury Manual Labor School near Fort Mitchell, Alabama. After removal to the West, Checote was a Methodist preacher, often persecuted by the traditional Creeks for his religious work. During the Civil War he reached the rank of lieutenant in the Confederate army. In 1867 he was elected principal chief and was reelected in 1871. He was elected to a third term in 1879. Checote died on September 3, 1884. John Bartlett Meserve, "Chief Samuel Checote, With Sketches of Chiefs Locher Harjo and Ward Coachman," Chronicles of Oklahoma, 16 (September, 1938), 401-409; O. A. Lambert, "Historical Sketch of Colonel Samuel Checote, Once Chief of the Creek Nation," Chronicles of Oklahoma, 4 (September, 1926), 275-280.

CHICO, ANTONIO (Papago)
Antonio Chico graduated from Sherman Institute in 1919.

CHIEF, ANNIE (Sioux)
Annie Chief was a student at the Oglala Boarding School in 1900.

CHIEF EAGLE, ALBERT (Pine Ridge Sioux)
In 1919 Albert Chief Eagle, from Pine Ridge, South Dakota, was a student at the Genoa Indian School, Genoa, Nebraska.

CHILDERS, CLARENCE (Creek)
From Broken Arrow, Oklahoma, Clarence Childers was an engineering student at the Chilocco Indian Agricultural School at Chilocco, Oklahoma, from which he graduated in 1918.

CHILDS, CHRISTINE (Crow)
Christine Childs was from Montana and graduated from Carlisle Indian Industrial School in 1906. Arrow, March 30, 1906.

CHILSON, DANIEL O. (Citizen Band Potawatomi)
Daniel O. Chilson lived at Shawneetown, Indian Territory. He entered Hampton Institute in 1885 and graduated in 1889. He married Madeline Tapaw. Chilson taught for several years at the Absentee Shawnee School, worked at the Sac and Fox Agency, and was clerk in a store. 52 Congress, 1 Session, Senate Executive Document 31, 25, 44-45; Oklahoma Historical Society, Archives Division, Sac and Fox Volume 16, 310, Volume 15, 148, and Volume 20, 79; Sac and Fox--Employees, September 30, 1889.

CHIMAL, ETTA (Mescalero Apache)
Etta Chimal was a student at Hampton Institute in 1902-1903.

Thirty-Fifth Annual Catalogue of the Hampton Normal and Agricultural Institute (Hampton: Hampton Institute Press, 1903), 111.

CHINGWA, LOUIS F. (Chippewa)
Louis Chingwa, from Michigan, was a 1908 graduate of the Carlisle Indian Industrial School. He then went to work at the Indian School at Mt. Pleasant, Michigan. Arrow, April 3, 1908; Indian Craftsman, 1 (April, 1909), 53.

CHOOROMI, JOHN (Hopi)
John Chooromi attended the Phoenix Indian School and then went to Hampton Institute. Thirty-Fifth Annual Catalogue of the Hampton Normal and Agricultural Institute (Hampton: Hampton Institute Press, 1903), 111.

CLAIRMONT, PHILIP (Sioux)
Philip Clairmont was a student at Carlisle Indian Industrial School in 1908.

CLANCY, ALLAN (Sioux)
No information is available.

CLARK, HOMER (Crow Creek Sioux)
The son of Killed Dead, Homer Clark entered Hampton Institute in 1888 at the age of 19. He remained until 1890, after which he was a catechist in the Episcopal church. 52 Congress, 1 Session, Senate Executive Document 31, 29, 48-49.

CLARKE, MALCOLM W. (Piegan)
Malcolm Clarke was from the Blackfeet Reservation in Montana. After graduation from Carlisle in 1893, he graduated from the normal school at Valparaiso, Indiana. He worked for a number of years as a clerk in the Indian Service but gave up the service and made his home in Midvale, Montana, where he ranched and took a leading part in the councils of his people. Indian Craftsman, 1 (April, 1909), 53.

CLEMENTE, JOHN C. (Mission)
John C. Clemente was a student at the Banning Mission School in 1895.

CLEVELAND, MARCHELL (Mission)
Marchell Cleveland was a native of Somerton, California.

CLIFFORD, JOHN (Pine Ridge Sioux)
John Clifford was a student at Hampton Institute, Hampton, Virginia, 1902-1904. Thirty-Fifth Annual Catalogue of the Hampton Normal and Agricultural Institute (Hampton: Hampton Institute Press, 1903), 111.

CLIFFORD, MARY (Sioux)
Mary Clifford attended the Santee Normal Training School.

CLOUD, BENEDICT D. (Sioux)
Benedict D. Cloud graduated from Carlisle in 1912. After graduation, he lived for a number of years at Bismarck, North Dakota, where he continued his education. In 1917 he was a sergeant-major in the North Dakota State Militia.

CLOUD, ELIZABETH (Bad River Chippewa)
See BENDER, ELIZABETH

CLOUD, HENRY C. ROE (Winnebago)
Henry Cloud was born in Thurston County, Nebraska, on December 28, 1884, of Winnebago parents, Nah'ilayhunkay and Hard-to-see. He attended the Genoa Indian School, the Santee Mission School, and Dwight Moody's Academy at Mount Hermon, Massachusetts. He was befriended by the Rev. and Mrs. Walter C. Roe, long-time missionaries to the Indians, who urged him to attend Yale, from which he graduated in 1910, the first Indian to earn a bachelor of arts degree from the institution. He later studied at Oberlin and Auburn Theological Seminary and earned a master of arts degree from Yale. Because of his gratitude to the Roes, he added their name to his. A Presbyterian clergyman, Cloud founded the American Indian Institute at Wichita, Kansas, where he remained for a number of years. He held several advisory posts in the government, and he became superintendent at Haskell Institute and made a reputation as a reform administrator. In 1936 he became supervisor of Indian education and in the 1940's supervisor of the Umatilla Agency. He married Elizabeth A. Bender (q.v.), a Chippewa. Cloud died on February 9, 1950. Marion E. Gridley, Indians of Today (Chicago: The Lakeside Press, 1936), 33; Stuart Levine, "Henry Roe Cloud," in John A. Garraty and Edward T. Jones, eds., Dictionary of American Biography: Supplement Four (New York: Charles Scribner's Sons, 1974), 165-166.

COACHMAN, WARD (Creek)
Ward Coachman (Co-cha-my) was born in Wetumpka, Alabama, in the Creek lands in 1823. His parents died when he was young, and he was reared by his uncle Lachlan Durant of Macon County, Georgia, where he received a limited education in the neighborhood schools. He moved to the West almost a decade after the tribe, returning to Alabama in 1848 to guide to the West a group of Creeks that had been held in slavery by the whites. Coachman was an interpreter and a farmer. During the Civil War he fought with the Confederate regiment of Chilly McIntosh. He held several public offices: clerk of Deep Fork District, member and speaker of the House of Warriors, clerk of Wewoka District, member and president of the House of Kings, delegate to Washington, and principal chief (1876). He was married to Lizzie Carr and Lizzie Yohler. He died on March 13, 1900. John Barlett Meserve, "Chief Samuel Checote, with Sketches of Chiefs Lochar Harjo and Ward Coachman," Chronicles of Oklahoma, 16 (December, 1938), 401-409; H. F. O'Beirne and E. S. O'Beirne, The Indian Territory (St. Louis: C. B. Woodward Company, 1892), 341-342.

COLBERT, GEORGE (Chickasaw)
It is uncertain which Colbert this is, but he is probably the George Colbert who was Probate and County Judge of Pontotoc County, Chickasaw Nation, in 1902.

COLBERT, HUMPHREY (Chickasaw)
Humphrey Colbert was born in the Choctaw Nation in 1842, the son of Daugherty (Winchester) Colbert, a well-known Chickasaw leader. During the Civil War he served in the Chickasaw Confederate battalion under Colonel Lem Reynolds. After the war he served terms as sheriff and judge of Pontotoc County, three terms as a member of the Chickasaw House of Representatives, interpreter in the House, and county and district clerk. Colbert was married to Elmira Parker and Selina Hamilton. He made his home near Frisco, Oklahoma. H. F. O'Beirne, Leaders and Leading Men of the Indian Territory (Chicago: American Publishers' Association, 1891), 250.

COLE, COLEMAN (Choctaw)
Coleman Cole was born about 1800 in present-day Yalobusha County, Mississippi, the son of Robert Cole, a half-blood Chickasaw and Sallie, a Choctaw. He was sent to school in Georgetown, Kentucky. In 1845, Cole moved to the West, settling in the Kiamichi Mountains in the Choctaw Nation. He was elected to the Choctaw National Council from Cedar County in 1850, 1855, 1871, and 1873. He was elected principal chief in 1874 and 1876. Cole made his living by raising livestock. He died in 1886. John Bartlett Meserve, "Chief Coleman Cole," Chronicles of Oklahoma, 14 (March, 1936), 9-21.

COLEMAN, FRANCIS E. (Chippewa)
Francis E. Coleman graduated from the Carlisle Indian Industrial School in 1911. In 1912 he was night manager of the Cumberland Valley passenger station at Carlisle, Pennsylvania. Carlisle Arrow, April 21, 1911; Red Man, 5 (November, 1912), 129.

COLHOFF, LIZZIE (Sioux)
In 1894 Lizzie Colhoff was a student at the Holy Rosary Mission School, Pine Ridge, South Dakota.

COLONAHASKI, ABRAHAM C. (Eastern Band Cherokee)
In 1906, Abraham C. Colonahaski was a student at Carlisle Indian Industrial School.

COLVARD, MYRTLE (Cherokee)
Myrtle Colvard was from Pryor, Oklahoma. She studied home economics at Chilocco Indian Agricultural School, from which she graduated in 1919.

COMMAND, JOSEPH (Leech Lake Chippewa)
Joseph Command was born at Leech Lake, Minnesota, on September 25, 1897. He attended the Leech Lake boarding school from

1905 to 1911. He then entered the Pipestone Indian School, from which he graduated in 1916. Peace Pipe, 5 (June, 1916), 9.

CONEPACHO, BILLY (Florida Seminole)
Billy Conepacho was a student at Carlisle Indian Industrial School in 1882. He also received some private education at Fort Meyers. At the time, he was the only one of his tribe to have had any formal education. Morning Star, 4 (April, 1884), 4.

CONGER, ALICE CORA (Santee Sioux)
Alice Cora Conger was born at Chouteau Creek, South Dakota, on May 4, 1875, the daughter of Cassius and Julia Bruguiere Conger. Conger served as the agent at Yankton. Julia Conger was a Santee, the daughter of War Eagle. The family lived at Yankton and later at Dubuque, Iowa. Alice Conger attended Santee Normal Training School at Santee, Nebraska, graduating in 1895, and later worked as a cook at the government school at Greenwood, South Dakota. She married John Kealer, and in 1920 she was a nurse at Greenwood. Word Carrier, 20 (June, 1891), 24 and 39 (March-April, 1910), 7; Iapi Oaye, 49 (June-July, 1920), 23; Thirty-Fifth Annual Catalogue of the Hampton Normal and Agricultural Institute (Hampton: Hampton Institute Press, 1903), 111.

CONGER, JENNIE IONE (Sioux)
Jennie Ione Conger attended Santee Normal Training School for eight years, graduating in 1902. She died at Andrus, South Dakota, in 1903. Iapi Oaye 49 (June-July, 1920), 23; "Girls' Literary Society," Word Carrier, 32 (November-December, 1903), 24.

CONGER, LUCILLE I. (Santee Sioux)
Lucille Conger was the daughter of Cassius and Julia Bruguiere Conger. Her mother was Santee, the daughter of War Eagle, but the family lived at Yankton where her father served as agent. Conger graduated from Hampton Institute in 1897 and taught at the Yankton and Sisseton schools. In 1902 she entered the postgraduate department at Hampton. She married A. O. Bonnin and lived at Lake Andes, South Dakota. Thirty-Fifth Annual Catalogue of the Hampton Normal and Agricultural Institute (Hampton: Hampton Institute Press, 1903), 111, 118; Word Carrier, 20 (June, 1891), 24.

CONGER, MERCY I. (Santee Sioux)
Mercy I. Conger Bonnin (or Wicantbuwin) was the daughter of Cassius Conger and Julia Bruguiere Conger. Conger was at one time the agent at Yankton and Mrs. Conger was a Santee, the daughter of War Eagle. Mercy Conger attended the Santee Normal Training School at Santee, Nebraska, and then Hampton Institute at Hampton, Virginia from 1881 to 1888. She taught for three years in the government school at Yankton. She married Charles H. Bonnin and in 1922 lived at Wagner, South Dakota, where she was elected clerk of the district court of Charles Mix County. Talks and Thoughts, May, 1897; Word Carrier 20 (June, 1891), 24; 52 (September-October, 1922),

20; 52 Congress, 1 Session, Senate Executive Document 31, 6, 32-33, 34-35.

CONGER, SYBIL (Sioux)
Sybil Conger attended Hampton Institute.

CONGWHIO, LOMO (Hopi)
Lomo Congwhio was a student at Haskell Institute in 1902.

COODALOOK, ANNIE (Eskimo)
Annie Coodalook attended Carlisle Indian Industrial School. She returned to her home at Barrow, Alaska, in 1907, and taught in the local school. In 1912 she lived in Riverside, California. Red Man and Helper, July 22, 1904; Carlisle Arrow, September 25 and November 12, 1908; Red Man, 5 (October, 1912), 86.

COODEY, DANIEL ROSS (Cherokee)
Daniel Ross Coodey was the son of Joseph and Jennie (Ross) Coodey. He served as senator from Canadian District, Cherokee Nation, in 1859. He died that year. Emmet Starr, History of the Cherokee Indians and Their Legends and Folk Lore (Oklahoma City: The Warden Company, 1921) 270, 410; Carolyn Thomas Foreman, "The Coodey Family of Indian Territory," Chronicles of Oklahoma, 25 (Winter, 1947-1948), 324, 325, 337.

COOK, CHARLES SMITH (Pine Ridge Sioux)
Charles Smith Cook, an Oglala, was an 1881 graduate of Trinity College. He studied theology at Seabury Divinity School, was ordained, and worked as a minister and teacher on the Pine Ridge Reservation in the 1880's. He died at the Pine Ridge Agency on April 15, 1892, and was buried at Greenwood, South Dakota. Red Man, 11 (June-July, 1892), 3.

COOK, PHILLIP (Southern Cheyenne)
Phillip Cook was a native preacher and served as an interpreter for missionaries. He was active in the Cheyenne and Arapaho Wigwam Society, served as delegate to Washington in 1913, and was on the committee on bylaws for the Cheyenne and Arapaho tribes. Oklahoma Historical Society, Archives Division, Cheyenne and Arapaho --Churches, June 15, 1904; Cheyenne and Arapaho--Federal Relations, June 5, 1912; Cheyenne and Arapaho--Indian Council, June 20, 1912, October 1, 1913.

COOKE, MARY (Mohawk)
Mary Cooke was from New York and attended Carlisle Indian Industrial School in 1909.

COOKE, MAUDE (Mohawk)
Maude Cooke was from New York and was a student at Carlisle Indian Industrial School in 1917.

COOLIDGE, SHERMAN S. (Northern Arapaho)

Sherman Coolidge was born at Goose Creek, Wyoming, in 1863, the son of Arapaho parents, Banasda and Ba-ah-noce. When he was seven or eight years old, he was taken in, following a battle, by General Coolidge and his wife. He received his education at Shattuck Military School in Faribault, Minnesota, Seabury Divinity School, and Hobart College. An Episcopal priest, Coolidge was a missionary to the Arapahoes and Shoshonis of Wyoming and to the tribes in western Oklahoma. He was well known as a lecturer on Indian affairs and served on national committees dealing with Indian matters. He married Grace D. Wetherbee. Coolidge died in January, 1932. Oklahoma Historical Society, Archives Division, Cheyenne and Arapaho--Carlisle, August 24 and September 21, 26, 27, and 28, 1911; "Rev. Sherman Coolidge," Indian Progress, 1 (March 1, 1909), 1, 4.

COONS, ARTHUR (Pawnee)

Arthur Coons, from Oklahoma, was a student at Carlisle Indian Industrial School in 1908 and 1909. In 1923 he was a member of the Business Committee of the Skeedee Band of Pawnees. Oklahoma Historical Society, Archives Division, Pawnee--Indian Council, February 26, 1923.

COOPER, MEDORA (Citizen Band)

From Newkirk, Oklahoma, Medora Cooper was a student of domestic arts at the Chilocco Indian Agricultural School, from which she graduated in 1918. Oklahoma Historical Society, Archives Division, Chilocco--Enrollment, December 29, 1913.

COPWAY, GEORGE (Chippewa)

George Copway (Kah-ge-ga-gah-bowh) was born in Ontario in 1818. A hereditary chief of the Ojibwa, he was educated traditionally but was later converted to Christianity. In 1838-1839 he attended Ebenezer Academy in Illinois. He served as an assistant to a Methodist missionary and then became a missionary himself, serving in Illinois, Iowa, Michigan, Minnesota, and Wisconsin. He traveled to Europe in 1850 and wrote extensively. He married Elizabeth Howell. Copway died in Michigan in 1863. George Harvey Genzmer, "George Copway," in Allan Johnson and Dumas Malone, eds., Dictionary of American Biography (New York: Charles Scribner's Sons, 1930), 4: 433.

CORNELIUS, BRIGMAN (Oneida)

Brigman Cornelius (also known as Buchanan) was born in Wisconsin about 1878. After graduating from Carlisle in 1897, Cornelius returned to Wisconsin where he farmed and interpreted for the Episcopal church. He married Elizabeth Skenadore. Red Man, 14 (April, 1897), 4; Red Man and Helper, October 22, 1901, and February 21, 1902.

CORNELIUS, ISABELLA C. (Oneida)

Isabella Cornelius, the daughter of Elijah Cornelius, graduated

from Carlisle Indian Industrial School in 1892 and then taught in the
East. In 1897 she was alleged to be the only Indian teacher of white
children. In 1900, she lived in Wisconsin. Her married name was
Denny. Red Man and Helper, October 12, 1900; National Archives
Microfilm, Microcopy 595 (Indian Census Rolls, 1885-1940), Roll 315,
Oneida 1900; Indian Craftsman, 1 (June, 1909), 50.

CORNELIUS, LAURA MINNIE (Oneida)
      Laura Minnie Cornelius, from Seymour, Wisconsin, attended
Carlisle Indian Industrial School. In 1903 she became an instructor
at Sherman Institute. Her married name was Kellogg.

CORNELIUS, LAVINIA (Oneida)
      Lavinia Cornelius, the daughter of Samson Cornelius, was from
Wisconsin. She entered Hampton Institute in November, 1888, at the
age of 17. She remained until 1891. She was later trained in nursing at New Haven, Connecticut. 52 Congress, 1 Session, Senate Executive Document 31, 36-37; Talks and Thoughts, October, 1898.

CORNELIUS, LEILA (Oneida)
      Leila Cornelius was from Wisconsin and graduated from Carlisle
Indian Industrial School in 1896. Red Man, 13 (March, 1896), 1.

CORNELIUS, LILLIAN (Oneida)
      Lillian Cornelius, from Wisconsin, was the daughter of Elijah
Cornelius. She graduated from Carlisle Indian Industrial School in
1903. Red Man and Helper, February 20-27, 1903; National Archives
Microfilm, Microcopy 595 (Indian Census Rolls, 1885-1940), Roll 315,
Oneida 1900.

CORNELIUS, REBECCA (Oneida)
      Rebecca Cornelius, from Wisconsin, was a student at Hampton
Institute from 1900 to 1903. Thirty-Fifth Annual Catalogue of the
Hampton Normal and Agricultural Institute (Hampton: Hampton Insti-
tute Press, 1903), 112.

CORNELIUS, ROSE (Oneida)
      Rose Cornelius, who was from Wisconsin, was a student at Has-
kell Institute in 1905. Her married name was Smith, and she lived
at West De Pere, Wisconsin. Indian Leader, 17 (September, 1913), 21.

CORNTASSEL, BERTHA (Cherokee)
      In 1917, Bertha Corntassel was a student at the Cherokee Or-
phan Training School near Tahlequah, Oklahoma.

COSAR, GALVOS (Creek)
      Galvos Cosar was born at Sapulpa, Creek Nation, in 1902, the
son of Tom and Jennie Cosar. He attended Bacone College.

COUNTING, DORA (Sioux)
      Dora Counting was born about 1894 and attended Oahe Mission
School in South Dakota.

CRANE, JAMES (Umatilla)
   James Crane was a student at Carlisle Indian Industrial School in 1908.

CRAZY GHOST, JULIA (Sioux)
   Julia Crazy Ghost was a student at the Oglala Boarding School in 1920.

CROOKS, OLIVE (Crow)
   Olive Crooks was born about 1883. In 1899 she was a student at the Crow Agency School.

CROTZER, ETHEL (Wyandot)
   Ethel Crotzer was a 1907 graduate of Haskell Institute. In 1922 she lived at the Wyandot Indian School in Oklahoma.

CROTZER, MARTHA BAIN (Sisseton Sioux)
   Martha Bain attended Santee Normal Training School at Santee, Nebraska, and Armour Institute of Technology in Chicago. In 1904 she married Archibald Crotzer, and the couple lived at Darlington, Oklahoma, where she was seamstress at the Indian School. Word Carrier, 33 (September-October, 1904), 17.

CROWE, NONA (Cherokee)
   Nona Crowe was a student at the Carlisle Indian Industrial School in 1908.

CROWE, WESLEY (Cherokee)
   Wesley Crowe was a student at Hampton Institute, Hampton, Virginia, in 1895.

CROW-EAGLE, THOMAS (Sioux)
   In 1894, Thomas Crow-Eagle was a student at the Standing Rock Agricultural Boarding School.

CROWSGHOST, MORGAN (Gros Ventre)
   Morgan Crowsghost, who was from the Fort Berthold Reservation in North Dakota, entered the Carlisle Indian Industrial School in 1901 and graduated in 1908. Red Man and Helper, November 8, 1901; Arrow, April 3, 1908.

CULBERTSON, MOSES (Sioux)
   Moses Culbertson, who was from South Dakota, attended Carlisle Indian Industrial School before he entered Hampton Institute in 1886 at the age of nineteen. He remained there until 1890. He farmed and worked as a policeman at the Flandreau agency. 52 Congress, 1 Session, Senate Executive Document 31, 27, 46-47; Red Man, 10 (June, 1890), 3.

DAJIDA (San Carlos Apache)
   See BULLIS, LON S.

DALE, WILLIAM (Caddo)
    William Dale, from Oklahoma, attended Carlisle.

DAUGHERTY, MATHEW (Cherokee)
    Mathew Daugherty, who was of Cherokee descent, was born in
Arkansas on September 24, 1839, the son of James Daugherty. His
family lived in Missouri until 1849, when they moved to Denton County,
Texas. Daugherty attended McKenzie College at Clarksville and later
studied law. In the late 1890's he lived in Muskogee, Creek Nation.
H. F. O'Beirne and E. S. O'Beirne, The Indian Territory (St. Louis:
C. B. Woodward Company, 1892), 366-368.

DAVIS, RICHARD (Southern Cheyenne)
    Richard Davis was born about 1867, the son of Bull Bear and
his wife Elsie. He lived the life of a plains Cheyenne until 1879 when
he went to Carlisle. In 1881 he entered the outing program and
learned farming at Danboro, Pennsylvania, and in 1882 learned fruit
culture. He also studied printing and worked on the school's paper,
The Morning Star, and later worked as a coachman in Philadelphia.
In 1888 he married Nannie Aspenall, a Pawnee, and he and his wife
took farm jobs at West Grove, Pennsylvania. He was induced, finally,
to return to the reservation with his family. He took a job at the
agency but soon lost it to other office seekers. A good farmer and
dairyman, he lived at Seger's Colony, Oklahoma, in 1904. He served
as special interpreter for the Cheyenne Indians. In 1907 he was a
member of the 101 Wild West Show. Morning Star, 6 (December,
1885), 5; Red Man, 8 (April, 1888), 4, 9 (February, 1889), 8, and
13 (September-October, 1895), 3. Oklahoma Historical Society, Archives Division, Chilocco--Fair, December 14, 1903, May 14, 1904;
Cheyenne and Arapaho--Indians with Wild West Shows and Exhibition,
July 22, 1907.

DAVIS, SAMUEL G. (Haida)
    Samuel G. Davis was from Kasaan, Alaska.

DAWSON, ANNA R. (Arickara)
    Anna Dawson, from the Fort Berthold Reservation, was the
daughter of Mary Dawson. Her Indian name was Spahananadaka.
She entered Hampton in 1878 at age eight and graduated in September, 1887. After graduation, she taught a year at Hampton Institute
before entering the Framingham (Massachusetts) Normal School, from
which she graduated after two years. In 1890 she became a teacher
at the Santee Normal Training School at Santee, Nebraska. Her married name was Wilde. 52 Congress, 1 Session, Senate Executive Document 31, 4, 32-33; Twenty-Two Years' Work of the Hampton Normal
and Agricultural Institute (Hampton: Normal School Press, 1891),
28, 55.

DAY, EUGENE (Paiute)
    Eugene Day was from Columbia, California, and attended Sher-
man Institute from which he graduated in 1916. Sherman Bulletin,
May 24, 1916.

DAY, MARTHA (Pueblo)
Martha Day was a student at Carlisle Indian Industrial School in 1908.

DAY-DODGE (White Earth Chippewa)
Day-Dodge was described in 1888 as "Grand Sachem and Medicine Seer of the White-Earth Ojibways, now about 90 years of age." Articles attributed to him in the White Earth Progress were probably written by Theo H. Beaulieu (q.v.), who later published several articles on the same topics under his own name.

DE CORA, ANGEL (Winnebago)
Angel De Cora was born on the Winnebago Reservation in Nebraska on May 3, 1871, the daughter of David De Cora. She was educated for four years at the reservation school and then entered Hampton Institute, from which she graduated in 1891. She attended Miss Burnham's School at Northampton, Massachusetts, and then studied art at Smith College, Drexel Institute, and the Boston Museum of Fine Arts. She maintained a studio in New York where she illustrated books. In 1906 she went to Carlisle as an art teacher and stayed there until 1915. She then worked for the New York State Museum at Albany and in 1918 returned to New York where she again worked as an illustrator. She married William Deitz, a Sioux, who illustrated the covers of the Carlisle Red Man. She died on February 6, 1919. "American Indian Artist," Outlook, 124 (January 14, 1920), 64-66; E. L. Martin, "The Story of Two Real Indian Artists," Red Man, 5 (February, 1913), 231-241; Some Results of Hampton's Work (Hampton: The Institute Press, 1915), 21; 52 Congress, 1 Session, Senate Executive Document 31, 7; Southern Workman, 49 (March, 1919), 104-105; Frederick J. Dockstader, Great North American Indians (New York: Van Nostrand Reinhold Company, 1977), 71.

DE CORA, JULIA (Winnebago)
Julia De Cora was from Nebraska and attended Hampton Institute at Hampton, Virginia, from 1895 to 1898. Her married name was Lukeheart. In 1922 she was an employee at the government hospital at Winnebago, Nebraska.

DE COTEAU, LIEN (Sisseton Sioux)
Lien De Coteau graduated from the Santee Normal Training School at Santee, Nebraska, in 1916. In 1920 he lived at Greenwood, South Dakota, where he farmed. Iape Oaye, 49 (June-July, 1920), 23.

DE COTEAU, LOUIS (Sioux)
Louis De Coteau attended the Santee Normal Training School, and in 1907 he was secretary of the association of former students. He lived at Wilmot, South Dakota. Word Carrier, 38 (September-October, 1909), 17.

DEER, JAMES H. (Caddo)
James H. Deer was a student at Carlisle Indian Industrial School

in 1880. He served as butcher at the Kiowa Agency and in 1886 became interpreter, in which capacity he still served in 1900. Oklahoma Historical Society, Archives Division, Kiowa Volume K, August 28, 1880; Kiowa--Issues, February 11, 1879, and May 15, 1885; Cherokee Volume 412, March 15, 1886; Kiowa--Indian Houses, April 11, 1898; Kiowa--Interpreters, September 12, 1900.

DE FOND, SAMUEL C. (Yankton Sioux)
Samuel De Fond (or Cingekerdan), from the Yankton Reservation, was born about 1870, the son of Battice De Fond. He attended Hampton Institute from 1885 to 1888. In 1890 he taught at St. Paul's School on the Yankton Reservation. He assisted local missionaries in translating and later served as agency farmer and clerk. 52 Congress, 1 Session, Senate Executive Document 31, 24, 44-45.

DEGAN, LILLIAN (Chippewa)
Lillian Degan graduated from the Pipestone Indian School in 1914.

DEGAN, LOUISE (Chippewa)
Louise Degan graduated from the Pipestone Indian School in 1914.

DE GRASSE, ALFRED L. (Mashpee)
Alfred De Grasse, born about 1889, was from New Bedford, Massachusetts. He was the grandson of Watson F. Hampton, a Cape Cod Indian elected to the Massachusetts State Legislature in 1885. De Grasse entered Carlisle Indian Industrial School in 1904 and graduated in 1911. In 1912 he lived at New Bedford, Massachusetts. Carlisle Arrow, April 21, 1911 and February 2, 1912; Red Man 4 (March, 1912), 306.

DE LODGE, VICTORIA (Ponca)
Victoria De Lodge, from Oklahoma, was full Ponca. Also known as Cora De Lodge, she attended Ponca Training School until she was fourteen. She then entered Haskell Institute, where she was a student in 1907. She married Stands Black. Victoria Stands Black died on May 5, 1912. Word Carrier, 41 (November-December, 1912), 1.

DE LONEY, ELLA (Chippewa)
Ella De Loney, who was from Minnesota, attended Carlisle Indian Industrial School in 1908 and 1909.

DELORIA, ELLA CARA (Yankton Sioux)
Ella Cara Deloria, a Yankton, was born at Wakpala, South Dakota, on January 3, 1888, the daughter of Philip Deloria. After attending local schools, she went to Oberlin and Columbia, where she received a bachelor's degree in 1915. She then taught and worked in Indian health for a number of years. In 1929 she returned to Columbia and worked with Franz Boaz on Siouan languages. In the years that followed she wrote extensively on Siouan linguistics; she

also lectured during that time. Besides her linguistic and ethnolog-
ical studies, Miss Deloria wrote Speaking of Indians (1944). Marion
E. Gridley, Indians of Today (Chicago: ICFP, Inc. 1971), 348;
Frederick J. Dockstader, Great North American Indians (New York:
Van Nostrand Reinhold Company, 1977), 74-75.

DE LORIMIERE, MARGARET I. (Mohawk)
    Margaret I. De Lorimiere was from Hogansburg, New York, and
was a 1911 graduate of the business department at Carlisle Indian Industrial School. Carlisle Arrow, April 21, 1911.

DEMARRIAS, MATT (Sioux)
    Matt Demarrias was a native missionary at Lodge Pole, Montana,
in 1913.

DENNY, JOSEPH H. (Oneida)
    Joseph Denny was a student at Carlisle Indian Industrial School
in 1908 and 1909.

DENNY, WALLACE (Oneida)
    Wallace Denny, from Wisconsin, was the son of Josh Denny.
He was a 1906 graduate of Carlisle Indian Industrial School. He mar-
ried Nellie Robertson, an employee at the school, and worked as dis-
ciplinarian for young boys at Carlisle. Arrow March 30, 1906, and
June 14, 1907; Red Man, 7 (October, 1914), 74; National Archives
Microfilm, Microcopy 595 (Indian Census Rolls, 1885-1940), Roll 315,
Oneida 1900.

DENOMIE, ALICE H. (Chippewa)
    Alice H. Denomie graduated from Carlisle Indian Industrial
School in 1908. Arrow, April 3, 1908.

DE PELTQUESTANGUE, ESTAIENE M. (Chippewa)
    Estaiene M. De Peltquestangue, a graduate of Carlisle, was su-
perintendent of the Lakeside Hospital at Cleveland, Ohio, from 1905
to 1910. She worked for a number of years in the World War I period as a private nurse in Massillon, Ohio.

DE POE, ROBERT R. (Siletz)
    Robert De Poe was an 1897 graduate of the Carlisle Indian In-
dustrial School. He taught at Fort Peck and at the Chemawa Indian
School. He then entered the normal department at Haskell Institute
and studied law at the University of Kansas. In 1908 and 1909 he
was bandmaster at Haskell. He married Mary Hauser (q.v.). In
1914 he lived at Orton, Oregon. Red Man, 14 (April, 1897), 4;
Indian Leader, April 16, 1909; Red Man, 7 (November, 1914), 112.

DESGEORGES, PATRICK (Pueblo)
    Patrick Desgeorges was a student at Haskell Institute, Lawr-
ence Kansas, from 1902 to 1905.

DOCTOR, MILO (Seneca)
Milo Doctor attended the Carlisle Indian Industrial School and then served with the U.S. Army in the Philippines.

DOCTOR, NANCY (Sioux)
Nancy Doctor attended the Santee Normal Training School.

DODSON, JOHN (Shoshoni)
John Dodson graduated from the Phoenix Indian School in 1904 and later from Hampton Institute. He returned to Phoenix and worked as assistant carpenter at the school, leaving there in 1914 to take a similar post at the Fort Apache School, Whiteriver, Arizona. He married Myra Valenzuela. In 1921 he was farming at Lehi, Arizona, Mrs. Dodson's home.

DOLPHUS, AMY E. (Sioux)
Amy E. Dolphus was from South Dakota and graduated from the Carlisle Indian Industrial School in 1903. Red Man and Helper, February 20-27, 1903.

DOOR, FRANK C. (Cheyenne River Sioux)
Frank C. Door (Tiyopa) entered Hampton Institute in 1884 at age fifteen and remained there until he died in June, 1888. 52 Congress, 1 Session, Senate Executive Document 32, 21, 42-43.

DORIAN, ELWOOD (Iowa)
Dorian Elwood was a student at Carlisle Indian Industrial School in 1881.

DORMAN, EBEN (Ukie, i.e., Yuki)
Eben Dorman was a 1909 graduate of Sherman Institute, Riverside, California. Sherman Bulletin, May 24, 1916.

DORMAN, ELLEN (Ukie, i.e., Yuki)
Ellen Dorman was a 1910 graduate of Sherman Institute, Riverside, California. She married Ben Neafus and lived at Covelo, California. Sherman Bulletin, May 24, 1916.

DOW, LEE (Hupa)
Lee Dow was a 1908 graduate of Sherman Institute, Riverside, California. Later, he lived at Trinity Center, California. Sherman Bulletin, May 24, 1916.

DOWNIE, FORDIE (Clallam)
Fordie Downie attended Chemawa Indian School at Salem, Oregon.

DOWNIE, REGINALD (Clallam)
Reginald Downie was from Tacoma, Washington, and attended Chemawa Indian School at Salem, Oregon. Chemewa American, 16 (June, 1914), 6.

DOWNING, LOUIS (Cherokee)
Louis Downing, who was from Chelsea, Oklahoma, was a 1918 graduate of Chilocco Indian Agricultural School.

DOWNING, LOUISE (Cherokee)
Louise Downing was from Chelsea, Oklahoma. She studied domestic arts at Chilocco Indian Agricultural School, graduating in 1918.

DOXON, CHARLES (Onandaga)
Charles Doxon, from New York, was orphaned at age six. He spoke no English until he was eighteen, when a missionary obtained a job for him on a farm. During the three years that he worked as a laborer, the farm family helped him with his English. Doxon then made his way to Hampton, which he had heard about, but upon arrival there he was disappointed to learn that the federal government would not support Indians from New York. Nevertheless, Doxon remained at Hampton from 1883 to 1886, working during the day and going to school at night. From Hampton, he went to Syracuse, New York, where he worked in a railroad shop for fifteen years. He was admitted to the union, which barred blacks, and was active in the labor movement around the turn of the century. After he was injured on the job, he returned to Hampton for a time and then returned to Syracuse where he worked as an "automobile expert" for the Thomas Manufacturing Company. Doxon served as president of the Six Nations Temperance League and as a member of the Executive Council of the Society of American Indians. He died on February 3, 1917. "Address by Mr. Charles Doxon," Red Man, 5 (May, 1913), 423-426; Some Results of Hampton's Work (Hampton: The Institute Press, 1915), 27; 52 Congress, 1 Session, Senate Executive Document 31, 21; The American Indian Magazine, 5 (January-March, 1917), 32, 33-35.

DOXTATER, EDNA (Seneca)
Edna Doxtater was a student at Carlisle Indian Industrial School in 1908.

DOXTATER, FRED (Oneida)
Fred Doxtater, from Wisconsin, was the son of Truman Doxtater. He attended Carlisle Indian Industrial School. National Archives Microfilms, Microcopy 595 (Indian Census Rolls, 1885-1940), Oneida, 1900.

DU BRAY, JOSEPH (Yankton Sioux)
Joseph Du Bray (or Cankaksa), from the Yankton Reservation, was born about 1872, the son of Peter Du Bray. He entered Hampton Institute in 1890. Du Bray married Mary Placek and lived at Greenwood, South Dakota. 52 Congress, 1 Session, Senate Executive Document 31, 50-51; Red Man and Helper, July 13, 1900.

DUEL, D. W. (Cherokee)
D. W. Duel, a graduate of the Bacone Indian University, lived at Coody's Bluff, Cherokee Nation.

DUNBAR, JOSEPH (Snohomish)
Joseph Dunbar was from the Tulalip Reservation in Washington and attended Chemawa Indian School at Salem, Oregon.

DUNCAN, DE WITT CLINTON (Cherokee)
De Witt Clinton Duncan was born in 1829 at Dahlonega in the Cherokee Nation in Georgia, the son of half-blood John Duncan and Elizabeth Abercrombie Duncan. Duncan was educated in mission and Cherokee national schools before he went to Dartmouth College, from which he graduated with honors in 1861, a member of Phi Beta Kappa. Because of the Civil War, Duncan did not return to the Indian Territory but taught school in New Hampshire, Wisconsin, and Illinois, finally settling in 1866 at Charles City, Iowa, where he practiced law, served as mayor for a year, and taught school. By 1880 Duncan was again in the Cherokee Nation, where, during the next several years he served the Cherokees in various capacities: legal counsel, teacher and principal of the Cherokee Male Seminary, and political writer and poet. He studied Cherokee history and linguistics, and writing under his English name and under Too-qua-stee, he contributed widely to Cherokee and U.S. publications. He died at Vinita, Oklahoma, in November, 1909. Kathleen Garrett, "Dartmouth Alumni in the Indian Territory," Chronicles of Oklahoma, 32 (Summer, 1954), 130-132; Muriel H. Wright, "An Open Letter from Too-Qua-Stee to Congressman Charles Curtis, 1898," Chronicles of Oklahoma, 47 (Autumn, 1969), 298; Carolyn Thomas Foreman, "Notes on De Witt Clinton Duncan and a Recently Discovered History of the Cherokees," Chronicles of Oklahoma, 47 (Autumn, 1969), 305-311.

DUNCAN, JAMES W. (Cherokee)
James W. Duncan was born at Knobnoster, Missouri, in 1861, the son of Morgan H. and Penelope C. Craig Duncan. Because of the civil strife that followed removal, his family had moved to Missouri. In 1869 they were readmitted to the Cherokee rolls. The family settled in Delaware District, where Duncan attended Cherokee neighborhood schools. He graduated from the Male Seminary in 1885. After teaching for a short time he entered Emory College, receiving his bachelor's degree in 1890. He returned to the Cherokee Nation where he became a professor at the Male Seminary and often spoke out on behalf of education. He served as the U.S. government surveyor and as alloting agent in the Cherokee Outlet. H. F. O'Beirne and E. S. O'Beirne, The Indian Territory (St. Louis: C. B. Woodward Company, 1892), 335-356.

DUNCAN, MYRTLE (Ukie, i.e., Yuki)
Myrtle Duncan graduated from Sherman Institute, Riverside, California, in 1914. She later lived at Los Angeles. Sherman Bulletin, May 24, 1916.

DUNCAN, WALTER ADAIR (Cherokee)
Walter Adair Duncan was born in the Eastern Cherokee Nation in March, 1823, the son of John and Elizabeth Abercrombie Duncan.

His family removed to the West in 1838 and settled in Flint District. He attended school near Evansville, Arkansas. In 1847 he was licensed to preach and became a circuit rider. In the early 1850's he was private secretary to Chief John Ross (q.v.) and later served as a member of the National Council. From 1872 to 1884, he was superintendent of the Cherokee Orphan Asylum, and in his later years he lived at Park Hill. Duncan married Martha Bell, Martha Wilson, and Catherine A. L. Caleb. He died on October 17, 1907. Tahlequah Arrow, October 26, 1907; N. B. Johnson, "The Cherokee Orphan Asylum," Chronicles of Oklahoma, 44 (Autumn, 1966), 278, 279.

DUNDAS, ARCHIE (Tsimshian)

Archie Dundas graduated from Carlisle Indian Industrial School in 1908, returned to Alaska, and became a carpenter at Metlakatla near his home. He married Mercie Allen, a Carlisle graduate. Arrow, April 3, 1908; Carlisle Arrow, February 5, 1909; Indian Craftsman, 1 (February, 1909), 37.

DUNLAP, SADIE (Caddo)

Sadie Dunlap was from Oklahoma and entered Carlisle Indian Industrial School in 1903.

DUPUIS, LOUIS (Iowa)

Louis Dupuis, who was from Oklahoma, was a student at Carlisle Indian Industrial School in 1910 and 1911, when he graduated. In 1912, he lived at Horton, Kansas. Carlisle Arrow, April 21, 1911; Red Man, 5 (December, 1912), 177.

DURAN, JACOB (Pueblo)

Jacob Duran attended Haskell Institute.

DWIGHT, JONATHAN EDWARDS (Choctaw)

Jonathan Edwards Dwight was born in Mississippi and emigrated to the Indian Territory in 1833. He entered Moor's School at Dartmouth college in 1838. After his return to the Indian Territory, he learned the printing trade while reading proof for Choctaw publications at the Park Hill Mission Press in the Cherokee Nation. Dwight was editor and owner of The Choctaw Intelligencer in 1850 and 1851. He wrote the Shullyville Constitution for the Choctaws in 1857 and translated hymns for the 1858 edition of the Choctaw Hymn Book. He died at Boggy Depot, Choctaw Nation, in 1878. D. C. Gideon, Indian Territory (New York: The Lewis Publishing Company, 1901), 683-684; Kathleen Garrett, "Dartmouth Alumni in the Indian Territory," Chronicles of Oklahoma, 32 (Summer, 1954), 138.

EADES, BESSIE (Nisenan)

Bessie Eades was a 1912 graduate of Sherman Institute, Riverside, California. She later lived at Alturas, California. Sherman Bulletin, May 24, 1916.

EAGLE, DANIEL D. (Sioux)
     Daniel D. Eagle, who was from South Dakota, graduated from
Carlisle Indian Industrial School in 1904. Red Man and Helper, February 26-March 4, 1904.

EAGLE, SIMON F. (Pawnee)
     Simon F. Eagle, from Oklahoma, was a student at Carlisle In-
dian Industrial School in 1909.

EAGLEBEAR, EDWARD (Sioux)
     Edward Eaglebear was a student at Carlisle Indian Industrial
School in 1909.

EAGLEMAN, THOMAS AHSLEY (Crow Creek Sioux)
     Thomas Eagleman graduated from Carlisle Indian Industrial
School in 1908 and then worked as an engineer at the Flandreau Indian School. In 1913 he lived at Chamberlain, South Dakota. Arrow, May 22, 1908; Red Man, 5 (February, 1913), 265.

EASTMAN, CHARLES ALEXANDER (Santee Sioux)
     Charles Eastman (Ohiyesa) was born at Redwood Falls, Minne-
sota, in 1858, the son of Jacob Eastman (Many Lightnings), a Santee,
and Nancy Eastman, a half-blood Sioux. His father and uncle saw
to his early education, instilling in him a knowledge of the traditions
of the tribe. He later attended mission schools near his home and at
the Santee Agency. In 1876 he was sent for further study to Beloit
College in Wisconsin, where he remained three years before entering
Knox College in Illinois. He returned to Dakota and taught school
before receiving a scholarship to Dartmouth, where he pursued a
premedical course from 1883 to 1887. After graduation he attended
Boston University, from which he received an M.D. degree. He
served as the physician at the Pine Ridge Agency from 1890 to 1893.
He married Elaine Goodale, a reservation teacher who later became
a well-known writer. In his later life, Eastman wrote extensively,
lectured, and held national posts in the Y.M.C.A. and Boy Scouts
of America. During the Coolidge administration he served as U.S.
Indian Inspector. Eastman died in 1939. Marion E. Gridley, Indians
of Today (Chicago: The Lakeside Press, 1936), 48-49; Raymond Wilson, "Dr. Charles Alexander Eastman (Ohiyesa), Santee Sioux" (Ph.D.
dissertation, University of New Mexico, 1977); Frederick J. Dockstader, Great North American Indians (New York: Van Nostrand
Reinhold Company, 1977), 82.

EASTMAN, FRANCIS R. (Sioux)
     Francis R. Eastman, from South Dakota, graduated from the
Carlisle Indian Industrial School in 1913. He then attended Conway
Hall. Red Man, 5 (May, 1913), 435; 7 (October, 1914), 74.

EASTMAN, GRACE OLIVE (Sioux)
     Grace Olive Eastman graduated from the Santee Normal School
in 1905 and then attended Miami University at Oxford, Ohio. She

then taught at the Presbyterian Mission School at Goodwill, South Dakota; at Nuyaka Mission, Creek Nation; and, in 1910, at Dwight Mission at Marble, Oklahoma. Her married name was Moore, and in 1920 she taught at Wolf Point, Montana. "What Santee Graduates Are Doing," Word Carrier, 34 (September–October, 1905), 17; 39 (March–April, 1910), 7; Iapi Oaye, 49 (June–July, 1920), 23.

EASTMAN, JOHN (Sisseton Sioux)

The Reverend John Eastman was born in Bloomington, Minnesota, in March, 1849. In December, 1870, Eastman walked from Flandreau to Santee, Nebraska, to attend the school (later called Santee Normal Training School) conducted by the Reverend Alfred L. Riggs. He later attended Beloit College. In 1873, Eastman married Viola Frazier, who died shortly thereafter of smallpox. The following year he married Jane Faribault. Ordained in 1876, he was pastor of the Presbyterian Indian church in Flandreau for thirty years. In 1906 he moved to Sisseton and became pastor of the Goodwill Indian Church. In 1915 he became general missionary for Presbyterian Indian churches in South Dakota. Eastman died at Sisseton on October 5, 1921. Word Carrier 50 (September–October, 1921), 17.

ECHO HAWK, ELMER (Pawnee)

Elmer Echo Hawk was a student at the Carlisle Indian Industrial School in 1908.

EDDLEMAN, ORA V. (Cherokee)

Ora V. Eddleman was the daughter of David J. and Mary Daugherty Eddleman, the latter of Cherokee descent. In 1898, at age twenty, Ora Eddleman became editor of Twin Territories: The Indian Magazine, established at Muskogee, Indian Territory, in December of that year. The magazine contained a section titled "Round the Center Fire of the Wigwam," in which were published Indian poetry, stories, and folklore. Several Indian writers contributed to the Twin Territories. Miss Eddleman herself contributed numerous pieces to that magazine and to other publications as well under the pen name of Mignon Schreiber. When Sturm's Statehood Magazine was established at Tulsa, Indian Territory, in 1905, she became editor of the "Indian Department" section, attracting to that journal a number of Indian writers. Ora Eddleman Reed, "Pioneer Publisher, First Daily Newspaper in Indian Territory," Chronicles of Oklahoma, 23 (Spring, 1945), 36–39; Daryl Morrison, "Twin Territories: The Indian Magazine and Its Editor, Ora Eddleman Reed," Chronicles of Oklahoma, 60 (Summer, 1982), 136–166.

EDDLEMAN, S. GEORGE (Cherokee)

S. George Eddleman was the son of David J. and Mary Daugherty Eddleman, the latter of whom was of Cherokee descent. In 1897, he was editor of the Muskogee Morning Times at Muskogee, Creek Nation. Eddleman served in the Spanish-American War. Ora Eddleman Reed, "Pioneer Publisher, First Daily Newspaper in Indian Territory," Chronicles of Oklahoma, 23 (Spring, 1945), 36–39.

EDENSHAW, RUFUS (Haida)
Rufus Edenshaw, from Klinquan, Alaska, attended the Chemawa Indian School in 1910. Weekly Chemawa American, February 17, 1911.

EDER, CHARLES JAMES (Sioux)
Charles James Eder was from Montana and graduated in 1914 from the Chemawa Indian School.

EDGE, MARY (Caddo)
Mary Edge was from Fort Cobb, Oklahoma. She was a home economics student at Chilocco Indian Agricultural School, from which she graduated in 1919. Oklahoma Historical Society, Archives Division, Chilocco--Students Returning Home, June 30, 1917.

EDICK, CHARLES (Chippewa)
Charles Edick, from Wisconsin, graduated from Haskell Institute in 1902. He became an electrician and lived at Oshkosh.

EDWARDS, JAMES (Choctaw)
Although he was Choctaw, James Edwards was raised among the Indians of the Wichita Agency and spoke several languages. He died in February, 1890. Indian Missionary, 6 (April, 1890), 3.

ELGIN, STANFORD (Chippewa)
Stanford Elgin was a student at Carlisle Indian Industrial School in 1908.

ELK, HENRY (Cayuse)
Henry Elk, who was from Oregon, attended Chemawa Indian School at Salem, Oregon.

ELLIOTT, HAZEL (Pomo)
Hazel Elliott was a student at Sherman Institute, in 1911.

ELM, ANDREW N. (Oneida)
Andrew N. Elm, who was from Wisconsin, was the son of Nicholas Elm. He attended Carlisle Indian Industrial School from 1897 to 1899. National Archives Microfilm, Microcopy 595 (Indian Census Rolls, 1885-1940), Oneida, 1900.

ELM, IDA (Oneida)
Ida Elm, from Wisconsin, was the daughter of Nicholas Elm. She attended Carlisle Indian Industrial School and Hampton Institute. Red Man and Helper, October 31, 1902; National Archives Microfilms, Microcopy 595 (Indian Census Rolls, 1885-1940), Oneida, 1900.

ENMEGAHBOWH (Ottawa)
Although an Ottawa, Enmegahbowh spent most of his life among the Chippewas of Wisconsin and Minnesota. Also known as John Johnson, Enmegahbowh was born about 1808 in Canada. He moved first to La Pointe, Wisconsin, and then to Rabbit Lake as minister to the

Chippewas. He worked in lumber camps to support himself. He
then took over the Gull Lake mission near Brainerd, Minnesota, where
he stayed until 1862. He then moved to Crow Wing, twelve miles
away, where he lived until 1868, when he moved to White Earth where
he remained for the rest of his life. He died on June 14, 1902. Tomahawk, January 8, 1904; Chippeway Herald, 2 (April, 1903), 1, 6.

ENOS, JOHNSON (Pima)
    Johnson Enos, also known as John E. Johnson, was born about
1886 and attended Carlisle, from which he graduated in 1910. He
made his home at Blackwater, Arizona. Red Man, 4 (September,
1911), 42, and (February, 1912), 259.

ENOUF, JAMES (Citizen Band Potawatomi)
    James Enouf was born about 1865, the son of John Enouf. He
was a student at Hampton Institute from 1889 to 1891. Enouf was
postmaster at Curry, Oklahoma, in 1899-1900. 52 Congress, 1 Session, Senate Executive Document 31, 48-49. Grant Foreman, "Early
Post Offices in Oklahoma," Chronicles of Oklahoma, 7 (March, 1929),
9.

ESTES, ALEXANDER H. (Yankton Sioux)
    Alexander Estes, the son of Benjamin Estes, entered Hampton
Institute, Hampton, Virginia, in 1885 at age 22. He died on February
3, 1887. Talks and Thoughts, 1 (February, 1887), 2; 52 Congress,
1 Session, Senate Executive Document 31, 24, 44-45.

ESTES, GRACE (Lower Brule Sioux)
    Grace Estes received a grammar school certificate from Haskell
Institute in 1914. Indian Leader, 17 (June, 1914), 26.

ETTAWAGESHIK, J. WILLIAM (Ottawa)
    J. William Ettawageshik was born about 1889 and graduated
from Carlisle in 1911. In 1913 he was assistant editor of the Ona-
way, Michigan Outlook, and in 1914 he settled at St. Ignace, Michigan, where he worked as a job printer for the St. Ignace Enterprise.
Carlisle Arrow, April 21, 1911; Red Man, 5 (February, 1913), 265,
and 6 (January, 1914), 205.

EUBANKS, R. Roger (Cherokee)
    R. Roger Eubanks taught at various schools in the Cherokee
Nation, including the Male Seminary in 1902-1905. Oklahoma Historical
Society, Archives Division, Cherokee Volume 544, December 9, 1898;
Cherokee Volume 566, January 25, 1901; Cherokee Schools--
Miscellaneous, April 9, 1903; Cherokee--Cherokee Male Seminary,
Spring Term, 1902, 2870A.

EXENDINE, ALBERT ANDREW (Delaware)
    Albert Andrew Exendine was born at Bartlesville, Cherokee
Nation, on January 27, 1884. He attended Mautame Presbyterian
Indian Mission School at Anadarko before entering Carlisle Indian

Industrial School, where he became well known as a football player. After graduation in 1907, he remained as assistant coach and in 1909 became head coach at Otterbein College, where he coached three years while studying law at Dickinson College. He later practiced law and coached high school football at Anadarko. He then entered a long, distinguished career as a football coach: assistant at Carlisle, 1913; head coach at Georgetown University, 1914-1922; head coach at Washington State College, 1923-1925; coach at Occidental College, 1926-1927; coach at Northeastern Oklahoma State College, 1928; backfield coach (1929-1933) and head coach at Oklahoma A & M College, 1934-1935, after which he retired. John L. Johnson, "Albert Andrew Exendine: Carlisle Coach and Teacher," Chronicles of Oklahoma, 43 (Autumn, 1965), 319-331.

FAIRBANKS, WILLIAM (Chippewa)
    William Fairbanks attended the Pipestone Indian School.

FARR, JOHN B. (Chippewa)
    John B. Farr was a 1908 graduate of the Carlisle Indian Industrial School. He entered the University of Pennsylvania in 1912. Arrow, April 3, 1908; Red Man, 5 (September, 1912), 42.

FAST HORSE, WILLIAM (Sioux)
    William Fast Horse was a student at the Oglala Boarding School in 1919 and 1920.

FAULKNER, CLARENCE L. (Shoshoni)
    Clarence L. Faulkner, from Idaho, graduated from Carlisle Indian Industrial School in 1906. Arrow, March 30, 1906.

FEATHER, JOHN (Menominee)
    John Feather was a 1909 graudate of Carlisle Indian Industrial School.

FIELDER, HENRY W. (Cheyenne River Sioux)
    Henry W. Fielder attended Hampton Institute at Hampton, from 1894 through 1899. After graduation he returned to North Dakota. He married Clara Price and in 1902 was a teacher at Rosebud, South Dakota, one of a number of positions he held in government service. In 1909 he was appointed to the commission to appraise lands on the Cheyenne River Reservation, and in 1912 received a patent to his land. He was a successful farmer and a partner in a store. Red Man and Helper, July 27, 1900; Talks and Thoughts, January, 1902; Some Results of Hampton's Work (Hampton: The Institute Press, 1915), 18.

FIELDS, DELILAH (Cherokee)
    No information is available.

FIELDS, RICHARD F. (Cherokee)
    Richard F. Fields was the son of Thomas and Nannie Downing

Fields. He married Rachel Goss and Minerva Kerr. Emmet Starr,
History of the Cherokee Indians and Their Legends and Folk Lore
(Oklahoma City: The Warden Company, 1921), 310, 344, 406.

FIGHT, FRANK (Pine Ridge Sioux)
     No information is available.

FIRE THUNDER, ANGELIQUE (Pine Ridge Sioux)
     Angelique Fire Thunder was a student at Hampton Institute,
1902-1904. Thirty-Fifth Annual Catalogue of the Hampton Normal
and Agricultural Institute (Hampton: Hampton Institute Press, 1903),
112.

FIRE THUNDER, ELLA (Lower Brule Sioux)
     Ella Fire Thunder (or Ziyawin), the daughter of Charging Hawk,
was from the Lower Brule Reservation. She was born about 1878
and entered Hampton Institute in 1890 at age 13, graduating in 1896.
She then went to the Osage Agency to teach. The following year
she returned to Hampton. She married Joel Littlebird. 52 Congress,
1 Session, Senate Executive Document 31, 36-37.

FIRECLOUD, DANIEL (Crow Creek Sioux)
     Daniel Firecloud entered Hampton Institute in 1885 at age 30.
He left in October, 1886, as a result of his wife's illness. Upon
his return home, Firecloud served as a catechist. 52 Congress,
1 Session, Senate Executive Document 31, 23, 44-45.

FIRECLOUD, GEORGE T. (Fort Totten Sioux)
     George T. Firecloud, from North Dakota, graduated from the
Santee Normal Training School in 1904. In 1910, he was a missionary
at Harlem, Montana, and in 1920 at Savoy, Montana. "What Santee
Graduates Are Doing," Word Carrier, 39 (March-April, 1910), 7;
Iapi Oaye, 49 (June-July, 1920), 23.

FIRETHUNDER, LYDIA (Sioux)
     Lydia Firethunder, who was from South Dakota, graduated
from the domestic science department of Haskell Institute in 1914.
Indian Leader, 17 (June, 1914), 25.

FIRETHUNDER, WILLIAM (Sioux)
     William Firethunder, who was from South Dakota, received his
grammar school certificate from Haskell Institute in 1914. Indian
Leader, 17 (June, 1914), 25.

FISH, CHARLES L. (Lower Brule Sioux)
     Charles L. Fish, from Lower Brule, North Dakota, was born
about 1886. He graduated from Carlisle Indian Industrial School
in 1911. He worked as school farmer at White Earth, Minnesota, after
which he returned to Lower Brule, where he farmed and followed
his trade as a painter. Carlisle Arrow, April 21 and October 6,
1911; Red Man, 7 (October, 1914), 73.

FISH, FRANK (Peoria)
Frank Fish, from Oklahoma, graduated from Haskell Institute in 1906. He married Lulu Moore.

FISHER, JOSIAH (Creek)
Josiah Fisher attended Tullahassee Mission School. In 1898 he was a trustee of the Pecan Creek Mission. Oklahoma Historical Society, Archives Division, Creek--Pecan Creek Mission, August 5, 1898, No. 36759.

FITE, NANCY DANIEL (Cherokee)
Nancy Daniel Fite was born in 1862, the daughter of Carter and Katherine Benge Daniel. She was educated at the Cherokee Orphan Asylum and at the Cherokee Female Seminary, from which she graduated in 1880. She taught for three years before marrying Dr. Richard L. Fite. They lived at Tahlequah, where she died on December 26, 1946. Eula E. Fullerton, "Mrs. R. L. Fite, 1862-1946," Chronicles of Oklahoma, 27 (Spring, 1949), 122-124; D. C. Gideon, Indian Territory (New York: The Lewis Publishing Company, 1901), 724-725.

FLOOD, THOMAS J. (Pine Ridge Sioux)
Thomas J. Flood was educated at the Oglala Boarding School and at Haskell Institute. In 1909 he worked as a stenographer in the Haskell superintendent's office. Indian Leader, April 16, 1909.

FLORES, VIRGINIA (Mission)
Virginia Flores was a student at the Banning Mission School in 1895.

FLY, JOSEPH (Sioux)
Joseph Fly attended Hampton Institute.

FLYINGEARTH, EVA (Standing Rock Sioux)
Eva Flyingearth was a student at the Santee Normal Training School in 1914-1915. Word Carrier, 44 (May-June, 1915), 9.

FOBB, RHODA (Choctaw)
Rhoda Fobb was from Oklahoma and attended Carlisle Indian Industrial School, graduating in 1917.

FOLSOM, DANIEL (Choctaw)
Daniel Folsom was born in the Choctaw Nation in Mississippi. At age thirteen, he entered the Choctaw Academy at Blue Springs, Kentucky. He returned to his home in Mississippi in 1829. In 1848 and 1849, he edited the Choctaw Telegraph at Doaksville, Choctaw Nation. James D. Morrison, "'News for the Choctaws,'" Chronicles of Oklahoma, 27 (Summer, 1949), 208n.

FOLSOM, DAVID (Choctaw)
David Folsom was born in Mississippi on January 25, 1791,

the son of Nathaniel Folsom and Ai-ni-chi-ho-yo. He married Rhoda
Nail. Folsom urged Christianity and English education among the
Choctaws. He served as chief of the Choctaws and as their delegate
to Washington. "David Folsom," Chronicles of Oklahoma, 4 (December,
1926), 340-355.

FOLSOM, DON JUAN (Choctaw)
    Don Juan Folsom was born at Atoka, Choctaw Nation, in 1866,
the son of Julius Folsom. He attended high school at Denison, Texas,
and Roanoke College at Salem, Virginia. He returned to Atoka in
1884 and served as clerk of the Choctaw House of Representatives.
In 1886 he bought half interest in The Indian Citizen, which he helped
edit. In 1888 he served as private secretary to Chief B. F. Smallwood (q.v.) and later read law and practiced at Paris, Texas. He
married Deboriah Louisa Brown. Oklahoma Historical Society, Archives Division, Choctaw Volume 1, November 14, 1886; H. F. O'Beirne,
Leaders and Leading Men of the Indian Territory (Chicago: American
Publishers' Association, 1891), 71.

FOLSOM, ISRAEL (Choctaw)
    The Reverend Israel Folsom was born in the Choctaw Nation
in Mississippi on May 1, 1802, the son of Nathaniel Folsom, a white
trader, and his Choctaw wife. He assisted in moving the Choctaws
to their lands west of the Mississippi and settled near old Fort Wash-
ita in the western Choctaw Nation. He died at Perryville, Choctaw
Nation, on April 24, 1870.

FOLSOM, J. T. (Choctaw)
    No information is available. However, this may be Jacob Fol-
som (q.v.).

FOLSOM, JACOB (Choctaw)
    Jacob Folsom was born about 1809 and was educated at the
Choctaw Academy. In later years he lived at Westend, Choctaw Nation, and was a member of the Skullyville Constitutional Convention
in 1857. Carolyn Thomas Foreman, "The Choctaw Academy," Chronicles
of Oklahoma, 6 (December, 1928), 455.

FOLSOM, L. S. W. (Choctaw)
    L. S. W. Folsom, who for several years after 1872 was judge
of the Third Judicial Circuit of the Choctaw Nation, was a well-known
political figure among the Choctaws. Oklahoma Historical Society,
Archives Division, Choctaw--Elections, August 3, 1887, (16513);
Choctaw--Courts, 3rd District, August 1, 1872 (15402A), August 22,
1876 (15405), and February, 1882 (15402A).

FOLSOM, PETER (Choctaw)
    In 1852 Peter Folsom was a member of the Choctaw Commission
to treat with the Chickasaws, in 1854 he was chief of Mosholatubbee
District, and in 1861, 1871, and 1887, he was a Choctaw delegate
to Washington. Oklahoma Historical Society, Archives Division,

Choctaw--National Council, November 11, 1852 (18295); November 16, 1854 (18297); October 27, 1858 (18300); June 12, 1861 (18304).

FOLSOM, S. (Choctaw)
It is uncertain which Folsom this is, but it is probably Sampson N., the son of David (q.v.).

FONTAINE, PETER (Blackfeet)
Peter Fontaine was a student at the Chemawa Indian School, Salem, Oregon, in 1913.

FOREMAN, JOHNSON (Cherokee)
Johnson Foreman served as national attorney and senator in the Cherokee Nation. He died in 1872. Oklahoma Historical Society, Archives Division, Cherokee--Citizenship, December 6, 1870, No. 359-1; Cherokee Volume 259, 1871, p. A-1; Cherokee Volume 258, December 17, 1870, p. 91; Litton, Cherokee Papers, 1815-1874, July 20, 1872, p. 217.

FOREMAN, STEPHEN (Cherokee)
Stephen Foreman was born in the Eastern Cherokee Nation on October 22, 1807, the son of Anthony Foreman, a Scot, and his Cherokee wife, Elizabeth Gurdaygee. He studied at Brainerd Mission school under the Reverend Samuel Austin Worcester and then went on to the College of Richmond and Princeton Theological Seminary. Licensed to preach by the Presbyterians, he preached at Brainerd in the 1830's and helped Worcester translate the New Testament. In the West, in addition to his work as a clergyman, Foreman organized the Cherokee national public school system and was its first superintendent. He also served as a Supreme Court judge in 1844 and on the Executive Council from 1847 to 1855. After the Civil War he established Park Hill Mission near his home at Park Hill where he died on November 20, 1881. Foreman was married to Sarah Watkins Riley and Ruth Riley Candy. Besides his work as a translator, Foreman wrote under the pen name of "Old Man of the Mountain." "Biography," Cherokee Advocate, December 23, 1881; Minta Ross Foreman, "Reverend Stephen Foreman, Cherokee Missionary," Chronicles of Oklahoma, 18 (September, 1940), 229-242; Frederick J. Dockstader, Great North American Indians (New York: Van Nostrand Reinhold Company, 1977), 86-87.

FOSTER, SAM (Creek)
Sam Foster was a student at the Tullahassee Mission School in 1870.

FRASS, ROSA (Cheyenne)
Rosa Frass graduated from Haskell Institute in 1901. She entered Indian Service but soon married Isaac Seneca, who worked at Chilocco Indian Agricultural School.

FRAZIER, DAVID (Santee Sioux)
David Frazier was the son of Francis (q.v.) and Margaret

Frazier. From 1902 to 1920, the elder Frazier was pastor of the Pilgrim Church (Congregational) at Santee, Nebraska, where David Frazier attended Santee Normal Training School.

FRAZIER, FRANCIS (Santee Sioux)
The Reverend Francis Frazier was born near Redwing, Minnesota, in 1853, the second son of Artemas Ehnamani and his wife Winyan Hiyayewin. He was educated at St. Peter Mission school. On July 27, 1873, he married Margaret, daughter of Wakanhdiǵi (Brown Thunder) and Wastedawin. He first was a miller. In 1885, he became pastor of the Ponca Creek Church in South Dakota. In 1902 he replaced his father as pastor of Pilgrim Church (Congregational) at Santee, Nebraska. In 1920 he became assistant superintendent of mission work on the Cheyenne River Reservation. Frazier died on February 3, 1924. Word Carrier, 53 (January-February, 1924), 1.

FRAZIER, FRANCIS PHILIP (Santee Sioux)
Francis Philip Frazier was the son of Francis (q.v.) and Margaret Frazier. From 1902 to 1920, the elder Frazier was pastor of the Pilgrim Church (Congregational) at Santee, Nebraska. Philip Frazier graduated from the Santee Normal Training School in 1910 and served in Europe during World War I, after which he attended Oberlin. He was an ordained Congregationalist minister, and he and his wife Susie Meek Frazier were missionaries to the Kickapoos in Oklahoma. He later became a missionary to the Sioux and was general superintendent of the missions in South Dakota and Nebraska. He then superintended adult education at Santee, Nebraska. During World War II, he worked in Los Angeles. Afterward, he served as missionary to the Osages before going to the Standing Rock Reservation where he was minister of five churches. Word Carrier, 53 (January-February, 1924), 1; Iapi Oaye, 49 (June-July), 1920), 23; Marion E. Gridley, Indians of Today (Chicago: Towertown Press, 1960), 201-203.

FRAZIER, GEORGE J. (Santee Sioux)
George J. Frazier (Haupu) was the son of Francis (q.v.) and Margaret Frazier. The elder Frazier was for many years pastor of the Pilgrim Church (Congregational) at Santee, Nebraska. George Frazier entered Hampton Institute in 1890 at age 14, and in 1896 entered Kimball Academy at Meridan, New Hampshire. He later graduated with a medical degree from Denver Homeopathic Medical College and practiced for a time in western Nebraska. After ten years, he became a physician for the Indian Service at the Santee, Lower Brule, Crow Creek, and Rosebud reservations. Frazier married Emma Scott. Word Carrier, 53 (January-February, 1924), 1; 52 Congress, 1 Session, Senate Executive Document 31, 50-51; Red Man, 12 (May, 1895), 6; Marion E. Gridley, Indians of Today (Chicago: Towertown Press, 1960), 203-204.

FRAZIER, HOWARD E. (Santee Sioux)
Howard E. Frazier graduated from the Santee Normal Training

School in 1904 and later lived at Oacoma, South Dakota, where he was a carpenter. "What Santee Graduates Are Doing," Word Carrier, 39 (March-April, 1910), 7; Iapi Oaye, 49 (June-July, 1920), 23.

FRAZIER, JESSIE H. (Sioux)
Jessie H. Frazier graduated from the Santee Normal Training School in 1905 and then entered Miami University, Oxford, Ohio. Her married name was Simmons, and in 1920 she lived at Greenwood, South Dakota. "Our Last Year's Class," Word Carrier, 34 (September-October, 1905), 17; Iapi Oaye, 49 (June-July, 1922), 23.

FRAZIER, STELLA M. (Santee Sioux)
Stella M. Frazier was the daughter of Charles Frazier of Herrick, South Dakota. She graduated from the Santee Normal Training School in 1912 and then attended school at St. Johnsbury, Vermont. She then returned to Santee, Nebraska, to live. Iapi Oaye, 49 (June-July, 1920), 23, and 51 (May, 1922), 18.

FREMONT, HENRIETTA R. (Omaha)
Henrietta R. Fremont (Nedawe) was born about 1870 on the Omaha Reservation in Nebraska, the daughter of Wajaepa. She had several years of education at the mission school on the reservation and at Elizabeth, New Jersey, before entering Hampton Institute in 1884. She left the school because of illness in 1887, studied at home for two years, and then entered Carlisle from which she graduated in 1895. She then took courses in stenography and typing at Banks' Business College in Philadelphia and briefly attended Swarthmore. She entered government service and worked for a time at Pierre and Crow Creek, South Dakota. She returned to Nebraska and lived at Walthill. 52 Congress, 1 Session, Senate Executive Document 31, 8.

FRENCH, DORA (Chippewa)
Dora French was a student at the Pipestone Indian School in 1914.

FRENCH, GRACE (Chippewa)
Grace French graduated from the Pipestone Indian School in 1915.

FRENIER, JAMES (Sioux)
James Frenier was a student at the Santee Normal Training School in 1884.

FRIDAY, MOSES L. (Northern Arapaho)
Moses Friday was born about 1888 and graduated from Carlisle Indian Industrial School in 1911. He was interpreter for the Arapaho Indians at the Crow Creek Council in 1918. Carlisle Arrow, April 21, 1911; Oklahoma Historical Society, Archives Division, Cheyenne and Arapaho--Indian Council, May 31, 1918.

FRIDAY, ROBERT (Northern Arapaho)
Robert Friday, who was from Wyoming, attended Carlisle Indian

Industrial School. He married Matilda J. Metoxen. Arrow, December 21, 1906; Red Man, 2 (March, 1910), 46.

FRITTS, JOHN (Klamath)
In 1913, John Fritts was a student at Chemawa Indian School.

FRYE, CHARLES OLIVER (Cherokee)
Charles Oliver Frye was born in the Cherokee Nation on November 2, 1854, the son of Edward M. and Nancy (Puppy) Frye. He was a well-known public official, serving as clerk of Sequoyah District, senator (1883, 1892), president of the Cherokee Board of Education (1885-1897), and postmaster at Sallisaw (1897-1906, 1910-1913). Frye was married twice, to Eliza J. Thornton and Sadie A. Quesenbury. He died at Sallisaw, Oklahoma, on August 17, 1913. "Charles Oliver Frye," Chronicles of Oklahoma, 6 (March, 1928), 94-95; D. C. Gideon, Indian Territory (New York: The Lewis Publishing Company, 1901), 880-882.

FRYE, LEONA (Creek)
Leona Frye graduated from the commercial department at Haskell Institute in 1914. Indian Leader, 17 (June, 1914), 24.

GABRIEL, CHRISTIANA (Serrano)
Christiana Gabriel, from California, was born about 1887. She attended Carlisle Indian Industrial School.

GADDY, VIRGINIA (Delaware)
Virginia Gaddy, from the Indian Territory, was born about 1886. She entered Carlisle Indian Industrial School in 1903. Red Man and Helper, August 28, 1903.

GANSWORTH, HOWARD EDWARD (Tuscarora)
Howard Gansworth, from Lewiston, New York, was an 1894 graduate of Carlisle Indian Industrial School. After graduation, he took courses at Dickinson College at Carlisle, Pennsylvania, preparatory to entering Princeton in 1897. At Princeton, he was appointed Junior Orator in 1900; he graduated in 1901. After graduation he returned to Carlisle as assistant disciplinarian and was placed in charge of the outing program. In 1905 he began working for the Baldwin Locomotive Works while writing his master's thesis. Princeton granted him a master's degree in 1906. Gansworth then lived in Buffalo, New York, where he was a department manager of the General Specialty Company, which he bought in 1929. He served on the advisory committee of the Society of American Indians and was a contributing editor of the Quarterly Journal. In 1921, he was also president of the New York Indian Welfare Society. Red Man, 6 (February, 1914), 241; Marion E. Gridley, Indians of Today (Chicago: The Lakeside Press, 1936), 58.

GANSWORTH, WILLARD N. (Tuscarora)
Willard N. Gansworth attended Carlisle Indian Industrial School

and entered Dickinson College Preparatory School in Pennsylvania.
In 1915 he was farming in New York. Red Man and Helper, March
29, 1901; Red Man, 7 (February, 1915), 219.

GARCIA, NAZARIA (Mission)
     Nazaria Garcia was a student at St. Anthony Industrial School,
San Diego, in 1895.

GARDNER, LUCIE (Sioux)
     Lucie Gardner was a student at Haskell Institute in 1902. She
married Joseph Goden and lived in Winthrop, North Dakota.

GARFIELD, EVA (Sioux)
     No information is available.

GARGIE, LEWIS (Creek)
     Lewis Gargie was a student at the Tullahassee Mission School
in 1870.

GARGIE, WASHINGTON (Creek)
     Washington Gargie was a student at the Tullahassee Mission
School in 1870.

GARLOW, WILLIAM (Tuscarora)
     William Garlow, from Lewiston, New York, was born in 1890
and was a 1913 graduate of Carlisle Indian Industrial School. Carlisle
Arrow, December 20, 1912; Red Man, 5 (May, 1913), 435.

GARLOW, WINIFRED (Tuscarora)
     Winifred Garlow, from New York, graduated from the commer-
cial department of Haskell Institute in 1914. Indian Leader, 17 (June,
1914), 24.

GARNETTE, RICHARD (Sioux)
     Richard Garnette was a student at the Oglala Boarding School
in 1900.

GARRETT, ROBERT BRUCE (Cherokee)
     Robert Bruce Garrett graduated from the Cherokee Seminary
in 1901 and became a teacher at the Cherokee Orphan Asylum. He
married Cherokee Edmondson. Oklahoma Historical Society, Archives
Division, Cherokee--Cherokee Orphan Asylum, April 30 and September
30, 1903, Nos. 134 and 147; Cherokee Volume 571, November 26,
1902, No. 9.

GARVIE, JAMES (Santee Sioux)
     James Garvie was one of the native-language editors of The
Word Carrier of Santee Normal Training School.

GATES, JOSEPHINE (Sioux)
     Josephine Gates, from North Dakota, entered Carlisle Indian

Industrial School in 1902 and graduated in 1909. <u>Arrow</u>, April 3, 1908.

GATES, NAKWALETZOMA (Hopi)
No information is available.

GEFFE, EUGENE C. (Alaska Native)
Eugene C. Geffe graduated from the Carlisle Indian Industrial School in 1908. <u>Arrow</u>, April 3, 1908.

GEISDORF, LOUISE (Crow)
Louise Geisdorf graduated from Carlisle Indian Industrial School in 1896. (<u>Red Man</u>, 13 (March, 1896), 1.

GEORGE, HAL B. (Quileute)
Hal B. George was a student at the Quileute Day School, La Push, Washington, in 1909.

GEORGE, LEWIS (Klamath)
Lewis George graduated from Carlisle Indian Industrial School in 1899 and then entered West Chester Normal School at Carlisle, Pennsylvania.

GEORGE, SAMUEL (Cattaraugus Seneca)
Samuel George, from New York, was a student at Hampton Institute in 1896.

GHANGRAW, FRANCES A. (Wallawalla)
Frances A. Ghangraw, from Washington, graduated from Carlisle Indian Industrial School in 1907. <u>Arrow</u>, March 29, 1907.

GIBEAU, MARY (Flathead)
Mary J. Gibeau was from Arlee, Montana. She attended the St. Ignatius Mission School in Montana and the Chemawa Indian School at Salem, Oregon. In 1910 she entered the Indian school at Genoa, Nebraska, from which she graduated in June, 1911.

GIBSON, CHARLES (Creek)
Charles Gibson was born near Eufaula, Creek Nation, on March 20, 1846, the son of John C. Gibson, who emigrated from Alabama in 1832. The family first settled on Grand River near Fort Gibson and farmed. Charles Gibson, who was self-taught, obtained what little formal education he had in the common schools of the Creek Nation and at Asbury Mission. He ran a store in the western part of the nation for a short time and then worked twenty years as head clerk and buyer in the Grayson Brothers store at North Fork Town. In 1896 he established his own store in Eufaula. At age 55 he married Mrs. Modeania Aultman, by whom he had one child. After 1900, he wrote extensively for Indian Territory newspapers and journals. Gibson died in 1923. "Creek Fable Writer," <u>Twin Territories</u>, 5 (July, 1903), 255; <u>Indian Journal</u>, February 8, 1901; "Three Indian

Writers of Prominence," Sturm's Statehood Magazine, 1 (October, 1905), 84-85, 88-90; H. F. O'Beirne and E. S. O'Beirne, The Indian Territory (St. Louis: C. B. Woodward Company, 1892), 296-298; D. C. Gideon, Indian Territory (New York: The Lewis Publishing Company, 1901), 891-892.

GIBSON, JOHN (Pima)
    John Gibson attended Carlisle Indian Industrial School and in 1914 entered Mercerburg (Pennsylvania) Academy on a Rodman Wanamaker scholarship. Red Man, 7 (January, 1915), 184.

GIBSON, JULIA (Pima)
    Julia Gibson was a student at Sherman Institute in 1912.

GILBERT, ISAAC (Sioux)
    Isaac Gilbert graduated from the Pierre Indian School in South Dakota in 1903.

GILLIS, ALFRED C. (Wintu)
    Alfred C. Gillis lived in Shasta County, California, and was active in the Indian Board of Co-Operation.

GIVEN, JOSHUA H. (Kiowa)
    Joshua H. Given was the son of the Kiowa leader Satank but took the name of a government physician. He attended reservation school before being sent to Carlisle Indian Industrial School. In 1887 he attended Lincoln University in Chester, Pennsylvania. The following year he acted as interpreter for the Presbyterian mission near Lawton, Indian Territory. He was ordained a minister on August 27, 1889. In 1892 he was the official interpreter for the Jerome commissioners at Fort Sill. He contracted tuberculosis, as did many Indians who returned from the East, and died in March, 1893. Morning Star, 6 (June, 1886), 7; Arrow, September 6, 1907; Oklahoma Historical Society, Archives Division, Kiowa--Trial of Santanta and Big Tree, November 21, 1885; Volume Kiowa 39, January 9 and April 27, 1893, pp. 13, 155; Volume Kiowa 40, February 2, 1894, p. 197; Volume Kiowa 74, January 5, 1900, p. 399.

GOFF, ROSE (Assiniboin)
    Rose Goff was a student at the Pipestone Indian School in 1916.

GOLSH, MARY (Mission)
    Mary Golsh, from California, graduated from Sherman Institute in 1912 and from Haskell Institute in 1914. She married Bert Jamison of Tiff City, Missouri. In 1916 she lived at Fort Defiance, Arizona. Sherman Bulletin June 2, 1915, and May 24, 1916; Indian Leader, 18 (June, 1914), 24.

GOLSH, ROSA (Mission)
    Rosa Golsh graduated from Sherman Institute, Riverside, California, in 1910. She then entered Haskell Institute at Lawrence,

Kansas, where she remained in 1916. Sherman Bulletin, May 24, 1916.

GONZALES, FELIX (Mission)
Felix Gonzales was a student at the Banning Mission School in 1896.

GOODBOY, BESSIE (Sioux)
Bessie Goodboy attended Santee Normal Training School.

GOODBOY, SARA (Sioux)
Sara Goodboy attended Santee Normal Training School. After leaving there she attended school at Bismarck, North Dakota. Iapi Oaye, 49 (June-July, 1920), 23.

GOODCLOUD, FRANK (Standing Rock Sioux)
Frank Goodcloud lived at Fort Yates, North Dakota.

GOODE, ANDREW (Mono, i.e., Monache)
Andrew Goode, who was from North Fork, California, graduated from Sherman Institute in 1919.

GOODEAGLE, CHARLES (Quapaw)
Charles Goodeagle was a 1906 graduate of Haskell Institute. He married Helen Lockley and lived near Baxter Springs, Kansas.

GOODEAGLE, FANNIE (Quapaw)
Fannie Goodeagle attended Haskell Institute and in 1910 lived at Wyandotte, Oklahoma. Indian Leader, September 9, 1910.

GOULD, ISAAC R. (Alaska Native)
Isaac R. Gould graduated from Carlisle Indian Industrial School in 1907. In 1915 he ran a fox farm at his home in Unga Island, Alaska. Arrow, March 29, 1907; Red Man, 7 (May-June, 1915), 327.

GOWDY, APIS (Yakima)
From Washington, Apis Gowdy was a student at Chemawa Indian School in 1911.

GOYITNEY, ANNIE (Pueblo)
Annie Goyitney, from New Mexico, graduated from Carlisle Indian Industrial School in 1901 and then attended Bloomsbury Normal School. Her married name was Canfield, and in 1909 she and her husband were teaching at Zuni. In 1913 and for several years thereafter, she worked at the Paraje Day School at Casa Blanca on the Laguna Reservation. Red Man, 6 (February, 1914), 241.

GRANDE, ENCARNATION (Mission)
In 1895, Encarnation Grande was a student at St. Anthony's Industrial School, San Diego.

GRAYSON, GEORGE WASHINGTON (Creek)
George Washington Grayson was born near Eufaula, Creek Nation, in 1843, the son of James and Jennie Wynn Grayson. He attended Creek public schools, Asbury Manual Labor School, and Arkansas College at Fayetteville. He served as national treasurer for eight years and delegate to Washington several times. He was also a member of the House of Warriors and a delegate to the International Council at Okmulgee. In 1877 he edited the "Creek Department" of the Indian Journal, of which he was associate editor in 1889. Grayson married Georgiana Stidham. In 1917 he was named Creek chief by the president. He served as chief until his death on December 2, 1920, at which time he was writing a history of his tribe.
H. F. O'Beirne and E. S. O'Beirne, The Indian Territory (St. Louis: C. B. Woodward Company, 1892), 131-134; Indian Journal, July 31, 1919, and December 9, 1920.

GREENBRIER, ADELINE (Menominee)
Adeline Greenbrier, from Wisconsin, was born about 1891 and graduated from Carlisle Indian Industrial School in 1910. Her married name was Shawandosa, and in 1915 she was living in Cleveland, Ohio.

GREENBRIER, CARLYSLE (Menominee)
Carlysle Greenbrier, born about 1889, was from Wisconsin. She attended Carlisle Indian Industrial School.

GREENWOOD, T. C. (Sioux)
T. C. Greenwood was a student at Hampton Institute, Hampton, Virginia, in 1887.

GREY CLOUD, DAVID (Santee Sioux)
In 1878, David Grey Cloud was a scribe of the Dakota Presbytery at the Santee Agency, Nebraska. He later served as pastor at Mayasan. Iapi Oaye, 7 (August, 1878), 4; 10 (May, 1881), 40.

GREYBEARD, SALLIE (Eastern Band Cherokee)
Sallie Greybeard graduated from Carlisle Indian Industrial School in 1917.

GUNTER, KEE KEE (Cherokee)
Kee Kee Gunter was active in protesting against the establishment of a territorial government in the Indian Territory.

GURULE, RALPH E. (Pueblo)
Ralph E. Gurule graduated from the blacksmithing course at Haskell Institute in 1906.

GUTIERREZ, CARLOTTA (Navajo)
Carlotta Gutierrez, from Nacimiento, New Mexico, was a student at Hampton Institute, Hampton, Virginia, from 1903 to 1906. Thirty-Fifth Annual Catalogue of the Hampton Normal and Agricultural Institute (Hampton: Hampton Institute Press, 1903), 112.

GUY, JAMES HARRIS (Chickasaw)
James Harris Guy, from the Indian Territory, was the son of
William Guy. He was a deputy U.S. Marshal and a member of the
Indian police force in the Chickasaw Nation. He was killed in a gun
battle with outlaws on May 1, 1885. He supposedly wrote a great
deal of poetry, but apparently little of it has survived. H. F.
O'Beirne, Leaders and Leading Men of the Indian Territory (Chicago:
American Publishers' Association, 1891), 213.

HAMILTON, ROBERT J. (Piegan)
Robert J. Hamilton, from the Blackfeet Reservation in Montana,
attended Carlisle Indian Industrial School. He made his home near
Browning, Montana. For a while, he was a clerk in a trading house
and then ranched. He was active in tribal affairs, urging his people to attend nonreservation schools. In 1925, he was elected to
the Business Council of the Blackfeet tribe from the Browning District.

HAMLIN, GEORGE H. (White Earth Chippewa)
George Hamlin, from Mahnomen on the White Earth Reservation
in Minnesota, graduated from Hampton in 1903. He died in 1905.
Thirty-Fifth Annual Catalogue of the Hampton Normal and Agricultural
Institute (Hampton: Hampton Institute Press, 1903), 111.

HAMLIN, LOUIS C. (White Earth Chippewa)
Louis C. Hamlin graduated from Hampton Institute in 1905.
He lived at Mahnomen, Minnesota. Thirty-Fifth Annual Catalogue
of the Hampton Normal and Agricultural Institute (Hampton: Hampton
Institute Press, 1903), 111.

HANCOCK, BENJAMIN (Choctaw)
Benjamin Hancock was full Choctaw and in 1877 was a teacher
at Double Spring, Coal County, Choctaw Nation.

HANCOCK, SIMON (Choctaw)
Simon Hancock was the son of Lewis and Betsy Hancock. He
graduated from Bacone College in 1916.

HAND, HARRY (Crow Creek Sioux)
Harry Hand, or Crazy Bull, was the son of Burnt Prairie.
He entered Hampton Institute in 1889 at age 18. 52 Congress, 1
Session, Senate Executive Document 31, 48-49.

HANKS, ROBERT T. (Cherokee)
Robert T. Hanks of Webbers Falls, Cherokee Nation, was a
well-known public figure. He held several positions after 1881: member of the House of Representatives, clerk of the Senate, and executive secretary. He wrote under the name Black Fox. Oklahoma Historical Society, Archives Division, Cherokee Volume 274, November
7, 1881, p. 186; Cherokee Volume 284, November 14, 1885, p. 37;
Cherokee Volume 283, February 15, 1892, p. 76.

HANSKAKAGAPI, JOSEPH (Sioux)
No information is available.

HARE, DAVID (Yankton Sioux)
David Hare graduated from the Santee Normal Training School and then from Huron College. In 1905 he lived in Greenwood, South Dakota, where he was a stenographer for an attorney. Word Carrier, 34 (September–October, 1905), 17.

HARE, DE WITT (Sioux)
De Witt Hare attended Santee Normal Training School at Santee, Nebraska. In 1903 he attended Commercial College at Grand Junction, Colorado, and in 1905 he was a stenographer in the attorney general's office at Wagner, South Dakota. He was a newspaper editor for a time in North Dakota, and in 1918 he lived in Minneapolis. He engaged in several kinds of businesses, studied law, and became a promoter. In 1922 he was in Sioux City, Iowa, selling buffalo for the well-known "Scotty" Phillips herd. Word Carrier, 51 (July–August, 1922), 14; Red Man, 6 (February, 1914), 241.

HARJO, HENRY M. (Creek)
Henry M. Harjo graduated from the Indian University in 1886 and became a teacher in the Creek Nation.

HARJO, IDA (Creek)
Ida Harjo graduated from Haskell Institute in 1908. She married John Goat and lived at Holdenville, Oklahoma.

HARKINS, GEORGE W. (Chickasaw)
George W. Harkins was the son of Willis J. Harkins, a Choctaw, but lived in the Chickasaw Nation most of his life. He was educated at Center College, Danville, Kentucky, and received a law degree from Cumberland University. In 1834 he was judge of Red River District, and in 1856 he was chief of Apuckshunubbee District. He served as superintendent of the Chickasaw Board of Education and as delegate to Washington. He was an effective speaker, and his speeches before the U.S. Congress earned him the title of "Rawhide Orator." Harkins died in August, 1890. H. F. O'Beirne, Leaders and Leading Men of the Indian Territory (Chicago: American Publishers' Association, 1891), 254; Oklahoma Historical Society, Archives Division, Choctaw--Principal Chief, No. 19457; Chickasaw--Federal Relations, 1888, No. 7072.

HARLIN, NONA P. (Cherokee)
Nona P. Harlin was a teacher in the Cherokee Nation. Oklahoma Historical Society, Archives Division, Cherokee Volume 544, June 26 and December 25, 1896, pp. 1, 5.

HARPER, ALFRED (Cherokee)
No information is available.

HARRIS, COLONEL JOHNSON (Cherokee)

Colonel Johnson Harris was born in Georgia on April 19, 1856, the son of William Harris and Susan Collins, the latter of Cherokee descent. After his father died, his mother moved to the Cherokee Nation in the early 1870's. Harris was educated in the common schools of Canadian District and at the Male Seminary. He was married three times--to Nannie E. Fields, daughter of Richard F. Fields; Mary E. Adair, the daughter of William Penn Adair (q.v.); and Mrs. Caroline A. (Hall) Collins. He was elected to the Cherokee Senate in 1881, 1883, and 1899, serving as its president from 1883 to 1885. He was a delegate to Washington in 1886 and 1895, and in 1891 he was elected principal chief of the nation. John Bartlett Meserve, "Chief Colonel Johnson Harris," Chronicles of Oklahoma, 17 (March, 1939), 17-21.

HARRIS, EDITH (Catawba)

Edith Harris was a student at Carlisle Indian Industrial School in 1908 and 1909.

HARRIS, HARVEY C. (Eel River)

Harvey Harris graduated from Sherman Institute in 1909. In 1916 he lived at Moreno. Sherman Bulletin, May 24, 1916.

HARRIS, HENRY E. (Pyramid Lake Ute)

Henry E. Harris, who was from Silver City, Nevada, entered the Indian Industrial School at Grand Junction, Colorado, after having attended public school for four years. Red Man, 8 (June, 1888), 7.

HART, JOSEPH C. (Umatilla)

Joseph C. Hart was a student at Haskell Institute in 1908.

HASHOLY, NANCY (Sioux)

Nancy Hasholy was born in 1888 in North Dakota, the daughter of Henry Owns Medicine and his wife Louise. She began school at age seven or eight and entered Carlisle Indian Industrial School in 1904. She was still there in 1909.

HASTINGS, CATHERINE (Cherokee)

Catherine Hastings, who wrote under the name of "Na-li," was full Cherokee. She was given her English name by missionaries at Dwight Mission. She was sent to the Cherokee Female Seminary, from which she graduated in 1855. She married Jenkins Whitesides Maxfield. Emmet Starr, History of the Cherokee Indians and Their Legends and Folk Lore (Oklahoma City: The Warden Company, 1921), 233, 678.

HASTINGS, WILLIAM WIRT (Cherokee)

William Wirt Hastings was born in Arkansas on December 31, 1866, the son of William Archibald Yell and Louisa J. (Stover) Lynch Hastings, the latter a member of the Cherokee tribe. He was reared

at Beatties Prairie, Cherokee Nation, and attended Cherokee common
schools and the Cherokee Male Seminary, from which he graduated
in 1884. After teaching in Cherokee schools for one year, Hastings
entered Vanderbilt, receiving a law degree in 1889. He formed a
partnership with E. C. Boudinot (q.v.) and served as attorney for
the Cherokee Nation. After Oklahoma statehood, he represented
the state in Congress for eighteen years. He married Lulu Starr.
Hastings died on April 8, 1938. William P. Thompson, "W. W. Hastings," Chronicles of Oklahoma, 16 (June, 1938), 269-270; H. F.
O'Beirne and E. S. O'Beirne, The Indian Territory (St. Louis: C.
B. Woodward Company, 1892), 441-443.

HATCH, AGNES (Chippewa)
      Agnes Hatch, who was from Michigan, was a student at Carlisle
Indian Industrial School in 1917.

HATCH, NICK (Aleut)
      Nick Hatch was a 1913 graduate of Chemawa Indian School.

HAUSER, ANNA (Southern Cheyenne)
      Anna Hauser, from Oklahoma, was born about 1891. She was
a 1913 graduate of Carlisle Indian Industrial School, after which she
attended Metzger College. In 1911 she attended the founding meeting of the American Indian Association in Columbus, Ohio. Oklahoma
Historical Society, Archives Division, Cheyenne and Arapaho--Carlisle,
October 13, 1910, and July 13 and August 17, 1911; Red Man, 5 (May,
1913), 435.

HAUSER, MARY (Southern Cheyenne)
      A Southern Cheyenne, Mary Hauser was educated at Darlington,
Oklahoma, a convent school in Leavenworth, Kansas, and Haskell
Institute, from which she graduated in 1903. In 1905 she married
Robert De Poe (q.v.). She returned to Haskell in 1907 as a substi-
tute teacher. The De Poes later lived at Ford, Washington. Indian
Leader, April 16, 1909.

HAUSER, PETER (Southern Cheyenne)
      Peter Hauser, who was from Oklahoma, graduated from the
Carlisle Indian Industrial School in 1910. In 1912, he lived at Calumet, Oklahoma, where he farmed. Oklahoma Historical Society,
Archives Division, Cheyenne and Arapaho--Carlisle, December 28,
1907; Red Man, 5 (October, 1912), 85.

HAWK, BERTHA B. (Sioux)
      Bertha B. Hawk was a student at Carlisle Indian Industrial
School in 1909.

HAWKINS, DIANA (Southern Cheyenne)
      Diana Hawkins was from Geary, Oklahoma. She studied house-
keeping at Chilocco Indian Agricultural School, from which she

graduated in 1918. Oklahoma Historical Society, Archives Division, Cheyenne and Arapaho--Chilocco Indian School, October 27, 1911, and September 10, 1918; Cheyenne and Arapaho--Haskell Institute, April 30, 1919, and January 16, 1923.

HAYES, AXTELL (Nez Percé)
Axtell Hayes was born in 1890. He entered Carlisle Indian Industrial School in 1904 and remained as late as 1908.

HEBRON, ELSIE (Paiute)
Elsie Hebron was a 1910 graduate of Sherman Institute. Her married name was Carter, and in 1916 she lived in Danville, Illinois. Sherman Bulletin, May 24, 1916.

HEMLOCK, JULIA (Seneca)
Julia Hemlock was a student at Carlisle Indian Industrial School in 1908 and 1909.

HENRY, LEVI J. (Cherokee)
Levi J. Henry was born about 1860 and lived in Indian Territory.

HENTOH (Wyandot)
See WALKER, BERTRAND N. O.

HERMAN, JAMES (Rosebud Sioux)
No information is available.

HERROD, MARY LEWIS (Creek)
Mary Herrod was born in the western Creek Nation in the early 1840's, the daughter of John and Louisa Kernels Lewis. She attended Tullahassee Mission near present-day Muskogee, Oklahoma, and later taught there, at Wewogufkee Town, among the Euchees, and at the Old Agency School. She married Goliath Herrod and settled at North Fork Town. After his death, Mrs. Herrod returned to teaching and had a long and distinguished career in the Creek public schools. She died at Wagoner, Oklahoma, in 1917. Carolyn Thomas Foreman, "Two Notable Women of the Creek Nation," Chronicles of Oklahoma, 35 (Autumn, 1957), 315-325.

HESCHINYA, MARY H. (Pueblo)
Mary H. Heschinya attended Carlisle Indian Industrial School.

HEWITT, JOHN NAPOLEON BRINTON (Tuscarora)
John Napoleon Brinton Hewitt was born at Lewiston, New York, on December 16, 1859, the son of David Hewitt and Harriet Brinton Hewitt, the latter of whom was of Tuscarora descent. He attended schools in Niagara Falls, Lockport, and Lewiston. He had plans for a medical career but in 1880 began working for Ermine A. Smith, whom he helped collect Iroquois myths during the next four years. When Smith died in 1886, Hewitt was called on by the

Bureau of American Ethnology to help complete Smith's work. Hewitt was associated with the Bureau for a half century, during which time he wrote extensively on the Six Nations. He was one of the founders of the American Anthropological Association. He was fluent in Tuscarora, Onandaga, and Mohawk. Hewitt died on October 14, 1937. Quarterly Journal of the Society of American Indians, 2 (April-June, 1914), 146-150; Frederick J. Dockstader, Great North American Indians (New York: Van Nostrand Reinhold Company, 1977), 107-108.

HEYL, RICHARD D. (Apache)
    Richard D. Heyl was captured in Arizona about 1872 by the U.S. Army. The child was reared by Colonel C. H. Heyl and his family in the East. Heyl lived in Camden, New Jersey, where he worked in the office of the assistant engineer of the Amboy Division of the Pennsylvania Railroad. He married Louise Eaton Odenheimer. Red Man and Helper, January 10, 1902, and January 16, 1903.

HICKS, AARON (Cherokee)
    Aaron Hicks was an Old Settler Cherokee and lived in Skin Bayou District of the Cherokee Nation.

HICKS, ED D. (Cherokee)
    Ed D. Hicks was a teacher and in the 1890's was director of the Tahlequah Public Schools in the Cherokee Nation. Oklahoma Historical Society, Archives Division, Cherokee Volume 545, September 4, 1896, p. 26.

HICKS, ELIJAH (Cherokee)
    Elijah Hicks was born in the Eastern Cherokee Nation on June 20, 1796, the son of Charles Renatus Hicks, who was principal chief in 1827. In 1822, he served as clerk of the National Council; in 1826-1827, he was president of that body. In 1832, John Ross (q.v.), whose sister Margaret he married, appointed him editor of the Cherokee Phoenix. In 1839, Hicks settled near present-day Claremore, Oklahoma. He was one of the framers of the 1839 constitution and was several times a delegate to Washington. Hicks died on August 6, 1856. Grant Foreman, ed., "The Journal of Elijah Hicks," Chronicles of Oklahoma, 13 (March, 1935), 68-99.

HICKS, GEORGE WASHINGTON (Cherokee)
    George Washington Hicks graduated from the Indian University and then completed a course of study at the Rochester Theological Seminary in New York. He was sent by the New York Home Board as a missionary to the Anadarko Agency, where he remained several years. He married Jane Ballew. Indian Missionary, 3 (May, 1887), 6, and (July, 1887), 3; 4 (November, 1888), 1.

HICKS, VICTORIA SUSAN (Cherokee)
    Victoria Susan Hicks graduated from the Cherokee Female Semi-

nary in 1856. Emmet Starr, History of the Cherokee Indians and
Their Legends and Folk Lore (Oklahoma City: The Warden Company,
1921), 233.

HICKS, WILLIAM, SR. (Cherokee)
    William Hicks was born in the Eastern Cherokee Nation, the
son of Nathan Hicks, a Scots trader, and Nancy, the daughter of
Broom. Hicks was the second chief of the Cherokees to serve under
the constitution of 1827, having finished the term of his brother,
who died in office.

HIGHEAGLE, ROBERT PLACIDUS (Standing Rock Sioux)
    Robert Placidus Higheagle, whose Indian name was Kahektakiya,
was born about 1873, the son of High Eagle. An 1895 graduate of
Hampton Institute, he became a teacher at Lower Brule. In 1896,
he was an interpreter and assistant clerk at Standing Rock. He
reentered the teaching field at Bull Head, South Dakota, on the Standing Rock Reservation and remained there for about two decades.
During this time, he also assisted in the work of the Bureau of American Ethnology on the music of the Teton Sioux. Higheagle married
Mary Louisa Ribble. Talks and Thoughts, August and November,
1896; Red Man, 12 (May, 1895), 6; 51 Congress, 1 Session, Senate
Executive Document 31, 50-51.

HIGHTOWER, JOSHUA (Chickasaw)
    In 1878 Joshua Hightower was superintendent of schools in
the Chickasaw Nation, a position he held for a number of years.
Oklahoma Historical Society, Archives Division, Chickasaw--Chickasaw
Orphan Home, February 11, 1881, No. 11832.

HILDEBRAND, ORAGONIA B. (Osage)
    Oragonia B. Hildebrand was a 1914 graduate of Sherman Insti-
tute. In 1916 she lived at Chickasha, Oklahoma. Sherman Bulletin,
May 24, 1916.

HILDEBRAND, SUSAN C. (Osage)
    Susan C. Hildebrand was a 1913 graduate of Sherman Institute.
In 1916, she lived at Emporia, Kansas. Sherman Bulletin, May 24,
1916.

HILL, DAVID RUSSELL (Oneida)
    Born about 1874, David Russell Hill was the son of William Hill
of Onondaga, New York. He entered Hampton Institute in 1890 and
graduated in 1895. 52 Congress, 1 Session, Senate Executive
Document 31, 50-51; Red Man, 12 (May, 1895), 6.

HILL, ISRAEL (Oneida)
    Israel Hill, who was from Wisconsin, was the son of Charles
Hill. He entered Hampton Institute in 1889 at age nineteen. 52 Congress, 1 Session Senate Executive Document 31, 48-49.

HILL, JESSE (Seneca)
Jesse Hill, a native of New York, attended Hampton Institute.

HILL, JOSEPHINE (Oneida)
Josephine Hill, who was from Wisconsin, was a student at Hampton Institute in 1904. After graduation, she taught in the government school at Oneida and then for several years taught lacemaking under the Sybil Carter Lace Association. She married Isaac N. Webster (q.v.). Thirty-Fifth Annual Catalogue of the Hampton Normal and Agricultural Institute (Hampton: Hampton Institute Press, 1903), 111; Some Results of Hampton's Work (Hampton: The Institute Press, 1915), 24.

HILL, MARIE (Onandaga)
Marie Hill was a student at Carlisle Indian Industrial School in 1909.

HILL, MINA (Klamath)
Mina Hill was a 1908 graduate of Sherman Institute. Sherman Bulletin, May 25, 1916.

HILLMAN, LEVI (Oneida)
Levi Hillman was from Wisconsin and attended Carlisle Indian Industrial School in 1909 and 1910.

HITCHCOCK, RAYMOND (Hupa)
Raymond Hitchcock was a 1910 graduate of Carlisle Indian Industrial School. He later resided in San Francisco.

HODJKISS, WILLIAM D. (Cheyenne River Sioux)
William D. Hodjkiss, from the Cheyenne River Reservation, was half Sioux. He served as clerk at Cheyenne, Arapaho, and Quapaw agencies.

HOFFMAN, JOHANNA E. (Red Lake Chippewa)
Johanna E. Hoffman attended Chemawa Indian School.

HOLT, LITTLE BEAR H., JR. (Sioux)
No information is available.

HOLT, R. D. (Yakima)
No information is available.

HOMEHOYOMA, NORA (Hopi)
Nora Homehoyoma was a student at Sherman Institute in 1912 and 1913.

HOMER, MARY (Choctaw)
Mary Homer was from Atoka, Choctaw Nation.

HONYOUST, WILLIAM (Oneida)
William Honyoust was a student at Hampton Institute in 1894.

HOOD, TENA M. (Klamath)
In 1908, Tena M. Hood was a student at Carlisle Indian Industrial School.

HOPPER, RICHARD (Cherokee)
Richard Hopper was a 1913 graduate of Haskell Institute.

HOXIE, SARA G. (Nomlaki)
Sara G. Hoxie was born at Covelo, California. She attended the Round Valley School and then entered the Phoenix Indian School from which she graduated in 1907. She then attended Carlisle Indian Industrial School, graduating in 1910. She later lived at Round Valley. Red Man, 4 (October, 1911), 86.

HUBBARD, CHESTER (Oklahoma Seneca)
Chester Hubbard was from Wyandotte, Oklahoma. After serving in the Navy, he studied horticulture at Chilocco Indian Agricultural School, from which he graduated in 1919.

HUFF, MORRIS (Seneca)
Morris Huff was a student at Carlisle Indian Industrial School in 1909.

HUNT, ALFRED (Acoma Pueblo)
No information is available.

HUNT, IRVING (Pueblo)
Irving Hunt was a student at Haskell Institute in 1909.

HUNTER, FLORENCE D. (Fort Totten Sioux)
Florence D. Hunter graduated from the Carlisle Indian Industrial School in 1908. She then attended pharmacy school in Philadelphia. She married Alvah F. Greaves and in 1912 lived in Boyertown, Pennsylvania, where her husband owned a drug store. Arrow, April 3, 1908; Red Man, 4 (June, 1912), 485; Indian Craftsman 2 (November, 1909), 41.

HUNTER, LUCY E. (Winnebago)
Lucy E. Hunter graduated from Santee Normal Training School in 1910. She graduated from Hampton Institute in 1915 and entered the Training School for Christian Workers in New York. She was for several years the Y.M.C.A. secretary for Indian Work. Hunter married John Kennedy of Caughnawaga, Canada. Iapi Oaye, 49 (June-July, 1920), 23; Word Carrier, 50 (July-August, 1921), 15.

HUSS, JOHN (Cherokee)
John Huss was a native preacher at Honey Creek, Cherokee Nation. "About Some of Our First Schools in Choctaw Nation," Chronicles of Oklahoma, 6 (September, 1928), 378-379.

IKE, LUCINDA (Klamath)
In 1912, Lucinda Ike was a student at Sherman Institute.

INGALLS, SADIE M. (Sac and Fox)
Sadie M. Ingalls, born in the Indian Territory about 1889, was a 1913 graduate of Carlisle Indian Industrial School, after which she attended Metzger College for a short time. She then returned to her home at Cushing, Oklahoma. Red Man, 5 (May, 1913), 435; 7 (January, 1915), 184.

IRON, ERNEST (Crow)
In 1910, Ernest Iron was a student at Carlisle Indian Industrial School.

IRON CROW, AMELIA (Sioux)
In 1900, Amelia Iron Crow was a student at the Oglala Boarding School.

IRONROAD, IGNATIUS (Sioux)
Ignatius Ironroad was from North Dakota and graduated from the Carlisle Indian Industrial School in 1906. He lived at Cannon Ball. Arrow, March 30, 1906; Word Carrier, 51 (September-December, 1922), 20.

IRVING, JAMES (Yankton Sioux)
James Irving was educated at St. Paul's Mission School on the Yankton Reservation and at Haskell Institute. He studied law at the University of Oregon and the Illinois College of Law at Chicago. He was admitted to the bar in 1922. Irving was judge of the juvenile court of Pipestone County, Minnesota, and in 1924 he was elected judge of the probate court. Word Carrier, 53 (November-December, 1924), 21.

IRVING, JOHN W. (Yankton Sioux)
John W. Irving was a student at Haskell Institute in 1907.

ISHAM, WILLIAM J. (Lac Courte Orielles Chippewa)
William J. Isham, who was from the Lac Courte Orielles Reservation in Wisconsin, entered Carlisle Indian Industrial School in 1903. He later entered the Indian Service and lived at Bena, Minnesota, where he worked in the lumber industry. Red Man and Helper, August 28, 1903; Red Man, 6 (January, 1914), 205.

IVEY, AUGUSTUS (Cherokee)
Augustus Ivey was born in the Cherokee Nation in 1855, the son of James W. and Charlotte Ivey. His father was white and his mother was of Cherokee descent. He married Julia A. Sixkiller (q.v.). He was by profession a newspaper man. In the 1890's, he edited the Tahlequah Telephone. In 1910 he published the Indian Home and Farm at Muskogee in English, Cherokee, Creek, and Choctaw.

Oklahoma Historical Society, Archives Division, Cherokee Volume
261, December 5, 1885, p. 174; Cherokee Volume 513, November 21,
1894, p. 240; Litton, Cherokee Papers, 1901-1925, December 13,
1906, p. 313.

JACK, NORA (Maidu)
    Nora Jack was a 1915 graduate of Sherman Institute. She lived
at Jonesville, California. Sherman Bulletin, May 24, 1916.

JACKSON, JONAS (Eastern Band Cherokee)
    Jonas Jackson was a 1907 graduate of Carlisle Indian Industrial
School. Arrow, March 29, 1907.

JACKSON, JULIA (Crow)
    Julia Jackson was a student at Carlisle Indian Industrial School
in 1907.

JACKSON, STELLA (Chippewa)
    In 1915, Stella Jackson was a student at the Pipestone Indian
School.

JAGO, FRANK (Pima)
    Frank Jago, from Sacaton, Arizona, was a 1916 graduate of
Sherman Institute.

JAMES, HATTIE (Winnebago)
    Hattie James was from Nebraska and was a student at Hampton
Institute from 1890 through 1893.

JANIS, ELLEN (Sioux)
    Ellen Janis was a student at the Oglala Boarding School in
1919 and 1920.

JEFFERSON, THOMAS (Mohave)
    Thomas Jefferson was a student at the Colorado River Agency
School in Arizona in 1897.

JEMISON, IRENE B. (Cattaraugus Seneca)
    Irene B. Jemison graduated from Hampton Institute in 1895
and later taught at Genoa, New York. Red Man, 12 (May, 1895),
6; Talks and Thoughts, November, 1896.

JEROME, ELMIRA C. (Chippewa)
    Elmira Jerome attended Carlisle Indian Industrial School. After
graduation, she became assistant seamstress at the government school
at Fort Totten, North Dakota.

JIMERSON, MARY (Onandaga)
    Mary Jimerson was a student at Carlisle Indian Industrial School
in 1909.

JOHN, ANDREW (Seneca)
No information is available.

JOHNSON, A. ELLA (Seneca)
A. Ella Johnson, born in New York about 1887, graduated from Carlisle Indian Industrial School in 1912. She lived in Batavia, New York.

JOHNSON, ADDISON E. (Eastern Band Cherokee)
Addison E. Johnson, from Cherokee, North Carolina, attended Carlisle Indian Industrial School.

JOHNSON, EDNA M. (Pit River)
Edna M. Johnson was a 1915 graduate of Sherman Institute. Sherman Bulletin, May 24, 1916.

JOHNSON, FRANK (Alaska Native)
Frank Johnson graduated from Chemawa Indian School in 1913.

JOHNSON, FRANK L. (Winnebago)
Frank L. Johnson was a student at Carlisle Indian Industrial School in 1910.

JOHNSON, JOHN (Seminole)
John Johnson was from Lima, Oklahoma. After serving in the Army, he studied horticulture at Chilocco Indian Agricultural School, from which he graduated in 1919.

JOHNSON, JOHN P. (Winnebago)
John Johnson graduated from Sherman Institute in 1911. In 1916 he lived in Los Angeles.

JOHNSON, VICTOR H. (Dalles)
Victor H. Johnson, from Washington, graduated from Carlisle in 1904. In 1907 he was a student at Dartmouth.

JONES, FLORA E. (Seneca)
Flora E. Jones, born about 1891, was a student at Carlisle, graduating in 1908. Arrow, April 3, 1908.

JONES, HENRY CLAY (Sac and Fox)
Henry Clay Jones served as interpreter for the Sac and Fox at the International Council in 1873, blacksmith at the Sac and Fox Agency, Supreme Court judge of the Sac and Fox Nation, and industrial teacher at the Pawnee School. Oklahoma Historical Society, Archives Division, International Council Files, December 1873, p. 3; Sac and Fox--Employees, July 13, 1885; Sac and Fox Volume 13, January 11, 1888, p. 386; Volume Pawnee 11, November 1, 1897, p. 223.

JONES, LUCY N. (Tuscarora)
Lucy N. Jones, who was from New York, attended Hampton
Institute. In 1896 she became a teacher in South Dakota. Talks
and Thoughts, October, 1896.

JONES, PENNINAH (Sioux)
Penninah Jones graduated from the Santee Normal Training
School in 1918. She married a man named McBride and lived at Dante,
South Dakota.

JONES, SIMON (Rosebud Sioux)
In 1914, Simon Jones lived at Pine Ridge, where his father
was a missionary. He was a student at the Santee Normal Training
School, Santee, Nebraska. Word Carrier, 44 (May-June, 1915), 9.

JONES, STEPHEN S. (Santee Sioux)
Stephen S. Jones was from the Santee Reservation. He attended
Hampton Institute, which he left in 1897, and entered Santee Normal
Training School at Santee, Nebraska. Later, he attended Haskell
Institute and then returned to the East to study at the Y.M.C.A.
Training School at Springfield, Massachusetts. Jones was appointed
secretary at large for Indian Work for the Y.M.C.A. Making his
home at Mitchell, South Dakota, he covered the field from Manitoba
to Oklahoma. He married Harriet Rouillard. Some Results of Hampton's Work (Hampton: The Institute Press, 1915), 28.

JONES, WILLIAM (Sac and Fox)
William Jones was born near present-day Stroud, Oklahoma,
in the Sac and Fox Reservation on March 28, 1871, the son of Henry
Clay (q.v.) and Sarah E. Penny Jones, from whom he inherited a
mixture of Fox, English, and Welsh blood. Sarah Jones died when
Jones was quite young, and for his first nine years he was raised
by his grandmother, Kitiqua, the daughter of the Fox Chief Wa-
shi-ho-wa, who taught Jones the traditions, language, and customs
of his Fox ancestors. At ten, Jones was sent to Indian school at
Newton, Kansas, and later spent three years at the Friends' boarding school in Wabash, Indiana. In 1889, he entered Hampton Institute and later enrolled in Philips Academy at Andover, Massachusetts.
In 1896, he entered Harvard, where he received his A. B. degree
in 1900. He received his A. M. degree in 1901 and went on to earn
a Ph.D. In 1906, he accepted an assignment from the Field Columbian
Museum in Chicago to study the native tribes of the Philippines.
He remained there for three years, living among the native peoples
of Luzon. On March 28, 1909, he was speared to death by members
of the Ilongot tribe, whom he was studying. "William Jones," American Anthropologist, 11 (January, 1909), 137-139; Henry Milner Ride-
out, William Jones: Indian, Cowboy, American Scholar, and Anthropologist in the Field (New York: Frederick A. Stokes Company,
1912), passim; Frederick J. Dockstader, Great North American Indians (New York: Van Nostrand Reinhold Company, 1977), 127-128.

JONES, WILSON N. (Choctaw)
    Wilson N. Jones was principal chief of the Choctaw Nation from
1890 to 1894.

JORDAN, HENRY M. (Mohawk)
    Henry M. Jordan was a student at Carlisle Indian Industrial
School in 1909.

JORDAN, JOHN W. (Cherokee)
    John W. Jordan was born in the Cherokee Nation in 1861, the
son of Levi and Malinda Jordan. Jordan farmed for a number of
years in Canadian District and then moved to the Cherokee Strip
in the early 1880's and began ranching. When the Cherokee Strip
was opened to settlement in 1893, Jordan and his family received
allotments near the town site of Kildare. Jordan married Sallie Bean
Thompson, Martha Rowland, and Tennessee Riley. Oklahoma Historical Society, Archives Division, Cherokee Census Card, No. 10279;
Emmet Starr, History of the Cherokee Indians and Their Legends
and Folk Lore (Oklahoma City: The Warden Company, 1921), 438.

JORDAN, PETER JOSEPH (Chippewa)
    Peter Joseph Jordan, born about 1885 in Wisconsin, was a 1914
graduate of Carlisle, after which he attended Keewaton Academy at
Prairie du Chien, where he also coached football. Red Man, 7 (October, 1914), 74.

JOSE, MAGELA (Papago)
    Magela Jose, from Arizona, graduated from the Phoenix Indian
School in 1910, after which she returned to the Papago Reservation.

JUMPER, JOHN (Seminole)
    John Jumper, a native preacher, was born about 1820. He
was head of the Confederate Seminoles during and after the Civil
War. He served as delegate to the International Council in 1870 and
in 1881 was elected principal chief of the Seminole Nation. Jumper
died in 1896. Frederick J. Dockstader, Great North American Indians
(New York: Van Nostrand Reinhold Company, 1977), 131-132; Oklahoma Historical Society, Archives Division, International Council File,
June, 1870; Creek--Foreign Relations, Seminole, March 31, 1881,
No. 30647, and July 4, 1882, No. 30676.

KACHIKUM, LOUISE (Menominee)
    Louise Kachikum graduated from Carlisle Indian Industrial School
in 1912.

KADASHON, MARY R. (Alaska Native)
    Mary R. Kadashon graduated from Carlisle Indian Industrial
School in 1905. She then attended Northfield Training School at
Northfield, Massachusetts, where she worked her way through by

giving mission talks to various missionary societies in the East. Red Man, 2 (February, 1910), 46.

KAUBOODLE, CHARLES (Kiowa)
Charles Kauboodle was a student at Carlisle Indian Industrial School in 1881.

KAY, SUSIE (Creek)
Susie Kay was a student at the Tullahassee Mission School in 1870.

KEALEAR, CHARLES H. (Yankton Sioux)
Charles H. Kealear was born in 1870, the son of Alex Kealear. A Yankton from South Dakota, he received several years of education at the Episcopal mission at the Yankton Agency and at Jubilee, Illinois, before entering Carlisle Indian Industrial School. In 1888, he attended Moody's School at Northfield, Massachusetts, and graduated from Hampton Institute the following year. After graduation, he assisted in the mission on the Standing Rock Reservation, worked as an industrial teacher at the government school there, taught at St. Paul's School, and then went to Genoa, Nebraska, where he was an employee and a student. In 1892, he moved to Wyoming where he later served as postmaster at Arapaho and worked for the Chicago and Northwestern Railroad. He died in November, 1922. 52 Congress, 1 Session, Senate Executive Document 31, 27, 46-47.

KEEL, WILLIAM (Chickasaw)
William Keel studied horticulture at Chilocco Indian Agricultural School, from which he graduated in 1919.

KENDALL, HENRY J. (Isleta Pueblo)
Henry Kendall attended Carlisle Indian Industrial School and in 1889 entered Rutgers. Red Man, 9 (June, 1899), 5.

KENNEDY, ALVIN W. (Seneca)
Alvin W. Kennedy, from Salamanca, New York, was born in 1892. A graduate of Carlisle in 1911, he joined the U.S. Navy and was stationed on the U.S.S. Jenkins and later in the Canal Zone as a wireless operator. He later worked as a telegrapher for the Chicago and Northwestern Railroad at Shawano, Wisconsin. Kennedy married Mary A. Bailey. Carlisle Arrow, April 22, 1911; Red Man, 4 (September, 1911), 42, and 7 (December, 1914), 148.

KENNEY, HELENA (Klamath)
Helena Kenney was a student at Sherman Institute in 1911.

KENNEY, LOUISA (Klamath)
Louisa Kenney attended Carlisle Indian Industrial School.

KEOKUK, FANNIE (Sac and Fox)
Fannie Keokuk, born about 1890 in the Indian Territory, attended

Carlisle Indian Industrial School, graduating in 1910. She married John Foote and lived at Stroud, Oklahoma. Carlisle Arrow, February 23, 1912.

KESHENA, ELIZA (Menominee)
    Eliza Keshena graduated from the Carlisle Indian Industrial School in 1911. Carlisle Arrow, April 21, 1911.

KESHOITEWA, CLARA TALAVENSKA (Hopi)
    Clara Talavenska Keshoitewa attended the Phoenix Indian School.

KEYES, JAMES M. (Cherokee)
    James M. Keyes was born in the Cherokee Nation on March 25, 1845, the son of Louis and Catharine (McDaniel) Keyes. He was educated in the Cherokee schools and became a merchant at Gibson Station. In 1879 and 1883 he was elected prosecuting attorney of Cooweescoowee District. In 1885 he was elected to the Supreme Court, on which he served as chief justice, and in 1891, he was elected to the Cherokee Senate. Keyes married Nannie J. Mayes. H. F. O'Bierne and E. S. O'Beirne. The Indian Territory (St. Louis: C. B. Woodward Company, 1892), 338; Oklahoma Historical Society, Archives Division, Cherokee Volume 19-C, May 28, 1890, p. 183, Cherokee Volume 53, September 21, 1880, p. 19, Cherokee Volume 287, November 11, 1885, p. 223.

KEYS, RILEY (Cherokee)
    In 1867 Riley Keys was a member of the Cherokee delegation that negotiated the Delaware Agreement. He held many posts in the Cherokee Nation, including delegate to the International Council of 1870, president of the board of trustees for the Male and Female Seminaries, and Chief Justice of the Supreme Court. He died in 1884 at the age of 103. Oklahoma Historical Society, Archives Division, Cherokee--Foreign Relations, April 8, 1867, p. 100; Cherokee Volume 512, December 20, 1876, p. 100; International Council File, September, 1870; Cherokee--Citizenship, August 3, 1874, p. 359.

KILLED, LOUIS (Standing Rock Sioux)
    Louis Killed, or Ktura, was the son of Good-toned Metal. He entered Hampton Institute in August, 1880 at the age of nineteen. 52 Congress, 1 Session, Senate Executive Document 31, 50-51.

KIMMEL HELEN (Sioux)
    Helen Kimmel was a student at Carlisle Indian Industrial School in 1910. She married L. C. De Cora and lived at Valentine, Nebraska. Red Man, 6 (February, 1914), 240.

KINGMAN, HARRY (Cheyenne River Sioux)
    Harry Kingman was a student at Hampton Institute in 1890.

KINGSLEY, EBENEZER (Winnebago)
    Ebenezer Kingsley graduated from Hampton Institute and in

1896 taught at the Cheyenne Agency School at Darlington, Oklahoma. Talks and Thoughts, November, 1896.

KINGSLEY, NETTIE MARY (Winnebago)
Nettie Kingsley attended school at Tomah, Wisconsin, and then entered Carlisle Indian Industrial School. She graduated in 1915 and then attended West Chester Normal School.

KINNINOOK, PAUL (Tlingit)
Paul Kinninook was born in March, 1892 at Port Tongas, Alaska. In 1895 or 1896, his people moved south of Ketchikan. In 1903, Edward Marsden (q.v.), a native missionary, took Kinninook and thirty-five other children to Carlisle Indian Industrial School. Kinninook was there for five years before transferring to Chemawa Indian School, from which he graduated in 1913. In 1914, he was a student at Willamette University. Chemawa American, 15 (June, 1913), 7-10; 16 (June, 1914), 34; Red Man, 6 (January, 1914), 205.

KIRK, SIMON J. (Sioux)
Simon J. Kirk attended Santee Normal Training School.

KNOX, STEPHEN W. (Pima)
Stephen W. Knox was a 1911 graduate of Sherman Institute. He then worked as a printer for The Arlington Times (California). In 1916, he resided at Sacaton, Arizona. Sherman Bulletin, May 24, 1916.

KOHPAY, HARRY (Osage)
Harry Kohpay, from Indian Territory, was an 1891 graduate of Carlisle. He then graduated from Eastman Business College at Poughkeepsie, New York. He made his home at Pawhuska in the Osage Reservation and worked for many years as an interpreter for the Osages. He also served as assistant clerk at the Osage Agency at Pawhuska.

KONKITAH, ROBERT HARRIS (Alaska Native)
No information is available.

KUDNOK, FRED THOMAS (Eskimo)
Fred Thomas Kudnok was from Noorvik.

KUTOOK, CHARLES (Eskimo)
In 1917, Charles Kutook lived in Nome, where he was an assistant teacher.

LACIE, ADAM L. (Cherokee)
Adam L. Lacie was not only a minister of the gospel but was also a Cherokee official, serving as a member of the House of Representatives and the Senate, as a member of the commission to negotiate with the Dawes Commission, and judge of Goingsnake District. Oklahoma Historical Society, Archives Division, Cherokee Volume

274, November 7, 1881, p. 185; Cherokee Volume 287, November 11, 1884, p. 185; Cherokee Volume 235, June 12, 1893, p. 6; Cherokee-- Federal Relations, April 3, 1897, p. 51, No. 1040-A; Indian-Pioneer History, 62:123.

LACK, BERRYMAN (Hupa)
Berryman Lack was from Hoopa, California, and graduated from Sherman Institute in 1910. Sherman Bulletin, May 24, 1916.

LACK, HIRAM (Hupa)
Hiram Lack was a student at Sherman Institute in 1909.

LA CROIX, KATIE (Yankton Sioux)
Katie La Croix was a student at the Genoa Indian School in 1881.

LA FLESCHE, FRANCIS (Omaha)
Francis La Flesche was born in 1857 on the Omaha Reservation in Nebraska, the son of Joseph La Flesche, a former head chief of the tribe, and Tianne. His early years were spent in the relative freedom of the Indian camp, where he was carefully taught in the ways and about the subjects that Omaha boys had been taught traditionally. He was then sent to the Presbyterian mission school at Bellevue, Nebraska, and he later went to Washington, D.C., where he worked as a clerk in the Bureau of Indian Affairs from 1881 to 1910. In 1881, he interpreted for Alice C. Fletcher, who undertook a study of the Omaha tribe and with whom he collaborated for years. He also studied law at the National University Law School in Washington, receiving his LL. B. in 1892 and his LL. M. in 1893. In 1910, La Flesche became an ethnologist for the Bureau of American Ethnology, in which capacity he served until his death on September 5, 1932. He was married to Alice Mitchell and Rosa Bourassa. Margot Liberty, "Francis La Flesche: The Osage Odyssey," in Liberty, ed., American Indian Intellectuals (St. Paul: West Publishing Co., 1978), 45-59; "General Gossip of Authors and Writers," Current Literature, 29 (October, 1900), 415; Elizabeth Luther Cary, "Recent Writings by American Indians," The Book Buyer, 24 (February, 1902), 23; Frederick J. Dockstader, Great North American Indians (New York: Van Nostrand Reinhold Company, 1977), 144-145.

LA FLESCHE, MARGUERITE (Omaha)
Marguerite La Flesche, from Nebraska, was born about 1863, the daughter of Joseph La Flesche. She graduated from Hampton Institute in 1887 and began teaching on the Omaha Reservation. In 1890 she became principal of the government school and served as an interpreter among her people. She married Charles Picotte (q.v.). 52 Congress, 1 Session, Senate Executive Document 31, 8-9.

LA FLESCHE, SUSAN (Omaha)
See PICOTTE, SUSAN LA FLESCHE

LA FLEUR, MITCHELL (Colville)
Mitchell La Fleur was a student at Carlisle Indian Industrial School in 1912.

LA FROMBOISE, JULIA (Sioux)
No information is available.

LA FROMBOISE, JUSTINE AMELIA (Sisseton Sioux)
Justine Amelia La Fromboise, or Mahpiyatowin, was a student at Carlisle Indian Industrial School in 1881 and 1882. Eadle Keahtah Toh, 1 (April, 1881), 4.

LA HAY, JOSEPH M. (Cherokee)
Joseph M. La Hay was born at Boggy Depot, Choctaw Nation, on August 27, 1865, the son of John D. and Helen (Martin) La Hay. He attended the Cherokee public schools and then worked for a time in coal mines in the Choctaw Nation. He then moved to Claremore, Cherokee Nation, and entered politics. He served as clerk of Cooweescoowee District, as senator during two terms, and as delegate to Washington. In 1899, he was elected Treasurer for the Cherokee nation. La Hay married Annie Russell. In 1905, he was an important member of the Sequoyah Convention. He moved to Muskogee in 1908 and practiced law. La Hay died in May, 1911. D. C. Gideon, Indian Territory (New York: The Lewis Publishing Company, 1901), 313-314; Emmet Starr, History of the Cherokee Indians and Their Legends and Folk Lore (Oklahoma City: The Warden Company, 1921), 663; Amos Maxwell, "The Sequoyah Convention," Chronicles of Oklahoma, 28 (Autumn, 1950), 299-340; Tahlequah Arrow, June 1, 1911.

LAMBERT, BAPTISTE P. (Yankton Sioux)
Baptiste P. Lambert entered Hampton Institute at age thirty-two in November, 1886, and left in July, 1889. He was made a catechist and worked with the missionary at Yankton. He then moved to White Swan, where he farmed and had charge of the Episcopal church. 52 Congress, 1 Session, Senate Executive Document 31, 27, 46.

LAMBERT, JESSE B. (Eastern Band Cherokee)
Jesse B. Lambert was a student at Hampton Institute in 1896 and 1897.

LAMBERTON, MAMIE (Klamath)
Mamie Lamberton graduated from Sherman Institute in 1919. She married Oliver Allen and lived at Orleans, California.

LAMOUREAUX, LOUISE G. (Sioux)
Louise G. Lamoureaux, who was from Winner, South Dakota, graduated from Sherman Institute in 1913. Sherman Bulletin, May 24, 1916.

LANE, HELEN F.   (Lummi)
      Helen F. Lane attended Carlisle Indian Industrial School in
1909.

LA POINTE, PIERRE   (Sioux)
      Pierre La Pointe attended the Santee Normal Training School.
In 1895 he lived at Pahata, South Dakota. Iapi Oaye, 24 (November,
1895), 1.

LA POINTE, ROSE   (Sioux)
      Rose La Pointe attended the Santee Normal Training School.
Her married name was Goodeagle, and in 1922 she lived in Dixon,
South Dakota. Word Carrier, 51 (September-December, 1922), 20.

LA POINTE, SAMUEL   (Rosebud Sioux)
      Samuel La Pointe graduated from the Santee Normal Training
School and served in the Army during World War I.

LA POINTE, SAMUEL O.   (Rosebud Sioux)
      Samuel O. La Pointe graduated from Santee Normal Training
School at Santee, Nebraska in 1898. He farmed on the Rosebud Res-
ervation. "What Santee Graduates Are Doing," Word Carrier, 39
(March-April, 1910), 7.

LARGE, ROY   (Shoshoni)
      Roy Large, who was from Wyoming, was a student at Carlisle
Indian Industrial School in 1908 and 1909. Carlisle Arrow, December
20, 1912.

LA ROQUE, DAVID   (Sioux)
      David La Roque was a student at Haskell Institute in 1901.

LASHEN, DAN M.   (Oto)
      No information is available.

LA VATTA, EMMA   (Fort Hall Shoshoni)
      Emma La Vatta, born about 1890 on the Fort Hall Reservation,
Idaho, was a 1911 graduate of Carlisle Indian Industrial School. After
graduation, she settled at Pocatello and married Alphonso Hutch of
Fort Hall. Carlisle Arrow, April 21, 1911.

LA VATTA, GEORGE P.   (Fort Hall Shoshoni)
      George P. La Vatta, born about 1894, attended Carlisle Indian
Industrial School. He graduated in 1913 and returned to his home
at Fort Hall, Idaho. He became a laborer for the Union Pacific Railroad and worked up through the ranks to a position in which he
helped organize safety and other programs. During this time, he
also conducted youth employment programs on his reservation. In
1929 he became assistant guidance and placement officer for the Bureau of Indian Affairs. Marion E. Gridley, Indians of Today (Chicago: The Lakeside Press, 1936), 72.

LA VATTA, PHILIP (Fort Hall Shoshoni)
Philip La Vatta, from the Fort Hall Reservation in Idaho, attended Carlisle Indian Industrial School. He lived at Pocatello in 1896 and worked in the office of the Idaho Herald.

LAWRENCE, P. M. (Sioux)
No information is available.

LAY, BLANCHE (Seneca)
Blanche Lay, who was from New York, was a 1906 graduate of the Carlisle Indian Industrial School. Arrow, March 30, 1906.

LAZELLE, DELLA (Citizen Band Potawatomi)
Della Lazelle, from Oklahoma, graduated from Haskell Institute in 1909. She then worked as a stenographer in Oklahoma City. Oklahoma Historical Society, Archives Division, Sac and Fox and Shawnee --Allotments, November 30, 1908.

LAZELLE, RUTH (Citizen Band Potawatomi)
Ruth Lazelle was from Shawnee, Oklahoma. She studied domestic arts at Chilocco Indian Agricultural School, from which she graduated in 1918.

LEACH, JOHN R. (Cherokee)
John R. Leach, born about 1862, was postmaster at Leach, Cherokee Nation. Grant Foreman, "Early Post Offices of Oklahoma," Chronicles of Oklahoma, 6 (September, 1928), 272.

LEE, ALONZO (Eastern Band Cherokee)
Alonzo Lee was a student at Hampton Institute from 1896 through 1899.

LEE, WILLIAM (Sioux)
No information is available.

LE FLORE, CARRIE (Choctaw)
Carrie Le Flore was the daughter of Forbis and Anne Marie (Maurer) Le Flore. She married Adolphus E. Perry. Mrs. A. E. Perry, "Colonel Forbis Le Flore, Pioneer and Statesman," Chronicles of Oklahoma, 6 (March, 1928), 83, 87.

LEMIEUX, AGNES (Chippewa)
Agnes Lemieux was a 1915 graduate of the Pipestone Indian School.

LEVERING, LEVI (Omaha)
Levi Levering, from Nebraska, was an 1890 graduate of Carlisle Indian Industrial School. He then attended Bellevue College in Nebraska. Levering entered the Indian service as a teacher and taught for a number of years on the Fort Hall Reservation in Montana. In 1912, he was appointed superintendent at the Nuyaka Boarding School

at Beggs, Oklahoma. By 1915, he had returned to Nebraska and settled at Macy. Red Man, 5 (November, 1912), 130; Arrow, December 24, 1905.

LEWIS, DOTY (Bannock)
Doty Lewis was a student at Sherman Institute in 1911.

LEWIS, MARIE (Cherokee)
Marie Lewis attended Carlisle Indian Industrial School.

LEWIS, WALLACE (Narragansett)
Wallace Lewis attended Carlisle Indian Industrial School.

LIBBY, JOSEPH (Chippewa)
From Minnesota, Joseph Libby graduated from the Carlisle Indian Industrial School in 1907, but he apparently remained for additional training. Arrow, March 29, 1907; Carlisle Arrow, February 2, 1912.

LITTLE CHIEF, LUCY (Pawnee)
Lucy Little Chief was a student at Haskell Institute in 1907. She died in 1909. Oklahoma Historical Society, Archives Division, Pawnee--Deaths, February 13, 1909; Pawnee--Estates, March 22, 1909.

LITTLE MOON, SARAH (Sioux)
Sarah Little Moon attended the Oglala Boarding School.

LITTLE WOLF, FELIX (Sioux)
Felix Little Wolf was a student at the Oglala Boarding School in 1900.

LOCUST, PETER (Cherokee)
Peter Locust attended Carlisle Indian Industrial School.

LOCUST, WILLIAM (Cherokee)
William Locust was full Cherokee. He graduated from the Indian University at Bacone, Indian Territory.

LOLORIAS, JOHN M. (Papago)
John Lolorias attended Hampton Institute in 1900 and 1901.

LOMAVITU, OTTO (Hopi)
Otto Lomavitu was from Oraibi.

LONG, SYLVESTER (Catawba-Cherokee)
Sylvester Long, from North Carolina, attended Carlisle Indian Industrial School, graduating in 1912. He entered St. John's Military School at Manlius, New York, where he assumed the name Long Lance. He graduated in 1915. After serving with Canadian forces in World War I, he entered the newspaper business as a reporter in Canada,

where he claimed to have been adopted by the Indians. He became
well known as a writer and published a fictionalized autobiography
called Long Lance. He died in 1932. Red Man 6 (January, 1914),
204, and 6 (June, 1914), 442; Chemawa American, 17 (June, 1915),
39. Hugh A. Dempsy, "Sylvester Long, Buffalo Child Long Lance,"
in Margot Liberty, ed., American Indian Intellectuals (St. Paul:
West Publishing Co., 1978), 197-203.

LONG, WILL WEST (Eastern Band Cherokee)
        Will West Long was born on January 25, 1870, the son of Gunaki
(John Long) and Ayosta (Sally Terrapin). He learned traditional
Cherokee culture from his mother. As a young man, he was employed
by James Mooney to organize and record Cherokee formulas and songs
for his Social Formulas of the Cherokees. Literate in English and
Cherokee, he worked with Mooney until 1920. In his later years,
he lived at Big Cove on the Qualla Reservation. Long died on March
14, 1947. "Notes and Documents," Chronicles of Oklahoma, 43 (Spring,
1965), 90-93; Frederick J. Dockstader, Great North American Indians
(New York: Van Nostrand Reinhold Company, 1977), 156-157.

LONG LANCE, CHIEF BUFFALO CHILD (Catawba-Cherokee)
        See LONG, SYLVESTER

LORENTZ, HENRY (Wichita)
        Henry Lorentz was a student at Carlisle Indian Industrial School
in 1910.

LOTT, HARRISON (Nez Percé)
        Harrison Lott was a student at Carlisle Indian Industrial School
in 1909.

LOWE, ADELIA (Sioux)
        Adelia Lowe graduated from the Carlisle Indian Industrial School
in 1896. Red Man, 13 (March, 1896), 1.

LOWREY, GEORGE (Cherokee)
        George Lowrey was born in the Eastern Cherokee Nation about
1770, the son of George and Nannie Lowrey. He was one of the
early members of the Presbyterian Church at Willstown. He was
a veteran of the War of 1812. Lowrey translated parts of the Book
of Isaiah into Cherokee, and he and his son-in-law David Brown
(q.v.) were working on a Cherokee spelling book in English charac-
ters when Sequoyah announced his syllabary. After removal, Lowrey
lived at Park Hill and was actively involved in Cherokee affairs.
Lowrey served as assistant principal chief from 1843 to 1851. He
married Lucy Benge. Lowrey died on October 20, 1852. Emmet Starr,
History of the Cherokee Indians and Their Legends and Folk Lore
(Oklahoma City: The Warden Company, 1921), 367, 472; Oklahoma
Historical Society, Archives Division, Indian-Pioneer History, 42:
424-426.

LOWRY, MAUDE (Washo)
Maude Lowry, from California, was a 1913 graduate of Chemawa Indian School.

LUCE, MAXIE (Nisenan)
Maxie Luce was a student at Carlisle Indian Industrial School in 1908.

LUDWICK, LENA (Oneida)
Lena Ludwick, from Wisconsin, was a student at Hampton Institute, 1902-1905. Thirty-Fifth Annual Catalogue of the Hampton Normal and Agricultural Institute (Hampton: Hampton Institute Press, 1903), 112.

LUGO, ASSIDRO (Mission)
Assidro Lugo was a student at the Banning Mission School in 1895.

LUGO, FRANK (Mission)
Frank Lugo was a student at the Banning Mission School in 1895.

LUJAN, MATTIE (Pueblo)
Mattie Lujan graduated from Sherman Institute in 1920.

LYDICK, HENRY (Chippewa)
Henry Lydick was a student at the Carlisle Indian Industrial School in 1908.

LYMAN, HENRY (Yankton Sioux)
Henry Lyman (Hoksiwa), the son of William P. Lyman, entered Hampton Institute in 1886 and graduated in 1889. He graduated from the Yale Law School and in 1891 practiced in New York City. 52 Congress, 1 Session, Senate Executive Document 31, 28, 46-47; Twenty-Two Years' Work of the Hampton Normal and Agricultural Institute (Hampton: Normal School Press, 1891), 56.

LYONS, JAMES F. (Onondaga)
James F. Lyons was a student at Carlisle Indian Industrial School in 1912.

MacARTHUR, LINDA (White Earth Chippewa)
Linda MacArthur graduated from Haskell Institute in 1902. She married Jacob Dugan.

McARTHUR, ROSABELLE (Umpqua)
Rosabelle McArthur was a student at Carlisle Indian Industrial School in 1908. She married Leonard A. Bolding and lived at Klamath Falls and then Gardiner, Oregon. Red Man 5 (October, 1912), 85, and 7 (March, 1915), 256.

McCARTHY, JOSEPHINE   (Standing Rock Sioux)
Josephine McCarthy, the daughter of Charles McCarthy, entered
Hampton Institute in October, 1881, at age thirteen. She left in
May, 1884, returned the next year, and continued until 1888. She
married a soldier and lived at Fort Yates. 52 Congress, 1 Session,
Senate Executive Document 31, 6, 32-33, 34-35.

McCAULEY, DORA   (Chippewa)
Dora McCauley studied domestic arts at Haskell Institute, from
which she graduated in 1913.

McCAULEY, ELLA   (Winnebago)
Ella McCauley, who was from Decatur, Nebraska, attended Haskell Institute.

McCLELLAN, WILLIAM A.   (Cherokee)
William McClellan, born about 1882, graduated from the Cherokee Male Seminary.

McCOY, JAMES   (Pawnee)
James McCoy, who was from Oklahoma, attended Hampton Institute in 1886 and 1887. He died on July 18, 1889, at age twenty-
two. 52 Congress, 1 Session, Senate Executive Document 31, 26,
46-47.

McCULLY, ELLA JULIA   (Kake, i.e., Tlingit)
Ella McCully attended Chemawa Indian School.

McCURTAIN, EDMUND   (Choctaw)
Edmund McCurtain was born near Fort Coffee, Choctaw Nation,
on June 4, 1842, the son of Cornelius and Mahayia McCurtain. During the Civil War, he served in the First Regiment of Choctaw and
Chickasaw Mounted Rifles (Confederate). After the war, he made
his home at San Bois. He served in various capacities such as county
judge, trustee of the schools, representative to the National Council,
Senator, and superintendent of education. In 1884, he replaced
his brother Jackson as Principal Chief and served two terms. Mc-
Curtain died November 9, 1890. He was married to Harriet Austin
and Clarissa LeFlore. John Barlett Meserve, "The McCurtains,"
Chronicles of Oklahoma, 13 (September, 1935), 297-312.

McCURTAIN, GREEN   (Choctaw)
Green McCurtain was born at Skullyville, Choctaw Nation, on
November 28, 1848, the son of Cornelius and Mahayia McCurtain.
He attended the common schools of the nation. McCurtain served
as sheriff of Skullyville county, three terms as a representative to
the National Council, trustee of schools for his district, district
attorney, two terms as treasurer, and one as a senator. He served
two terms as Principal Chief beginning in 1896 and was reelected
in 1902, that time serving until his death on December 27, 1910.
McCurtain was married to Martha A. Ainsworth and Kate Spring.

John Bartlett Meserve, "The McCurtains," Chronicles of Oklahoma, 13 (September, 1935), 297-312.

McDONALD, CHARLES F. (Chippewa)
Charles F. McDonald was a 1912 graduate of the Carlisle Indian Industrial School. Red Man, 6 (September, 1913), 42.

McDONALD, CLAUDIA E. (Chippewa)
Claudia McDonald was a 1908 graduate of the Carlisle Indian Industrial School. Arrow, April 4, 1908.

McDONALD, FLORA (Spokan)
Flora McDonald attended Carlisle Indian Industrial School.

McDRID, CHARLES (Ukiah, i.e. Pomo)
Charles McDrid was a 1912 graduate of Haskell Institute.

McDRID, SAVANNAH (Ukiah)
Savannah McDrid was a student at Haskell Institute in 1914.

McGAA, ALBERT D. (Sioux)
Albert D. McGaa attended the Oglala Boarding School in 1900.

McINNIS, JOHN (Washo)
John McInnis, born about 1888, attended Carlisle Indian Industrial School in 1911.

McINTOSH, DONALD (San Carlos Apache)
After Donald McIntosh graduated from Carlisle Indian Industrial School in 1901, he returned to the San Carlos Reservation, where he worked at the school. Red Man and Helper, March 14, 1902.

McINTOSH, ROLLIE (Creek)
Rollie (Roley) McIntosh was born April 22, 1858, the son of Colonel D. N. McIntosh. He served as district judge of Eufaula District, Creek Nation, and as Creek delegate to Washington.

McINTOSH, SADIE (Creek)
No information is available.

McKENZIE, MINNIE (Cherokee)
Minnie McKenzie was from Pryor, Oklahoma. She studied home economics at Chilocco Indian Agricultural School from which she graduated in 1919.

McKESSON, ISABELLE (Apache)
Isabelle McKesson graduated from Sherman Institute in 1915 and then lived at Kingman, Arizona. Sherman Bulletin, May 24, 1916.

McKINNEY, HENRY (Potawatomi)
Henry McKinney was a student at Chilocco Indian Agricultural

School in 1918. He later worked as a carpenter in Topeka, Kansas.

McKINNEY, THOMPSON (Choctaw)
Thompson McKinney (Red Pine) served as the Choctaw delegate to Washington for several years and as Principal Chief of the Choctaws from 1886 through 1888. Oklahoma Historical Society, Archives Division, Indian-Pioneer History, 36:247-248.

McLEAN, DINAH (Hopi)
Dinah McLean was a student at Sherman Institute in 1911.

McLEAN, SAMUEL J. (Rosebud Sioux)
Samuel J. McLean graduated from Carlisle Indian Industrial School in 1909. After graduation, he worked as a blacksmith before taking a position in 1913 as art and penmanship teacher at St. Mary's Mission near Omak, Washington. In 1922 he was employed at the Carson School, Stewart, Nevada, in charge of athletics and blacksmithing. Red Man, 6 (September, 1913), 40, and (February, 1914), 242.

MacLEOD, MICHAEL (Kenai, i.e., Tanaina)
Michael MacLeod was from Kodiak Island. He entered the Chemawa Indian School at Salem, Oregon, in 1912 and graduated in 1914. Chemawa American, 16 (June, 1914), 8.

MACHUKAY, MARTIN (Apache)
Martin Machukay, who was from Arizona, graduated from Carlisle Indian Industrial School in 1905.

MACK, JOHN A. (Pima)
John A. Mack graduated from Sherman Institute in 1911 and then worked in a tailor shop in Corona, California. In 1916 he lived at Banning. Sherman Bulletin, May 24, 1916.

MACK, MINNIE (Pima)
Minnie Mack attended Sherman Institute.

MADISON, LYMAN B. (Mashpee)
Lyman B. Madison, from Massachusetts, was a graduate of Carlisle Indian Industrial School. His home was at Fall River, Massachusetts. Red Man, 6 (January, 1914), 204.

MADRID, CARLOS (Pueblo)
Carlos Madrid was a 1910 graduate of Sherman Institute. In 1916 he lived in El Paso, Texas. Sherman Bulletin, May 24, 1916.

MAGASKAWIN, THERESA (Sioux)
Theresa Magaskawin was a student at the Standing Rock Agricultural Boarding School in 1892.

MAIN, LIZZIE E. (Blackfeet)
Lizzie E. Main was born at Browning, Montana, in 1894. She

entered the Indian school at Genoa, Nebraska, in 1905 and graduated in 1911.

MAKESITLONG, JOHN (Sioux)
    No information is available.

MANDAN, ARTHUR (Mandan)
    Arthur Mandan, from Fort Berthold Reservation, North Dakota, was a 1907 graduate of Carlisle Indian Industrial School. Red Man and Helper, August 28, 1903; Arrow, March 29, 1907.

MANITOWA, BERTHA (Sac and Fox)
    Bertha Manitowa, who was from Oklahoma, attended Chilocco Indian Agricultural School. She graduated from Haskell Institute in 1909 and married Walter M. Hodson. Oklahoma Historical Society, Archives Division, Chilocco--Enrollments, December 19, 1905.

MANRIQUEZ, JUANITA (Mission)
    Juanita Manriquez was a student at St. Anthony's Industrial School, San Diego, in 1896.

MANSFIELD, FRANCIS (Fort Apache Apache)
    Francis Mansfield was a student at Haskell Institute in 1902.

MANSUR, SARAH (Ousakie, i.e., Sauk)
    Sarah Mansur, from Oklahoma, entered Carlisle Indian Industrial School in 1903. She married a man named Thompson and in 1914 lived at Cushing, Oklahoma. Red Man and Helper, August 28, 1903; Red Man, 6 (January, 1914), 205.

MANTEL, JAMES (Bois Fort Chippewa)
    James Mantel, from Minnesota, was a student at Haskell Institute in 1913.

MARMON, ALICE (Pueblo)
    Alice Marmon was a 1905 graduate of Haskell Institute.

MARMON, BELLE (Laguna Pueblo)
    Belle Marmon was a student at Haskell Instiute in 1900 and 1901.

MARMON, FRANK (Laguna Pueblo)
    Frank Marmon was a 1915 graduate of Sherman Institute. Sherman Bulletin, May 24, 1916.

MARMON, HENRY C. (Laguna Pueblo)
    Henry C. Marmon was a 1912 graduate of Sherman Institute. Sherman Bulletin, May 24, 1916.

MARMON, KENNETH A. (Laguna Pueblo)
    Kenneth A. Marmon graduated from Sherman Institute in 1911

and then attended New Mexico State University. He served in World War I, after which he worked for many years as instructor of printing at Sherman, organization field agent for the Bureau of Indian Affairs, and superintendent of the Seminole Agency. He married Lucy Fay Doran. Marion E. Gridley, Indians of Today (Chicago: Towertown Press, 1960), 59.

MARMON, ROBERT (Pueblo)
Robert Marmon attended Haskell Institute.

MARSDEN, EDWARD (Tsimshian)
Edward Marsden was born on May 19, 1869, in northern British Columbia, the son of a native evangelist. He entered day school at New Metlakatla in 1880. His family moved to Alaska, and, in 1888, Marsden went to Sitka to resume his studies. He came to the United States in 1891. He graduated from Marietta College in Ohio in 1891 and later studied medicine and law. He returned to Alaska in 1898 as a Presbyterian missionary at Saxman. Red Man, 13 (June, 1895), 6; Red Man and Helper, April 10, 1903.

MARSHALL, ERNEST (Klamath)
In 1913 Ernest Marshall was a student at Sherman Institute.

MARTIN, BERTHA (Osage)
Bertha Martin Labadie graduated from Sherman Institute in 1914 and lived at Pawhuska, Oklahoma.

MARTIN, DANIEL (Assiniboin)
Daniel Martin was a 1915 graduate of Sherman Institute. In 1916 he lived at Frazer, Montana. Sherman Bulletin, May 24, 1916.

MARTIN, EDNA I. (Citizen Band Potawatomi)
Edna I. Martin was from Norman, Oklahoma. She studied domestic arts at Chilocco Indian Agricultural School, from which she graduated in 1918.

MARTIN, JOSEPH LYNCH (Cherokee)
Joseph L. Martin was born at the Cherokee town of Narcoochi, in present-day Habersham County, Georgia, in 1817, the son of John and Nellie McDaniel Martin. He was educated in mission schools and at St. Louis. In the West, he made his home at Green Brier on Grand River. During the Civil War, he commanded a company of cavalry in Bryan's Confederate Regiment. Martin was married to Julia Lombard, Sallie Childers, Lucy Brown Rogers, Caroline Garrett, and Jennie Harlin. Known in later life as "Greenbrier Joe," Martin died on November 6, 1891. Indian Chieftain, October 17, 1889; Emmet Starr, History of the Cherokee Indians and Their Legends and Folk Lore (Oklahoma City: The Warden Company, 1921), 310, 318; Oklahoma Historical Society, Archives Division Indian-Pioneer History, 81: 419-422; Cherokee Advocate, November 12, 1891.

MARTIN, MAUDE (Chippewa)
Maude Martin was a student at Haskell Institute in 1908.

MATHEWS, JOHN JOSEPH (Osage)
John Joseph Mathews was born at Pawhuska, Osage Nation, in 1894, the son of William Mathews. He attended the University of Oklahoma, graduating in 1920. He went on to distinguish himself as a historian, particularly of the Osages. Garrick Bailey, "John Joseph Mathews," in Margot Liberty, ed., American Indian Intellectuals (St. Paul: West Publishing Company, 1978), 205-213.

MATILTON, JOHN (Hupa)
John Matilton was a 1908 graduate of Sherman Institute. In 1916 he lived at Hoopa, California. Sherman Bulletin, May 24, 1916.

MATT, STEVENS (Flathead)
Stevens Matt was a student at Haskell Institute in 1913.

MAYBE, LILA (Seneca)
Lila Maybe attended Carlisle Indian Industrial School.

MAYES, SOGGIE (Cherokee)
Soggie Mayes graduated from the Cherokee Male Seminary and then taught school in the Cherokee Nation. Oklahoma Historical Society, Archives Division, Cherokee--Schools, Miscellaneous, June 12, 1905, 3035-B; Cherokee Volume 544, September 30, 1904, p. 142.

MEDICINE BULL, SAMUEL (Lower Brule Sioux)
Samuel Medicine Bull (Tatankawakau) was the son of Medicine Bull. He entered Hampton Institute in 1881 at age twenty and remained until 1884. In 1886 he began teaching at his father's camp and was a catechist there and at St. Albans. He was also a farmer. 52 Congress, 1 Session, Senate Executive Document 31, 18, 40-41.

MEDICINE EAGLE, BEN (Rosebud Sioux)
Ben Medicine Eagle attended the day school at Little Crow's camp on the Rosebud Reservation.

MEEK, RILLA (Sac and Fox)
Rilla Meek, from Oklahoma, graduated from the commercial course at Haskell Institute in 1914. She worked as a clerk at Seger's Colony and at the Shawnee Training School in Oklahoma. Indian Leader, 17 (June, 1914), 24; Oklahoma Historical Society, Archives Division, Cheyenne and Arapaho--Employees, October 31, 1916, and April 12, 1919, and Shawnee--Employees, April 17 and October 17, 1919.

MELOVIDOV, ALEX (Aleut, i.e., Chugach Eskimo)
Alex Melovidov was from the Pribiloff Islands. He attended the Chemawa Indian School at Salem, Oregon. In 1917 he toured the East as a member of a string quartet under the auspices of the Redpath Lyceum Bureau. Chemawa American, May 30, 1917.

MELTON, ANNA (Cherokee)
Anna Melton was born in the Cherokee Nation in 1892, the daughter of William T. and Louisa G. Melton. She was a 1912 graduate of Carlisle Indian Industrial School. She then attended St. Mary's Academy at Sacred Heart, Oklahoma, and, in 1914, began teaching in a rural school near Grove, Oklahoma. In 1918 she worked as matron at Cantonment School, Oklahoma. Oklahoma Historical Society, Archives Division, Cheyenne and Arapaho--Employees, April 21, 1918.

MELTON, CLARA (Cherokee)
Clara Melton attended Carlisle Indian Industrial School. In 1913 she was a teacher at Chilocco Indian Agricultural School. Oklahoma Historical Society, Archives Division, Chilocco--Teachers, February 1, 1913.

MENADALOOK, CHARLES (Eskimo)
In 1917, Charles Menadalook was a teacher at Kotzebue and at Nome, Alaska. In 1918, he transferred to Noatak. Eskimo, July, December, 1917; April-May, July-August, 1918.

MENAUL, JOHN (Laguna Pueblo)
John Menaul, or Kowsh-te-ah, was a student at Carlisle Indian Industrial School from 1881 to 1883. Eadle Keatah Toh, 1 (April, 1881), 4.

MENTZ, JOSEPH (Standing Rock Sioux)
Joseph Mentz was a student at Hampton Institute, 1902-1905. Thirty-Fifth Annual Catalogue of the Hampton Normal and Agricultural Institute (Hampton: Hampton Institute Press, 1903), 112.

MERRILL, GEORGE (Chippewa)
George Merrill, from Minnesota, was born about 1890. He entered Carlisle Indian Industrial School in 1910 and graduated in 1917.

MESKET, ANDERSON (Hupa)
Anderson Mesket attended Sherman Institute, graduating in 1904.

METOXEN, IVY E. (Oneida)
Ivy E. Metoxen, from Wisconsin, was born in 1890. She graduated from Carlisle Indian Industrial School in 1913. Red Man, 5 (May, 1913), 435.

METOXEN, JOSEPH (Oneida)
Joseph Metoxen, from Wisconsin, was born about 1888, the son of Simon W. and Lavinia Metoxen. He attended Haskell Institute.

MEZA, THECKLA (Mission)
Theckla Meza was a 1916 graduate of Sherman Institute. She lived at Valley Center, California. Sherman Bulletin, May 24, 1916.

MIGUEL, JEFFERSON (Yuma)
Jefferson Miguel was a student at Carlisle Indian Industrial School in 1907.

MILES, THOMAS J. (Sac and Fox)
Thomas J. Miles (Muckatuwishek), a member of the Sac and Fox tribe of the Indian Territory, was born about 1862, the son of John Miles. He attended public schools in Kansas before entering Hampton Institute in 1882. After graduating in 1885, he attended preparatory school at Meriden, New Hampshire, and then entered the medical department at the University of Pennsylvania, but after two years dropped out because of ill health. He went home and taught at the Sac and Fox school, returned to the East, attempted to finish school, but dropped out once more. He taught at the Sac and Fox school from 1889 to 1891 and then moved to Philadelphia, the home of his wife. Later, he returned to the Indian Territory and engaged in freighting. In 1909 he was secretary of the Sac and Fox Council. 52 Congress, 1 Session, Senate Executive Document 31, 20; Oklahoma Historical Society, Archives Division, Sac and Fox Volume 14, September 1, 1888, p. 238; Sac and Fox Volume 15A, August 12, 1891, p. 451; Sac and Fox--Freight and Transportation, November 26, 1894; Sac and Fox--Indian Council, May 3, 1909.

MILLER, EDWIN (Miami)
Edwin Miller, from Oklahoma, was a 1917 graduate of Carlisle Indian Industrial School.

MILLER, FLORENCE (Stockbridge)
Florence Miller was a student at Carlisle Indian Industrial School in 1894.

MILLER, IVA M. (Cherokee)
Iva M. Miller attended Chilocco Indian School before entering Carlisle Indian Industrial School from which she graduated in 1912. Oklahoma Historical Society, Archives Division, Chilocco--Enrollments, September 1, 1902.

MILLER, MARY (Chippewa)
Mary Miller attended Carlisle Indian Industrial School.

MILLS, EMMA (Sioux)
Emma Mills was a student at the Oglala Boarding School in 1919 and 1920.

MINTHORN, AARON (Cayuse)
Aaron Minthorn, born about 1890, attended Carlisle and Jenkins Institutes, Spokane, Washington. Red Man, 5 (November, 1912), 130.

MINTHORN, ANNA E. (Cayuse)
Anna E. Minthorn graduated from Carlisle Indian Industrial School in 1906. Arrow, March 30, 1906.

MITCHELL, CHARLES (Assiniboin)
Charles Mitchell was a 1909 graduate of Carlisle. He returned to Montana, where he worked as a store clerk at Wolf Point in 1913. Red Man, 7 (October, 1914), 76.

MITCHELL, HORACE (Ponca)
Horace Mitchell was a student at Haskell Institute in 1912.

MITCHELL, LAWRENCE J. (Penobscot, i.e., Eastern Abenaki)
Lawrence J. Mitchell attended Carlisle Indian Industrial School and in 1905 served with the Seventh U.S. Cavalry Band.

MODESTO, LOUISA (Mission)
Louisa Modesto was a student at the Banning Mission School in 1895.

MONCHAMP, CHARLES (Chippewa)
Charles Monchamp was a student at Carlisle Indian Industrial School in 1910.

MONROE, LYDIA (Sac and Fox)
Lydia Monroe was from Indian Territory. She entered Hampton Institute in 1886 at age 18. She stayed until 1889. She married Frank Hamblin. 52 Congress, 1 Session, Senate Executive Document 31, 10.

MONROE, MABEL (Blackfeet)
No information is available.

MONTEZUMA, CARLOS (Yavapai)
Carlos Montezuma was born in Arizona in the 1860's, the son of Co-lu-ye-vah of the Mohave-Apaches. As a young child, Montezuma, whose name was Wassaja, was captured by the Pimas, who later sold him to a photographer, C. Gentile, who took him to Chicago in 1872. He was educated in the public schools in Chicago, in Galesburg, Illinois, and in Brooklyn, New York. He received a B.S. degree from the University of Illinois in 1884 and an M.D. from Chicago Medical College in 1889. From 1889 until 1896, he was a physician in the U.S. Indian Service. He conducted a private practice and taught medicine in Chicago. He traveled widely, lectured, and founded and edited Wassaja, a magazine devoted to Indian affairs. His wife was Mary Keller. Montezuma died on January 31, 1923. Neil M. Clark, "Dr. Montezuma, Apache: Warrior in Two Worlds," Montana, the Magazine of Western History, 23 (Spring, 1973), 56-65; John A. Turcheneske, Jr., "The Southwest in La Follette Land: The Carlos Montezuma Papers," Manuscripts, 25 (Summer, 1973), 202-207; Frederick J. Dockstader, Great North American Indians (New York: Van Nostrand Reinhold Company, 1977), 178-180; Peter Iverson, "Carlos Montezuma," in R. David Edmunds, ed., American Indian Leaders: Studies in Diversity (Lincoln: University of Nebraska Press, 1980), 206-220.

MOORE, FRANK (Pine Ridge Sioux)
Frank Moore graduated from the wagon-making course at Haskell Institute in 1903.

MOORE, JOHN (Creek)
John Moore was a student at the Tullahassee Mission School in 1870.

MOORE, WILLIAM (Sac and Fox)
William Moore, from Oklahoma, was the son of Rienzi Moore. He entered Hampton Institute in 1888 at age fourteen. 52 Congress, 1 Session, Senate Executive Document 31, 48-49.

MOORE, WILSON D. (Pawnee)
Wilson D. Moore entered Hampton Institute in 1888 at the age of 17 and left in 1890. He returned to the Indian Territory where he farmed. 52 Congress, 1 Session, Senate Executive Document 31, 29, 48-49.

MOOSE, JOSEPH (Citizen Band Potawatomi)
Joseph Moose was a member of the business committee of the Oklahoma Potawatomis during the 1890's. In 1915 he was a member of the Potawatomi Tribal Council. Oklahoma Historical Society, Archives Division, Volume Sac and Fox 16B, January 26, 1892, p. 87; Sac and Fox--Potawatomi Indians, April 11, 1892, November 20, 1894, February 12, 1896, October 29, 1915.

MORAGO, EDITH J. (Pima)
Edith J. Morago was a student at Sherman Institute in 1909.

MORAGO, JAY ROE (Pima)
Jay Roe Morago was a student at Sherman Institute in 1910.

MORALES, NANCY A. (Mission)
Nancy A. Morales was a student at the Banning Mission School in 1896.

MORGAN, GIDEON (Cherokee)
Gideon Morgan was born on April 3, 1851, the son of William and Martha Mayo Morgan, the latter of Cherokee descent. He was educated by private tutors. In 1871, Morgan moved to Fort Gibson, Cherokee Nation. He was a farmer and rancher and owner of the Capital Hotel in Tahlequah and Morgan's Inn Resort north of Salina, Oklahoma. He died in March, 1937. His wife was Mary Llewallan Payne. H. F. O'Beirne and E. S. O'Beirne, The Indian Territory (St. Louis: C. B. Woodward Company, 1892), 427; Emmet Starr, History of the Cherokees and Their Legends and Folk Lore (Oklahoma City: The Warden Company, 1921), 636-637.

MORGAN, JACOB CASIMERA (Navajo)
Jacob Casimera Morgan, from Arizona, attended Teller Indian

School at Grand Junction, Colorado, and was a student at Hampton Institute from 1899 to 1902. He married Zahrina Tso. He was in business for himself and taught at Phoenix, Crownpoint, Shiprock, and Farmington. He then worked as boys' industrial teacher at the Christian Reformed Mission at Tohatchi, Arizona. In 1914 he became industrial teacher at Pueblo Bonita School at Crownpoint. He served over twenty years as a member of Navajo Tribal Council and served as tribal chairman. In 1944 he was ordained as a minister of the gospel. Thirty-Fifth Annual Catalogue of the Hampton Normal and Agricultural Institute (Hampton: Hampton Institute Press, 1903), 111; Marion E. Gridley, Indians of Today (Chicago: Millar, 1947), 61; Donald L. Parman, "J. C. Morgan, Navajo Apostle of Assimilation," Prologue: The Journal of the National Archives, 4 (Summer, 1972), 83-98.

MORRIS, L. PEARL (Cherokee)
    In 1910, L. Pearl Morris was a student at Sherman Institute.

MORSEA, CHARLES ROY (Lower Brule Sioux)
    No information is available.

MORTON, ANNIE M. (Laguna Pueblo)
    Annie M. Morton, from Laguna Pueblo in New Mexico, was born about 1879. She was an 1898 graduate of Carlisle Indian Industrial School. Her married name was Lubo and, in 1916, she lived in Riverside, California.

MOSELY, GARNETT (Chickasaw)
    Garnett Mosely was from Bromide, Oklahoma. He studied printing at Chilocco Indian Agricultural School, from which he graduated in 1918. Oklahoma Historical Society, Archives Division, Chilocco--Enrollment, June 30, 1912.

MOSES, HENRY (Washo)
    No information is available.

MT. PLEASANT, EDISON (Tuscarora)
    Edison Mt. Pleasant, born about 1890, was from New York and graduated from Carlisle Indian Industrial School in 1911. Carlisle Arrow, April 21, 1911.

MOUNTAIN SHEEP, BERTHA (Crow)
    Bertha Mountain Sheep attended Hampton Institute.

MOUSSEAU, JULIA (Sioux)
    Julia Mousseau was a student at the Oglala Boarding School in 1900.

MUMBLEHEAD, JAMES W. (Eastern Band Cherokee)
    James Mumblehead, born about 1882, graduated from Carlisle Indian Industrial School in 1911. In 1914, he was a bandmaster and

printer and was managing the Oglala Light at Pine Ridge, South Dakota. Carlisle Arrow, April 21, 1911; Red Man, 7 (November, 1914), 110, and (December, 1914), 148.

MURRAY, LAURA (Sioux)
Laura Murray, from Nebraska, graduated from the domestic arts department of Haskell Institute in 1914. Indian Leader, 17 (June, 1914), 25.

MURRAY, WALLACE (Sioux)
No information is available.

MUSKRAT, RUTH MARGARET (Cherokee)
Ruth Muskrat was born in 1897 at Grove, Cherokee Nation. She attended Carlisle Indian Industrial School and then the University of Kansas. While a student at Kansas, she was a delegate to the World's Student Christian Federation Conference at Peking. She also attended the University of Oklahoma and graduated from Mount Holyoke College. After graduation from college, she went to work for the Bureau of Indian Affairs, serving in several capacities, including guidance and placement officer. She also served as executive secretary of the National Congress of American Indians. She was active as a youth worker in the Y.W.C.A. Muskrat married John F. Bronson. She was the author of Indians Are People, Too (1947). "Indian Poet Delegate to China," University of Oklahoma Magazine, 10 (February, 1922), 14; Marion E. Gridley, Indians of Today (Chicago: ICFP, Inc., 1971), 475-476.

NAGOZRUK, ARTHUR (Eskimo)
Arthur Nagozruk was a teacher at Wales, Alaska, in 1917.

NAIL, ROBERT W. (Choctaw)
Robert W. Nail attended the Choctaw Academy in Kentucky. In 1849 he was Attorney of the Chickasaw District. Oklahoma Historical Society, Archives Division, Indian Affairs, Vol. 7, August 17, 1849, p. 439.

NAMEQUA, JOSIE (Comanche)
Josie Namequa was a student at Haskell Institute in 1914.

NARCHA, PABLO (Papago)
Pablo Narcha graduated from Haskell Institute in 1914. Indian Leader, 17 (September, 1913), 12.

NASH, AUGUSTA M. (Winnebago)
Augusta M. Nash graduated from Carlisle Indian Industrial School in 1901 and then returned to Nebraska, making her home at Thurston. Red Man and Helper, March 8, 1901, and February 26-March 4, 1904.

NATONI, PAULINE (Navajo)
Pauline Natoni was from Shiprock, New Mexico. She graduated from Sherman Institute in 1923.

NAVARRE, PETER (Prairie Band Potawatomi)
Peter Navarre was a graduate of Haskell Institute, where he learned printing. He worked as a printer at various places, including the Indian School at White Earth, Minnesota. In 1913 he bought The Rossville Reporter at Rossville, Kansas, and edited it for over forty years. Tomahawk, January 1, 1904; "New Publisher for Rossville Reporter," Kansas Publisher, 29 (March, 1953), 8.

NECKAR, ZELIA (Crow)
Zelia Neckar, born about 1883, was a student at the Crow Agency School in 1899.

NELSON, ALMA (Aleut)
Alma Nelson was a student at Chemawa Indian School at Salem, Oregon.

NELSON, WILLIAM (Pima)
William Nelson was a student at Carlisle Indian Industrial School from 1907 through 1909.

NEPHEW, EDITH L. (Seneca)
Edith L. Nephew was a student at Carlisle Indian Industrial School in 1909. She married Raymond Waterman. Carlisle Arrow, May 5, 1911.

NEWASHE, EMMA M. (Sac and Fox)
Emma M. Newashe was born in the Indian Territory about 1891. After graduation from Carlisle in 1912, she attended West Chester Normal School for a short time. In 1914, she married F. A. McAllister, moved to Oklahoma City, and became a housewife. Red Man, 5 (December, 1912), 177, and 6 (January, 1914), 206; Oklahoma Historical Society, Archives Division, Sac and Fox and Shawnee--Carlisle Indian School, July 29, 1906, and April 4, 1910.

NEWASHE, WILLIAM (Sac and Fox)
William Newashe attended Carlisle Indian Industrial School.

NEWBEAR, EVA (Crow)
Eva Newbear was a 1908 graduate of Sherman Institute. She married Eli Yellow Mule, and in 1916 she lived at Wyla, Montana. Sherman Bulletin, May 24, 1916.

NEWMAN, WALLACE (Mission)
Wallace Newman graduated from Sherman Institute in 1919 and then attended the University of Southern California.

NOMBRIE, LORENZO (Mission)
Lorenzo Nombrie was a student at Sherman Institute in 1910.

NORRIS, ELLEN L. (Klamath)
Ellen L. Norris graduated from Sherman Institute in 1919 and then entered the University of California, Berkeley.

NORRIS, SADIE C. (Chippewa)
Sadie C. Norris graduated from the Pipestone Indian School, Pipestone, Minnesota, in 1913.

NORTH, MARY (Arapaho)
Mary North was a student at Carlisle Indian Industrial School in 1881.

NORTHRUP, JOHN (Chippewa)
John Northrup attended Carlisle Indian Industrial School.

NUÑEZ, OCTAVIANO (Papago)
Octaviano Nuñez was a student at the San Xavier Mission School in 1896.

OAKES, FANNIE (Choctaw)
Fannie Oakes was a school teacher in the Choctaw schools. Oklahoma Historical Society, Archives Division, Choctaw Schools, 3rd District, Kiamitia County, November 28, 1885, No. 21928.

OCCOM, SAMSON (Mohegan)
Samson Occom was born near New London, Connecticut, in 1723. Converted during the Great Awakening, he studied under Eleazar Wheelock at Lebanon. He became a missionary to the Montauk tribe of Long Island and married one of its members, Mary Fowler. In 1761 and 1763, he was Wheelock's emissary to the Oneidas. In 1765, he went with Nathaniel Whitaker to England and Scotland where he preached and helped raise money for Moor's Indian Charity School conducted by Wheelock. Occom and Whitaker raised about twelve thousand pounds which became the financial base for Dartmouth College. After his return to America in 1768, he became an itinerant preacher. He was instrumental in the establishment of Brothertown in New York and removed to there from Connecticut in 1789. He remained there until he died on July 14, 1792. W. DeLoss Love, Samson Occom and the Christian Indians of New England (Boston: Pilgrim Press, 1899); Leon Burr Richardson, ed., An Indian Preacher in England (Hanover, N. H.: Dartmouth College Publications, 1933); Frederick J. Dockstader, Great North American Indians (New York: Van Nostrand Reinhold Company, 1977), 194-195.

OEQUA, VIRGINIA (Kiowa)
Virginia Oequa was a student at Carlisle Indian Industrial School in 1881 and 1882. Oklahoma Historical Society, Archives Division, Kiowa--Carlisle Indian School, September 11, 1882.

OFFIELD, FITSIMONS (Klamath)
Fitsimons Offield was a student at Sherman Institute in 1911.

OHMERT, ROSE (Delaware)
Rose Ohmert was a student at Carlisle Indian Industrial School.

OJIBWAY, FRANCIS (Chippewa)
Francis Ojibway, from Wisconsin, was a 1917 graduate of Carlisle Indian Industrial School.

OKILLOOK, ABRAHAM (Eskimo)
Abraham Okillook lived at Kotzebue, Alaska. He was a sled and harness maker and a tanner. Eskimo, May, 1917.

ONEBULL, C. (Standing Rock Sioux)
C. Onebull, born about 1893, was the son of Oscar Onebull. He attended Santee Normal Training School at Santee, Nebraska.

ONEROAD, AMOS (Sisseton Sioux)
Amos Oneroad, from South Dakota, graduated from Haskell Institute in 1909. He spent much of his time in religious work and attended Bible school in New York.

ONLIAY, WARREN (Zuni)
In 1910, Warren Onliay was a student at the Zuni school.

OQUILLUK, CUDLUK (Eskimo)
No information is available.

OREALUK, JAMES (Eskimo)
James Orealuk was from Selawik, Alaska.

OSHKENENY, MITCHELL (Menominee)
No information is available.

OSKISON, JOHN MILTON (Cherokee)
John Milton Oskison was born at Vinita, Cherokee Nation, on September 1, 1874, the son of John and Rachel Crittenden Oskison. Oskison attended Willie Halsell College at Vinita, where he was a classmate of his lifelong friend, Will Rogers. Oskison also attended Stanford University where he took his B.A. degree in 1899 before going on to do graduate work at Harvard. That year, he won the Century Magazine prize competition for college graduates and launched a long and successful writing career. He worked as an editorial writer on the New York Evening Post and later was associate editor and special writer for Collier's. From 1917 to 1919, Oskison served with the A.E.F. in Europe. He married Florence Ballard Day, the niece of Jay Gould; she divorced him in 1920. He later married Hildegarde Hawthorne. Oskison died in New York in 1947. Who Was Who in America with World Notables (Chicago: Marquis Who's Who, 1973), 5: 549.

OTTLEY, RALPH (Klamath)
Ralph Ottley was a 1909 graduate of Sherman Institute. In 1916 he lived at Orleans, California. Sherman Bulletin, May 24, 1916.

OVERTON, BENJAMIN FRANKLIN (Chickasaw)
Benjamin Franklin Overton was born on November 2, 1836, in Mississippi, the son of John Overton and Tennessee Allen, the latter of Chickasaw descent. Orphaned at an early age, Overton received little formal education, only six months at the old Chickasaw Male Academy at Tishomingo. He farmed in Pickens County, Chickasaw Nation, and served in both the Chickasaw House and Senate. Overton was elected to four terms as Governor of the Nation, 1874-1878 and 1880-1884. He died on February 8, 1884. John Bartlett Meserve, "Governor Benjamin Franklin Overton and Governor Benjamin Crooks Burney," Chronicles of Oklahoma, 16 (June, 1936), 221-233.

OWEN, ROBERT LATHAM (Cherokee)
Robert Latham Owen was born at Lynchburg, Virginia, on February 2, 1856, the son of Robert Latham and Narcissa Chisholm Owen. At age ten, he was enrolled in Merillat Institute near Baltimore. He later attended Washington and Lee from which he received an M.A. degree. In the 1870's, the widowed Mrs. Owen returned with her sons to the Cherokee Nation, where Owen taught at the Cherokee Orphan Asylum, practiced law, and served as secretary to the Board of Education. In 1884, he became owner and editor of the Vinita Indian Chieftain. From 1885 to 1889, Owen was union agent for the Five Civilized Tribes. In 1890, he organized the First National Bank of Muskogee. From 1907 to 1925, he was U.S. senator from Oklahoma. After retirement from the Senate, he kept a law office for a number of years in Washington, D.C. Owen died on July 19, 1947. Wyatt W. Belcher, "Political Leadership of Robert L. Owen," Chronicles of Oklahoma, 31 (Winter, 1953-1954), 361-371; George H. Shirk, "Tribute to Senator Robert L. Owen," Chronicles of Oklahoma, 49 (Winter, 1971-1972), 504-510. Dewey W. Grantham, "Robert Latham Owen," in John A. Garraty and Edward T. James, eds., Dictionary of American Biography: Supplement Four (New York: Charles Scribner's Sons, 1974), 640-642.

OWL, HENRY M. (Eastern Band Cherokee)
Henry Owl graduated from Hampton Institute and continued his studies at Columbia University. In 1922, he was a teacher at Bacone College.

OWL, WILLIAM J. (Eastern Band Cherokee)
William J. Owl, born about 1883, graduated from Carlisle Indian Industrial School in 1911 and, in 1912, was employed at the Cherokee Indian School in North Carolina. Carlisle Arrow, April 21, 1911.

PADIA, ONOFRE (Pueblo)
Onofre Padia (probably Padilla) was a student at Haskell Institute in 1899 and 1900.

PADILLA, POLITA (Pueblo)
Polita Padilla was a student at Haskell Institute, 1900 to 1904.

PAISANO, MABEL (Pueblo)
Mabel Paisano attended Haskell Institute from 1907 to 1912.

PALMER, JOHN (Skokomish)
No information is available.

PARKER, ARTHUR CASWELL (Seneca)
Arthur Caswell Parker was born at Iroquois, New York, on
April 5, 1881, the son of Frederick Ely and Geneva Griswold Parker.
He was educated in the day schools of the Cattaraugus Reservation
and at Dickinson Seminary. He also attended Harvard and the University of Rochester. In 1903-1904, he was an ethnologist for the
New York State Library; from 1905 to 1925 he was archaeologist for
the New York State Museum; and from 1925 to 1946, he was the Director of the Rochester Museum of Arts and Sciences. Parker held
a number of editorial positions including ones for the Transactions
of the New York State Archaeological Association (1916-1955), for
Museum Service (1926-1946), for Research Records (1926-1946), for
The Galleon (1949-1955), and for The Builder (1949-1955). He was
as well involved in numerous civic affairs, he was a practicing ethnologist, and he wrote extensively. Parker was married to Beatrice
Tahamont and Anna T. Cook. He died on January 1, 1955. Hazel
W. Hertzberg, "Arthur C. Parker," in Margot Liberty, ed., American Indian Intellectuals (St. Paul: West Publishing Co., 1978),
129-138; Marion E. Gridley, Indians of Today (Chicago: The Lakeside Press, 1936), 93-95; William A. Ritchie, "Arthur Caswell Parker,"
in John A. Garraty, ed., Dictionary of American Biography: Supplement Five (New York: Charles Scribner's Sons, 1977), 533-534;
Frederick J. Dockstader, Great North American Indians (New York:
Van Nostrand Reinhold Company, 1977), 203-204.

PARKER, GABRIEL E. (Choctaw)
Gabriel E. Parker was born at Fort Towson, Choctaw Nation,
on September 29, 1878, the son of John Clay and Eliza Willis Parker.
In 1899, he received a B.A. Degree from Henry Kendall College at
Muskogee, Creek Nation. He served as superintendent of the Spencer
Academy in 1899 and 1900, and as principal and superintendent of
Armstrong Academy for Boys in the Choctaw Nation (later Oklahoma)
between 1900 and 1913. He was a member of the Oklahoma Constitu-
tional Convention in 1906-1907 and was register of the U.S. Treasury,
1913-1915. In 1914, he was appointed superintendent of the Five
Civilized Tribes in which capacity he served for several years. Oscar H. Lipps, "Gabe E. Parker: An Appreciation," Red Man, 7 (December, 1914), 115-116; D. C. Gideon, Indian Territory (New York:
The Lewis Publishing Company, 1901), 694-695.

PARKER, LENA (Seneca)
Lena Parker, from New York, was a 1917 graduate of Carlisle
Indian Industrial School.

PARKER, MATTIE E. (Cayuga)
Mattie E. Parker, who was from New York, graduated from
Carlisle Indian Industrial School in 1901 and then entered high school
at Downington, Pennsylvania. Her married name was Nephew. Red
Man and Helper, March 8 and March 29, 1901; Red Man, 4 (October,
1911), 86.

PASCHAL, SARAH (Cherokee)
Sarah Paschal was the sister of John Ridge (q.v.). She married George W. Paschal, and during the factional struggle following
Cherokee removal, she and her family moved to Arkansas, where
she made her home.

PATONE, EDGAR (Zuni)
Edgar Patone attended the Zuni School in New Mexico in 1910.

PATTEE, JOHN (Crow Creek Sioux)
John Pattee, who was the son of John Pattee, entered Hampton
Institute in 1888 and graduated in 1891. After leaving Hampton,
he was a carpenter at the Chemawa Indian School at Salem, Oregon,
and worked there until he died in 1900. He married Lottie Smith
(q.v.). Talks and Thoughts, November, 1896; 52 Congress, 1
Session, Senate Executive Document 31, 30, 48-49; Red Man and
Helper, October 12, 1900.

PATTERSON, SPENCER (Seneca)
Spencer Patterson attended Carlisle Indian Industrial School,
graduating in 1911. He then lived in Buffalo, New York. Carlisle
Arrow, April 21, 1911; Red Man, 5 (November, 1912), 130.

PATTON, ALONZO A. (Alaska Native)
Alonzo A. Patton attended Carlisle Indian Industrial School
in 1909.

PATTON, MINNIE (Pima)
Minnie Patton was a student at Sherman Institute in 1913.

PATTON, SARAH (Pima)
Sarah Patton was a student at Sherman Institute, 1911 to 1914.

PAUL, EDWARD (Nez Percé)
Edward Paul was a student at Carlisle Indian Industrial School
in 1909.

PAUL, LOUIS F. (Tlingit)
Louis F. Paul, the son of Mrs. Matilda K. Paul (q.v.), graduated from Carlisle Indian Industrial School in 1906.

PAUL, MATILDA K. (Tlingit)
Mrs. Matilda K. Paul was reared at Killisnoo, about eighty miles
from Sitka. She lived a traditional life until she was converted as
a child and brought up in one of the early mission schools. She

and her husband did mission work, first at Chilcat and then at Tongass. When her husband died, Mrs. Paul was then transferred to Sitka, where she continued her work in the early years of the twentieth century.

PAUL, PAULINE (Chitimacha)
Pauline Paul was a student at Carlisle Indian Industrial School in 1908.

PAUL, SAMUEL (Chickasaw)
No information is available.

PAUL, WILLIAM L. (Tlingit)
William L. Paul, the son of Matilda K. Paul (q.v.), attended the Sheldon Jackson School in Sitka before going to Carlisle, from which he graduated in 1902. He then studied at Banks Business College in Philadelphia before entering Whitworth College at Tacoma, from which he graduated in 1909. After studying law at La Salle University, he was admitted to the bar. He later served in the Alaska Territorial Legislature. Red Man, 7 (May-June, 1915), 327.

PAXON, AL (Choctaw)
Al Paxon was a student at Jones Academy, Choctaw Nation, in 1903.

PAYNE, JAMES M. (Cherokee)
James M. Payne was a member of the Old Settler Cherokee party.

PEAKE, GEORGE C. (Chippewa)
Born in Aitkin County, Minnesota, George C. Peake attended school at Riggs Institute, Carlisle Indian Industrial School, and Haskell Institute. He worked at various occupations before entering military service during World War I. After the war he entered McPhail School of Dramatic Art. After graduating in 1921, he became a dramatist and was featured at the Stand Rock Indian Ceremonials at Wisconsin Dells. Red Man and Helper, February 14, 1902; Marion E. Gridley, Indians of Today, (Chicago: The Lakeside Press, 1936), 97.

PEAWO, WILBUR A. (Comanche)
Wilbur A. Peawo graduated from Carlisle Indian Industrial School in 1906. In 1915 he was the Comanche delegate to Washington. Arrow, March 30, 1906; Oklahoma Historical Society, Archives Division, Kiowa--Federal Relations, February 3, 1915.

PEAZZONI, ELI M. (Nisenan)
Eli M. Peazzoni, from California, was a 1907 graduate of Carlisle Indian Industrial School. He married Clara Scott. A mechanic by trade, in 1914 he lived at Wyebrooke, Pennsylvania. Arrow, March 29, 1907; Carlisle Arrow, September 10, 1909; Red Man, 7 (October, 1914), 75.

PECK, MARY I. (Pine Ridge Sioux)
Mary I. Peck graduated from the Genoa Indian School, Genoa, Nebraska, in 1913.

PEDRO, FRANCISCO (Mission)
In 1895, Francisco Pedro was a student at the Banning Mission School.

PENISKA, BELLE (Ponca)
Belle Peniska, from Nebraska, graduated from Carlisle Indian Industrial School in 1917.

PENN, WILLIAM (Quileute)
William Penn was sixteen years old when he was a student at the Quileute Day School in 1909.

PENNY, ELIZABETH (Nez Percé)
Elizabeth Penny graduated from Carlisle Indian Industrial School in 1908. She later attended business college at Lewiston, Idaho. Arrow, April 3, 1908; Carlisle Arrow, November 5, 1909.

PERRY, SAMUEL (Shawnee)
Samuel Perry, from the Indian Territory, entered Hampton Institute in August, 1885, at age 19. He left in July, 1889, and entered Haskell Institute. 52 Congress, 1 Session, Senate Executive Document 31, 25, 44-45.

PERRYMAN, DANIEL (Creek)
Daniel Perryman served as prosecuting attorney and judge of Arkansas District of the Creek Nation. At the time of his death in 1878 he was a judge of the Supreme Court. Oklahoma Historical Society, Archives Division, Creek--Courts, Arkansas District, February 26, 1867, No. 25489, and March 7, 1868, No. 25492; Creek--Courts, Supreme, October 7, 1878, No. 28748.

PERRYMAN, PHOEBE A. (Creek)
Phoebe A. Perryman attended the Tullahassee Mission School and then became a teacher at Coweta Town, Creek Nation. Oklahoma Historical Society, Archives Division, Creek--Schools, Neighborhood, May 10, 1872, No. 37722.

PERRYMAN, SUSIE (Creek)
Susie Perryman attended Tullahassee Mission School.

PETERS, MARGARET (Ottawa)
Margaret Peters was a student at Carlisle Indian Industrial School in 1909.

PETERS, MYRTLE (Stockbridge)
Myrtle Peters attended Carlisle Indian Industrial School in 1909.

PETERS, NELLIE H. (Stockbridge)
Nellie Peters, who was from Wisconsin, graduated from Carlisle Indian Industrial School in 1901. Red Man and Helper, March 8, 1901.

PETERS, ROSINA (Tonawanda Seneca)
Rosina Peters was from the Tonawanda Reservation in New York. She was a student at Carlisle Indian Industrial School in 1908.

PETERS, WILLIAM (Pima)
William Peters, from Gila Crossing, Arizona, graduated from the Phoenix Indian School in 1902. He later graduated from the Charles H. Cook Bible School in 1914. He was considered a progressive farmer and preached at the houses of Indians of the Gila River Reservation.

PETERSON, EDWARD W. (Klamath)
Edward W. Peterson was a student at Carlisle Indian Industrial School in 1897 and 1898. Red Man and Helper, 14 (March, 1898), 2.

PHELPS, GIDEON (Sisseton Sioux)
Gideon Phelps was the son of Edwin Phelps, a native missionary who lived on the Standing Rock Reservation. He attended Hampton Institute in 1886 and 1887 and then entered the mission school at Oahe, South Dakota. 52 Congress, 1 Session, Senate Executive Document 31, 28, 46-47.

PHILBRICK, MARY (Sioux)
Mary Philbrick was a student at the Santee Normal Training School in 1884.

PHILIPS, DANIEL (Standing Rock Sioux)
Daniel Philips, who was from Wappala, South Dakota, was a student at Carlisle Indian Industrial School in 1910.

PHILLIPS, ALICE (Klamath)
No information is available.

PHILLIPS, LUKE (Nez Percé)
Luke Phillips was a student at the Carlisle Indian Industrial School during the 1880's. Morning Star, 7 (January-February, 1887), 8.

PICARD, CHARLES (Chippewa)
Charles Picard was a student at Haskell Institute in 1899.

PICARD, JOSEPH (Chippewa)
Joseph Picard was a student at Carlisle Indian Industrial School in 1908.

PICKET PIN, EVA (Sioux)
    Eva Picket Pin attended the Oglala Boarding School.

PICOTTE, CHARLES F., JR. (Yankton Sioux)
    Charles F. Picotte, Jr. (or Miniskuya), from the Yankton Res-
ervation, was born about 1864, the son of Charles F. Picotte. He
attended Hampton Institute from 1879 to 1887, when he graduated.
He married Marguerite La Flesche, and they lived on the Omaha Reservation, where he was a successful farmer. 52 Congress, 1 Session,
Senate Executive Document 31, 15, 40-41.

PICOTTE, SUSAN LA FLESCHE (Omaha)
    Susan La Flesche Picotte was born on June 17, 1865, on the
Omaha Reservation, Nebraska, the daughter of Joseph La Flesche.
She graduated from Hampton Institute in 1886 and then spent three
years at the Woman's Medical College in Philadelphia, from which
she graduated in 1889. After a year of internship at Woman's Hospital, she returned to the Omaha Reservation to practice medicine
as the government physician, a position she held for five years.
She then entered private practice at Bancroft, Nebraska, and, in
1905, began combining medical practice with missionary work. She
married Henri Picotte. Dr. Picotte died on September 18, 1916. 52
Congress, 1 Session, Senate Executive Document 31, 9, 34-35; Word
Carrier, 53 (July-August, 1924), 1; "An Indian Woman Doctor," Red
Man, 11 (September-October, 1892), 7; Red Man, 12 (July-August,
1894), 8; Some Results of Hampton's Work (Hampton: The Institute
Press, 1915), 22; T. Finks, "First Indian Woman Physician," Southern
Workman, 53 (April, 1924), 169-172; Frederick J. Dockstader, Great
North American Indians (New York: Van Nostrand Reinhold Company,
1977), 145; Norma Kidd Green, Iron Eye's Family: The Children
of Joseph La Flesche (Lincoln: Johnson, 1969), 56-81, 97-162.

PIERCE, BEMUS (Cattaraugus Seneca)
    Bemus Pierce, who was from New York, attended Carlisle Indian
Industrial School in the 1890's and later lived at Irving, New York,
on the Cattaraugus Reservation. He married Annie Gesis. Red Man,
15 (December, 1899), 7; Red Man and Helper, March 1, 1901.

PIERCE, EVELYN (Seneca)
    Evelyn Pierce, who was from New York, was born about 1891.
She graduated from Carlisle Indian Industrial School in 1910 and
from the business department at Haskell Institute in 1914. Red Man
7 (May-June, 1915), 327; Indian Leader, 17 (September, 1913), 12,
and 18 (June, 1914), 24.

PILCHER, ETTA M. (Omaha)
    The daughter of John Pilcher, Etta Pilcher entered Hampton
Institute in July, 1887, at age fourteen, and graduated in 1890. She
then became a teacher at the government school for the Omahas.
52 Congress, 1 Session, Senate Executive Document 31, 11, 36-37.

PITCHLYNN, PETER PERKINS (Choctaw)

Peter Perkins Pitchlynn was born in the Choctaw Nation in Mississippi on January 20, 1806, the son of John Pitchlynn, a white man, and Sopha Folsom Pitchlynn, a Choctaw. Pitchlynn was educated at the Academy of Columbia, Tennessee, and the University of Tennessee. After graduation from the university, he returned to the Choctaw Nation, where he married his cousin, Rhoda Folsom. He was elected to the Choctaw National Council in 1825 and, in 1828, led an exploring and peace-making mission to the Osage country west of the Mississippi. Pitchlynn was active in Choctaw politics throughout his life. He served as Principal Chief from 1864 through 1866 and, after his term of office, stayed in Washington pressing Choctaw claims against the government. He died in Washington on January 17, 1881. David W. Baird, Peter Pitchlynn: Chief of the Choctaws (Norman: University of Oklahoma Press, 1972); Czarina C. Conlan, "Peter P. Pitchlynn: Chief of the Choctaws, 1864-66," Chronicles of Oklahoma, 6 (June, 1928), 215-224; Carolyn Thomas Foreman, "Notes of Interest Concerning Peter P. Pitchlynn," Chronicles of Oklahoma, 7 (June, 1929), 172-174; Frederick J. Dockstader, Great North American Indians (New York: Van Nostrand Reinhold Company, 1977), 213-214.

PLENTY HOLES, EUNICE (Sioux)

Eunice Plenty Holes was a student at the Oglala Boarding School.

PLENTY HORSES, GUY (Sioux)

Guy Plenty Horses was a student at Carlisle Indian Industrial School in 1909 and 1910.

POKAGON, JULIA (Potawatomi)

Julia Pokagon was a student at Haskell Institute in 1898.

POKAGON, SIMON (Pokaguns Potawatomi)

Simon Pokagon was born in 1830 in Pokagon Village in present-day Berrien County, Michigan. His father, Leopold Pokagon, who died in 1840, was chief of the Potawatomi for forty-two years, was present at the massacre at Fort Dearborn in 1812, and later represented the tribe in negotiations that led to the sale of lands on which Chicago sits. At fourteen, Simon Pokagon entered Notre Dame at South Bend, Indiana, where he remained for three years. He then spent one year at Oberlin and two years in school at Twinsburg, Ohio. As Chief of the Pokagon band of Potawatomis, Simon Pokagon made one of his prime concerns the payment of funds due the tribe for the sale of Chicago and its environs. The claim was finally settled in 1896. When Pokagon learned that the World's Fair was to be held in Chicago in 1893, he tried but failed to organize a congress of American Indians to meet in conjunction with the fair. He was, however, invited to speak at the fair. Pokagon devoted much time during his last years in recording his tribal cultural heritage and history. He died in 1899. Pokagon was married to Lonidaw Sinagaw and Victoria. David H. Dickason, "Chief Simon Pokagon: 'The Indian

Longfellow,'" Indiana Magazine of History, 57 (June, 1961), 127-140; Frederick J. Dockstader, Great North American Indians (New York: Van Nostrand Reinhold, 1977), 216-217.

POO, LAH (Hopi)
Lah Poo was a student at the Keams Canyon school in 1898.

POODRY, FANNIE C. (Seneca)
Fannie C. Poodry, from the Tonawanda Reservation in New York, was a student at Hampton Institute in 1902. Thirty-Fifth Annual Catalogue of the Hampton Normal and Agricultural Institute (Hampto (Hampton: Hampton Institute Press, 1903), 111.

POOR BEAR, PETER (Sioux)
Peter Poor Bear was a student at the Oglala Boarding School in 1920.

PORTER, JOSE (Navajo)
Jose Porter was a student at Carlisle Indian Industrial School in 1909.

PORTER, NANCY (Creek)
Nancy Porter attended Tullahassee Mission School and then taught in the Creek public schools. Oklahoma Historical Society, Archives Division, Creek--Schools, Neighborhood, December 12, 1871, No. 38130; November 1, 1873, No. 37702; February 3, 1876, No. 37828.

PORTER, PLEASANT (Creek)
Pleasant Porter was born near Clarksville, Creek Nation, on September 26, 1840, the son of Benjamin Edwin Porter and Phoebe, the daughter of Tahlopee Tustennuggee. Porter spent five years in Presbyterian mission schools and obtained the rest of his education through home study. Before the Civil War, he worked as a store clerk and a cattle driver. In the war, he served in D. N. McIntosh's Confederate Creek regiment. After the war, he reorganized the Creek school system and served as a delegate to Washington. Later, he was a Captain of the Creek Light-Horse Police, served four years in the House of Warriors, and was a member of the Creek commission that negotiated with the Dawes Commission. He served as Principal Chief from 1899 until his death on September 3, 1907. Porter was married to Mary Ellen Keys and Mattie L. Bertholf. Ralph William Goodwin, "Pleasant Porter and the Decline of the Muskogee Nation" (Ph.D. dissertation, Harvard University, 1960); John Bartlett Meserve, "Chief Pleasant Porter," Chronicles of Oklahoma, 9 (September, 1931), 318-334; H. F. O'Beirne and E. S. O'Beirne, The Indian Territory (St. Louis: C. B. Woodward Company, 1892), 161; Frederick J. Dockstader, Great North American Indians (New York: Van Nostrand Reinhold Company, 1977), 221-222.

PORTER, SUSIE (Chippewa)
Susie Porter was a student at Carlisle Indian Industrial School in 1908 and 1909.

POSEY, ALEXANDER LAWRENCE (Creek)

Alexander Lawrence Posey was born near Eufaula, Creek Nation, on August 3, 1873. He was the son of Lewis H. Posey, a Scot who had been born in Indian Territory, and Nancy Phillips, the full-blood daughter of Pohos Harjo of the Wind Clan of Creeks. During his early years, he preferred Creek to English but was forced to speak English by his teacher at age twelve or fourteen. He attended Creek public school in Eufaula and then graduated with honors from the Indian University (Bacone) at Muskogee in 1895. That year, he was elected to the House of Warriors, the lower house of the Creek legislature and the next year was appointed superintendent of the Creek National Orphan Asylum at Okmulgee. In 1896, he married Minnie Harris of Fayetteville, Arkansas, a matron at the Asylum. In 1897, he was appointed superintendent of Public Instruction of the Creek Nation, but soon left that office for a career in writing. However, he later served as principal at the Creek National High School in Eufaula and still later at Wetumpka. He edited the Eufaula weekly Indian Journal, a newspaper in which he published some of his most successful works. After two years with the Journal, he moved to Muskogee, where he assisted in editing the Muskogee Times and did a brief term of government service enrolling Creeks with the Dawes Commission. In 1905, he served as secretary of the Con-stitutional Convention for the proposed state of Sequoyah. A prolific writer, he wrote poetry under the name of Chinnubbie Harjo and political satire under the name of Fus Fixico. He drowned on May 27, 1908. "Alexander L. Posey, a Creek Bard," American Indian, April 23, 1925; Doris Challocombe, "Alexander Lawrence Posey," Chronicles of Oklahoma, 11 (December 1933), 1011-1018; S. M. Ruth-erford, "A Tribute to Posey," Muskogee Phoenix, July 23, 1908; O. P. Sturm, "The Passing of the Creek Poet," Sturm's Oklahoma Magazine, 4 (July, 1908), 13-17; "Three Indian Writers of Prominence," Sturm's Statehood Magazine, 1 (October, 1905), 84-85; Frederick J. Dockstader, Great North American Indians (New York: Van Nos-trand Reinhold Company, 1977), 222-223.

POSEYSEVA, JOHN (Hopi)

In 1910, John Poseyseva was a student at Sherman Institute.

POSTOAK, NANCY (Creek)

Nancy Postoak attended the Tullahassee Mission School.

POWERS, EDITH (Paiute)

Edith Powers graduated from Sherman Institute in 1919. She married Samson Dewey and lived at Stewart, Nevada.

POWLESS, ALFRED (Oneida)

Alfred Powless was a student at Hampton Institute in 1896.

POWLESS, DENNISON (Oneida)

Dennison Powless was a student at Haskell Institute in 1906.

POWLESS, ELLA (Oneida)
     Born about 1873, Ella Powless was the daughter of John D.
Powless of Wisconsin. She entered Hampton Institute in 1888 and
graduated in 1895. 52 Congress, 1 Session, Senate Executive
Document 31, 36-37; Red Man, 12 (May, 1895), 6; National Archives
Microfilm, Microcopy 595 (Indian Census Rolls, 1885-1940), Roll 314,
Oneida 1900.

POWLESS, GRACE (Oneida)
     Grace Powless, from Wisconsin, was born about 1897, the daugh-
ter of Joseph Powless. National Archives Microfilm, Microcopy 595
(Indian Census Rolls, 1885-1940), Roll 315, Oneida 1900.

POWLESS, LYMAN (Oneida)
     Lyman Powless (or Tamtolus), from Wisconsin, was born in
1869, the son of Peter Powless. He entered Hampton Institute in
July, 1888. 52 Congress, 1 Session, Senate Executive Document
31, 48-49; National Archives Microfilm, Microcopy 595 (Indian Census
Rolls, 1885-1940), Roll 315, Oneida 1900.

POWLESS, RICHARD S. (Oneida)
     Richard Powless, from Wisconsin, was the son of Henry Powless.
He attended Hampton Institute from 1886 to 1888. After teaching
school at home for a year, he went to Cambridge, Massachusetts,
where he worked as a printer for the Riverside Press. 52 Congress,
1 Session, Senate Executive Document 31, 226, 46-47.

PRADT, EDWIN (Pueblo)
     Edwin Pradt graduated from Sherman Institute in 1921 and
then worked for the Southern California Telephone Company at Los
Angeles.

PRADT, ELIZABETH (Laguna Pueblo)
     Elizabeth Pradt graduated from Sherman Institute in 1909.
Sherman Bulletin, May 24, 1916.

PRADT, GEORGE H. (Laguna Pueblo)
     George H. Pradt was a 1903 graduate of the Carlisle Indian
Industrial School. He lived at Grants and then Guam, New Mexico.
He served as a deputy forest ranger in the Manzano National Forest.
Red Man and Helper, February 20-27 and March 20, 1903; Red Man,
7 (March, 1915), 256; Indian Craftsman, 2 (October, 1909), 32.

PRADT, LAURA (Pueblo)
     Laura Pradt was a student at Sherman Institute in 1911.

PRIMEAU, LULU (Sioux)
     Lulu Primeau was a student at the Santee Normal Training
School in 1884.

PROPHET, EDNA (Chippewa)
     Edna Prophet, who was from Seneca, Missouri, studied home

economics at Chilocco Indian Agricultural School, from which she graduated in 1919.

PROPHET, WILLIAM (Shawnee)
William Prophet was a student at Haskell Institute in 1906.

PUGH, WILLIAM G. (Sioux)
William G. Pugh graduated from Sherman Institute. In 1914 he bought half interest in the Martin Messenger at Martin, South Dakota. He later owned the paper and established The Shannon County News. Sherman Bulletin, May 27, 1914; June 2, 1915; March 28, 1917.

QUICK BEAR, REUBEN (Rosebud Sioux)
Reuben Quick Bear was born about 1868, the son of Quick Bear. He was a student at Carlisle Indian Industrial School from 1879 to 1881. In 1900 he was part of a Rosebud delegation to Washington to discuss Rosebud school lands. In 1909 he was elected one of the commissioners of Melette County, South Dakota. Eadle Keahtah Toh, 1 (April, 1881), 4; Red Man, 15 (March, 1900), 6; Red Man 4 (June, 1912), 486.

QUINLAN, DELIA (White Earth Chippewa)
Delia Quinlan was born at White Earth, Minnesota, in 1891. She was reared by her grandparents and was taught English and French as well as her native language. She entered mission school at age six and later spent three years in school at Morris, Minnesota. She later entered Carlisle Indian Industrial School, where she was a student in 1908.

QUINN, RENA (Hupa)
Rena Quinn attended the Hoopa Indian School before entering Sherman Institute.

QUITAC, LORETTA (Mission)
Loretta Quitac was a student at Sherman Institute in 1911.

RABBIT, ELSIE M. (Chippewa)
Elsie M. Rabbit, from Minnesota, was a student at Carlisle Indian Industrial School in 1910.

RAFAEL, HARRY E. (Papago)
Harry E. Rafael graduated from Haskell Institute in 1911. Indian Leader, June 9, 1911.

RAMSEY, JOHN (Nez Percé)
John Ramsey, born about 1888, attended Carlisle.

RANDOLPH, GEORGE EDDY (Chippewa)
George Eddy Randolph, who was from International Falls, Minnesota, studied engineering at Chilocco Indian Agricultural School, from which he graduated in 1918.

RAVEN, ANNA   (Arapaho)
    Anna Raven was a student at Carlisle Indian Industrial School in 1880.

RAY, LEWIS J.   (Pueblo)
    Lewis J. Ray was from Bibo, New Mexico. He was a student at Carlisle Indian Industrial School in 1909. In 1913 he lived at Winslow, Arizona. Carlisle Arrow, November 5, 1909; Red Man, 5 (June, 1913), 480.

REBOIN, ALLEN   (Nez Percé)
    Allen Reboin was a student at Carlisle Indian Industrial School in 1910.

RED FOX   (Blackfeet)
    See SKIUHUSHU

REDBIRD, NED   (Cherokee)
    Ned Redbird, from Oklahoma, was born in the Cherokee Nation. He wrote his prizewinning essay for The Outlook in 1921.

REDDIE, WILLIE   (Haida)
    Willie Reddie, who was from Wrangell, Alaska, entered the Chemawa Indian School at Salem, Oregon, in 1908 and graduated in 1914. In 1917 he toured the East as a member of a string quartet under the auspices of the Redpath Lyceum Bureau. Chemawa American, 16 (June, 1914), 7-8; November 14, 1917.

REDEYE, ROSA   (Seneca)
    Rosa Redeye attended Carlisle Indian Industrial School in 1909.

REDTHUNDER, MARY M.   (Sisseton)
    Mary M. Redthunder, from Minnesota, entered the Carlisle Indian Industrial School in 1903 and remained until 1910. In 1912, she was in the dressmaking business at Sisseton, South Dakota, and in 1913 became assistant matron at the Indian school in Dulce, New Mexico. Red Man and Helper, August 28, 1903; Carlisle Arrow, January 12, 1912; Red Man, 6 (January, 1914), 206.

REED, KATIE   (Crow)
    Katie Reed, from Montana, graduated from the commercial department of Haskell Institute in 1914. Indian Leader, 17 (June, 1914), 24.

REID, NETTIE   (Washo)
    Nettie Reid graduated from Haskell Institute in 1910. Her married name was Walker, and she worked for a number of years at the Carson Indian School, Stewart, Nevada.

REINKEN, OLGA   (Alaska Native)
    Olga Reinken attended Carlisle Indian Industrial School in 1908 and 1909.

RENVILLE, GABRIEL (Sisseton Sioux)
Gabriel Renville was born at Sweet Corn's Village on Big Stone
Lake, South Dakota, in April, 1824, the son of Victor and Winona
Crawford Renville. He was the last chief of the Sisseton Sioux,
appointed by the War Department. He signed the treaty of 1867
as Chief of the Sisseton and Wahpeton Sioux. He received an allotment on the Santee Reservation. Renville died at the Sisseton Agency
on August 24, 1902.

RICE, SAMUEL J. (Mission)
Samuel Rice, from California, graduated from the Phoenix Indian School in 1909. In 1922 he was editor of The Indian, published
by the Mission Indian Federation, of which he was an active member.
Rice lived at Santa Rosa.

RICHARDSON, IDA (Klamath)
Ida Richardson was a student at Sherman Institute in 1911.

RIDGE, JOHN (Cherokee)
John Ridge was born about 1800 in the eastern Cherokee Nation, the son of Major Ridge and Susie Wickett Ridge. He attended
mission schools at Spring Place, Georgia, and Brainerd, Tennessee,
before going to school at Cornwall, Connecticut in 1819. He married
Sarah Bird Northrup of Cornwall. He was assassinated on June 22,
1839, for having signed the New Echota removal treaty of 1835.

RIDGE, JOHN ROLLIN (Cherokee)
John Rollin Ridge (Chees-quat-a-law-ny, or Yellow Bird) was
born in the Eastern Cherokee Nation in 1827, the son of John Ridge
(q.v.). After his father was killed in 1839 for having signed the
removal treaty, Ridge's family moved to Fayetteville, Arkansas, where
Ridge received a basic education. In 1849, he killed another Cherokee and fled to Missouri and went the next year to California, never
to return to the Cherokee Nation. There he edited several newspapers including the Sacramento Bee, the Marysville California Express
and Daily National Democrat, and Grass Valley National. He founded
the Trinity National. Ridge became widely known as a poet and as
the author of the Life and Adventures of Joaquin Murietta. He died
in 1867. Edward Everett Dale, "John Rollin Ridge," Chronicles of
Oklahoma, 4 (December, 1926), 312-321; Carolyn Thomas Foreman,
"Edward W. Bushyhead and John Rollin Ridge, Cherokee Editors
in California," Chronicles of Oklahoma, 14 (September, 1936), 295-
311.

RIGGS, ROLLA LYNN (Cherokee)
Rolla Lynn Riggs was born at Claremore, Cherokee Nation,
the son of William G. and Ella Riggs, the latter of Cherokee descent.
After high school, Riggs worked for newspapers in Chicago, New
York, and Los Angeles. In 1920, he entered the University of Okla-
homa, where he wrote for the university newspaper and magazine.
In the summer of 1922, he toured with a Chautauqua company and
that year taught part time, attended classes, and wrote, mainly poetry.

In the fall of 1923, he went to New Mexico for his health and wrote plays. His first play of significance was Green Grow the Lilacs (1930), that later became the Broadway musical Oklahoma! He went on to write such plays as The Cherokee Night (1933) and Russet Mantle (1936). Riggs died in New York on June 30, 1954. Joseph Benton, "Some Remembrances About Lynn Riggs," Chronicles of Oklahoma, 34 (Autumn, 1956), 296-299; Charles Aughtry, "Lynn Riggs at the University of Oklahoma," Chronicles of Oklahoma, 37 (Autumn, 1959), 280-284; Frederick J. Dockstader, Great North American Indians (New York: Van Nostrand Reinhold Company, 1977), 243-244.

RILEY, AGNES H. (Southern Cheyenne)
Agnes H. Riley, who was from Tologa, Oklahoma, studied domestic arts at Chilocco Indian Agricultural School, from which she graduated in 1918.

RILEY, MINNIE (Shawnee)
Minnie Riley attended Haskell Institute.

RIOS, VINCENTE STANISLAUS (Papago)
Vincente Stanislaus Rios was a student at the San Xavier School in Arizona in 1895.

ROBARDS, CHRISTOPHER C. (Cherokee)
Christopher Robards was born about 1848. He lived at Claremore, Cherokee Nation.

ROBERTS, ETHEL (Smith River, i.e., Tolowa)
Ethel Roberts, from California, was a senior student at Chemawa Indian School, Salem, Oregon, in 1913.

ROBERTS, HENRY E. (Pawnee)
Henry Roberts was a student at Haskell Institute in 1903. He graduated from Hampton Institute in 1908 and later worked as lease and land clerk at the Pawnee Agency.

ROBERTS, MAE A. (Pima)
Mae A. Roberts graduated from Sherman Institute in 1922.

ROBERTSON, BERTHA (Santee Sioux)
Bertha Robertson was a student at the Santee Normal Training School in 1914 and 1915. Word Carrier, 44 (May-June, 1915), 9.

ROBERTSON, EMILY (Sioux)
Emily Robertson was a student at Haskell Institute in 1909.

ROBERTSON, FLORENCE (Sioux)
No information is available.

ROBINETTE, PAUL (Santee Sioux)
Paul Robinette attended Haskell Institute.

ROBINSON, WILLIAM (Chippewa)
William Robinson was a student at Carlisle Indian Industrial School in 1911.

ROCQUE, LEO (Sioux)
Leo Rocque, from Colorado, graduated from Haskell Institute in 1912. He then entered the commercial course there and graduated in 1914. Indian Leader, June 9, 1911, June 14, 1912, and 17 (June, 1914), 24.

RODGERS, THOMAS L. (Cherokee)
Thomas L. Rodgers was a Headman of the Old Settler Cherokees. He operated a salt mill at present-day Spavinaw, Oklahoma.

ROE CLOUD, HENRY C. (Winnebago)
See CLOUD, HENRY C. ROE

ROGERS, EDWARD L. (White Earth Chippewa)
Edward L. Rogers, from the White Earth Reservation, was born in 1876 in Libby, Minnesota. He entered Carlisle in 1894 and graduated in 1897. He then studied law at the Dickinson Law School and then entered the University of Minnesota in 1901. He played football for the university and spent his summers working in a law firm in Minneapolis. After graduation in 1904, he returned to Carlisle as the head coach. He then entered law practice at Walker, Minnesota. He was quite active in Chippewa affairs and served several terms as County Attorney of Cass County. He was tribal attorney for the Minnesota Chippewas, 1941-1945. In 1963, he was named the Outstanding County Attorney in the United States. He retired from practice in 1966. Red Man, 14 (April, 1897), 4; Red Man and Helper, October 12, 1900, November 15, 1901, February 28, 1902, and March 11, 1904; Red Man, 7 (September, 1913), 41; Marion E. Gridley, Indians of Today (Chicago: The Lakeside Press, 1936), 101, and (Chicago: Towertown Press, 1960), 162-163.

ROGERS, WILLIAM CHARLES (Cherokee)
William Charles Rogers was born near Claremore, Cherokee Nation, on December 13, 1847, the son of Charles Coody and Elizabeth McCorkle Rogers. He attended tribal school and later took up farming near present-day Skiatook, Oklahoma. He was also a store owner and rancher. He served the Cherokee Nation as a councilman, twice as a member of the Senate, and as the last elected chief of the nation. His wife was Nannie Haynie. Rogers died on November 8, 1917. John Bartlett Meserve, "Chief Thomas Mitchell Buffington and Chief William Charles Rogers," Chronicles of Oklahoma, 17 (June, 1939), 140-146; Elzie Ronald Caywood, "The Administration of William C. Rogers, Principal Chief of the Cherokee Nation, 1903-1907," Chronicles of Oklahoma, 30 (Spring, 1952), 29-37.

ROMAN NOSE, HENRY CARUTHERS (Southern Cheyenne)
Henry Caruthers Roman Nose, born sometime in the 1850's, was

one of the prisoners sent to Florida from the Cheyenne Agency in 1870's. From prison at St. Augustine, he was sent to Hampton Institute in 1878. He was sent to Carlisle when it first opened in 1879 and stayed there two years. He returned to the West and, in 1890, was living in a tent at the agency where he was employed by the government as a tinner. His wife was Standing. Roman Nose died on June 13, 1917. Red Man, 10 (June, 1890), 3; Karen Daniels Peterson, "The Writing of Henry Roman Nose," Chronicles of Oklahoma, 47 (Winter, 1964-1965), 458-478.

ROMERO, ESTHER (Acomita Pueblo)
     Esther Romero, from Acomita, New Mexico, graduated from Sherman Institute in 1914. Sherman Bulletin, May 24, 1916.

ROOKS, GEORGE (Sioux)
     George Rooks was a student at the Oglala Boarding School in 1919 and 1920.

ROOT, CLARA (Northern Arapaho)
     Clara Root, who was from Fort Washakie, Wyoming, studied domestic arts at Chilocco Indian Agricultural School, from which she graduated in 1918.

ROSS, A. FRANK (Choctaw)
     A. Frank Ross was born in Mississippi on January 21, 1851, the son of Abraham and Martha J. (Moore) Ross, the latter of Choctaw descent. He graduated from Baylor College in Texas in 1873 and then attended the Southern Baptist Seminary at Greenville, South Carolina, and studied Theology at Louisville, Kentucky. He went to the Choctaw Nation as a missionary. From 1882 to 1886, he edited The Indian Missionary. Ross moved to Hartshorne, where he served as deputy clerk of Gaines County and examiner of teachers in the Choctaw schools. He was licensed to practice law before the Choctaw courts. Ross was elected to the first legislature of the new state of Oklahoma. He died in 1908. D. C. Gideon, Indian Territory (New York: The Lewis Publishing Company, 1901), 488-490; "A. Frank Ross," Chronicles of Oklahoma, 10 (March, 1932), 147-148.

ROSS, DANIEL H. (Cherokee)
     Daniel H. Ross was born in the Cherokee Nation in 1848, the son of Andrew Ross. In 1873, he was a delegate to the Okmulgee Convention, and in 1874, he was one of three people appointed to codify the Cherokee laws. He married Naomi Chisholm and Sarah Halfbreed.

ROSS, JOHN (Cherokee)
     John Ross (Cooweescoowee) was born near Lookout Mountain, Tennessee, in the Eastern Cherokee Nation on October 3, 1790, the son of David and Mary McDonald Ross. He was a veteran of the War of 1812, having served in Andrew Jackson's campaign against

the Creeks and held several offices in tribal government: member and
and president of the council, assistant principal chief, and Principal
Chief (1828-1866). He was instrumental in drafting both Cherokee
Constitutions (1827 and 1839) and was bitterly opposed to removal
of the Cherokees from the East. He tried to keep his tribe neutral
during the Civil War but was finally persuaded to sign a treaty with
the Confederacy. He was married to Quatie and to Mary Bryan Stapler. He died on August 1, 1866. Gary E. Moulton, "John Ross,"
in R. David Edmunds, ed., American Indian Leaders: Studies in
Diversity (Lincoln: University of Nebraska Press, 1980), 88-106;
Frederick J. Dockstader, Great North American Indians (New York:
Van Nostrand Reinhold Company, 1977), 246-247; John Bartlett Meserve, "Chief John Ross," Chronicles of Oklahoma, 13 (December,
1935), 421-437.

ROSS, JOSHUA (Cherokee)
    Joshua Ross was born in May, 1833, at Wills Valley, Alabama,
in the Eastern Cherokee Nation, the son of Andrew and Susan Lowrey
Ross. He attended Fairfield and Park Hill mission schools in the western
nation. After graduation from the Cherokee Male Seminary in 1855,
he attended Emory and Henry College, graduating in 1860. He taught
at the Cherokee Male Seminary and, during the Civil War, clerked
at a sutler's store at Fort Gibson. He married Muskogee Yargee,
a Creek, and, in 1871, moved to Muskogee, Creek Nation, where
he opened a store. He was a Cherokee delegate to the Okmulgee
Convention from 1870 to 1875 and sat in the Cherokee National Council. He died on February 12, 1924. D. C. Gideon, Indian Territory
(New York: The Lewis Publishing Company, 1901), 217-220; Muriel
H. Wright, "A Report to the General Council of the Indian Territory
Meeting at Okmulgee in 1873," Chronicles of Oklahoma, 34 (Spring,
1956), 12n.

ROSS, OLIVER C. (Pine Ridge Sioux)
    Oliver C. Ross was a student at Hampton Institute in 1902-
1903. Thirty-Fifth Annual Catalogue of the Hampton Normal and
Agricultural Institute (Hampton: Hampton Institute Press, 1903),
111.

ROSS, ROSA L. (Cherokee-Creek)
    Rosa L. Ross was the daughter of Joshua Ross (q.v.), and
Muskogee Yargee Ross, a Creek. She grew up in Muskogee, Creek
Nation, and attended Carlisle Indian Industrial School in the 1880's.
She married W. S. Miles. Morning Star, 2 (August, 1882), 4, and
5 (May, 1885), 5.

ROSS, S. W. (Cherokee)
    S. W. Ross was born near Tahlequah, Cherokee Nation, the
son of Lewis Anderson and Nellie Potts Ross. He attended private
schools, the Presbyterian mission school at Park Hill, and the Cherokee Male Seminary. In his teens, he began working for the Tahlequah Indian Arrow and did newspaper work for a number of years.

ROSS, WILLIAM POTTER (Cherokee)
William Potter Ross was born at Lookout Mountain, Tennessee, in the Eastern Cherokee Nation on August 28, 1820. He was educated in Presbyterian mission schools, at Greenville Academy in Tennessee, Hamil School, in Lawrenceville, New Jersey, and Princeton, from which he graduated with honors in 1842. In 1843, he was elected secretary of the upper house of the Cherokee Council. In 1844, he became the first editor of the Cherokee Advocate. He served in the Confederate army during the Civil War. He was a delegate to the Okmulgee Council in 1870, and, in 1873, he was elected Principal Chief of the tribe. He retired from public office in 1875 but maintained interests in newspaper work, including the Indian Journal, the Indian Chieftain, and the Indian Arrow. He died on July 20, 1891, at Fort Gibson, Cherokee Nation. John Bartlett Meserve, "Chief William Potter Ross," Chronicles of Oklahoma, 15 (March, 1937), 21-29.

ROUILLARD, ALEX (Santee Sioux)
Alex Rouillard was a student at Hampton Institute in 1896.

ROUILLARD, DAVID (Santee Sioux)
David Rouillard, from Santee, Nebraska, entered Hampton Institute in 1890. He died in April, 1897. Talks and Thoughts, May, 1897.

ROUILLARD, EUGENE (Santee Sioux)
Eugene Rouillard graduated from the Santee Normal Training School in 1917 and entered military service during World War I. In 1920, he was a printer at Santee, Nebraska. Iapi Oaye, 49 (June-July, 1920), 23.

ROUILLARD, LUCY (Santee Sioux)
Lucy Rouillard entered the Santee Normal Training School in 1909 and graduated in 1917. She then entered Hampton Institute where she was a student in 1920. Word Carrier, 44 (May-June, 1915), 9; Iapi Oaye, 49 (June-July, 1920), 23.

ROUILLARD, THOMAS J. (Santee Sioux)
No information is available.

ROWLAND, EMMA J. (Northern Cheyenne)
Emma J. Rowland, from the Northern Cheyenne Reservation in Montana, was born about 1892 and graduated from Carlisle Indian Industrial School in 1913. In 1914, she entered government service at the Pine Ridge School in South Dakota. She married George Harris.

ROY, MARY (Ponca)
Mary Roy graduated from Haskell Institute in 1901.

RUIZ, EMMA (Nisenan)
Emma Ruiz graduated from Sherman Institute in 1913. She

married Joseph Kie and in 1916 lived in San Bernardino, California. *Sherman Bulletin*, May 24, 1916.

RULO, CORA A. (Ponca)
The daughter of Charles Rulo, Cora A. Rulo entered Hampton Institute in 1885 at age 15 and remained there until 1888. She married David Sherman. 52 Congress, 1 Session, *Senate Executive Document 31*, 10, 34-35.

RULO, LOUIS (Oto)
Louis Rulo, from Oklahoma, graduated from the Phoenix Indian School in 1911. He took commercial courses at Haskell Institute. He worked at the Mescalero school in New Mexico and served in the Nineteenth Infantry during World War I. In 1921, he was assistant disciplinarian at the Santa Fe School.

RUNNELS, LOUIS H. (Sanpoil)
Louis H. Runnels, born about 1885, was a 1911 graduate of Carlisle Indian Industrial School. He worked for a short time as a traveling salesman for a Boston firm and then attended school at Keller, Washington. *Carlisle Arrow*, April 21, 1911; *Red Man*, 5 (February, 1913), 265.

RUNNELS, MARY E. (Sanpoil)
Mary E. Runnels, who was from Washington State, graduated from Carlisle Indian Industrial School in 1906. *Arrow*, March 30, 1906.

RYAN, CHARLES (Pokanoket, i.e., Wampanoag)
Charles Ryan attended Carlisle Indian Industrial School.

SAGE, ALEXANDER W. (Arickara)
Alexander W. Sage was from the Fort Berthold Reservation, North Dakota, and entered Carlisle Indian Industrial School in 1903. He later worked as a farmer at the Bismarck Indian School. *Red Man and Helper*, August 28, 1903; *Red Man*, 4 (September, 1911), 42.

ST. PIERRE, MARY (Chippewa)
Mary St. Pierre attended Haskell Institute.

SAKEASTEWA, VICTOR (Hopi)
Victor Sakeastewa was a student at Sherman Institute in 1911.

SANDERS, SAMUEL STEPHEN (Cherokee)
Samuel Stephen Sanders was elected to the Cherokee National Council from Illinois District in 1899 and 1903. Emmet Starr, *History of the Cherokee Indians and Their Legends and Folk Lore* (Oklahoma City: The Warden Company, 1921), 279.

SANDS, ROBERT (Kansa)
Robert Sands, a full-blood Kaw, was from Indian Territory.

SANGO   (Eskimo)
No information is available.

SANGSTER, MARGARET   (Navajo)
From Leupp, Arizona, Margaret Sangster graduated from Sherman Institute in 1923 and then studied nursing at the Methodist Hospital in Los Angeles. She next served three years as duty nurse at the Carson Indian School. Then after a year of further study in New York, she returned to the Navajo Reservation as the first full-blood Indian public health nurse. Marion E. Gridley, Indians of Today (Chicago: The Lakeside Press, 1936), 104.

SAUL, THOMAS T.   (Crow Creek Sioux)
Thomas T. Saul graduated from the Carlisle Indian Industrial School in 1909 and lived at Chamberlain, South Dakota. Red Man, 5 (February, 1913), 265.

SAUNOOKE, NAN E.   (Eastern Band Cherokee)
Nan Saunooke, from North Carolina, was born about 1889. She graduated from Carlisle Indian Industrial School in 1911. Carlisle Arrow, April 21, 1911.

SCHANANDOAH, CHAPMAN   (Oneida)
Chapman Schanandoah, who was from Nedro, New York, was the son of Abram Schanandoah. He entered Hampton Institute in November, 1888, at age 18 and left a year later. He was at Hampton again, in 1892-1894. In 1897 he joined the U.S. Navy and reached the rank of chief machinist; in 1904 he served aboard the U.S.S. Raleigh. He left the navy in 1912 and lived in Buffalo. He invented an explosive called Schanadite and a new kind of megaphone and a compressor. 52 Congress, 1 Session, Senate Executive Document 31, 48-49; Talks and Thoughts, November, 1898, and April, 1904; Red Man, 5 (December, 1912), 176; Marion E. Gridley, Indians of Today (Chicago: The Lakeside Press, 1936), 105.

SCHOOLCRAFT, JANE JOHNSTON   (Ojibwa)
Jane Schoolcraft was the daughter of John Johnston, an Irish trader at La Pointe, and Susan (Ozha-guscoday-way-quay). They later lived at Sault Ste. Marie. She was born in 1800 and as a child travelled with her father to Detroit, Montreal, and Quebec. In 1809 she was sent to Ireland for education. In 1823, she married Henry Rowe Schoolcraft. She died in 1841. She wrote under the names Rosa, Leelinau, and her Indian name Bame-wa-was-ge-zhik-a-quay. Philip P. Mason, ed., The Literary Voyager of Muzzeniegun (East Lansing: Michigan State University Press, 1962), xxi-xxii, xxiv.

SCHRAM, GRACE   (Chippewa)
Grace Schram was born at Milaca, Minnesota, on April 14, 1899. She attended school at Onamia and then entered the Pipestone Indian School in 1910.

SCOTT, COLBY (Creek)
Colby Scott was a student at Tullahassee Mission School in 1870.

SCREAMER, ALBERT MANUS (Eastern Band Cherokee)
Albert Screamer was a student at Carlisle Indian Industrial School in 1907. He married Nan Saunooke (q.v.). In 1910 he worked as a printer at Asheville, North Carolina. Arrow, January 24, 1908; Carlisle Arrow, October 7, 1910.

SEARS, LEE ALLEN (Sioux)
Lee Allen Sears graduated from Pipestone Indian School in 1913.

SEARS, ROSALIND (Assiniboin)
Rosalind Sears was from Poplar, Montana. She studied domestic arts at Chilocco Indian Agricultural School from which she graduated in 1918.

SEATTLE, MATTHEW (Puyallup)
No information is available.

SEDICK, EUDOCIA M. (Alaska Native)
Eudocia M. Sedick graduated from the Carlisle Indian Industrial School in 1906. Arrow, March 30, 1906.

SEKONIK, JOE (Eskimo)
Joe Sekonik, of Kivalina, Alaska, supposedly knew the traditional stories and was writing them down in 1918 so they would not be lost.

SELKIRK, CHARLES (White Earth Chippewa)
Charles Selkirk was from the White Earth Reservation in Minnesota.

SERVICE, ROBERT (Clatsop)
Robert Service, from Oregon, was a 1914 graduate of the Chemawa Indian School at Salem, Oregon.

SEVECK, CHESTER (Eskimo)
No information is available.

SHAMBOW, MARY (Chippewa)
Mary Shambow graduated from the Pipestone Indian School in 1914.

SHANGREAU, MARY (Pine Ridge Sioux)
Mary Sangreau was a student at the Oglala Boarding School in 1900 after which she attended Haskell Institute, graduating in 1909. She then worked at the Oglala Boarding School and at a day school on the Pine Ridge Reservation.

SHANGREAU, WILLIAM (Sioux)
William Shangreau was a student at the Oglala Boarding School in 1919 and 1920.

SHAW, EVALYN CALLAHAN (Creek)
Evalyn Callahan Shaw was the daughter of S. B. Callahan of Muskogee, Creek Nation. In 1900, she lived at Wagoner.

SHAWNEE, GEORGE (Shawnee)
In 1897, George Shawnee was a student at Haskell Institute, from which he graduated. He later worked as issue clerk at Haskell. He married Sadie Bland. Indian Leader, April 16, 1909.

SHEEHAN, JOSEPH (Alaska Native)
Joseph Sheehan worked in the printing shop at Carlisle Indian Industrial School in 1907. In 1908, he worked for the Waynesboro, Pennsylvania, Zephyr. The next year he worked at the Frederick, Maryland, Citizen and the Waynesboro Herald. In 1912 he gave up printing and went to work for a manufacturing firm. Carlisle Arrow, September 18, 1908, June 26, 1909, September 10, 1909, and November 5, 1909; Red Man, 4 (April, 1912), 355 and 7 (October, 1914), 75.

SHEPHERD, MASON (Sioux)
Mason Shepherd attended Haskell Institute.

SHEPPARD, GRACE (Sisseton Sioux)
Born near Waubay, South Dakota, on January 29, 1900, Grace Sheppard attended the Sisseton Reservation School before entering the Pipestone Indian School in 1913. She graduated in 1916. Peace Pipe, 5 (May, 1916), 11.

SHERIDAN, RACHEL (Omaha)
Rachel Sheridan, from Macy, Nebraska, was a student at Hampton Institute in 1905 and 1906.

SHEYAHSHE, GEORGE (Caddo)
George Sheyahshe was from Anadarko, Oklahoma. He studied blacksmithing at Chilocco Indian Industrial School, from which he graduated in 1919.

SHIELD, DAWSON (Sioux)
Dawson Shield was a student at the Oglala Boarding School in 1920.

SHIELDS, F. H. (Sioux)
F. H. Shields was from Fort Totten, North Dakota.

SHIELDS, MARY (Sioux)
Mary Shields was a student at the Oglala Boarding School in 1919 and 1920.

SHIPSHE, ROSA (Potawatomi)
Rosa Shipshe attended Haskell Institute.

SHOTLEY, EVA (Chippewa)
Eva Shotley was a student at the Pipestone Indian School in 1915.

SIFTSOFF, LUBOVA (Alaska Native)
Lubova Siftsoff was a senior student at Chemawa Indian School at Salem, Oregon, in 1914.

SILK, CARL E. (Gros Ventre)
Carl E. Silk was from North Dakota. He graduated from Carlisle Indian Industrial School in 1907. Arrow, March 29, 1907.

SILOOK, PAUL (Eskimo)
No information is available.

SILVAS, CARMELITA (Tule River, i.e., Yokuts)
Carmelita Silvas, who married Modesto Moreno, graduated from Sherman Institute in 1920.

SILVAS, MARTINA (Mission)
Martina Silvas was a student at the Banning Mission School in 1895.

SILVERHEELS, FLORENCE W. (Cattaraugus Seneca)
Florence W. Silverheels, who was from New York, was a student at Hampton Institute, 1902-1905. Thirty-Fifth Annual Catalogue of the Hampton Normal and Agricultural Institute (Hampton: Hampton Institute Press, 1903), 112.

SIMPSON, ALBERT H. (Arickara)
Albert Simpson graduated from the Carlisle Indian Industrial School in 1907. He lived at Elbowoods, North Dakota. Arrow, March 29, 1907; Red Man, 6 (February, 1914), 240.

SIMPSON, ELLA (Nisenan)
Ella Simpson was a student at Sherman Institute in 1910.

SIMPSON, PETER (Tlingit)
Peter Simpson resided at the Cottage Settlement at Sitka, Alaska, a mission enterprise established by the National Indian Association in the late 1890's. In 1902, the Sitka Bay Cannery refused to hire natives. The boys of Cottage Settlement made five fishing boats and under Simpson's leadership sailed to the cannery. When the superintendent refused to hire them, Simpson supposedly said, "You think we are like those Killisno natives, but we are not; we are Christian natives." The superintendent hired them; they built two more boats and had a good season. Simpson attended the Sitka Training School. Besides owning his own boat, he knew the sawmill

business, doing seasonal work as a mill foreman. He also received a contract to build a government native school.

SIXKILLER, JULIA A. (Cherokee)
Julia A. Sixkiller was an 1884 graduate of the Indian University at Tahlequah, Cherokee Nation.

SKENANDORE, AMELIA (Oneida)
Amelia Skenandore was from Wisconsin. The daughter of Solomon Skenandore, she entered Hampton Institute in July, 1888, at age 17. She remained until May, 1891. 52 Congress, 1 Session, Senate Executive Document 31, 36-37.

SKENANDORE, ELI (Oneida)
Eli Skenandore attended Hampton Institute.

SKENANDORE, JOEL W. (Oneida)
Joel W. Skenandore attended Hampton Institute.

SKENANDORE, WILSON (Oneida)
Wilson Skenandore was from Wisconsin. The son of Daniel Skenandore, he entered Hampton Institute in November, 1888, at the age of eighteen. 52 Congress, 1 Session, Senate Executive Document 31, 48-49.

SKIUHUSHU (Blackfeet)
The Rev. Skiuhushu (Red Fox) was general secretary of the Society of American Indians in 1922. He was long-time editor of Indian Teepee Magazine.

SKYE, ESTELLA (Peoria)
Estella Skye was a student at Carlisle Indian Industrial School in 1909.

SKYE, GLADYS (Peoria)
Gladys Skye, who was from Oklahoma, was a student at Haskell Institute in 1913.

SKYE, MAZIE L. (Seneca)
Mazie L. Skye, from New York, was born about 1890 and graduated from Carlisle in 1911. Carlisle Arrow, April 21, 1911.

SLOAN, THOMAS L. (Omaha)
Thomas L. Sloan, from Nebraska, was born about 1863. He entered Hampton Institute in 1886 and graduated in 1889. 52 Congress, 1 Session, Senate Executive Document 31, 27, 46-47; Twenty-Two Years' Work of the Hampton Normal and Agricultural Institute (Hampton: Normal School Press, 1891). 56-57.

SMALLWOOD, BENJAMIN FRANKLIN (Choctaw)
Benjamin Franklin Smallwood was born in the Choctaw Nation

in Mississippi in 1829, the son of William and Mary Leflore Smallwood. He attended the common schools and Spencer Academy in the Choctaw Nation. He was a farmer and store owner. Except for the war years, Smallwood held public office from 1847 to 1890, including positions as member of the Choctaw council, Speaker of the lower house, delegate to Washington, and Principal Chief, to which position he was elected in 1888. His wife was Abbie James. Smallwood died on December 15, 1891. John Bartlett Meserve, "Chief Benjamin Franklin Smallwood and Chief Jefferson Gardner," Chronicles of Oklahoma, 19 (September, 1941), 213-220.

SMITH, AMY (Little Lake, i.e., Pomo)
Amy Smith was a student at Carlisle Indian Industrial School in 1909.

SMITH, BURNHAM (Konkow)
Burnham Smith was a 1908 graduate of Sherman Institute and in 1916 lived at Covelo, California. Sherman Bulletin, May 24, 1916.

SMITH, CHARLES H. (Chemehuevi)
Charles H. Smith graduated from Sherman Intitute in 1919.

SMITH, CLARENCE (Arapaho)
Clarence Smith, born about 1887, attended Carlisle Indian Industrial School in 1908.

SMITH, FRANK (Chippewa)
Frank Smith was a student at the Pipestone Indian School in 1914.

SMITH, HARRISON B. (Oneida)
Harrison B. Smith, from Wisconsin, was born about 1890. He attended Carlisle Indian Industrial School.

SMITH, JAMES (Warm Springs, i.e., Shasta)
James Smith, from California, was a student at Haskell Institute from 1913 through 1915.

SMITH, JEFFERSON B. (Gros Ventre)
Jefferson B. Smith, from Elbowoods, North Dakota, entered Carlisle Indian Industrial School in 1903 and graduated in 1911. He then attended school in Minneapolis. He married Ruth Packineau, and they made their home at Elbowoods, where he ranched. Red Man and Helper, August 28, 1903; Carlisle Arrow, April 21, 1911.

SMITH, LOTTIE (Eastern Band Cherokee)
The daughter of Chief N. J. Smith, Lottie Smith entered Hampton Institute in 1889 at age 19. She remained until 1891. She married John Pattee (q.v.). 52 Congress, 1 Session, Senate Executive Document 31, 12, 36-37.

SOUCEA, HUGH (Pueblo)
Hugh Soucea graduated from Carlisle Indian Industrial School in 1894. After he left Carlisle, he went home to farm and later graduated from the normal department of the Indian school at Albuquerque. He then went to Wyoming and took charge of the engineering department at the Wind River School. He then moved to Denver, where he worked as a carpenter for several years. From 1912 to 1915 he was at the Shiprock School where he was employed as a carpenter. Red Man and Helper, February 26-March 4, 1904; Red Man, 4 (January, 1912), 216, and 6 (February, 1914), 242.

SPATZ, LEE (Hupa)
Lee Spatz, who was from Willow Creek, California, graduated from Sherman Institute in 1919.

SPICER, ALEX (Oklahoma Seneca)
Alex Spicer was from the Indian Territory.

SPLITLOG, JOHN (Cayuga)
John Splitlog was a student at Haskell Institute in 1900.

SPOTTED CROW, LIZZIE (Sioux)
Lizzie Spotted Crow was a student at the Oglala Boarding School in 1919 and 1920.

SPOTTEDBEAR, RUSSEL (Sioux)
Russel Spottedbear attended Carlisle Indian Industrial School.

SPOTTEDHORSE, CLARA (Crow)
Clara Spottedhorse attended Carlisle Indian Industrial School from 1907 to 1910. She married Robert Yellow Tail. Carlisle Arrow, October 21, 1910.

SPRADLING, ORA V. (Cherokee)
Ora V. Spradling died on the day she was to have graduated from the Baptist Indian University in 1887.

STABLER, ROY DORSEY (Omaha)
Roy Dorsey Stabler attended Hampton Institute, where he worked for the Indian students' newsletter, Talks and Thoughts. He graduated in 1896 and attended high school at Hampton, Massachusetts. In 1907, he established the Winnebago Chieftain at Winnebago, Nebraska. Talks and Thoughts, November, 1896.

STANDING BEAR, LUTHER (Pine Ridge Sioux)
Luther Standing Bear spent six years at the Carlisle Indian Industrial School, where he learned the tinner's trade. After leaving there in 1885, he worked at Wanamaker's store in Philadelphia before returning to the reservation, where he taught. Red Man, 10 (June, 1890), 4.

STANDING ELK, BESSIE (Chippewa)

Bessie Standing Elk was a student at Carlisle Indian Industrial School in 1909.

STANLEY, ARNOLD (Choctaw)

Arnold Stanley was a student at Jones Academy, Choctaw Nation, in 1903.

STANLEY, GRACE B. (Chippewa)

Grace B. Stanley graduated from Haskell Institute in 1906. She married Wallace Tourtillot and worked as a matron at Fort Hall, Idaho.

STARR, EMMET (Cherokee)

Emmet Starr was born in Going Snake District, Cherokee Nation, on December 12, 1870, the son of Walter Adair and Ruth A. Thornton Starr. He graduated from the Cherokee Male Seminary in 1888 and from Barnes Medical College at St. Louis in 1891. Starr practiced medicine for five years at Chelsea and Skiatook, Cherokee Nation, but gave up his medical practice to undertake his monumental work on Cherokee genealogy and history. In 1901, he was elected to a term in the National Council. He was a Mason and a Methodist. Starr never married. He died on January 30, 1930. R. Harper, "Dr. Emmet Starr--A Tribute," Chronicles of Oklahoma, 8 (March, 1930), 130-131; Rennard Strickland and Jack Gregory, "Emmet Starr: Heroic Historian," in Margot Liberty, ed., American Indian Intellectuals (St. Paul: West Publishing Co., 1978), 105-114; "Death of Dr. Emmet Starr," Chronicles of Oklahoma, 8 (March, 1930), 129-130.

STARR, JOHN CALEB (Cherokee)

John Caleb (Cale) Starr was born in Flint District, Cherokee Nation, in October, 1870, the son of James and Emma Rider Starr. He attended public schools and the Cherokee Male Seminary, from which he graduated in 1890. He also attended a commercial college in Fort Smith, Arkansas in 1891. He worked as a bookkeeper, a teacher, and clerk of the Cherokee Senate. Starr married Lillie B. Zimmerman.

STEPHENS, SPENCER SEAGO (Cherokee)

Spencer Seago Stephens was born in the Cherokee Nation in 1837, the son of Jess and Malinda Stephens. He attended the Old Baptist Mission School in Going Snake District. Orphaned in 1853, he was taken into the home of Mrs. Lizzie Bushyhead. He graduated from the Male Seminary in 1856. He was for many years Superintendent of Education in the Cherokee Nation and also served as National Auditor. Stephens married Sarah R. Hicks.

STEVENS, ADDIE (Winnebago)

Addie Stevens entered Hampton Institute at age 10 in 1883 and remained until June, 1887. She returned in 1888 and remained a year. She married Gabriel Robertson. 52 Congress, 1 Session, Senate Executive Document 31, 8, 32-33, 36-37.

STEVENS, BERTHA (Klamath)
Bertha Stevens was a student at the Carlisle Indian Industrial School in 1909.

STEWART, ROBERT W. (Creek)
Robert W. Stewart attended Tullahassee Mission School in the Creek Nation before entering Carlisle Indian Industrial School in 1881. He married Antoinette Williams, a Navajo, and in 1883 they went to New Mexico, where they taught in a Navajo school. In 1885, they lived at Muskogee, Creek Nation. Morning Star, 4 (November, 1883), 3, and 5 (January, 1885), 5.

STIDHAM, LEONIDAS (Creek)
Leonidas Stidham was a student at the Tullahassee Mission School in 1870.

STRIKE AXE, BENJAMIN E. (Osage)
No information is available.

STUART, MARION (Piegan)
Marion Stuart, from Montana, was a student at Chemawa Indian School at Salem, Oregon, in 1914.

STYLES, LOTTIE R. (Arickara)
Lottie Styles was from the Fort Berthold Reservation in North Dakota. She attended Hampton Institute in 1902 and entered Carlisle Indian Industrial School in 1903, graduating in 1908. Red Man and Helper, August 28, 1903; Thirty-Fifth Annual Catalogue of the Hampton Normal and Agricultural Institute (Hampton: Hampton Institute, 1903), 112; Arrow, April 3, 1908.

SUNDOWN, REUBEN (Seneca)
Reuben Sundown was a student at Carlisle Indian Industrial School in 1910.

SUTTON, MYRTLE (Seneca)
Myrtle Sutton was a student at Carlisle Indian Industrial School in 1910.

SWALLOW, IDA (Sioux)
Ida Swallow was from South Dakota. After graduation from Carlisle Indian Industrial School in 1901, she entered Drexel Institute to study stenography and typing. She then did clerical work for her father, who owned a store at Oelricks. She married a Dr. Merdaman at Oelricks. Red Man and Helper, March 8 and September 27, 1901; Red Man, 5 (February, 1913), 265.

SWAYNEY, ARIZONA (Eastern Band Cherokee)
Arizona Swayney was a student at Hampton Institute in 1902.

Thirty-Fifth Annual Catalogue of the Hampton Normal and Agricultural
Institute (Hampton: Hampton Institute Press, 1903), 111.

SWIMMER, GEORGE (Cherokee)
　　George Swimmer, who was from Fourteen Mile Creek, Cherokee
Nation, was a native preacher.

TAHAMONT, ROBERT J. (Abenaki)
　　Robert J. Tahamont, born about 1890, graduated from Carlisle
Indian Industrial School in 1911, after which he lived in Newark,
New Jersey. Carlisle Arrow, April 21, 1911.

TALKAHPUER, EUGENE (Comanche)
　　Eugene Talkahpuer entered the Fort Sill Agency school in 1875
when he was about twelve. In 1880 he entered Carlisle Indian
Industrial School and remained until 1887, spending much of his time
in the outing program in Pennsylvania and New Jersey. Red Man,
15 (July-August, 1899), 1.

TALL CHIEF, EVES (Osage)
　　Eves Tall Chief, who attended Haskell Institute, was from Gray
Horse, Oklahoma. Oklahoma Historical Society, Archives Division,
Chilocco-Haskell, December 14, 1902.

TALLCHIEF, MARY (Seneca)
　　Mary Tallchief was a student at Carlisle Indian Industrial School
in 1908.

TALLCRANE, FRED (Sioux)
　　Fred Tallcrane was a student at the Carlisle Indian Industrial
School in 1909.

TARBELL, JOE F. (Mohawk)
　　Joe F. Tarbell was a student at Carlisle Indian Industrial School
in 1908.

TAUTUK, THOMAS (Eskimo)
　　No information is available.

TAYLOR, CLIFFORD (Pawnee)
　　Clifford Taylor was a 1912 graduate of Carlisle Indian Industrial
School.

TEHEE, HOUSTON BENGE (Cherokee)
　　Houston Benge Tehee was born on October 14, 1874, in Sequoyah District, Cherokee Nation, the son of Stephen and Rhoda Benge
Tehee. He attended Cherokee common schools and the Male Seminary
and went one term to Fort Worth University. He served as Clerk
of Tahlequah District for ten years and, in 1906, became cashier
of a bank. Meanwhile, he studied law, specializing in oil and gas
matters. In 1910, he served as mayor of Tahlequah and was elected

to the Oklahoma State Legislature in 1910 and 1912. From 1914 to 1919, he served as register of the U.S. Treasury, and in 1926-1927, as assistant attorney general. He was vice-president, treasurer, and general manager of the Continental Asphalt and Petroleum Company of Oklahoma City. Tehee died on November 19, 1938. Marie L. Wadley, "Houston Benge Tehee," Chronicles of Oklahoma, 37 (Autumn 1959), 384-385; Marion E. Gridley, Indians of Today (Chicago: The Lakeside Press, 1936), 116.

TERRY, LIDDY (Sioux)
Terry Liddy was a student at the Holy Rosary School in 1894.

THOMAS, DANIEL N. (Pima)
Daniel Thomas, a 1911 graduate of Sherman Institute, graduated from Hampton Institute in 1916 and became disciplinarian at the government school at Fort Hall. He left after a year and then taught printing in New Orleans. He died about 1920. Sherman Bulletin, May 24, 1916.

THOMAS, FRED (Eskimo)
Fred Thomas was from Noorvik, Alaska.

THOMPSON, EMMA (Sioux)
Emma Thompson was a student at the Santee Normal Training School in 1884.

THOMPSON, NOBLE A. (Pueblo)
Noble A. Thompson was a student at Carlisle Indian Industrial School in 1908.

THOMPSON, WILLIAM ABBOTT (Cherokee)
William Abbott Thompson was a teacher. He was also business manager of the Telephone, a newspaper at Tahlequah, Cherokee Nation, in 1888 and edited the Indian Sentinel in 1892. He died in 1899. Indian Sentinel November 14, 1899.

THORPE, JAMES FRANCIS (Sac and Fox)
James F. Thorpe was born on May 28, 1888, in Oklahoma, the son of Hiram and Charlotte (View) Thorpe. He was educated on the Sac and Fox Reservation and at Haskell Institute. He attended Carlisle Indian Industrial School where he distinguished himself as an athlete. He went on to win the pentathlon and the decathlon in the 1912 Olympics, but was stripped of his medals because of his involvement in professional sports. He played professional football and baseball until 1929. In the late 1930's, he lived in Oklahoma, where he was involved in tribal affairs. He lectured and served in the Merchant Marines during World War II. After the war, he lived in California, where he died on March 28, 1953. Marion E. Gridley, Indians of Today (Chicago: The Lakeside Press, 1936), 117.

THREE STARS, CLARENCE (Pine Ridge Sioux)
Clarence Three Stars went to Carlisle Indian Industrial School

from the Pine Ridge Reservation in 1879 and stayed nearly five years.
He returned to the Pine Ridge Agency and, after working for a trader
for a time, entered government service. He taught for many years
in the day school at Pine Ridge and for a time was a merchant there.
In 1912, Three Stars married Jennie Dubray. Red Man, 10 (February-
March, 1891), 8, and 11 (November-December, 1892), 1; Red Man
and Helper, February 28, 1902; Red Man, 5 (January, 1913), 222,
and 6 (February, 1914), 241.

THUNDER BEAR, JULIA (Sioux)
     Julia Thunder Bear was a student at the Oglala Boarding School
in 1920.

THUNDER HAWK, MAGGIE (Sioux)
     Maggie Thunder Hawk was a student at the Standing Rock Agri-
cultural Boarding School in 1892.

TIAOKASIN, JOHN (Standing Rock Sioux)
     John Tiaokasin (or Looks-into-the-Lodge), from the Standing
Rock Reservation, was born about 1865, the son of Porcupine. He
attended Hampton Institute from 1881 to 1884 and from 1885 to 1889.
After his return to the West, he was a carpenter at the agency. He
married Rosa Pleets. 52 Congress, 1 Session, Senate Executive
Document 31, 19, 40-41.

TIBBETTS, ARTHUR T. (Sioux)
     Arthur T. Tibbetts graduated from the Santee Normal Training
School in 1894 and in 1897 entered the Y.M.C.A. Training School at
Springfield, Massachusetts, which he attended for three years. He
served as general secretary of the Indian Y.M.C.A. and for many
years was pastor of a church at Cannon Ball, North Dakota, on the
Standing Rock Reservation. Red Man, 15 (May, 1900), 4; "What Santee Graduates Are Doing," Word Carrier, 39 (March-April, 1910),
7; Iapi Oaye, 49 (June-July, 1920), 23.

TIBBETTS, GEORGE (Chippewa)
     George Tibbetts, who was from Minnesota, was a 1917 graduate
of Carlisle Indian Industrial School.

TIBBETTS, JESSE J. (Chippewa)
     Jesse J. Tibbetts graduated from the Pipestone Indian School
in 1913 and also attended Haskell Institute.

TIBBETTS, LUZENIA (Leech Lake Chippewa)
     Luzenia E. Tibbetts, from the Leech Lake Reservation in Minne-
sota, graduated from Carlisle Indian Industrial School in 1901 and
spent the next two years at Bloomsburg Normal School. Her married
name was Isham, and she lived in later years at Bena, Minnesota.
Red Man and Helper, March 8 and April 5, 1901.

TINKER, GEORGE EDWARD (Osage)
     George Edward Tinker was born on September 24, 1868, at

Osage Mission, Kansas, the son of George and Lucille Lessert Tinker. In the 1890's he was a member of the Osage Tribal Council and engaged in publishing ventures. In 1893 he was co-founder of The Wah-shah-she News. In 1909 he was co-founder of The Osage Magazine at Pawhuska. Tinker died on October 31, 1947. Louis F. Burns, The Turn of the Wheel: A Genealogy of the Burns and Tinker Families (Fallbrook, CA: The Author, 1980), 152, 154.

TOMEY, JOSEPHINE   (Prairie Band Potawatomi)
    Josephine Tomey, who was from Kansas, was a student at Haskell Institute in 1913 and 1914. Indian Helper, 17 (September, 1913), 12.

TOO-QUA-STEE
    See DUNCAN, DE WITT CLINTON

TOURTILLOTTE, EDITH   (Menominee)
    Edith Tourtillotte graduated from Haskell Institute in 1901. She married Robert Gauthier.

TOWNS, IDA   (Crow)
    Ida Towns was a student at Carlisle Indian Industrial School in 1909.

TREPANIA, CLARA   (Chippewa)
    Clara Trepania was a student at Carlisle Indian Industrial School in 1909.

TRIPP, DORA   (Klamath)
    Dora Tripp was born in California in 1883. She attended school on the Hupa Reservation and then entered the Phoenix Indian School, graduating in 1903.

TROTTERCHAUD, LIZZIE D.   (Chippewa)
    Lizzie D. Trotterchaud was born at Fort Snelling, Minnesota. She attended St. Benedict's School, White Earth School, and then the Genoa Indian School at Genoa, Nebraska. She attended the latter from 1902 to 1904 and again from 1907 to 1911, when she graduated. She took a job as a cook at Beaulieu School in Minnesota.

TRUCHOT, LOUISE   (Shoshoni)
    Louise Truchot graduated from Sherman Institute in 1919.

TRUDELL, LUCY   (Santee Sioux)
    Lucy Trudell was the daughter of Charles Poicolle. She entered Hampton Institute in September, 1890, at age nineteen. 52 Congress, 1 Session, Senate Executive Document 31, 36-37.

TUBBS, LAURA   (Cherokee)
    Laura Tubbs was a student at Carlisle Indian Industrial School in 1909.

TUCKER, GEORGE (Cherokee)
George Tucker was three-quarters Cherokee.

TUNGOK, LESTER (Eskimo)
Lester Tungok was from Selawik, Alaska.

TUPPER, HOBSON (Choctaw)
Hobson Tupper graduated from Carlisle Indian Industrial School in 1917.

TURNER, HATTIE (Choctaw)
Hattie Turner, from Oklahoma, graduated from the business department at Haskell Institute in 1915. Indian Leader, 18 (June, 1915), 6.

TURRISH, BLANCHE (Chippewa)
Blanche Turrish was a 1910 graduate of Haskell Institute. She married Frank Cournoyer. Indian Leader, June 9, 1911.

TWISS, FRANK W. (Pine Ridge Sioux)
Frank W. Twiss, from the Pine Ridge Reservation in South Dakota, attended the Genoa, Nebraska, Indian School, where he worked before entering Carlisle Indian Industrial School, which he left in 1884. After he returned to the reservation, he worked at the agency as a butcher, painter, and tinsmith. In 1892, he was a clerk in a store on the reservation. He married Adelia Lowe and lived at Porcupine, South Dakota. Red Man, 10 (February-March, 1891), 8, and 11 (November-December, 1892), 1; Arrow, March 29, 1907.

TWOGUNS, EVELYN R. (Seneca)
Evelyn R. Twoguns was from Brent, New York. She graduated from Hampton Institute in 1909. In 1915, she worked as assistant nurse at White Earth, Minnesota, and, in 1920, was matron at the government hospital in Winnebago, Nebraska. In 1923, she was a nurse at Rochester, New York.

TWOGUNS, SELINA (Seneca)
Selina Twoguns, from New York, was born about 1887 and graduated from Carlisle Indian Industrial School in 1910. She then entered the Indian Service as boys' matron at the boarding school in Greenville, California.

TYNDALL, VICTORIA A. (Omaha)
Victoria A. Tyndall was born at Decatur, Nebraska. In 1900 she entered the Genoa Indian School at Genoa, Nebraska, and remained until 1911, when she graduated.

TYNER, JOHN (Shawnee)
From Oklahoma, John Tyner was a student at Hampton Institute, 1902-1905. Thirty-Fifth Annual Catalogue of the Hampton Normal and Agricultural Institute (Hampton: Hampton Institute Press, 1903), 111.

TYNER, RACHEL K. (Shawnee)
    Rachel K. Tyner, from Oklahoma, was a student at Hampton Institute, 1902-1906. Thirty-Fifth Annual Catalogue of the Hampton Normal and Agricultural Institute (Hampton: Hampton Institute Press, 1903), 112.

UN-A-QUA (Menominee)
    Un-a-qua was August A. Breuninger, who attended Haskell Institute. He was active in the Progressive Indian Association of Wisconsin and in 1911 established The Indian Observer in Washington, D.C. Indian Leader, July 2, 1909; Indian Observer, 1 (January, 1911), 3.

UNQAROOK, ANDY (Eskimo)
    No information is available.

UPHAM, MYRTLE S. (Blackfeet)
    Myrtle S. Upham was born at Browning, Montana, in 1893. From 1901 to 1909 she attended mission schools. From 1909 to 1911 she attended Genoa Indian School at Genoa, Nebraska, from which she graduated.

UPSHAW, ALEXANDER B. (Crow)
    Alexander B. Upshaw, from St. Xavier, Montana, was born about 1875, the son of Crazy Pend d'Orielle. He graduated from Carlisle Indian Industrial School in 1897, and he then attended Bloomsburg State Normal School. He worked as an industrial teacher at the Genoa, Nebraska, Indian School. In 1901, he helped survey the Crow Reservation, and he later farmed in the Pryor Valley, sixteen miles north of old Fort C. F. Smith. In 1906, he became associated with Edward S. Curtis, assisting him in gathering information for his works on the North American Indians, and with Curtis, toured the northwest coastal area in 1909. Red Man, 14 (April, 1897), 4; Red Man and Helper, September 5, 1902.

VALENSKI, CHAY SHERMAN (Navajo)
    Chay Sherman Valenski was born near Manuelito, New Mexico. In 1907 he entered Carlisle Indian Industrial School. From 1912 to 1915 he lived at Fort Defiance, Arizona, where he was employed as an interpreter and general worker at the hospital. Red Man, 4 (March, 1912), 306.

VALENZUELA, THOMAS (Pima)
    Thomas Valenzuela, from Lehi, Arizona, was the son of Mrs. Encarnacion Valenzuela. After graduation from the Phoenix Indian School in 1909, he returned to Lehi.

VANN, CLEMENT NEELEY (Cherokee)
    Clement Neeley Vann was born in the Cherokee Nation, the son of David (q.v.) and Martha McNair Vann. Before the Civil War, he served as a Senator from Saline District. During the war, he was

a colonel in the Second Cherokee Confederate Regiment. After the war, he served as clerk of the Council, Treasurer of the Nation, delegate to the Okmulgee Council, and delegate to Washington for the Southern Cherokees.

VANN, DAVID (Cherokee)
David Vann was born in the Eastern Cherokee Nation on January 1, 1800, the son of Avery and Margaret McSwain Vann. Before the Civil War, he served four terms as national treasurer, and during the war, he ran a salt works on Dirty Creek until he was killed on December 23, 1863. Vann was married to Jennie Chambers and Martha McNair. Emmet Starr, History of the Cherokee Indians and Their Legends and Folk Lore (Oklahoma City: The Warden Company, 1921), 468.

VANN, JAMES SHEPHERD (Cherokee)
The son of Joseph Vann, James Shepherd Vann edited The Cherokee Advocate in 1848 and 1849, 1851 and 1852, and 1853.

VEIX, BESSIE L. (Munsee)
Bessie L. Veix graduated from Haskell Institute in 1908 and worked in Indian Service until 1916, when she went to work for the Ottawa Manufacturing Company, Ottawa, Kansas.

VEIX, CORA E. (Munsee)
Cora E. Veix graduated from Haskell Institute in 1914. Indian Leader, 17 (June, 1914), 24; 18 (June, 1915), 6.

VEIX, KATIE (Munsee)
Katie Veix attended Haskell Institute. She married a man named Warner and lived at Ottawa, Kansas.

VEIX, ROSE (Munsee)
Rose Veix was a student at Haskell Institute in 1913.

VENNE, ALFRED MICHAEL (Chippewa)
Alfred Michael Venne was born in 1880, of Chippewa and French parentage, on the Fort Totten Reservation. He spoke only his native language and French until he was twelve. At age thirteen, he entered the Fort Totten School and finished the elementary grades. He remained there as disciplinarian and bandmaster for four years. In 1901, he entered Carlisle Indian Industrial School, from which he graduated in 1903. While he was a student, he also took on the duties of assistant physical director. After graduation, he became physical and athletic director for the school and remained at that post for five years. In 1909, he was transferred to Chilocco as disciplinarian and band leader, athletic director, and Y.M.C.A. secretary. He took summer courses at the School of Physical Education at Lake Chautauqua, New York, and at Kansas State University. In 1912, he worked briefly at Haskell Institute and then returned to Chilocco. Venne married Sara Williams. Red Man and Helper, February 26–March 4, 1904.

VENNE, ERNESTINE   (Chippewa)
     Ernestine Venne, born about 1891, graduated from Carlisle in
1912.

VERIGAN, FRANCIS   (Tlingit)
     Francis Verigan graduated from Carlisle Indian Industrial School
in 1918. He then attended Hampton Institute and Phillips Academy
at Andover, Massachusetts.

VERNEY, PATRICK   (Tsimshian)
     Patrick Verny, from Metlakatla, Alaska, entered Carlisle Indian
Industrial School in 1901 and graduated in 1909. He went to Ketchi-
kan to work in his father's curio shop and, in 1911, worked for the
Ketchikan Miner. Later that year he moved to Gallup, New Mexico.
He married Grace Kie, a Navajo, and in 1912 moved back to Ketchikan.
Verney was the nephew of Edward Marsden (q.v.). Red Man and
Helper, November 8, 1901; Carlisle Arrow, September 10, 1909, April
7, 1911, November 3, 1911, and January 5, 1912; Red Man, 4 (June,
1912), 486.

WACKER, VICTOR   (Alaska Native)
     Victor Wacker was from Wacker, Alaska.

WAGGONER, RAMONA   (Standing Rock Sioux)
     Ramona Waggoner was a student at Haskell Institute in 1905.

WAGNER, FRED   (Wasco)
     Fred Wagner graduated from Haskell Institute in 1907. He farmed
and did guard work in the forest before settling down as a farmer
and rancher. Indian Leader, June 9, 1911.

WAGNER, VERA   (Alaska Native)
     Vera Wagner graduated from Carlisle Indian Industrial School
in 1908. Arrow, March 4, 1908.

WAITE, AGNES V.   (Serrano)
     Agnes V. Waite, from Banning, California, was born about 1889
and graduated from Carlisle Indian Industrial School in 1912, after
which she attended high school at Glendale, California. After graduating in 1914, she entered the Indian Service as a teacher at the
Indian School at Fort Yuma. Red Man, 5 (June, 1913), 478.

WALKER, BERTRAND N. O.   (Wyandot)
     Bertrand N. O. Walker, who wrote under the name of Hen-
Toh, was a Wyandot of the Big Turtle Clan. Born in Wyandot County,
Kansas, on September 5, 1870, he was the son of Isaiah and Mary
Walker and a descendant of a number of important men in Wyandot
history dating back to Colonial times. In 1874, Walker's family moved
to lands assigned the Wyandots in extreme northeastern Indian Territory, southwest of Seneca, Missouri. He attended the Friends Mission School near present-day Wyandotte, Oklahoma, and public schools

and a private academy at Seneca. Walker taught school for several years and served as an Indian Service teacher and clerk in the Indian Territory, Kansas, Oklahoma, California, and Arizona. He also maintained the family farm, which was on his allotment. He read widely and talked to older Indians of various tribes about traditions, legends, myths, customs, and manners. From 1917 to 1924, he wrote, publishing a book of legends and a volume of poetry. In 1924, he became clerk at the Quapaw Agency at Miami, Oklahoma, and served until his death on June 27, 1927. B. N. O. Walker, "Sketch of B. N. O. Walker, Written by Himself," Chronicles of Oklahoma, 6 (1928), 89-93.

WALKER, JOHN B. (Miami)
John B. Walker was a 1906 graduate of Haskell Institute.

WALKER, JOHN GREEN (Navajo)
John G. Walker graduated from Hampton Institute in 1898 and became a businessman in Arizona. In 1912, he went to Los Angeles to study law. Talks and Thoughts, July-August, 1905.

WALKER, TULIE (Navajo)
Tulie Walker was a student at Hampton Institute in 1902. Thirty-Fifth Annual Catalogue of the Hampton Normal and Agricultural Institute (Hampton: Hampton Institute Press, 1903), 112.

WALKINGSTICK, SIMON RALPH, JR. (Cherokee)
Simon Ralph Walkingstick was born in the Cherokee Nation in 1896. He graduated from Bacone College in 1914 and entered Dartmouth, but left in 1918 without taking a degree. He was the first secretary for Indian work under the State Committee of the Y.M.C.A. of Oklahoma and spent two years as war work secretary of the Y.M.C.A. with the British Expeditionary Force in India and Mesopotamia. In the 1950's, Walkingstick made his home in Syracuse, New York. American Indian Magazine, 5 (April-June, 1917), 178.

WARD, JIM (Quileute)
No information is available.

WARREN, EUGENE J. (Chippewa)
Eugene J. Warren, from Minnesota, graduated from the Carlisle Indian Industrial School in 1901. Red Man and Helper, March 8 and 29, 1901.

WARRINGTON, GEORGE (Menominee)
George Warrington was a 1917 graduate of Carlisle Indian Industrial School.

WARRINGTON, JENNIE (Menominee)
Jennie Warrington, who was from Keshena, Wisconsin, attended Carlisle Indian Industrial School. She married Eugene Funmaker. Carlisle Arrow, November 26, 1909.

WASHINGTON, CHARLES (Oto)
Charles Washington was the son of Panecoge. In October, 1889, at age 17, he entered Hampton Institute. 52 Congress, 1 Session, Senate Executive Document 31, 50-51.

WATERMAN, LEILA (Seneca)
Leila Waterman, from Gowanda, New York, was born about 1894 and graduated from Carlisle in 1913. Red Man, 5 (May, 1913), 435.

WATIE, STAND (Cherokee)
Stand Watie was born in the Eastern Cherokee Nation, the son of Oo-watie. He received some education in mission schools. Watie on occasion assisted his brother, Elias Boudinot (q.v.) in publishing the Cherokee Phoenix at New Echota, Georgia. After removal, he was marked for assassination because he had signed the removal treaty, but he escaped and became a leader of the Treaty Party Cherokees. During the Civil War, he commanded a regiment of Cherokee cavalry and reached the rank of brigadier-general. He was the last Confederate general to officially surrender. Edward Everett Dale, "Stand Watie," in Dumas Malone, ed., Dictionary of American Biography (New York: Charles Scribner's Sons, 1936) 19: 537-538; Kenny A. Franks, Stand Watie and the Agony of the Chero-kee Nation (Memphis: Memphis State University Press, 1979), passim.

WATKINS, BEN (Choctaw)
Ben Watkins, who lived at Mountain Home, Choctaw Nation, helped compile the laws of the Choctaw Nation in 1894.

WATTA, VENTURA (Mission)
Ventura (or Ben) Watta, from California, graduated from the Phoenix Indian School in 1905. He worked as a ranch hand and was grand secretary of the Mission Indian Federation at San Jacinto California, where he lived in 1912.

WAWA CHAW (Luíseño)
Wawa Calac Chaw was born on December 25, 1888, at Valley Center, California. She was active in Indian affairs and supported many of the causes espoused by Carlos Montezuma (q.v.). She married Manuel Carmonia-Núñez, and went by the name Benita Núñez. Well known as a lecturer, she died in New York on May 12, 1972. Frederick J. Dockstader, Great North American Indians (New York: Van Nostrand Reinhold Company, 1977), 327-328.

WEATHERSTONE, ROBERT (Sioux)
Robert Weatherstone was a student at Carlisle Indian Industrial School in 1910.

WEAVER, HENRY (White Earth Chippewa)
Henry Weaver was born at White Earth, Minnesota, on June 14, 1900, and was reared at Bena. He entered the Pipestone Indian School in 1908.

WEBSTER, ISAAC N. (Oneida)
Isaac N. Webster was born about 1877, the son of August Webster. He was a student at Hampton Institute in 1902. After he left Hampton, he held positions in government service before developing his farm at Oneida, Wisconsin. He married Josephine Hill (q.v.). National Archives Microfilm, Microcopy 595 (Indian Census Rolls, 1885-1940), Roll 315, Oneida 1900; Some Results of Hampton's Work (Hampton: The Institute Press, 1915), 24; Thirty-Fifth Annual Catalogue of the Hampton Normal and Agricultural Institute (Hampton: Hampton Institute Press, 1903), 111.

WEEKS, WILLIAM H. (Gros Ventre)
William Weeks graduated from the Carlisle Indian Industrial School in 1909. In 1914 he was a farmer at Wolfe Point, Montana. Red Man, 7 (October, 1914), 76.

WELCH, GUSTAVUS (Chippewa)
Gustavus Welch was a student at Carlisle Indian Industrial School from 1909 through 1912, when he graduated. In 1914 he took law courses at Dickinson College. Carlisle Arrow, September 22, 1911, and December 12, 1912; Red Man, 7 (December, 1914), 147.

WELLINGTON, JAMES (Maricopa)
No information is available.

WELLS, ALFRED (Oneida)
Alfred Wells graduated from Sherman Institute in 1919.

WELLS, FLORENCE (Alaska Native)
Florence Wells was a student at Carlisle Indian Industrial School in 1894.

WELSH, HERBERT (Standing Rock Sioux)
Herbert Welsh, or Mahpiya-mato, was the son of Two-Packs. In November, 1888, he entered Hampton Institute at age 22. He remained until October, 1891. Upon his return home, he assisted at the Episcopal school at Oak Creek, where he had charge of the boys, and preached in the place of the regular preacher. 52 Congress, 1 Session, Senate Executive Document 31, 48-49.

WEMARK, GRANT (Eskimo)
No information is available.

WHEELER, JOHN CALDWELL (Cherokee)
John Caldwell Wheeler was born in 1843, the son of John Foster Wheeler and Nancy Watie. The elder Wheeler was the first printer of the Cherokee Phoenix, edited by Elias Boudinot (q.v.), whose sister he married. The younger Wheeler edited the Fort Smith Picayune at Fort Smith, Arkansas, in 1860 and, during the Civil War, served in the Confederate Cherokee Regiment of his uncle Stand Watie (q.v.). In 1872 he served as local editor of his father's paper, Wheelers'

Independent and later was the junior partner with his father. He edited the paper until his death on July 3, 1880. Indian Record, 1 (October, 1886), 1; Fred W. Allsopp, History of the Arkansas Press for a Hundred Years and More (Little Rock: Parke-Harper Publishing Company, 1922), 416.

WHEELOCK, JOEL H. (Oneida)
Joel H. Wheelock, from Wisconsin, was born about 1889, the son of James A. Wheelock. He graduated from the Carlisle Indian Industrial School in 1912, after which he attended Lebanon Valley College at Annville, Pennsylvania. Red Man, 6 (September, 1913), 42; 7 (January, 1915), 184; National Archives Microfilms, Microcopy 595 (Indian Census Rolls, 1885-1940), Roll 315, Oneida 1900.

WHEELOCK, LEHIGH (Oneida)
Lehigh Wheelock was from Wisconsin. The son of Isaac Wheelock, he entered Hampton Institute in November, 1888, at age 30. 52 Congress, 1 Session Senate Executive Document 31, 48-49.

WHEELOCK, PERCY MAE (Oneida)
Percy Mae Wheelock, from Wisconsin, was a 1912 graduate of the Carlisle Indian Industrial School.

WHITE, HUGH (Nisenan)
Hugh White was a student at the Carlisle Indian Industrial School in 1908.

WHITE, JEFFERSON (Sioux)
Jefferson White was a student at the Oglala Boarding School in 1920.

WHITE, JOHN (Mohawk)
John White, born about 1886, attended Carlisle Indian Industrial School from 1906 to 1909, when he graduated.

WHITE, MELVINA K. (Blackfeet)
Melvina K. White was born in 1895 and attended the Fort Hall, Montana, Indian School in 1908. She entered the Genoa Indian School at Genoa, Nebraska, in 1910 and graduated in June, 1911.

WHITE, MINNIE O. (Mohawk)
Minnie O. White, from the St. Regis Reservation in New York, was born about 1888 and graduated from Carlisle in 1911. She returned to New York and taught at the reservation school at Hogansburg, her home town. Carlisle Arrow, April 21, 1911; Red Man, 4 (March, 1912), 308.

WHITE, RALPH (Standing Rock Sioux)
Ralph White was a student at the Santee Normal Training School, Santee, Nebraska, in 1903 and 1904. He then entered Hampton Institute.

WHITE BULL, LEVI (Sioux)
Levi White Bull was a student at the Oglala Boarding School in 1920.

WHITECROW, GERTRUDE (Oklahoma Seneca)
Gertrude Whitecrow was from Oklahoma.

WHITETREE, JESSE WILLIS (Oklahoma Seneca)
Jesse Willis Whitetree was from Turkeyford, Oklahoma, and attended Chilocco Indian Agricultural School, from which he graduated in 1919.

WHITTAKER, HORACE (Pima)
Horace Whittaker attended Sherman Institute.

WILBUR, EARNEY E. (Menominee)
Earney Wilbur was a 1903 graduate of the Carlisle Indian Industrial School. She married James M. Phillips, a Cherokee, who was a judge and justice of the peace at Aberdeen, Washington. Red Man, 7 (May-June, 1915), 328.

WILBUR, LAVINA CHRISTINA (Klikitat)
Lavina Christina Wilbur was from Oregon. She attended Chemawa Indian School at Salem, Oregon, in 1914. Chemawa American, 16 (June, 1914), 8.

WILLIAMS, JAMES P. (Ponca)
James Williams, from Oklahoma, studied at Haskell Institute, at Hampton Institute in 1898 and 1899, and at other Indian schools.

WILLIAMS, NATHAN (Navajo)
Nathan Williams was a student at Hampton Institute in 1901.

WILLIAMS, SPENCER F. (Seneca)
Spencer F. Williams, who was from New York, was a 1905 graduate of Carlisle Indian Industrial School. In 1914 he lived in Philadelphia, where he played trombone in an orchestra. Red Man, 7 (December, 1914), 146.

WILLIS, PERRY M. (Choctaw)
Perry M. Willis was a student at Jones Academy, Choctaw Nation, in 1903. He edited the school's newsletter.

WILSON, ALFRETTA (Nisenan)
Alfretta Wilson was a 1909 graduate of Sherman Institute.

WILSON, ETHEL (Columbia River Tribe)
Ethel Wilson, who was from Washington, graduated from Chemawa Indian School in 1913.

WILSON, SOPHIA (Nisenan)
Sophia Wilson was a student at Sherman Institute in 1910.

WINSLETT, KIZZIE (Creek)
   Kizzie Winslett was a student at the Tullahassee Mission School
in 1870.

WINSLETT, NANCY JANE (Creek)
   Nancy Jane Winslett was a student at the Tullahassee Mission
School in 1870.

WISACOBY, JOSEPH (Menominee)
   Joseph Wisacoby was a student at Carlisle Indian Industrial
School in 1881.

WOLF, FLORA (Crow)
   Flora Wolf, from Montana, graduated from Sherman Institute
in 1909.

WOLFE, EDWARD (Eastern Band Cherokee)
   Edward Wolfe was a student at Carlisle Indian Industrial School
in 1908.

WOLFE, KATHERINE E. (Eastern Band Cherokee)
   Katherine Wolfe, born about 1885, attended Carlisle Indian
Industrial School in 1909 and 1910. After she graduated she worked
as a seamstress at the Cherokee School in North Carolina. Carlisle
Arrow, May 13, 1910.

WOOD, ISAAC (Quileute)
   In 1909, Isaac Wood was a student at the Quileute Day School
at La Push, Washington.

WOODFACE, HARRY (Cheyenne River Sioux)
   Harry Woodface, the son of Iron Foot, entered Hampton Institute in June, 1884, at age fifteen. He remained until September,
1888. He returned to Cheyenne River to serve as a clerk and an
interpreter. He then enlisted as a soldier. 52 Congress, 1 Session,
Senate Executive Document 31, 22, 42-43.

WOOTHTAKEWAHBITTY, OWEN (Comanche)
   Owen Woothtakewahbitty was from Fletcher, Oklahoma, and graduated from Chilocco Indian Agricultural School in 1919.

WRIGHT, ALLEN (Choctaw)
   Allen Wright was born in the Choctaw Nation in present-day
Attala County, Mississippi, in November, 1826, the son of Ishtemahilvbi
and Ahepat. He went by the name of Kiliahote until 1834 when he
entered the Choctaw school at Bok-tuk-lo in the western Choctaw
Nation. He later attended Pine Ridge School and Spencer Academy
in the nation and then went on to Delaware College and Union College
at Schenectady, New York, where he graduated with an A.B. degree
in 1852. He then entered Union Theological Seminary, from which
he received an M.A. in 1855. Wright returned to the Choctaw Nation

where he served his people in various capacities: principal of Armstrong Academy, member of the National Council, national treasurer, superintendent of schools. He was Principal Chief from 1866 through 1870. Wright was a scholar. In 1872, he translated Choctaw laws from English to Choctaw; in 1883-1884, he translated the Psalms from Hebrew to Choctaw; and in 1885, he was editor and translator for the Indian Champion at Atoka. He was an ordained Presbyterian minister and a Mason. His wife was Harriet Mitchell, a white woman. He died on December 2, 1885. John Bartlett Meserve, "Chief Allen Wright," Chronicles of Oklahoma, 19 (December, 1941), 314-321; Frederick J. Dockstader, Great North American Indians (New York: Van Nostrand Reinhold Company, 1977), 342-344.

WRIGHT, DAVID (Pawnee)
From Pawnee, Oklahoma, David Wright studied carpentry at Chilocco Indian Agricultural School, from which he graduated in 1919.

WYLY, PERCY (Cherokee)
Percy Wyly was the son of R. F. and Mary Jane (Buffington) Wyly.

YELLOW BOY, ROSA (Sioux)
In 1920, Rosa Yellow Boy was a student at the Oglala Boarding School.

YELLOW ROBE, CHAUNCEY (Yankton Sioux)
Chauncey Yellow Robe was born about 1870 near Rapid City, South Dakota, the son of Yanktonai Sioux parents, Tasi Nagi (Yellow Robe) and Tahcawin (The Doe). In 1890, he was in Washington, translating for the Indians traveling with Buffalo Bill's Wild West Show. He entered Carlisle in 1891 and graduated in 1895. He became disciplinarian at the Genoa, Nebraska, Indian School and then at the Fort Shaw School, where he introduced football. In 1897, he returned to Carlisle as assistant disciplinarian. In 1903, he became disciplinarian at the Rapid City School and remained in that position for many years. Yellow Robe took an active interest in Indian affairs. He died on April 6, 1930. Red Man and Helper, January 21 and September 19, 1902; Red Man, 7 (February, 1915), 218; American Indian Magazine, 4 (January-March, 1916), 50-53; Frederick J. Dockstader, Great North American Indians (New York: Van Nostrand Reinhold Company, 1977), 345-346.

YELLOWBIRD, EDWARD (Yankton Sioux)
Edward Yellowbird, or Tunkaw-wangapapi, was the son of Hemkenisin. He entered Hampton Institute in August, 1885, at age 19. He remained there until October, 1886. He then attended Haskell Institute for a year and later worked at the Yankton agency before enlisting in the Army. 52 Congress, 1 Session, Senate Executive Document 31, 25, 44-45.

YELLOWFISH, ADA (Comanche)
Ada Yellowfish was a student at Haskell Institute in 1910.

YELLOWFISH, BESSIE (Comanche)
Bessie Yellowfish, who was from Apache, Oklahoma, was a 1918 graduate of Chilocco Indian Agricultural School.

YELLOWTAIL, ROBERT (Crow)
Robert Yellowtail, from Lodge Grass, Montana, attended Carlisle Indian Industrial School. He later graduated from Sherman Institute at Riverside, California, in 1907. He then returned to the Crow Reservation in Montana, improved his allotment, became a successful farmer, and played an active role in tribal affairs. In 1934 he was appointed Superintendent of the Crow Reservation. Sherman Bulletin, May 24, 1916; Red Man (April, 1916), 265; Marion E. Gridley, Indians of Today (Chicago: The Lakeside Press, 1936), 128.

YOUNG MAN, FRANK (Sioux)
Frank Young Man was a student at the Oglala Boarding School in 1900.

YUDA, MONTREVILLE (Oneida)
Montreville Yuda was a student at Carlisle Indian Industrial School in 1910.

YUKKATANACHE, DOCK G. (Mohave)
Dock G. Yukkatanache was a 1906 graduate of Carlisle Indian Industrial School. Arrow, March 30, 1906.

ZANE, OLIVE (Wyandot)
Olive Zane was a student at Haskell Institute in 1912.

ZEIGLER, CORA (New River Tribe, i.e., Ipai)
From California, Clara Zeigler graduated from Chemawa Indian School in 1914. Chemawa American, 16 (June, 1914), 8.

ZITKALA-SA (Yankton Sioux)
See BONNIN, GERTRUDE SIMMONS

INDEX OF WRITERS BY
TRIBAL AFFILIATION

(Underlines indicate pseudonymous
writers listed in Part II)

Goodeagle, Charles
Goodeagle, Fannie

QUILEUTE
Black, Thompson
George, Hal B.
Penn, William
Ward, Jim
Wood, Isaac

SAC AND FOX
Battice, C. Walter
Bigwalker, Lelia
Ingalls, Sadie M.
Jones, Henry C.
Jones, William
Keokuk, Fannie
Manitowa, Bertha
Meek, Rilla
Miles, Thomas J.
Monroe, Lydia
Moore, William
Newashe, Emma M.
Newashe, William
Thorpe, James F.
See also SAUK

SANPOIL
Runnels, Louis H.
Runnels, Mary E.

SAUK
Mansur, Sarah
See also SAC AND FOX

SEMINOLE
Conepacho, Billy (Florida)
Johnson, John
Jumper, John

SENECA
Bishop, Lucius
Brooks, Emily
Butler, Charles W. (Cattaraugus)
Charles, Reuben (Tonawanda)
Doctor, Milo
Doxtater, Edna
George, Samuel (Cattaraugus)
Hemlock, Julia
Hubbard, Chester (Oklahoma)
Huff, Morris
Jemison, Irene B. (Cattaraugus)
John, Andrew
Johnson, A. Ella
Jones, Flora E.
Kennedy, Alvin W.
Lay, Blanche

Maybe, Lila
Nephew, Edith L.
Parker, Arthur Caswell
Parker, Lena
Patterson, Spencer
Peters, Rosina (Tonawanda)
Pierce, Bemus (Cattaraugus)
Pierce, Evelyn
Poodry, Fannie C. (Tonawanda)
Redeye, Rosa
Silverheels, Florence W. (Cattaraugus)
Skye, Mazie L.
Spicer, Alex (Oklahoma)
Sundown, Reuben
Sutton, Myrtle
Tall Chief, Mary
Twoguns, Evelyn R.
Twoguns, Selina
Waterman, Leila
Whitecrow, Gertrude (Oklahoma)
Whitetree, Jesse Willis (Oklahoma)
Williams, Spencer F.

SERRANO
Gabriel, Christiana
Waite, Agnes V.

SHASTA
Bagnell, Amy T.
Brown, Fannie
Smith, James

SHAWNEE
Alford, Pierrepont (Absentee)
Alford, Reese (Absentee)
Alford, Thomas Wildcat (Absentee)
Alford, Webster (Absentee)
Perry, Samuel
Prophet, William
Riley, Minnie
Shawnee, George
Tyner, John
Tyner, Rachel

SHOSHONI
Dodson, John
Faulkner, Clarence L.
Large, Roy
LaVatta, Emma (Fort Hall)
LaVatta, George (Fort Hall)
LaVatta, Philip (Fort Hall)
Truchot, Louise

SILETZ
Adams, John F.
DePoe, Robert R.

Shepherd, Mason
Shield, Dawson
Shields, F. H.
Shields, Mary
Spotted Crow, Lizzie
Spottedbear, Russel
Swallow, Ida
Tall Crane, Fred
Terry, Liddy
Thompson, Emma
Thunder Bear, Julia
Thunder Hawk, Maggie
Tibbetts, Arthur T.
Weatherstone, Robert
White, Jefferson
White Eagle
Whitebull, Levi
Yellow Boy, Rosa
Young Man, Frank

SKOKOMISH
Bishop, Thomas G.
Palmer, John

SNOHOMISH
Dunbar, Joseph

SPOKAN
McDonald, Flora

STOCKBRIDGE
Brushel, Samuel J.
Butler, Bessie
Miller, Florence
Peters, Myrtle
Peters, Nellie H.

TANAINA
MacLeod, Michael

TLINGIT
Kinninook, Paul
McCully, Ella Julia
Paul, Louis F.
Paul, Matilda K.
Paul, William L.
Simpson, Peter
Verigan, Francis L.

TOLOWA
Roberts, Ethel

TSMISHIAN
Dundas, Archie
Marsden, Edward
Verney, Patrick

TUSCARORA
Gansworth, Howard Edward
Gansworth, Willard N.
Garlow, William
Garlow, Winnifred
Hewitt, John Napoleon Brinton
Jones, Lucy N.
Mt. Pleasant, Edison

UMATILLA
Crane, James
Hart, Joseph C.

UMPQUA
McArthur, Rosabelle

UTE
Burson, Rachel
Harris, Henry E. (Pyramid Lake)

WALLAWALLA
Ghangraw, Frances A.

WAMPANOAG
Ryan, Charles

WASCO
Wagner, Fred

WASHO
Bender, Tiffany
Lowry, Maude
McInnis, John
Moses, Henry
Reid, Nettie

WICHITA
Lorentz, Henry

WINNEBAGO
Armell, Josephine
Armell, Louis H.
Blackhawk, Joseph (Nebraska)
Bruce, Harold E. (Nebraska)
Cloud, Henry C. Roe (Nebraska)
DeCora, Angel (Nebraska)
DeCora, Julia (Nebraska)
Hunter, Lucy E.
James, Hattie (Nebraska)
Johnson, Frank L.
Johnson, John P.
Kingsley, Ebenezer
Kingsley, Nettie Mary (Wisconsin)
McCauley, Ella
Nash, Augusta M. (Wisconsin)
Stevens, Addie

LIST OF PERIODICALS CITED

The Adair Ledger. Adair, Cherokee Nation. 1904-1912. Also published as Adair Weekly Ledger.

The Afton News. Afton, Cherokee Nation. 1894-1895.

The Alaskan Fisherman. Ketchikan and Petersburg, Alaska. 1923-1932.

The Albuquerque Indian. Albuquerque, New Mexico. 1905-1906.

The American Indian Advocate. Yakima and Tacoma, Washington; Independence, Missouri; Wheeling, West Virginia. 1920-1928. Also published as American Indian Tepee and Indian Teepee Magazine.

The American Indian Magazine. Washington, D.C., and Cooperstown, New York. 1913-1920.

American Indian Tepee. See The American Indian Advocate.

American Indian YMCA Bulletin. Lawrence, Kansas; New York, New York; Denver, Colorado. 1911-1927. Also published as Haskell Bulletin and Haskell Institute YMCA Bulletin.

The Apache Scout. White River, Arizona; El Paso, Texas; Decatur, Indiana; Milwaukee, Wisconsin; Green Lake, Wisconsin; Bylas, Arizona. 1923+. Also published as The Apache Lutheran.

Arkansas Gazette. Little Rock, Arkansas. 1819+.

Arkansas Intelligencer. Van Buren, Arkansas. 1842-1860.

The Arkansian. Fayetteville, Arkansas. 1859-1861.

Atoka Independent. Atoka, Choctaw Nation. 1877-1878.

The Arrow. See The Carlisle Arrow.

The B.I.U. Instructor. Bacone, Indian Territory. 1892-1893.

The Baconian. Bacone, Indian Territory. 1898-1907.

The Baptist Home Mission Monthly. New York, New York. 1878-1909.

California Indian Herald. San Francisco, California. 1923-1924.

The Carlisle Arrow. Carlisle, Pennsylvania. 1904-1918. Also published as The Arrow and The Carlisle Arrow and Red Man.

Chemawa American. Chemawa, Oregon. 1897+. Also published as Weekly Chemawa American.

The Cherokee Advocate. Tahlequah, Cherokee Nation. 1844-1906.

Cherokee Rose Buds. See A Wreath of Cherokee Rosebuds.

Cherokee Telephone. Tahlequah, Cherokee Nation. 1887-1896. Also published as The Telephone and Weekly Capital.

The Chippeway Herald. White Earth, Minnesota. 1902-1909.

The Choctaw Intelligencer. Doaksville, Choctaw Nation. 1850-1852.

Connecticut Mirror. Hartford, Connecticut. 1809-1832.

The Council Fire. Philadelphia, Pennsylvania, and Washington, D.C. 1878-1889. Also published as The Council Fire and Arbitrator.

The Council Fire and Arbitrator. See The Council Fire.

The Craftsman. Eastwood, New York. 1901-1916.

The Creek Boys' and Girls' Monthly. See Our Monthly.

Daily Alta California. San Francisco, California. 1849-1891.

Daily Indian Chieftain. Vinita, Cherokee Nation. 1891.

The Daily Bee. Sacramento, California. 1857+. Now published as The Sacramento Bee.

Daily Oklahoman. Oklahoma City, Oklahoma. 1894+.
The Daily Union. Sacramento, California. 1851+.
Eskimo. Nome, Alaska; Seattle, Washington; Eugene, Oregon. 1916-1947.
Fort Smith Elevator. Fort Smith, Arkansas. 1878-1909.
Fort Smith Herald. Fort Smith, Arkansas. 1847-1862.
Fort Smith Times. Fort Smith, Arkansas. 1861-1862.
Golden Era. San Francisco and San Diego, California. 1852-1893.
The Hesperian. See Pacific Monthly.
Home Mission Monthly. New York, New York. 1886-1924.
Hutchings' California Magazine. San Francisco, California. 1856-1861.
Iapi Oaye. Greenwood, South Dakota; Santee, Nebraska; Yankton, South
    Dakota. 1871-1939.
The Indian. Riverside, California. 1921-1957.
The Indian Advance. Stewart, Nevada. 1899-1903.
The Indian Advocate. Louisville, Kentucky. 1846-1855.
The Indian Advocate. Sacred Heart, Oklahoma. 1889-1910.
Indian Arrow. See The Tahlequah Arrow.
The Indian Chieftain. Vinita, Cherokee Nation. 1881-1912. Also published
    as Vinita Weekly Chieftain and Weekly Chieftain.
The Indian Citizen. Atoka, Choctaw Nation, later Oklahoma. 1886-1956.
    Also published as Atoka Independent and The Indian Citizen-Democrat.
The Indian Herald. Tama, Iowa. 1903-1905.
The Indian Journal. Muskogee and Eufaula, Creek Nation, later Oklahoma.
    1876+.
The Indian Leader. Lawrence, Kansas. 1897+.
The Indian Missionary. Eufaula, Creek Nation, and McAlester, Choctaw Na-
    tion, simultaneously; McAlester and Canadian, Choctaw Nation, and
    Tahlequah, Cherokee Nation, simultaneously; Atoka, Choctaw Nation.
    1884-1891.
The Indian Moccasin. Afton, Cherokee Nation. 1893-1894.
The Indian News. Genoa, Nebraska. 1897-1920.
The Indian Observer. Washington, D.C. 1911.
The Indian Orphan. Atoka and Bacone, Oklahoma. 1903-1919. Also pub-
    lished as Indian Education.
The Indian Progress. Bacone, Oklahoma. 1923-1927.
The Indian School Journal. Chilocco, Oklahoma. 1900-1980.
Indian Sentinel. Webbers Falls and Tahlequah, Cherokee Nation. 1890-1902.
The Indian's Friend. Philadelphia and Lancaster, Pennsylvania; New Haven,
    Connecticut; New York, New York. 1888-1951.
The Interpreter. Park Hill, Oklahoma. 1916-1918.
Jones Academy Herald. Dwight, Choctaw Nation. 1902-1903.
The Literary Voyager. Sault Ste. Marie, Michigan. 1826-1827.
Mentor. New York, New York. 1913-1931.
The Mission Indian. Banning, California. 1895-1906.
The Missionary Herald. Boston, Massachusetts. 1805-1951.
The Mistletoe. Athens, Georgia. 1849.
Monthly Repository and Library of Entertaining Knowledge. New York, New
    York. 1830-1834.
The Morning Star. See The Red Man and Helper.
Muskogee Morning Times. Muskogee, Creek Nation, later Oklahoma. 1896-
    1971. Also published as Muskogee Evening Times and Muskogee Times-
    Democrat.
Muskogee Phoenix. Muskogee, Creek Nation, later Oklahoma. 1888+.
The Native American. Phoenix, Arizona. 1900+.
The New Era. Stilwell, Cherokee Nation. 1906.
The New Indian. Stewart, Nevada. 1903-1908.
Niles' Register. See Niles' Weekly Register.

Niles' Weekly Register. Philadelphia, Pennsylvania. 1811-1849.
The North Star. Sitka, Alaska. 1887-1898.
Ogalalla Light. See Oglala Light.
Oglala Light. Pine Ridge, South Dakota. 1900-1902. Also published as
    Ogalalla Light.
Oklahoma Star. See The Star-Vindicator.
The Osage Journal. Pawhuska, Osage Nation, later Oklahoma. 1897-1960.
The Osage Magazine. Pawhuska, Oklahoma City, and Muskogee, Oklahoma.
    1909-1921. Also published as The Wide West and The Oklahoma Maga-
    zine.
Our Monthly. Tullahassee, Creek Nation. 1870-1875. Also published as
    The Creek Boys' and Girls' Monthly.
Pacific Monthly. San Francisco, California. 1858-1864. Also published as
    Hesperian.
The Peace Pipe. Pipestone, Minnesota. 1912-1918.
The Progress. White Earth, Minnesota. 1886-1889.
The Quileute Chieftain. La Push, Washington, 1910.
Quileute Independent. La Push, Washington. 1908-1909.
Red Lake News. Red Lake, Minnesota. 1912-1920.
The Red Man. See The Red Man and Helper.
The Red Man and Helper. Carlisle, Pennsylvania. 1880-1904. Also pub-
    lished as Eadle Keatah Toh, The Morning Star, and The Red Man.
The Religious Intelligencer. New Haven, Connecticut. 1816-1837.
The Sallisaw Star. Sallisaw, Cherokee Nation. 1895-1907.
The San Francisco Herald. San Francisco, California. 1850-1862.
School News. Carlisle, Pennsylvania. 1880-1883.
The Sequoyah Memorial. Park Hill, Cherokee Nation. 1855-1856.
The Sherman Bulletin. Riverside, California. 1907+.
Sina Sapa Wocekiye Taeyanpaha. Fort Totten, North Dakota. 1892-1923.
The Southern Workman. Hampton, Virginia. 1872-1939.
The Southern Workman and Hampton School Journal. See The Southern Work-
    man.
The Standard-Sentinel. Stilwell, Cherokee Nation, later Oklahoma. 1898-
    1928. Also published as Stilwell Standard.
The Star-Vindicator. Caddo and McAlester, Choctaw Nation. 1874-1879.
    Also published as Oklahoma Star.
The State Herald. Claremore, Oklahoma. 1905.
Stilwell Standard. See The Standard-Sentinel.
The Tahlequah Arrow. Tahlequah, Cherokee Nation, later Oklahoma. 1888-
    1930. Also published as Indian Arrow and Tahlequah Democratic Ar-
    row.
Tahlequah Democratic Arrow. See The Tahlequah Arrow.
Tahlequah Leader. Tahlequah, Oklahoma. 1921-1923.
Talks and Thoughts. Hampton, Virginia. 1886-1907.
The Teepee Book. Sheridan, Wyoming. 1915-1916.
The Telephone. See Cherokee Telephone.
Twin Territories. Muskogee, Creek Nation; Fort Gibson, Cherokee Nation;
    Oklahoma City, Oklahoma. 1898-1904.
University of Oklahoma Magazine. Norman, Oklahoma. 1911-1924.
Van Buren Press. Van Buren, Arkansas. 1859-1916.
The Vinita Leader. Vinita, Cherokee Nation, later, Oklahoma. 1895-1921.
Wassaja. Chicago, Illinois. 1916-1922.
Weekly California Express. Marysville, California. 1857-1859.
Weekly Chemawa American. See Chemawa American.
The Weekly Review. Flandreau, South Dakota. 1902-1916.
Western Christian Advocate. Ardmore and Ada, Chickasaw Nation. 1900-
    1906.

Western Independent. See Wheelers' Western Independent.

Wheelers' Western Independent. Fort Smith, Arkansas. 1872-1877. Also
    published as Western Independent and Wheelers' Independent.

The Word Carrier of the Santee Normal Training School. Santee, Nebraska.
    1884-1937. Also published as The Word Carrier.

Wowapi. Boston, Massachusetts. 1883.

A Wreath of Cherokee Rose Buds. Park Hill, Cherokee Nation. 1854-1857.
    Also published as Cherokee Rose Buds.

Basketry 54, 1025, 2053; in
  Alaska 2166
Baskets 1186
Beans 627; legend of 1134
Bear 198, 354, 562, 727, 1006,
  1354, 1712, 1893
Bear Star 1548
Beaver County, Oklahoma 2035
Bee 1231
Behavior, proper 134
Bells 137, 677
Bermuda Islands 356
Betting 2045
Bible 1048
Big Dipper 145, 1417
Birds 1651; see also names of
  birds
Black Hawk 94
Black Snake 1316
Blackfeet 2121, 1359; reservation
  2047
Blacks 1544, 1550, 1814; see also
  Negroes
Blacksmithing 639, 828, 1464,
  1493, 2002, 2202
Blaine, James G. 252
Blake, Lillian 1794
Bland, T. A. 1792
Blankets 1129
Block Island 439
Bloomfield, Connecticut 1405
Blue Earring 801
Blue Jay 79
Bluebird 564, 1258, 1259
Boar 1279
Boarding School 1476
Bois Fort Chippewas 1270
Bone Ghost 519
Boston 146, 748, 1029
Botkin, B. A. 1749
Boudinot family 2187
Brave Bear 1127
Bread 676, 2147; lye 777; making
  of 1196
Brewer, Thomas F. 2143
Brook 1036
Brotherhood of Christian Unity
  269
Brown Eyes 666
Brule Sioux 660
Bryant, William Cullen 2151
Budget, household 102
Buckskin 191
Buffalo 847, 1944, 2070
Buffalo, New York 1168
Buffalo Heena 1235
Buffalo Rock 2121

Building trades 950
Burials 1791, 2125; customs concern-
  ing 216, 1691
Burro 1633
Businessmen, Indian 679
Butler School 535
Butter 579
Buzzard 1514

Cadahoun 2028
Caddo Indians 577, 1347
Caddo Resolutions 238, 243
California 1717, 1726, 1727, 1731;
  Cherokees in 2329
California Indians 790; conditions of
  220, 222, 785; meeting of 1373;
  treaties of 221
Calumet 1551
Camel 1630
Camp meeting 1136
Camp Pike, Arkansas 1034
Camping 599
Canada 1188
Cane 967
Canktewin 1123
Canoes 1129; birch 596; first birch
  119, 476; flying 820; kinds and
  uses 127
Cape Fox Indians 1292
Captive 635
Career goals 60, 69, 613
Carlisle Indian Industrial School 32,
  285, 556, 884, 976, 1038, 1040,
  1059, 1124, 1125, 1146, 1187,
  1189, 1337, 1360, 1466, 1554,
  1640, 1780, 2122, 2165; athletics
  at 625; band at 296, 367; build-
  ings at 427, 875; campus of
  1207, 1317, 1469; Christmas at
  2059; courses at 431, 448, 507,
  576, 639, 795, 821, 864, 950, 1170,
  1191, 1205, 1558, 1565, 1592, 1681,
  1682, 2081, 2182, 2196, 2202; harness shop at 371; improvements at
  586; literary society at 440; news
  of 2044; outing system at 326,
  498, 752, 882, 947, 1008, 1009,
  1082, 1093, 1323, 1326, 1346,
  1471, 1491, 1504, 1616, 1688,
  2042, 2061, 2062, 2158, 2256;
  poem about 171; praised 1080;
  sports at 341, 1494, 1613, 2091,
  2155; students at 333, 423, 683,
  1318, 1324, 1473, 1515, 2013,
  2115, 2126, 2157, 2181, 2220; students returned from 300, 301